Reference and Online Services Handbook

Reference and Online Services Handbook:

Guidelines, Policies, and Procedures for Libraries

Edited by Bill Katz and Anne Clifford

Neal-Schuman Publishers, Inc.

Published by Neal-Schuman Publishers, Inc.
23 Cornelia Street
New York, NY 10014

Copyright © 1982 by Neal-Schuman Publishers, Inc.

Printed and bound in the United States of America.

Library of Congress Cataloging in Publication Data

Katz, William A., 1924–
  Reference and online services handbook.

  Bibliography: p.
  Includes index.
    1. Reference services (Libraries)—United States
—Handbooks, manuals, etc.   2. On-line bibliographic
searching—Handbooks, manuals, etc.   I. Clifford,
Anne (Anne Marie)   II. Title.
Z711.K33   025.5'2   81-11290
ISBN 0-918212-49-9   AACR2

Contents

Acknowledgments

The editors would like to extend their thanks to Mary Donnery, former student at the School of Library and Information Science, SUNY-Albany, and now a public librarian, who did much of the initial work in developing this project; Kay Flanagan, who typed the manuscript; and all of the librarians and information scientists who took the time to send us their policies.

Sources of Information

ACADEMIC LIBRARIES

University of Alberta, Edmondton, Alberta, Canada T6G 2J8. Margaret H. Farnell, Head, Reference Services (February 1980).* "Policy for the Selection and Maintenance of the Reference Books Housed in the Humanities and Social Sciences Library."

Arizona State University, Tempe, AZ 85281. Kay F. Jones, Chair, Reference Services. "Role, Scope and Goals of the Reference Service," 1976. "We have general guidelines which apply to the Reference Collection as a whole and specific guidelines for materials to be placed on Index Tables."

Ball State University, Bracken Library, University Ave., Muncie, IN 47306. "Library Guides," 1976–78.

University of British Columbia, 1956 Main Mall, Vancouver, British Columbia V6T 1Y3. Doug McLuna, Assistant Librarian, Public Services (March 1980). There is no "current general policy statement on reference services . . . [but] concern is reflected in the enclosed materials" among which: "UBC Library Service to External Users" and "Faculty Library Guide," 1979–1980.

Case Western Reserve University, Freiberger Library, Cleveland, OH 44106. Yadwiga Kuncaitis, Chief of Reference Department (March 1980). "Policies and Procedures for Reference Desk Service," which are "provisional statements for reference desk service."

Colorado State University, William E. Morgan Library, Fort Collins, CO 80523. "Reference—Selected Policies and Procedures," 1979.

Georgia Institute of Technology, Price Gilbert Memorial Library, Atlanta, GA 30332. Ruth C. Hale, Head, Bibliographic Services Division. "Literature Searches and Other Reference Services," 1980. "We have no single, comprehensive reference service policy statement. . . . I am enclosing copies of the bits and pieces we do have."

University of Illinois at Urbana-Champaign, Wright St., Urbana, IL 61801. Maureen Pastine, Reference Librarian. "Public Services Manual" 1979 [section on "reference services" from that manual]. "Over the next year . . . [we] will be working on a policy and procedural manual for Reference. Presently we do not have such a manual." Enclosed "copies of some suggested guidelines . . . ."

Kent State University Libraries, Kent, OH 44240. Neal L. Edgar, Associate Curator, Special Collections. "Reference" sections from "Policy and Procedures Manual," various dates, 1973 to 1980. Also included here are other related sections.

Louisiana State University, Troy H. Middleton Library, Baton Rouge, LA 70803. D. W. Schneider, Associate Director (March 1980). "Reference Services Division Policy Statement (Draft)," 1980. "Prepared from memos issued by the Head, Reference Services. . . . I plan to have this draft worked into a more complete document."

University of Massachusetts, Amherst, MA 01003. Marjorie Karlson, Head, Reference Department (February 1980). "Reference Service Manual," revised 1980.

McGill University, McLennan Library, 3459 McTavish St., Montreal, PQ, Canada H3A 1Y1. Elizabeth Silvester, Head, Reference Department. "Reference Manual Extracts," revised February 1980. "We don't have a nice tidy policy statement but a collection of policies and procedures which we keep in two big yellow binders called Reference Manual and update bit by bit as the occasion arises." [Note: The 4th edition of the "Reference Collection Policy," 1980, is not included in the excerpts.]

Miami University, Edgar W. King Library, Oxford, OH 45056. Donald E. Oehlerts, Director of Libraries. "University Services: Libraries," 1978, which is part of the faculty "Information Manual," distributed to all university faculty.

Michigan State University, East Lansing, MI 48824. Thomas E. Albright, Assistant Director, General Readers' Services (February 1980). No policy, but "the basics of such policy are expressed or implied in the enclosed departmental and unit goals and objective statements." Includes "General Readers' Services: Statement of Goals and Objectives," 1979.

University of North Carolina, Walter Clinton Jackson Library, Greensboro, NC 27412. Nancy C. Fogarty, Head Reference Librarian (March 1980). "Reference Policy Statements." Various policies, including "Services of the Reference Department," n.d.

Northwestern University, Library, 1935 Sheridan Rd., Evanston, IL 60201. Sandy Whiteley, Head, Reference Department (February 1980). These are "reference policies from the ... library Policies and Procedures Manual." Includes "Goals of the Reference Department."

University of Oklahoma, Memorial Library, 401 W. Brooks, Norman, OK 73019. "Guide to the Libraries," n.d.

Potsdam, College of, State University of New York, Frederick W. Crumb Memorial Library, Pierrepont Ave., Potsdam, NY 13676. Edith Frankel, Head, Reference Department. "Reference Service Policy," 1978, from the Reference Desk Handbook, "always a mixture of policies and procedures, [which] over the years [has] become the library handbook. The enclosed pages are the ones that include some reference policy statements."

Rice University Library, Box 1892, Houston, TX 77001. Richard H. Perrine, Head, Reference/Collection Development Department. "Rice University Library Reference Procedures," 1980. (This is printed in full at the end of the compilation.)

San Diego State University, San Diego, CA 92182. Kathy Coleman, Reference and Instructional Services. "Reference Service Policy," 1978. "This is a very general document ... more a statement of philosophy than a list of operational guidelines."

The University of South Carolina, Thomas Cooper Library, Columbia, SC 29208. Joyce C. Werner, Head, Reference Department (March 1980). "Copy of our Library Guide and the information leaflets from the Reference Department, Interlibrary Loan, and ACCESS, the computerized bibliographic search service." 1978.

The University of Texas at Austin, The General Libraries, Austin, TX 78712. Linda Beaupre, Acting Assistant Director for Public Services (February 1980). "Guidelines for Reference and Information Services," 1977. The "guidelines are primarily for the use of library staff."

University of Toledo, Carlson Library, 2801 W. Bancroft St., Toledo, OH 43606. "Reference Department Goals," 1978.

University of Western Ontario, A. B. Weldon Library, 1151 Richmond St., N., London, Ontario N6A 3K7. Various documents: includes "Self study Objectives," n.d.

The following statements were received, but it was either too late for inclusion or repetitious of other material:

  University of Southern Mississippi, Hattiesburg, 39401. Virginia Toliver, Coordinator, Southern's Computer Assisted Retrieval Services (November, 1980). "Reference," four pages included in the Policies and Procedural Manual. "These are in the process of being revised." See Online Section.

  Temple University, Philadelphia, Pennsylvania 19122. Jack L. Gotlobe, Associate Director (June, 1980). Material from "Public Services Division Policy Handbook." "Policies from our reference department are still being developed." See Online Section.

  Two libraries have policies, but do not want to release them for publication in this compilation (there may be many more who did not respond). The two: University of California, Berkeley. Rita Kane, Acting Associate University Librarian (October 10, 1980). "The policy will only be available for internal distribution," and the University of Chicago, Patrician Swanson, Head of Reference Services (February 21, 1980). "We are undecided about submitting our ... statement." There followed a number of perceptive questions about the intent of the book. The questions were answered, but there was no further correspondence.

  The following libraries responded, but stated they do not have statements, although many do have memorandums, directives, etc.: Columbia University; University of California, Davis; Duke University; University of Iowa; Notre Dame; Ohio State University; University of Oregon; Pennsylvania State University; University of

Pennsylvania; Purdue; Princeton; Southern California; Vanderbilt; University of Virginia; Washington University; Yale.

These libraries are working on statements (as of late 1980): University of Alabama; Boston University; Bowling Green State University; Wichita State University.

PUBLIC LIBRARIES

Ann Arbor Public Library, 343 S. Fifth Ave., Ann Arbor, MI 48104. "Reference Department Policy Manual," 1978.

Atlanta Public Library, 10 Pryor St., S.W., Atlanta, GA 30303. Virginia H. Weaver, Librarian, Coordinator for Research and Training (November 1980). "Information Line Service [i.e., Telephone]," n.d.

The Berkeley Public Library, 2090 Kittredge St., Berkeley, CA 94704. Norine Gerber, Reference. "Reference Service Guidelines," 1980.

Birmingham Public, 2020 Park Place, Birmingham, AL 35203. George R. Stewart, Director (August 1980). "Reference Service Policy," n.d. The policy "is currently being reviewed. While there will probably be some changes . . . the present statement does generally reflect our policies."

Charlotte & Mecklenburg County, Inc., Public Library of, 310 N. Tryon St., Charlotte, NC 28202. "Main Library Public Service," n.d.

Chicago Public Library, 425 N. Michigan Ave., Chicago, IL 60611. Bronwyn Parhad, Head, Information Center. "Reference/Information Service Policy Manual for Staff of the Chicago Public Library," 1978.

Cleveland Public Library, 325 Superior Ave., Cleveland, OH 44114. Helen V. Azusenis, Head, Planning and Research (October, 1980). "Guidelines for Reference Service," n.d., a part of the library "Procedures Manual."

The Dayton and Montgomery County Public Library, 215 E. Third St., Dayton, OH 45402. Jeremy R. Buck, Assistant Director. "Reference and Readers' Aid Practice," 1977, from the library "Procedure Manual."

Denver Public Library, 3840 York St., Denver, CO 80205. Richard G. Akeroyd, Jr., Assistant City Librarian. "Reference Service Policy Statement," February 1976.

Dunedin Public Library, 223 Douglas Ave., Dunedin, FL 33528. Sally White Ward (formerly Reference Librarian, Dunedin Public Library, now head of Adult Services, Collier County, Florida, Public Library). "Information Service Policy and Procedures Manual," 1978.

Inglewood Public Library, City of, 101 W. Manchester Blvd., Inglewood, CA 90301. Suzanne Schippleck. "Library Reference Service," 1976.

Kingsport Public Library, J. Fred Johnson Memorial Library, Kingsport, TN 37660. Maryalice Waldrip, Reference Librarian. "Reference Service Policy," 1980. "Under consideration for adoption."

Knoxville-Knox County Public Library, 500 W. Church Ave., Knoxville, TN 37902. Patricia S. Rugg (September 1980). "General Reference Guidelines" from the "Procedures Manual," n.d.

Los Angeles Public Library, 630 W. Fifth St., Los Angeles, CA 90071. Linda M. Wood, Assistant City Librarian. "Reference and Advisory Service Guidelines," 1980. (This is published in full at the end of the compilation.)

Louisville Free Public Library, Fourth & York Sts., Louisville, KY 40203. "Reference Work," 1979.

Memphis Public Library, 1850 Peabody Ave., Memphis, TN 38104. "Information Desk Procedures," 1975.

New Castle County Department of Libraries, 6000 Kirkwood Hwy., Wilmington, DE. Anne L. Hampton, Executive Assistant. "Cooperative Information Services–Committee Goals and Objectives of SPSS Study (Statistical Programs in the Social Sciences)," 1978. This is not a policy statement per se, and in September 1980, Ms. Hampton suggested a policy might be formulated following completion of a study.

New Orleans Public Library, Simon Heinsheim & Fisk Libraries, 219 Loyola Ave., New Orleans, LA 70140. "Policies and Procedures: Readers' Services," 1978.

The New York Public Library, The Research Libraries, Fifth Ave. & 42nd St., New York, NY 10018. Faye Simkin, Executive Officer. "Standards of Research Library Service: Technical Memorandum No. 8," 1977.

Orlando Public Library, Ten North Rosalind, Orlando, FL 32801. Glenn Miller, Director. "Reference Policy Statement," 1979.

Philadelphia, The Free Library of, Logan Square, Philadelphia, PA 19103. J. Randall Rosensteel, Administrative Assistant to the Director. "Policies and Procedures," 1979.

Providence Public Library, 150 Empire St., Providence, RI 02903. "Service Code," 1976.

St. Louis Public Library, 1301 Olive St., St. Louis, MO 63103. Anna E. Horn, Manager, Main Library. "St. Louis Public Library Reference Work," 1975.

San Diego Public Library, 820 E St., San Diego, CA 92101. "Information-Reference Service Policy," 1976.

The following statement was received too late for inclusion:

Troy Public Library, Troy, New York 12180. Scott Baker, Head, Reference Department. "Reference Room—Policies and Procedures," 1975. Eleven pages. In process of revision.

The following public libraries responded, but reported they do not have statements, although many have memorandums, directives, etc.: Buffalo & Erie County (New York); Charleston County (South Carolina); Hartford (Connecticut); Houston (Texas); County of Orange (California); Schenectady County (New York).

ONLINE

Birmingham Public Library, 2020 Park Place, Birmingham, AL 35203. George R. Stewart, Director (August 1980). "Online Reference Service Policy," n.d. Policy being reviewed.

Brigham Young University, Provo, UT 84602. Richard Jensen, Life Science Librarian (November 1980). Copies of online searching services brochure and search request forms. "We do not have a formal written policy other than what appears in the handout."

CITE, Coordinating Information for Texas Educators, 211 E. 7 St., Austin, TX 78701 (1980–81). Jan Anderson, Manager (November 1980). Enclosed a "summary of our services."

Colorado State University, William E. Morgan Library, Fort Collins, CO 80523. "Reference–Selected Policies and Procedures," 1979.

Columbus Technical Institute (ERIC), Box 1609, Columbus, OH 43216. Susan Pyle, Reference Librarian (October 1980).

Dow Chemical U.S.A., Texas Division, Freeport, TX 77541. Leonard Levine, 17 November 1980. "We have no policy statement, nor do we have any forms" (quotes in collection are from Mr. Levine's summary of policy).

The Free Library of Philadelphia, Logan Square, Philadelphia, PA 19103. Vilma M. Lieberman, Head, Computer Based Information Center, October 1980. Various forms. "Although we never set out to write a policy statement as such, the first paragraph of the Fees and Charges sheet functions as one."

Georgia Institute of Technology, Price Gilbert Memorial Library, Atlanta, GA 30332. Ruth C. Hale, Head, Bibliographic Services Division. "Literature Searches and Other Reference Services," 1980.

Hennepin County Medical Center, Thomas Lowry Health Sciences Library, 701 Park Ave., Minneapolis, MN 55415. Judi Urich, Librarian (November 1980). Enclosed statements and forms. "We are in the process of rewriting our policy statement and developing new forms."

Kansas State Department of Education, 120 E. 10th St., Topeka, KS 66612. Nancy L. Flott, Director, KEDDS Resources (November 1980). "We do not have a written policy," but do have brochures explaining services.

Massachusetts Institute of Technology, Cambridge, MA 02139. Mary E. Pensyl, Head, Computerized Literature Search Service (January 1981). Forms, brochures and price schedules. Has not developed "a formal online policy statement for in-house use."

Michigan State University, East Lansing, MI 48824. Thomas E. Albright, Assistant Director, General Readers' Services (February 1980).

Northwestern University, Library, 1935 Sheridan Rd., Evanston, IL 60201. Sandy Whiteley, Head, Reference Department (February 1980).

State University of New York at Albany, Albany, NY 12222. Sara Knapp. Policy dated January 23, 1981.

State University of New York College at Potsdam, Frederick W. Crumb Memorial Library, Pierrepont Ave., Potsdam, NY 13676. Edith Frankel, Head, Reference Department.

Suffolk University College Library, Beacon Hill, Boston, MA 02114. E. G. Hamman, College Librarian (March 1980). "We don't have one . . . We did, however, start out with one [memo to the faculty enclosed—and republished here] but soon discovered that, so far, its limiting provisions are not necessary."

Temple University, Berks & 13 St., Philadelphia, PA 19122. Jack L. Gotlobe, Associate Director, June 1979. Online policies are from the "Public Services Division Policy Handbook," 1979, and in draft form.

Texas A & M University, Automated Information Retrieval Service (AIRS), College Station, TX 77843.

Tulsa City County Library, 400 Civic Center, Tulsa, OK 74103. Martha Gregory, INFO II Librarian (December 1980). Enclosed sample forms and brochures. Do not have a policy manual.

United States Environmental Protection Agency, Cincinnati, OH 45268. JoAnn Johnson, Chief, Library Services (November 20, 1980). "Online Literature Searching and Databases," compiled by Mary L. Calkins in October, 1978. Of the 35 pages some 30 are description of databases.

University of British Columbia, 1956 Main Mall, Vancouver, British Columbia V6T 1Y3. Doug McLuna, Assistant Librarian, Public Services (March 1980).

University of Connecticut, Storrs, CT. Linda Polcan, December 1980. Does not have a policy statement except for handouts.

University of Houston, Houston, TX. "Policy Manual for a Computerized Search Service in an Academic Library," by William J. Jackson (March 15, 1979). Reprinted in full at the end of this compilation.

University of Illinois at Urbana-Champaign, Wright St., Urbana, IL 61801.

University of Massachusetts Libraries, Amherst, MA 01003. "Computer Search Service Group Policy Manual," June, 1977.

University of Missouri-Columbia, Columbia, MO 65201. Jeanmarie Lang Fraser, Coordinator, Online Search Service, December 5, 1980. Policy in process of development. Enclosed forms and service brochure.

University of North Carolina, Walter Clinton Jackson Library, Greensboro, NC 27412. Nancy C. Fogarty, Head Reference Librarian (March 1980). "Reference Policy Statements." Various policies, including "Services of the Reference Department," n.d.

University of North Carolina at Chapel Hill, Chapel Hill, NC. "Online Information Service Policy," January 1978; September 1980.

The University of South Carolina, ACCESS, Computerized Bibliographic Search Service, Columbia, SC 29208.

University of Southern Mississippi, Hattiesburg, MS 39401. Virginia Toliver, Coordinator, SCARS (November 1980). Enclosed "policies and procedures . . . for our Online Information Retrieval Service."

The University of Texas at Austin, The General Libraries, Austin, TX 78712. "Computer Based Information Services," May, 1979 (brochure).

The University of Texas Health Science Center at Dallas, 5323 Harry Hines Blvd., Dallas, TX 75235. Sharon Shekha (December 1980). Copies of forms, documents and brochures. "Our policies have not yet been collected into one statement."

Veterans Administration West Side Hospital, Box 8195, Chicago, IL
  60680. Lynne D. Morris, Chief, Library Services. November 1978
  (December 1980).

———————

Various forms, brochures, brief explanations, fee schedules, etc. are
available from the following—*none of which is reprinted here*:

  University of Alberta, Edmonton, Canada
  Arizona State University, Tempe, AZ
  University of Colorado, Boulder, CO
  University of Illinois at Urbana-Champaign, Urbana, IL
  Kansas State University, Manhattan, KS
  Boston College Libraries, Chestnut Hill, MA
  Miami University, Oxford, OH
  University of Toledo Libraries, Toledo, OH
  University of South Carolina, Columbia, SC
  University of Houston, Central Campus, TX
  The University of Vermont, Burlington, VT

———

*NOTE: Dates in parentheses indicate the date of the major correspondence
with the library, and are employed to indicate date of quotes or relative
period suggested by the undated policy.

Introduction

This collection of reference services policy statements is compiled and organized to assist reference librarians, administrators, teachers, students, and interested laypersons. The material provides the essential guidelines, procedures, and policies necessary in the day-to-day operations of an effective reference services operation in the academic, public, and, to a lesser extent, special library. (School libraries are not included, not for lack of the editors' interest, but for apparent lack of policies. See further on.)

This work represents material from 53 academic libraries, 33 public libraries, and online statements from a combination of 40 academic, public, and special libraries. Having spent over a year (early 1980 to March 1981) in gathering statements, the editors are convinced the present book is at least representative of what is now available in American and some Canadian libraries; but no claim is made that this is a definitive collection.

The term "reference services policy statement" needs a close definition. Librarians customarily divide the statements into procedures and policies. In fact, the term "policy" tends to be the overall title when the primary focus is on a broad overview or philosophy of reference services.

The statements may take one of two basic forms. One form, the exception, is the detailed manual (i.e., over 12 and up to 40 or more pages). In the present survey, only five of the 53 academic libraries had such manuals, the three most impressive being Massachusetts, McGill, and Rice. Among public libraries, the focus on the distinguishable, separate manual or statement is more pronounced. Of the 33 respondents, 14 had such policies. Direct administrative control of public libraries by city or regional bodies, coupled with a more heterogeneous public than the academic library, accounts for the added reliance on such statements.

The majority of respondents, however, depend upon memorandums, directives, minutes of meetings, and numerous other formal and informal individual bits and pieces which over a period of time tend to shape policy and procedures. Numerous times these become a part, or section, of the library public services manual or in-house policy and procedures manual.

Where libraries lack a neat, tidy policy or manual, most turn to collections of policies and procedures kept in big binders called the "reference manual" and updated bit by bit when the occasion required it. Even those with model statements or manuals are aware of the constant necessity for revision, deletion, and addition.

The various approaches sometimes lead to difficulty in definition and it is not unusual to find a reference service policy unavailable as such, yet subdivided in individual memorandums and decisions made over the years. Many of these, made on an ad hoc basis, have never been collected and codified. A spokesperson for Michigan State University explains: "We have no policy statement on reference service, however, the basics of such policy are expressed or implied in the enclosed departmental and unit goals and objectives statements." Robert Balay, Head, Reference Department, Yale, had much the same comment: "Although reference service is mentioned in various library policy statements, we have no written statement of reference service policy."

The Knoxville-Knox County Public Library uses material from their "Procedures Manual" as guidelines, as do many other public libraries. Even where a manual may exist, there is a chance it will not reflect current policy. Jeremy Buck, Assistant Director of the Dayton and Montgomery Public Library, notes that both he and the director were appointed since the manual was prepared. Mr. Buck carefully pointed out that he took exception to some provisions in the old manual.

A third section of this collection is devoted to online policy statements. Again, these are not likely to be codified, but made up of directives, memorandums, and still another form. This is the informational brochure, pamphlet, or broadside produced for the public. Some are printed, others mimeographed.

Vilma Lieberman, Head, Computer Based Information Center, The Free Library of Philadelphia, notes that: "Although we never set out to write an [online] policy statement as such, note that the first paragraph of the 'Fees and Charges' sheet [see p. 502] functions as one."[1] And at Brigham Young University: "We do not have a formal written policy statement other than what appears in the CARS (Computer Assisted Research Services) handout" [see p. 401].[2]

The real difficulty is that the service is relatively new. The situation for most libraries is similar to that at the Birmingham Public Library, where Director George R. Stewart writes: "Online reference is a new service for us. Consequently our policy for such service is really in the draft stage." A typical response is from the University of Texas Health Science Center at Dallas Library: "[We] are in the process of evolving a policies and procedures manual. My estimate is that it will be another year before we have finished the section on online services."[3] And the Tulsa City County Library notes that work is going forward on a statement to be completed within the next year.[4]

Faye Simkin of the New York Public Library adds another reason for lack of such statements—lack of online services. If online is a regular feature for many academic libraries, it is more the exception for public libraries.

The most succinct statement regarding online searches is offered by Leonard Levine of Dow Chemical: "Anyone who has a need to know has access to online searching. We have no other policy statement, nor do we have any forms."

The limited aspects of the online operation with usually small staffs accounts, too, for the lack of a formal policy. As MIT librarian Mary E. Pensyl puts it: "As a small centralized office with two full-time searchers and one full-time assistant, our rather collegial service has not yet felt the need to develop a formal online policy statement for in-house use. Nor do the MIT Libraries at present have a system-wide reference policy."[5] Here, though, as in many libraries, Ms. Pensyl adds that a committee is at work in an attempt "to draw together some of the disparate policy-related materials of the various library units and services. One such memo [is] the description of guidelines on the use of the online service for quick reference referrals" [see p. 486].

If full online policy statements are rare, they do exist; see the 12-page manual from the University of Houston which is printed in full at the end of this compilation. An earlier effort, and one often used as a guideline, is the University of Massachusetts' "Computer Search Service Group. Policy Manual" prepared in 1977 and quoted in part here.

PURPOSE OF POLICY & PROCEDURES

No matter what form, the purpose of the policy and procedures "is to state guidelines for providing reference service in order to insure a uniform standard of service of the highest possible quality consistent with available resources." (University of Massachusetts/Amherst). At McGill it is noted that "the manual is designed both to orient new staff members and to be an information resource for . . . reference librarians." Beyond the pragmatic justification for statements, they serve to indicate the basic philosophy of service envisioned by the librarians and administration, and in most cases establish a number of goals and objectives.

Reasons for having a policy are almost as numerous as the librarians who draw them up, but essentially:

- The drafting or modification of a policy requires some appreciation of the overall goals, purpose, and direction of reference service. The systematic analyses of service given, or not given, helps to formulate these necessary objectives.
- Standards are established, not only for service but for such things as building the collection, the handling of interlibrary loan materials, and preparation of correspondence.
- A better view of the audience served (or not served) is achieved by considering objectives and standards. Obviously, neither can be analyzed without a careful study of the library patrons.
- Levels of service must be considered, i.e., just how much assistance is given the user in finding information and/or in actually finding the information for the user?
- Without a view of the world beyond the scope of the reference desk, services may become less than ambitious, locked more into routine and daily expediency than long-range needs of the community and the individuals the librarian hopes to serve.
- As Kathy Coleman of San Diego State University puts it: "Most of our policy statements are developed to resolve controversies . . . [such as] why the microforms staff cannot do all the threading of film readers; why advance notice of class assignments is necessary."
- The policy serves as a touchstone of continuity for new staff, helps to refresh the memory of even veterans who may not be aware of rarely recurrent problems.
- Since there rarely are enough staff members for ideal service, the statement establishes priorities in the hierarchy of services.

- And this leads to probably the most useful aspect of the policy statement: it serves to clarify, if not always answer, nagging queries about the limits of service that the librarian faces daily. For example, a good policy should consider (to name only a few) such things as: What type of material is considered reference and what does this mean in terms of use, circulation, storage, etc.?; Who comes first when the telephone rings, the person standing at the desk or the individual with a question on the phone?; What's to be done when a person wants legal, medical, or consumer advice?; Are the rules different for children, young people, and adults?

Addressing himself to public library statements, Childers concludes that:

Reference and information service policy has been shown to be uneven. Even within a given reference department, it would not be unusual to find two of the service staff harboring quite divergent ideas about the services that clients are entitled to....Matters that should have been settled through formal policy have been left to individual whim and...each librarian...is creating his own set of policies....There are, however, forces at work that may be precipitating the formation of more explicit reference and information service policy for the library agency. First, restricted reference and information service budgets may be forcing a reconsideration of how much of the library's resources should be expended on a client's questions and which client's questions should be dealt with.... Second, studies of reference and information service continue; moreover, the practice of locally collecting reference and information statistics grows ....It is my experience that early unobtrusive studies of reference performance have not only prompted further investigations on the local level but have impelled some librarians to revise their reference and information processes and policies.[6]

Is it valid to use, or at least modify, statements in X library when they are developed for the need of Y library? The answer is "yes" if it is a question of philosophy and broad goals of service; "no" if it is a problem of minor procedure. Obviously, for example, all libraries, regardless of size, type, location, or staff, are dedicated to information services. This is a goal, but it is another thing to turn to procedures and say that in giving those services the telephone should be in use from 8:00 a.m. to 5:00 p.m., answered only by professional librarians, etc. Still, even the smallest detail about a procedure may be useful as a point of departure for consideration and discussion by a librarian in another situation; many of these procedures are reprinted here.

ORGANIZATION OF THE BOOK

This compilation opens with a series of articles, which were requested by the editors. Except for the RASD guidelines, none has been published before. It was also decided to reprint three detailed manuals in their entirety and in the order prescribed by the compilers: Rice University Library, Los Angeles Public Library, and University of Houston, Texas Library. These offer an overall view of what the editors consider some of the better statements.

In addition, a detailed list of the libraries who contributed or are otherwise involved in this compilation is provided. The name of each library is given in full, as well as the person with whom the editors had correspondence, at least when material included a covering letter. The name of the statement is given, as well as the date. (Where the statement was not dated, the date of the correspondence is indicated.) Here and there some explanatory material from a letter is included.

With the exception of the three policy statements reprinted in full, reliance is on excerpts from manuals, statements, directives, and the like. It was early decided to use the excerpt approach, rather than simply printing the statements as received, because the excerpt method was considered by far the most useful by librarians consulted, and the excerpts save useless duplication. Understandably, many of the policies and/or sections within the policies are almost exact duplicates of those found in other libraries. It is understandable because many librarians model their efforts after ones used successfully by other libraries.

The organization of the various approaches to reference policy and procedures in this compilation follows that suggested in several sources: The Reference and Adult Services Division "Draft Guidelines Outline of Information Service Policy Manual" (see p. 8), and the organization employed by the University of Massachusetts/Amherst, Rice University, and the Los Angeles Public Library. A much modified version of these approaches was employed to organize the online materials.

Within this pattern, excerpts are divided by academic, public, and online services—the latter including statements from both types of libraries as well as a few special libraries. The outlines are models and can be of great value, for, as one expert put it, "they are a tremendous step toward the development of the necessary service policy statements for libraries."[7]

A few libraries include collection statements in the service policy,[8] but these are not reprinted, since many are already available in another collection—Elizabeth Futas' *Library Acquisition Policies and Procedures* (Neal-Schuman/Oryx Press, 1977). Futas' index shows some two dozen entries for "reference collection" or "reference materials." Acquisition of reference materials tends to be treated differently; often it is not part of the policy statement itself, but may be a separate document.

The best, most complete collection policy is available from the reference department at McGill University: "Reference Collection Policy," fourth edition. Revised in late 1980, it consists of 23 single-spaced, tightly packed pages. The one concession made to acquisitions is inclusion of the last part of the Rice University Library "Reference Procedures."[9]

HOW TO DEVELOP A POLICY

Readers are advised to turn to the articles preceding this collection for the best advice on policy development—and to the readings on p. xxxvi. There are no magic methods, but those who have drawn up statements do have a few major suggestions.

Preparing a statement is a time-consuming affair. Typical is the experience of the Los Angeles Public Library. As the Assistant City Librarian explained: "These guidelines . . . reflect the work of a staff committee which spent several years developing them, seeking comments from staff at all agencies, and responding to those comments and concerns."[10]

Depending upon the situation, the best initial approach to drawing up or modifying a statement is to organize a small committee. Each member should be responsible for studying one or more operations or procedures of the reference section on a daily basis. This should be accomplished by discussion with the librarians involved, and sometimes, depending upon the situation, a representative group of users. Necessary documents, previous rules, standards, guidelines, etc., should be collected—but only those relevant. Statements from other similar libraries should be considered—a service of this collection; but one which may be augmented, of course, by direct contact with libraries in the immediate area or region.

One of the major problems is separating policy from procedures. As Marjorie Karlson of the University Massachusetts notes elsewhere in this compilation: "In our work we had no real difficulties in coming to an agreement in principle on policy questions. Our solution was to include a lot of material on procedures."[11] Once the parts pertinent to reference service are collected, a rough draft should be drawn and compared with operational procedures throughout the library, for example, statements employed in cataloging, circulation, and/or by individual subject divisions or departments or sections.

Every individual involved should have the opportunity to make suggestions for additions and deletions. And from there, the draft should be developed into the final statement, which, once again, should be examined carefully by the entire staff and—in some cases—by the lay public. The latter may seem advisable where there is a helpful board of trustees.

WHY NO POLICY

One may assume that a basic reason that 58 percent of the libraries queried did not respond is that they do not have a policy statement. But even of the 42 percent that did answer, five of the 33 public libraries and eight of the 52 academic libraries do not have policies. Only two of the 40 respondents to online queries lack any type of policy.

There are numerous reasons, both expressed and unexpressed, for the showing of less than enthusiastic interest in a codified policy. Commonly expressed reasons are:

- It is a time-consuming and sometimes costly business and, in a period of short staff and small budgets, the time and money are better spent elsewhere.
- Often even the most detailed statement will not answer once-a-year type problems, i.e., problems arise which are not covered.
- The statements should be precise and lacking ambiguity. This is not always possible, particularly as some situations do not lend themselves to simple solutions.
- Procedures, if not overall policies, tend to date quickly and there is little point in codification of rapid change.
- Even with a procedure/policy statement, few of the staff bother to use the statement, and rely primarily upon experience and advice from peers to solve problems.
- As Alice's endless tea party, policy statements constantly are in need of revision—so much so that some librarians find it a major check against even thinking about a written policy. As a librarian from Northwestern University put it, "I have mixed feelings about policy manuals since they continually have to be updated—I wonder if they are worth the amount of time invested."[12]

The policy statement is not a monolithic set of rules and regulations. It is subject to constant change, but this is not always possible. Today, the lack of revision and modification is more due to lack of staff and budget than to the will. For example, a probably typical case is described by Kathy Coleman of San Diego State University: "Since 1974 when the policy was written, we have suffered several major budget cuts; these have affected both our staff and our materials. Consequently, there are now unwritten policies which limit our services."

All of the reasons are apparent, but there are more persuasive arguments against written policy statements—persuasive at least to those who defend lack of such policies. Fear of overt regulation as a check to the imaginative is clearly stated in a letter from the Houston Public Library: "We have not developed a written policy because we would not wish to place a limit on what our reference staff might wish to do in serving the patron. Our philosophy generally, in regard to public service, is to make every effort to satisfy the information needs of the public we serve. In some cases, we think a written policy statement would not be consistent with our philosophy and intent."[13] Merrily E. Taylor, the Director, Library Services Group at Columbia, implied much the same thing: "We do not have any formal written statement. . . . Columbia has a long tradition of skilled and outgoing reference service, something which we try to encourage by peer example, dialogue among reference librarians on ways to improve reference approaches, and administrative support."

Summarizing these attitudes, a spokesperson for the University of Western Ontario library observes:

> I am personally opposed to lengthy and detailed policy statements and/or procedural manuals for reference services. While it is true that there exists a body of unwritten policy which is passed on more or less formally during the training program for new Reference staff members, writing it down causes two major problems.
> 1. There might well be a tendency for some staff to regard the statements as prescriptive: i.e., "I can only do what it says here." This would destroy the initiative and ad hoc situational judgements which are so important in our line of work.
> 2. Any such statement would require not only lengthy internal negotiations to insure the agreement of all to its basic principles, but also passage through at least two further levels of bureaucracy in the Library System. Aside from the obvious problems of time wastage, there might be problems caused by making explicit some of our services.
> We have, through the eight years of our existence, developed a very good overall reputation for providing service. I'm not terribly inclined to tinker with success.[14]

THE SURVEY

Statements to be included in this compilation were collected over a period of 14 months from the first part of 1980 to March 1981. A letter requesting the statements was sent to 120 academic, 100 public, and 80 school librarians. These letters also requested the policy for bibliographic data base use, if the library had such a statement. Follow-up letters went to 50 special libraries, in the expectation of receiving their data base policy statements.

The academic libraries receiving letters were chosen from a list of the ranking research libraries that appeared in the *Chronicle of Higher Education* (February 20, 1979). In addition, 25 letters were sent to librarians who had written articles for *RQ* in the past four years and who worked at institutions other than those on the *Chronicle* list. The public libraries were chosen out of the *American Library Directory*, 32nd edition, by a random sample method. School library systems with enrollment of 10,000 and over were chosen from the *Education Directory* compiled by the National Center for Education Statistics. The special libraries were chosen from the "User Group Directory" that appeared in *Online* (July 1979, January 1980, July 1980), the *New England On-Line Users Group Directory of Members*, and the *Directory of Libraries Providing Computer-Based Information Services in the New York Metropolitan Area.*

In a negative sense, perhaps the most interesting—although hardly unexpected—finding was that school libraries apparently do not have reference service guidelines. Of the 80 inquiries sent to schools (both elementary and secondary), there were only 15 responses. None were applicable.[15] Most who responded noted they had no such policy, or simply sent material about collections and acquisitions. The reader is referred to Patricia Payne's article for one explanation of this less-than-wild interest by school librarians in reference policies. The editors hope to explore this situation in more depth at a later date.

Of the 120 academic libraries to which a query was sent requesting reference statements, there were 52 responses, of which about one-half (24) were found useful for the present compilation. Others were not used because they were not available, repetitious of existing material, dated, they arrived too late, etc.[16]

Of the 100 public libraries which were sent letters, there were 33 responses, of which 24 were of use and reprinted in part. Of the 270 online inquiries sent to 120 academic libraries, 100 public libraries, and 50 special libraries, there were 40 responses, of which 23 (12 academic, 3 public, and 8 special) are reprinted in part here.

If one examines the results, libraries represented here *with* documents fall into fairly well-defined categories:

Academic
These libraries are broken down by the number of volumes in the collection:
Small (under 1 million volumes)—20%
Medium (between 1 million and 2 million volumes)—60%
Large (over 2 million volumes)—20%
Public
Circulation figures are used for the breakdown here:
Small (under 1 million circulation)—21%
Medium (between 1 million and 2 million circulation)—33%
Large (over 2 million circulation)—46%
Online
Public Libraries—the three represented here have circulations of well over 1.5 million
Academic—four with volumes under 1 million
—four with between 1 and 2 million
—four with 2 million and over
Special Libraries—these eight libraries are distinguished by their specializations in the sciences and education.

It becomes apparent that medium- to large-sized libraries are more likely to have policy statements detailing their reference and online services to the public. The problems and procedures of reference work can grow more complicated as the number of patrons increases. It seems that some of the larger libraries have attempted to deal with these problems by clarifying and codifying methods of service.

Although the excerpts included in this compilation seem to cover most situations, there are four areas the editors have identified where more attention is needed:

- Security of reference materials is a recurrent theme in letters to the editor. But how can a policy statement prevent theft? More is needed. Should the statement then call for rigorous guard controls, or what?
- Continuing education of staff, particularly with increased on-line activities, seems increasingly important, but is *not* found in many of the statements.
- The use of OCLC, RLIN, etc. (related, of course, to online service) at the reference desk requires specific attention.
- Services to handicapped people is an area that must be addressed by all types of libraries.

Further editions of this compilation are planned. Therefore, the editor would welcome statements prepared by libraries for consideration in the next edition, as well as revisions of statements included in this first edition. Any communication about policies is most welcome. Correspondence should be directed to the editor at: School of Library and Information Science, State University of New York, 135 Western Ave., Albany, NY 12222.

Bill Katz

Anne Clifford

FOOTNOTES

1. Ms. Lieberman, letter to editor, October 30, 1980. She goes on to explain that "In 1977 the library received funds to implement a two-year project of online searching through Lockheed, SDC, and BRS. . . . I reviewed the material and did not find anything that could be called a policy statement."
2. Richard Jensen, Life Sciences Librarian, letter to editor, November 20, 1980.
3. Sharon Shekha, letter to editor, December, 1980.
4. Martha Gregory, Info II Librarian, letter to editor, December 8, 1980. "Since the policy for the entire library system is to be updated in 1981, we are going to add the Info II service to that project."
5. Mary E. Pensyl, Head, Computerized Literature Search Service, MIT, letter to editor, January 7, 1981. Martha Gregory, letter to editor, December 8, 1980, reports the same situation in the Tulsa City County Library: "Since we have a rather small operation, one person and a half-time person, it has not been a problem [not to have a policy statement.]"
6. Thomas Childers, "The Future of Reference and Information Service in the Public Library," *The Library Quarterly*, October, 1978, pp. 467–68.
7. Thelma Freides, "Report from Dallas . . .," *RQ*, Winter, 1979, p. 132. The quote is from Janet Bean.
8. Of those reprinted in part here, the academic libraries: Alberta, Arizona State, Ball State, Brigham Young, Case Western Reserve, and Illinois; and public libraries: Louisville, Philadelphia.
9. Although somewhat dated, the best outline to date for a reference collection policy is that by Kathleen Coleman and Pauline Dickinson, "Drafting a Reference Collection Policy," *College & Research Libraries*, May 1977, pp. 227–233. While for an academic library, most of the outline is equally applicable to other types of libraries.

The authors give a succinct justification for such a policy, p. 227: "A reference collection policy is a useful tool for several reasons. First, it sets uniform guidelines for the collection, including subject scope, depth of coverage, and types of material to be included. Second, it provides an opportunity for coordinating the reference collection with reference service. Since the reference collection is a working collection, materials should be chosen, located, and, if necessary, duplicated, to serve the needs of reference librarians and users. Third, the reference collection policy is an effective orientation device for training new staff in making reference decisions. Finally, the policy spells out the cooperation and division of labor which takes place between public service departments or, in very large institutions, between libraries, so that duplication is planned rather than unintentional."

10. Linda Wood, Assistant City Librarian, Letter to editor, February 28, 1980.
11. Marjorie Karlson, p. 17 of this compilation.
12. Sandy Whiteley, Head, Reference Department, letter to editor, February 13, 1980. Northwestern does have policies and procedures in written form, but even those libraries with such statements sometimes question their validity.
13. James L. Mayfield, Administrative Assistant, Houston Public Library, letter to editor, February 27, 1980.
14. George T. Robinson, Librarian-in-charge, Reference/Government Publications, University of Western Ontario Library, London, Canada, letter to editor, March 24, 1980.
15. Documents sent by schools included such things as "Evaluation and selection of instructional materials and equipment"; a board policy on "The selection and adoption of library books and instructional materials"; statements on academic freedom; selection policies.
16. For comparison: Mary Jo Lynch ("Academic Library Reference Policy Statement," *RQ*, Spring, 1972, pp. 222–226) surveyed 60 academic libraries (of the same type and approximate size as the University of Massachusetts) and found that only three replied with documents which could be useful for Massachusetts.

In 1976, Elizabeth Futas (*Library Acquisition Policies and Procedures.* Neal Schuman/Oryx Press, 1977) requested acquisition policy statements from about 3,600 academic and public libraries. She received material from about 15 percent of the total.

The primary source of reference services policy statements has been the limited collection at the American Library Association library. It is limited because there are seven statements available from academic libraries and six from public libraries, and not all of these consist of full statements of policy. There are no online statements, although "a packet of information sheets collected in 1978 from libraries on their policies and methods of charging for online bibliographic services" is available on interlibrary loan.

Readings

The literature is no gauge of need for reference service policies. Or if it is, the result is negative in that a search, both manual and online, of major services for the past 10 years reveals little.

Writing in 1971, Mary Jo Lynch noted that a ten-year search of *Library Literature* "and scanning the major books on reference service and university library administration did not provide any leads to model policy statements or advice on how to develop one." ("Academic Library Reference Policy Statement," *RQ*, Spring 1972, p. 222.)

GENERAL

"California Library Association Draft—Statement of Professional Responsibility for Librarians," *California Librarian*, January, 1978, pp. 35–38. Guidelines which detail five principles to be followed by librarians. All may be modified and/or adopted in a reference services statement.

Coleman, Kathleen and Pauline Dickinson. "Drafting a Reference Collection Policy," *College & Research Libraries*, May, 1977, pp. 227–233. A detailed outline of the collection policy at San Diego State University. Also a brief indication is given of procedures employed in drawing up the policy.

"Goals and Guidelines for Community Library Services," *PLA Newsletter*, June, 1975, p. 12+. Points here still useful for consideration in reference policy statements.

Lynch, Mary Jo. "Academic Library Reference Policy Statement,"
RQ, Spring, 1972, pp. 222–226. A report on the development of one
of the best and most complete reference service manuals now available (since revised). Particularly helpful: "Draft outline of reference service policy manual," pp. 217–220.

McKinnon, Katherine. "Policies for Public Libraries," *Ontario Library
Review*, December 1973, pp. 231–233. A guide for library trustees,
and while dated it offers a simple, direct outline of topics to cover.

ONLINE

Atherton, Pauline and Roger Christian. *Librarians and Online Services*. White Plains, New York: Knowledge Industries, 1977. One of
the best general guides to the field with much which is applicable
to planning an online service policy.

Daniels, Linda. "A Matter of Form," *Online*, October, 1978, pp. 31–
38. A collection of search request forms.

Gardner, Trudy. "Effect of On-Line Data Bases on Reference Policy,"
RQ, Fall, 1979, pp. 70–74. A discussion of levels of reference service,
online searches, and the future of teaching people how to use the
library. An argument on user education which will influence online policy statements.

Kranich, Nancy. "Fees for Library Service: They Are Not Inevitable,"
Library Journal, May 1, 1980, pp. 1048–1051. In opposition to
charging for online searches. One of scores of articles (pro and con)
on the subject which will influence online policy statements.

McClure, Charles. "A Planning Primer for Online Reference Service
in a Public Library," *Online*, April, 1980, pp. 57–65. A clear explanation of basic planning steps for establishment and maintenance of
online services. Useful for both public and small- to medium-sized
academic libraries. Applicable, at least in part, to online search
policy statements.

ERIC DOCUMENTS

ED 116/701 Reference Service Manual. Massachusetts Univ. Amherst. June, 1975. 46pp. (1980 revision ED 200211.)

135/409 Standards for Reference Service at the University of
Michigan—Dearborn Library. Feb. 1977. 7pp.

144/557 Computer Search Service Group. Policy Manual. Massachusetts Univ. Amherst. June, 1977. 29pp.

150/983 A Model Reference Service Manual for a Law School
Library. M.A., Univ. of California at Los Angeles. June,
1977. 35pp.

160/120 Procedures for Processing Requests for Computerized
Literature Searches. New York State Dept. of Education, Division of Library Development. January 1976.
36pp.

174/221 Policy Manual for a Computerized Search Service in an
Academic Library. University of Houston, Texas, March
15, 1979.

Policy Statements:
An Overview

After the Guidelines and Reference Policy

Bernard Vavrek, Professor
School of Library Science
Clarion State College

Librarians can generally be faulted for a historical failure to establish priorities. This is a particularly acute matter when it is related to the development of reference services in the United States. Dutifully, the reference librarian has pursued his/her perception of assumed responsibilities in an honest, but not necessarily direct, fashion. This circuity has not been created by a lack of motivation or professionalism, but because there has been frequently little opportunity to think about and plan for what reference service means in a particular library. It is not uncommon to overhear a reference librarian saying, "There is no need for a reference policy in a library because reference service is a creative process and, therefore, defies neat description."

Every library needs a reference policy. Not because it will offer the framework to answer every procedural or philosophical matter that

3

arises, but because it provides a basis for continuity. That is, a policy enables the patron, as well as the librarian, to expect that certain things will be done and likewise, that certain things fall outside the normal expectations of what is known as reference service. There is no more compelling long-range priority than for the immediate development of a reference policy or the improvement of an existing policy to improve service.

Although it has been now five years since "Commitment for Information Services . . ." was published by RASD, this author has not lost enthusiasm over the importance of that document. There is little question that both philosophically and practically the "Guidelines" are as important as the inception of institutionalized reference service itself.

The significance of the "Guidelines" lies with the fact that they were published. For the first time, reference service emerged from the closet of historical discussion to enable a basis for "detailed" consideration to take place. The reader must remember that while the standards issued for types of libraries do include some direct mention of reference service, the "Guidelines" were the first pronouncement aimed at normalization, i.e., attempting to generalize reference service by common elements, to all types of libraries.

Critics of the "Guidelines" probably have not been dissuaded from their 1976 positions. Frankly, there is considerable room for criticism because there are plenty of weaknesses in that publication. Undoubtedly, the most significant omission is in relation to reference evaluation. The "Guidelines" provide little more to the reader than the admonition: do it. Another critical area which was not addressed by RASD's Standards Committee in promulgating the "Guidelines" was the technological application of online reference service, although it is more than hinted in the document; consider the title, "Commitment to Information Services . . ." Further, the "Guidelines" express nothing directly about information services provided in a community information center (I&R) context. Here the author believes, however, that enough information can be gleaned generally from the "Guidelines" to help those interested in I&R centers.

But with weaknesses aside, the reader is cautioned to remember that the utility derived from the "Guidelines" is based on its generalness, that is, its ability to be applied in a variety of different circumstances. And in this broad application or in the effort to do all things for all libraries, specificity, is sacrificed.

This last matter, after all, must be considered one of the reasons that it took so long for any compromise document to be published by

RASD that would approximate standards. If it is unclear how the "Guidelines" represent a compromise, it should be noted that the rather cumbersome "reference librarian/information specialist" appears in the document—an effort to satisfy both perceptions of the reference person.

For the record, this author would like to state the view that the "Guidelines" represent standards of service. In fact, in many ways they are a part of the general trend that has developed in casting standards for types of libraries in a philosophical rather than quantitative framework. And, of course, in describing standards it should be clear that minimal levels of service are being suggested.

It is my contention that reference departments or services should be accredited just as the American Library Association accredits schools of library science. Otherwise there is no really satisfactory means of reference librarians evaluating or helping other reference librarians.

It has been assumed that reference people work conscientiously with the best interests of their clients centrally in mind. Unfortunately, there is also evidence that some reference librarians perform poorly and are content to provide less than minimally acceptable service. Certainly, an accreditation process will not cure all shortcomings, but it would at least have the tendency to insure minimal levels of preparation and acceptance.

The question of "What is the incentive?" still lingers. An answer would be that libraries would be professionally blacklisted if they did not meet standards. Blacklisted by whom? By both the state library organizations as well as ALA. It would provide an opportunity for some library associations to begin or to recapture their lost sense of professional direction. ("Lost" because some library associations exist for few reasons other than maintaining the status quo and existence of the organization.)

The idea of accrediting reference services in all types of libraries initially creates an impression of an overwhelming bureaucratic mess if not a sheer impossibility. But let's assume that if the mechanism were established for even one type of library, considerable accomplishment would be achieved. Public libraries, for example, represent the largest category of library in the United States and generally represent the institution needing the greatest amount of assistance. The responsibilities for implementing accreditation in public libraries would be shared by at least three components: The American Library Association, state libraries and state library agencies, and district or county library systems. Practically speaking, the actual techniques could, and probably by necessity would, vary from state to state, but the important thing is that the ultimate goal be kept alive: insuring good reference service.

Another step in improving reference service would be for the RASD's Standards Committee to update the "Guidelines." This author would like to suggest two areas in the "Guidelines" for direct improvement. One topic in need of change has already been suggested— reference evaluation. My own biased view (actually shared by others) is that evaluation, if it is to be of any significant impact, must be based on individual reference programs which have goals, objectives, a budget, and a basis for evaluation. An example would be the public library that wants to augment its ability at providing telephone reference service. It would have to determine the means to achieve this, and determine how to judge its success. Many librarians have simply failed to establish program objectives and the appropriate follow-through. It is not surprising that uncertainty has overwhelmed the discussions dealing with techniques of reference evaluation because of the tendency to want to do everything at the same time.

The other category for improvement in the "Guidelines" pertains to the size of reference collections. This individual has fought (at least in writing) against the appropriateness of devising an arbitrary minimum for collection development. My argument followed the logic that the effort at establishing national norms was without purpose. Age and, hopefully, additional insight into library matters has now tempered this author's view that identifying minimal collection size is of merit largely because this bit of practical information does not exist.

Interestingly, while bibliographies and guides for collection development are available, such as *Reference Books for Small and Medium-Sized Libraries*, these resources do not really answer the question of which reference books constitute a basic reference collection and should be purchased first before any others. So while it will provide some controversy, librarians, particularly those in small- and medium-sized libraries, need some practical insight into the basis of collection development. As to what this minimal figure is, this author will leave comfortably to the deliberations of the Standards Committee. Parenthetically, it is not enough to determine optimal size; specific reference titles must be identified for initial purchase (understanding that there will be bitter disagreements on the matter), with some sense of what will be purchased the second year, etc.

Assuming that updating the "Guidelines" can be done expeditiously, the next phase would be for the state libraries and state library organizations to develop a modus operandi for implementing the "Guidelines." Because of the uniqueness of public library service across the United States, the approaches will be different. But whether the direction is by district or county system or individual library, "enforcement" of the "Guidelines" has to be achieved through state initiative. A logical approach, in my view, is to allocate some LSCA funds to assure minimal levels of reference service consistent with the "Guidelines." While many readers may be taken aback with the notion of using already thinly distributed LSCA funds for additional purposes, consider for a moment the fact that many projects funded with Library Services and Construction Act funds are directed toward reference utilization anyway.

Verification of implementation would be the final step in the process being suggested. State libraries cooperating with state agencies would have this responsibility. One can envisage a situation where the extension librarian or county librarian and a committee of individuals would be accountable for individual libraries. And accountability would mean on-site verification that libraries are meeting these standards.

Assuring the quality of reference service may be a step many believe has been taken; the reality is that it has not.

A Commitment to Information Services: Developmental Guidelines 1979

Standards Committee, RASD, American Library Association

INTRODUCTION

The emergence of entirely new and sophisticated information retrieval systems has required rethinking of established concepts and methods of reference and information services. The institutional framework for those services becomes less important than the delivery of services of high quality. In addition, the increasing diversity of the user populations requires a change in the traditional modes of the delivery of information services, particularly in relation to cooperative endeavors and networking arrangements where back-up levels of information resource capability are provided.

The librarian/information specialist must be the intermediary or the negotiator for unlocking these multifarious information resources.

This responsibility places the concept of good service on the ability of the librarian/information specialist to be an effective facilitator in this transaction. In all transactions the librarian/information specialist must be impartial and nonjudgmental.

It is recognized that service strategies need to be designed that are more sophisticated and sensitive to the complex user patterns never known to our profession before. The guidelines for services reflect a suggested level of performance in meeting the needs of users in those institutions and agencies which need practical methods of procedure and self-evaluation for the delivery of information services.

The guidelines are directed to all those who have any responsibility for providing reference and information services, including the reference or information specialist, supervisors or department heads, administrators, educators, and trustees. In providing services, they shall consider the needs and interests of all users, including children, young adults, adults, people who do not come to a library information center, and potential clients.

SCOPE

Providing reference services in a library or information center should be recognized as a critical responsibility in meeting the information needs of users and prospective users.[1] It should be organized to provide, as appropriate, for the coordinated access to the information resources existing within an area or a given field of endeavor.

Since all functions of a library or information center should be viewed, in ultimate terms, as facilitating the transfer of information, the distinguishing feature of reference services is that it specifically ensures the optimum uses of information resources through substantive interaction with the users on direct and indirect levels cited below:

A. *Reference or information services* consist of personal assistance provided to users in pursuit of information. The character and extent of such services will vary with the kind of library or information center; with the user the institution is designed to serve; with the skill, competence, and professional training of the librarian/information specialist providing the service; and with the resources available both inside and outside the institutional framework to which the user has come. This service may range from answering an apparently simple query to supplying information based on a bibliographical search combining the library/information specialist's competence in information-handling techniques with competence in the subject of inquiry. The feature of information service, irrespective of its level or its intensity, is to provide an end-product in terms of information sought by the user.

B. *Formal and informal instruction in the use of the library or information center and its resources* may range from the explanation of the use of the bibliographical aids (e.g., catalogs, information data bases, traditional reference works) to more formal assistance through interpretative tours and lectures designed to provide guidance and direction in the pursuit of information, rather than providing the information itself to users.

C. *Indirect reference service* reflects user access to a wide range of informational sources (e.g., bibliographies, indexes, information data bases) and may be the extension of the library's information service potential through cooperation with other library or information centers. This type of service recognizes the key role of interlibrary and interagency cooperation to provide adequate information service to users.

DEVELOPMENTAL GUIDELINES

1.0 *Services*

1.1 Reference or information services are to be developed not only to meet user needs and to improve present services but to anticipate user needs and demands.

1.2 A published service code with stated objectives is to be used to carry out information services and is to be available to all users. The code is to detail the circumstances under which services and resources are to be offered, the extent to which they are to be provided, any limitation on their provision, and to whom and by whom such services are to be provided. (See Appendix A for a sample draft outline)

1.3 Reference or information services are to be reviewed at regular intervals to identify those individuals who are and are not being served and to determine how individuals not utilizing such services can be reached.

1.4 Provision is to be made for continuous feedback from users concerning their satisfaction with services and success in locating information.

1.5 A specific plan for the instruction of individuals in the use of information aids is to be developed and coordinated among all types of libraries, information centers, or units of library activity.

1.6 Bibliographical and other information access guides are to be developed by librarians/information specialists as an active "alert" service signifying the potential of the information resource base available to users.

1.7 Access to reference or information services is to be promoted and provided in adaptable settings, including person-to-person contact, correspondence, and/or through other communication media.

1.8 Formal cooperation among other information handling units, centers, or agencies at local, regional, state, and national levels is essential to provide for the needs of all users and potential users.

1.9 Referrals to other sources and agencies are to be a standard level of information service operation. The effectiveness of these referrals should be evaluated at selected intervals to determine the effectiveness of the delivery service and the quality of the response to the user.

2.0 *Resources*

2.1 A selection policy is to be developed which addresses the needs and anticipated needs of the user and reflects the available resources to the user within an accessible area. Consideration should be given to a cooperative selection policy within a given service area.

2.2 Materials are to be added which reflect a diversity in format, levels of information service activity (e.g., general information service, resource back-up and research capability), and known user patterns of the past.

2.3 Frequently used materials are to be available in multiple copies in order to address user demands more quickly.

2.4 All information materials are to be examined regularly for condition, usefulness and currency, and either retained, discarded, or replaced.

3.0 *Environment*

3.1 The importance of information services requires that service points be as near as possible to the main focal point of activity in the library or information center. In some instances, this will be near the main entrance.

3.2 The reference or information collection should be situated so that it is near an open area where access allows for quick and effective service.

3.3 Individual carrels or other provisions for quiet concentrated study are to be available for users of the reference or information collection.

3.4 The main reference or information area is to be situated so that the necessary conversation between library users and librarians/information specialists is not disturbing to others.

3.5 Additional service points are to be located so that access to librarians/information specialists is available throughout the library with communication equipment and techniques provided when appropriate.

4.0 *Personnel*

4.1 Staffing patterns and hours open are to reflect directly the needs of the users.

4.2 A professional librarian/information specialist should be available to users during all hours the library is open.

4.3 The reference or information staff is to promote actively the use of all library services. This should be done by whatever means are appropriate to the institutional setting, e.g., canvassing a public library area to offer assistance.

4.4 When staff size permits, individual librarians/information specialists should have training in specific subject fields.

4.5 Staff members are to be chosen with consideration given not only to their academic background and knowledge, but also to their ability to communicate easily with people.

4.6 Continuing education of the librarian/information specialist is basic to professional growth and is the responsibility of the individual, the institution, and the policymaking body of the institution.

5.0 *Evaluation*

5.1 User data are to be collected on a regular basis to determine effectiveness of information service patterns. This implies the budgeting for such analysis through user surveys and other analytic measures.

5.2 The measurement and evaluation of reference or information services should be the responsibility of one or more staff members with some skills in this field.

5.3 Statistics are to be collected on a systematic basis for use in evaluation, policy decision, reports, and in budget preparation.

6.0 *Ethics of Service*

6.1 Information provided the user in response to any inquiry must be the most accurate possible. Type of question or status of user is not to be considered. Eligibility of users will be determined by the role, scope, and mission of individual institutions.

6.2 Personal philosophies and attitudes should not be reflected in the execution of service or in the extent and accuracy of information provided.

6.3 Information contacts with users, whether reference or directional, are to be treated with complete confidentiality.

6.4 All rules and practices regarding availability and use of information or resources must be administered impartially. Rules and practices must be codified (i.e., reference policy statement) and made available to the user in written form.

6.5 No personal financial gain should result because of the librarian/ information specialist role as a representative of the library in dealing with the user.

Appendix A

Draft Outline of Information Service Policy Manual

I.   Introduction
    A. Nature of Information Service
    B. Statement of Objectives
    C. Purpose of the Policy Manual
      1. Guidance
      2. Standards

II.   Types of Service
    A. General Statement
    B. List of Services
      1. Information Service at Desk
        a. Information service—answers to specific questions, statistics, biographies, etc.
        b. Instruction in the use of the library—how to use the card catalog, periodical indexes, bibliographies, services, etc.
        c. Bibliographic verification of items in the library or not in the library—including assistance in obtaining items by purchase, copy, or loan of items not in the collection.
        d. Instruction in methodology and bibliography—how to do a literature search, how to bibliographically cite a publication or article.
        e. Assistance in locating library material.
      2. Interlibrary Service
        a. Borrowing
        b. Lending
        c. Answering inquiries from other libraries

3. Bibliographic Service
   a. Bibliographies
   b. Demand bibliographies
   c. Current awareness services
4. Correspondence—answering inquiries from individuals
5. Document Service
6. Orientation and Instructional Services

III.   Library Users
   A. General Statement
   B. Categories of Users
IV.   Priorities
V.   Desk Service Policies and Instructions
   A. General Guidelines for Desk Duty
      1. Nature and extent of responsibilities
      2. Guidelines for handling inquiries
         a. General inquiries
         b. Problem inquiries
      3. Behavior and attitudes
         a. Approachability
         b. Mobility
      4. Recording statistics and questions
      5. Reporting problems
   B. General instructions for information assistants on desk duty (Limitations concerning responsibilities outlined in Section I).
   C. Telephone
      1. Incoming Calls
         a. General guidelines
            (Time involved in answering phone, priority to user in building, etc.)
         b. Paging patrons
         c. Checking public catalog
         d. Circulation inquiries (checking shelf for material)
         e. General library information (switchboard function)
         f. Personal calls
         g. Emergency and nuisance calls
      2. Outgoing calls
         a. General guidelines for making calls
         b. Patron use of phone
         c. Personal calls
   D. Circulation Functions of Information Staff
      1. Reference books and other restricted materials

       a. Reference collection
       b. Stack Reference
       c. Archives
    2. Authorizing extended loans of periodicals
    3. Documents
    4. Vertical file
    5. Microforms
    6. Unprocessed materials
  E. Responsibility for service at nights, on weekends, and during skeleton coverage
    1. Public service areas
    2. Closed area
  F. Inquiries for "In Process" materials
  G. Referrals
    1. Information
    2. Other libraries and services
  H. "Special Information Collections"
    1. Documents
    2. Microforms
    3. Archives
    4. Vertical file
  I. Card catalog service
    1. Inquiries
    2. Surveillance of user at catalog
  J. Questions for exams, quizzes, puzzles
  K. Genealogical questions
VI. Interlibrary Loan Service
VII. Bibliographic Services
  A. Reference initiated
  B. Users' requests
    1. Individuals
    2. Courses
    3. Administrative staff
  C. Current awareness services
VIII. Information Correspondence
  A. Incoming
    1. General information
    2. Bibliographical information (holdings)
    3. Surveys
  B. Outgoing
    1. Preparation and review of replies
    2. Letters of introduction

IX.   Document Services
X.   Orientation and Instructional Services

FOOTNOTE

1. The term information center in this document includes any service point from which a user or prospective user may seek information on any level or type through direct or electronic means. Information services is a term used in the guidelines to include all traditional reference and information services and to be the broadest term possible.

The Reference Service Manual

Marjorie Karlson, Head
Reference Department
University of Massachusetts

The Reference Department of the University of Massachusetts/
Amherst Library has had a *Reference Service Manual*, incorporating
our reference policy, since 1975. (Available as ERIC document ED 116
701.) It has been reviewed several times and a revised version, with a
few changes in content and an improved format, was issued in
January, 1980. Work on the *Manual* began in 1971. An account of the
early stages of its preparation appears in an article by Mary Jo Lynch
who was a senior reference librarian in the department at that time
("Academic Library Reference Policy Statements," *RQ*, Spring 1972,
pp. 222–226). Its completion was delayed because of a change in
department head, a large turnover and a significant increase in the
staff of the department, and a move into a new building.

The many requests for copies which came from other reference
librarians were constant reminders of our unfinished task. We began
work again in 1974, using the original outline and drafts of some

sections of the *Manual* which had been prepared earlier. The sections of the outline on which no work had been done were distributed among the reference librarians in the department for the preparation of the remaining preliminary drafts. The drafts were discussed over a period of several months in our weekly departmental meetings and revised as a result of those discussions. Subsequent reviews of the text, which we have tried to do every year, have been handled in much the same way.

In our work on the *Manual* we had no real difficulties in coming to an agreement in principle on policy questions. The biggest problem was in trying to separate policy from procedure. Our solution was to include a lot of material on procedures, but even so, many references to additional procedures (texts of which are filed in our Staff Vertical File) are incorporated in the *Manual*.

How has the *Manual* been used since it was completed? It has, of course, been a basic tool for the orientation of new reference librarians. I do not think it is actually referred to very often by experienced reference librarians to answer questions about policy or procedures which come up in the course of daily work. I expect this is so because much of the content of the *Manual* has become internalized over a period of time. On occasion when there has been some continuing problem which we have discussed in a staff meeting we have referred back to the *Manual* to see if there is a policy statement which covers the situation. We have extracted from the *Manual* a two-page statement on departmental services and service policies which is available for public distribution. The parts of the *Manual* which deal with standards of service might be used as a tool for self-evaluation by each reference librarian, but we have not done this formally.

It is easy enough to state some of the uses to which the *Manual* has been or might be put. Its *value* is harder to determine. It is my own opinion that it is important to take the time to systematically think through what we are trying to do and what our priorities are and to wrestle with the problem of trying to state them in writing. And doing it once is not enough. There should be a continuing review in order to keep one's objectives, priorities, and standards clearly in focus and to allow for the possibility of changes as staff and circumstances change.

Whether the *Manual* could insure its stated purpose—"a uniform standard of service of the highest possible quality"—is another question. The only assurance of quality is excellent staff. I do not think it is possible, even with excellent staff, to achieve a "uniform standard of service." When one considers the size of collections even in a medium-sized academic library, the universe of knowledge those collections cover, and the pressures under which we work, such an expectation is unrealistic. Furthermore, each staff member will have individual strengths and weaknesses, and individual points of view. We cannot all be equally good at measuring up to each of the standards we set. But it does seem to me to be of unquestionable importance that we clearly know what our standards are so that we can continually work in trying to meet them. For this reason, I think that the considerable amount of time we have spent on our *Reference Service Manual* has been time well spent.

Drafting the Reference Services Policy Statement

Billie M. Connor, Principal Librarian, Science and Technology
Thomas E. Alford, Assistant City Librarian
Los Angeles Public Library

Library reference service as a concept has existed for a century.[1] Nevertheless, it has never had "an accepted body of theory which would delimit its field of activity, name and organize its basic concepts, formalize its techniques, and so lead us in the formulation of guidelines and standards."[2] In recent years, libraries have been forced to begin to articulate reference service policy. Factors bringing this about have been: the arrival of the post-industrial society, termed "an information society,"[3] the emergence of automated information retrieval systems,[4] which are revolutionizing the practice of reference service more than any other innovation, and the looming of serious fiscal limits.

Probably the greatest impetus was the adoption of the first working document which approximates standards of reference service,[5] "A Commitment to Information Services: Developmental Guidelines."[6] This statement, prepared by the Standards Committee, Reference and Adult Services Division, American Library Association, after almost ten years of discussion, was adopted by the Division in January 1976 and amended to include a section on ethics of service in January 1979. It serves as a useful guide for the formulation of a specific statement of reference and information policy for the individual library. Basic considerations for a local statement are listed in *Introduction to Reference Work*, by Katz.[7]

Faced with the task of drawing up a statement for the medium-sized to large public library, how does one proceed? Ideally, the institution should first establish its level of service. Three levels of reference service were outlined by James Wyer in 1930:[8] (1) conservative, which is to direct the patron to a source; (2) moderate, to show the patron the source that might answer his need and instruct him on how to use it; and (3) liberal, to provide the information or the actual answer to his question. Wyer's concepts are the basis for the scope of RASD's "Guidelines,"[9] and should assist the library in clarifying its philosophy of reference service.

Once the library has formulated its policy, drafting of the statement can begin. Major goals will be to produce a statement embodying the concepts in RASD's "Guidelines," one that will insure uniformity and a high quality of service throughout the institution (based on its level of service), and offer guidance to staff in all aspects of reference service. Following a statement of basic service philosophy and ethics, factors which must have general stated guidelines are: in-person reference service, telephone reference, mail requests, bibliographic services, reader's advisory service, information and referral, use of online data bases, updating information, and anticipating questions.

Problem areas which need to be dealt with are: quantitative guidelines for telephone reference limits; distinguishing between ready reference and call-backs; reserves and interlibrary loan; photocopy requests; school assignments; contest questions; reference questions which require special approaches; ratings and evaluations; critical analyses; medical, legal, statistical, and technical information; patent, trademark, and copyright searches; genealogies; translations; compilations and literature searches; mathematical calculations; and any other areas of significance to the specific library.

Methods used to produce a written statement may vary depending on the size and circumstances of the institution in question. The process used by the Los Angeles Public Library in drawing up its *Reference and Advisory Service Guidelines* was very effective. It required considerable time and effort, some of which could have been saved with better intitial planning; for example, a statement of philosophy evolved from the process rather than having preceded it. Nevertheless, the endeavor involved reference staff throughout the library system and resulted in a practical document which addresses basic needs of the reference librarian for guidance yet leaves room for professional judgment.

Initially, the project arose out of a need for guidelines for telephone reference policy for the Central Library. A committee of three Central Library reference supervisors was appointed to produce a draft statement. Very quickly the group came to the realization that guidelines for all aspects of reference service were needed and for the entire library system. A request for expansion of the charge and make-up of the committee was granted. The expanded committee consisted of representatives from varying information service components system-wide: the initial three, a reference supervisor in a regional branch, a reference supervisor in a community branch, a branch reference librarian, and a subject specialist in the federally funded extended reference service which serves Los Angeles Public Library as well as a network of other southern California libraries.

Work of the committee involved many steps. First, a thorough literature search was done relative to written statements of reference policy or guidelines and the development of such. Although the literature was very sparse, and RASD's "Guidelines" had not yet been published, a few bits of useful information were found. Libraries working on such a project today will find considerably more published information. Second, all Central Library subject departments and the branch libraries were surveyed to collect any existing written statements. Third, inquiries were sent to 24 libraries, some chosen for size and others for proximity, asking if a written statement of guidelines or policy existed and, if so, requesting a copy. The American Library Association Headquarters Library was also contacted to determine if a central file of such statements existed. Although ALA does maintain a collection today, at the time there were no examples on file. However, information was supplied that the University of Massachusetts Reference Department had such a statement and the committee was able to acquire that directly.

Of the 24 libraries contacted, only five did not respond. Of the respondents, four had no written statement, five were working on preparing one or anticipated doing so very soon, and ten had something in writing (ranging from a one-paragraph policy statement to two excellent sets of written guidelines). All were eager to receive the Los Angeles Public Library's statement when completed.

Next, a draft outline of what should be contained in a reference policy statement was devised, utilizing RASD's "Guidelines," which by that time had had their initial appearance in *RQ*, Summer 1976, and ideas gleaned from existing in-house statements, as well as those from other libraries.

With the outline as a basis, a questionnaire was prepared for use in interviews throughout the library system in an effort to determine current practice, problem areas, and expressed needs which should be addressed in a written statement. The committee then divided up the 13 Central Library departments and seven regions and in-person interviews were conducted with librarians with administrative responsibility and, in many cases, reference supervisors. Findings from the interviews were summarized in writing and a subcommittee prepared an overall summary of practice, problems, and consensus of opinion for the entire system. Due to the uniform questionnaire and in-person approach, the committee felt that the information had considerable validity.

The initial outline for reference guidelines was divided among three subcommittees for preparation of a draft of each part, taking into consideration the summary information from interviews, existing in-house statements, and sample statements from other libraries. Once completed, each draft was reviewed and refined by the committee as a whole, the statement was polished and a complete draft emerged.

The proposed guidelines were presented to Library administration with a request from the committee that librarians throughout the system be given an opportunity to review and comment on them before their revision and/or adoption as policy.

Many responses were received from staff, all of which were carefully reviewed by the committee. In some cases, changes were made in the proposed guidelines. The newly revised draft was then presented to Library administration for review and consideration of certain basic policy issues. A few more changes were made to the document following administrative review. On receipt of the final draft by administration it was decided that the statement should be redrafted in the format of the Library's *General Manual*, of which it was to be a part.

Finally, with this task completed, the guidelines were adopted. Copies were forwarded to all library agencies for inclusion in their *General Manual* and for routing and discussion at staff meetings. Copies were also sent to all libraries previously contacted and to California library schools. The process was completed for the present.

In the future, periodic review and evaluation of the philosophy and practice of reference service is a necessity. Changed concepts must be incorporated into the written reference service policy. Online information service and any changes in service resulting from it must be blended into it. Policy, as any living thing, should not be static.

Every library need not follow all the steps used in this particular instance. However, it is important that all basic factors of reference service and problem areas be addressed. And, since RASD's "Guidelines" are the only statement approximating reference and information standards, their use must be an essential part of the drafting process.

REFERENCES

1. Katharine G. Harris, "Reference Service in Public Libraries," *Library Trends*, January 1964, pp. 373–387.
2. Archie G. Rugh, "Reference Standards & Reference Work," *Library Journal*, July 1976, pp. 1497–1500.
3. Daniel Bell, *The Coming of the Post-Industrial Society: A Venture in Social Forecasting*. New York: Basic Books, 1973, pp. 466.
4. Trudy A. Gardner, "Effect of On-Line Data Bases on Reference Policy," *RQ*, Fall 1979, p. 70–74.
5. Bernard Vavrek, "Bless You Samuel Green!" *Library Journal*, April 15, 1976 p. 971.
6. "A Commitment to Information Services: Developmental Guidelines," *RQ*, Summer 1976, pp. 327–30, and *RQ*, Spring 1979, pp. 275–78.
7. William A. Katz, *Introduction to Reference Work*, V.2, "Reference Services and Reference Processes," 3d ed. New York: McGraw-Hill, 1978, p. 249.
8. James I. Wyer, *Reference Work*. Chicago: American Library Association, 1930, pp. 6–13.
9. "A Commitment to Information Services . . .," op. cit.

The Online Policy Manual

Mary E. Pensyl, Head
Online Services
Massachusetts Institute of
Technology

The introduction of online services into the reference departments of libraries within the last decade was a major happening in our profession, creating shock waves that are only now subsiding. Out of the upheaval wrought by the introduction of this new tool has emerged a more sophisticated and complex practice of reference service. But with the wide-spread adoption of computerized searching has also come the need to clarify and actively rethink the theory and practice of traditional reference service. The terminal in the reference department has challenged many previously sacrosanct assumptions and little-questioned modes of operation. For the first time, librarians at large have had to address such major policy issues as whether computer searching is simply another information tool or a totally different and specialized service. And they have had to come to grips with perhaps the single biggest controversy ever to confront them: whether or not to charge for online services.

In addition to these philosophic quandaries, the sheer number of new tasks that the computer introduces into reference work—from publicity to extensive record-keeping and accounting—implies fundamental and far-reaching changes in the operation of reference departments. The necessity for new policies and procedures is implicit in all of these activities, whether theoretical or operational. As Gardner has suggested, now that the early excitement and experimental phase is past, it is time to "stop and consider what the concept of computerized searching is doing to the traditional philosophy of reference service."[1]

It seems obvious that computer-based reference, with all of its practical and philosophic complexities, requires well-thought-out guidelines for its practitioners even more than does traditional reference service. It has only been within the last decade that libraries have found it important to articulate what they have been doing and taking for granted in non-computerized activities. A critical look at these activities led to articulated guidelines for suggested levels of performance, and general criteria for information service, culminating in RASD's "A Commitment to Information Services." A written policy statement for online searching services seem an even greater necessity. It is critical for formalizing the respective procedures, setting priorities, and providing continuity—and, above all, consistency—for these ever-evolving services. It should identify the objectives and standards of the service, describe the policies and procedures in detail, and include examples of the forms and documentation used. A policy manual can quickly acquaint new staff members with the modus operandi of their organization without having to rely upon oral tradition or tribal knowledge, remove ambiguity from the duties of all connected with the service, and provide a codified justification of procedures should users question them. It is also a valuable management tool for the administrator of the library's online reference service.

Despite these advantages, it would appear that few libraries presently have such published guidelines. (The University of Houston, Stanford University, and the University of Massachusetts are notable exceptions.[2]) In a written survey of 200 members of the New England Online Users Group, for example, the author found 6 organizations (all universities) which indicated that they presently had some kind of online policy manual. When questioned more closely, however, it was found that they were either in a very rudimentary stage of development or were not detailed enough to serve as a model for an online service policy statement. If extrapolated nationally, this would suggest, as Mary Jo Lynch found in her 1972 survey of general reference policies in ARL libraries,³ that online services are operating on a very informal basis at present.

It is, however, a daunting prospect to draw up such guidelines. Lynch found that many of the librarians questioned in her survey considered it a truly formidable task; some gave it up because they found it impossible to arrive at an agreement of the professional staff on key issues. One might suggest that this is all the more reason to attempt to hammer out some kind of written policy. Something in this case is doubtless better than nothing, and it could be a valuable exercise for staff members to have to face and resolve issues over which there are recognized conflicts. Otherwise, in the jargon of the '60s, *not* to decide *is* to decide, and people will continue to attempt to operate in a policy-less vacuum, each according to his or her personal interpretation of what online services should be.

There are several ways to go about drafting computerized guidelines. One is to have the person most directly responsible for the service—the Coordinator or Head of Reference—draw up a preliminary manual, which the reference staff could critique and amend. This would probably be the fastest and least painful way to get something into writing. The second, and undoubtedly more tedious (although more democratic) approach would be for all who are involved with the service to sit down together and break out the essential elements which address the needs of both users and librarians. Although time-consuming, a staff-generated manual would assure a consensus on most major points.

Naturally the size, organizational structure and internal needs of the library will influence the development of an online reference policy. Obviously, no two will be alike. But there are a number of common questions, both philosophic and practical, that can be examined in each setting. Below are some considerations that might be used in formulating computerized guidelines:

BACKGROUND AND OBJECTIVES

Perhaps the leading question in establishing an online reference facility is: What is its purpose? Its goals and mission? If this simple but important question is begged at the beginning, it may mean that the service may merely exist to "respond to queries with startling speed or to generate bargain-basement bibliographies."[4] Therefore a general statement of purpose is useful at the beginning of a policy statement, even if it is as simple as "the computerized literature search service exists to support the research efforts of University X." Such goals are measurable and provide a yardstick for evaluating progress.

Other questions to be asked might include: How can online searching most effectively enhance traditional reference services? How can it be most effectively integrated with traditional reference? What clientele does the service intend to reach? What level of service should be provided? What criteria should be used to identify when a literature search should be performed by computer rather than by manual means?[5] What measures should be used to monitor the service's effectiveness? Should the service have cost recovery goals?

SERVICE ORGANIZATION AND MODES OF OPERATION

One of the primary questions to be resolved in setting up a search service is whether the online function should be autonomous and separate from regular reference services, or integrated with them. This will determine where the service is located: at a central point, distributed in department or branch libraries, or available through some combination of these arrangements.

At what times will the service be available (specific days and hours)? Will there be evening or weekend service? Will the service require making advance appointments or will it accommodate walk-in, on-demand searches? Should users be present for the search or will searches be batched and done at the discretion of the librarians? Will the service accept requests over the phone or by mail? Are there specified goals or standards for through-put time? (For example, some services have statements to the effect that no user will have to wait more than three days for a search.)

What information systems will be used? Databases? What types of services will be provided? For example, will the library limit itself to retrospective searches or also provide SDI's? Will the databases accessed be solely bibliographic or also non-bibliographic (factual, numeric, statistical)? Will librarians access these services only to provide service to users or will they also make use of them for their own purposes, such as for quick reference or bibliometrics? If librarians do perform discretionary searches, what guidelines for use should be followed? A statement of purpose might outline this, such as: "Short reference searches by staff members may be conducted as part of comprehensive reference services, to further the traditional reference function of assisting the user in locating relevant information as efficiently and expeditiously as possible and to provide access to a wide range of reference and bibliographic sources than may be available in one's own library." It might further articulate guidelines for use (e.g. "To verify a citation, when a reference is garbled, difficult, elusive, incomplete, or too new, particularly when it requires searching several sources or many years of a reference tool.")

An additional operations procedures section should address policies for setting fees, if cost recovery is attempted. A policy statement regarding payment may be as simple as: "Payment is due when the search is completed and the print-out picked up." Some services may spell out specific policies for user fees (e.g., "All customers associated with for-profit organizations are charged an additional $25.00 service fee.") Other financial policy considerations might include establishing procedures for handling delinquent accounts, refunds, and other fiscal contingencies. The manual should also describe the specific mechanisms for payment and collection of revenue. For example, are credit cards legal tender in this context? Should users of the service be required to sign a statement agreeing to pay for searches provided, whether or not they are satisfied with the results? How should the myriad clerical duties be handled—by the staff?—by the departmental secretary? What statistics should be maintained? What forms are needed? What equipment is necessary? What is the rationale for 1200 vs. 300 baud terminals? Who is responsible for the security of the terminal(s)? Whose duty is it to select and order search aids (thesauri, manuals), route vendor communications, etc.?

STAFF SELECTION AND TRAINING

Often it is necessary to reorganize staff assignments to accommodate these new duties. Sometimes new responsibilities are added on without there being formal acknowledgement of the fact. The policy statement should spell out who is in charge of the service and what that person's duties and responsibilities are vis à vis everyone else involved in online searching. The guidelines should also indicate to whom that person reports and what proportion of his or her time should be dedicated to the online service.

The manual should also delineate clear lines of authority within the library organization. In some libraries, for example, reference staff members find themselves caught in a "matrix" situation where they report to two heads—the person in charge of the search service and their departmental librarian. This problematic situation can only be resolved by addressing the issues and getting them into writing. Another important question with regard to staff is how the work load is to be distributed. For example, how are searches assigned—on a rotating basis?—by subject expertise?

Many policy issues revolve around the training of searchers. What criteria should be used to determine who should become a searcher? In some libraries the policy is to choose searchers solely on the basis of their subject expertise; in others it may be the policy to train all reference librarians, based upon the philosophy that online retrieval is only a part of the overall reference process. Further policy issues may involve determining which searchers are to be trained on what databases and how they will be expected to maintain skills.

SEARCH PROCEDURES

The more practical aspects of the online reference manual involve the actual procedures involved in conducting the online searching. These specific tasks should be addressed in as much detail as possible, illustrated by forms in use:

1. handling initial inquiries
2. orienting librarians not actually engaged in searching
3. referring potential users to the appropriate searcher and determining useful databases
4. conducting the search interview
5. preparing for the search (consulting search aids, reviewing user request forms, etc.)
6. conducting the online search
7. delivering the printout
8. following and evaluating the search results
9. handling potential problems—technical, as well as patron complaints, etc.

SPECIFIC SEARCH POLICIES

Some of the more controversial issues could be handled in a separate section of the manual, or be integrated into the body of the document dealing with individual elements of the service's operations. Specific search policies might include guidelines on how to handle patron complaints, or how to deal with inquiries relating to controversial areas of law, religion, confidential material, or other sensitive issues. The University of Houston's policy manual,[6] for example, outlines concrete procedures for dealing with complaints:

a. Complaints about service should be directed initially to the searcher who performed the search.

b. Patrons who remain dissatisfied after speaking with a searcher about a complaint should be directed to the Coordinator.

c. If the Coordinator is unable to resolve a patron complaint, the patron will be referred to the Assistant Director for Public Services and Collection Development.

A very important policy issue in the operation of online services is confidentiality. Many librarians today do searches for users outside the parent organization, including industry. A client may request a patent search on a topic which she or he wishes to keep strictly private. Online searches dealing with confidentiality should have well thought-out guidelines for protecting user files and information generated in searches, not to mention defending the searcher's potential liability in this regard.

A service manual should also address the question of when a search is inappropriate. This may range from setting guidelines for appropriate questions for computer entry (i.e., specific, well-defined, non-global questions) to setting policies for how to handle a user who has a large unpaid debt, or who has a serious illness and requests a medical search in the hopes of finding a nostrum in the online bibliography.

Priorities of the service should also be clearly articulated in the manual. A policy, for example, might include a clear-cut statement as to which category of users should receive priority service (e.g., "All faculty, enrolled students and staff of University X [the home institution] will be served first. If time permits, the following categories of users will also be served, in order of priority: 1. alumni; 2. courtesy card holders; 3. persons enrolled at other universities; 4. industrial and business affiliates").

Finally, the manual should be sufficiently comprehensive and detailed to be useful on a day-to-day basis, but should also be an organic document, allowing room for expansion, since nothing is truer of online services than their capacity for growth and change.

A well-done policy manual serves a dual purpose: it can be used as an operations handbook for the information services librarians, but it can also provide management with documentation of the specific duties and issues involved with online searching. Those not searching themselves sometimes have a hazy impression of what is actually involved in providing these new services, and frequently underestimate the time, complexities, and philosophic issues involved. A properly done manual can serve as a basis for performance reviews (documenting specific, and often entirely new responsibilities), as well as provide "ammunition" when recommending adjusted workloads and schedules.

Whether a formal online policy manual stands alone or is part of a more general reference manual, librarians who have gone through the process of drawing up computerized guidelines have been forced to take a fresh view of the *whole* reference process. It may be that certain cherished attitudes and modes of operation get jettisoned along the way, but this self-imposed scrutiny can ultimately only benefit the practice of information services.

REFERENCES

1. Trudy A. Gardner, "Effect of Online Data Bases on Reference Policy," *RQ*, Fall 1979, pp. 70–74.
2. A draft of the table of contents from Stanford University Libraries' policy manual appears in Pauline Atherton and Roger Christian's book, *Librarians and Online Services*. The online policy manuals of the University of Houston and the University of Massachusetts at Amherst Libraries are available as ERIC documents ED 174 221 and ED 144 557, respectively. Excerpts of the University of Massachusetts's manual are also reprinted here, and the entire manual from the University of Houston is reprinted here as well.
3. Mary Jo Lynch, "Toward a Definition of Service: Academic Library Reference Policy Statements," *RQ*, Spring 1972, pp. 222–226.
4. Pauline Atherton and Roger W. Christian, *Librarians and Online Services*. New York: Knowledge Industry Publications, 1977, p. 109.
5. An excellent unpublished paper on this topic, "Print or Computer: Non-Monetary Criteria" by Guy T. Westmoreland, Stanford University, was presented at the 1978 Machine Assisted Reference Section's (MARS) program at the annual ALA Conference.
6. William J. Jackson, *Policy Manual for a Computerized Search Service in an Academic Library*. Houston University, 1979, ED 174 221, p. 11.

Why School Libraries Lack Reference Policy Statements— And What's To Be Done About It

Patricia C. Payne, Assistant Professor
School of Library Science
Clarion State College

The new technology of microcomputers and online bibliographic control present exciting challenges for school library programs and services. One critical area of library service, however, is both timeless and ever changing. Providing reference service, whether carried out through traditional reference interviews or sophisticated delivery systems, is the cornerstone of library programming. Why then, in this era of information explosion, is there such a dearth of reference service policy statements in the elementary and secondary schools?

The purpose of this paper is to identify the significant role of the reference function in school libraries today, as well as to suggest a few reasons for the reluctance of librarians to design policy statements.

School librarians face numerous challenges in the 1980s and beyond. The first national conference of the American Association of School Librarians in Louisville, Kentucky, last September, provided an opportunity for 2,000 librarians and educators to attend meetings and share ideas in a variety of workshops and presentations. A broad spectrum of media programs and services was presented, including the potential of microcomputers in the classroom and the media center, demonstrations of computer games to integrate media skills with the curriculum, networking, the creation of data banks for computer-based resource sharing, humanization, and education and accountability.

This current emphasis on computer technology and networking may be the method by which school librarians break away from their self-imposed professional isolation and take another step closer toward realizing the goals proposed by the 1975 national guidelines, *Media Programs: District and School.*

> Programs of media services are designed to assist the learners to grow in their ability to find, generate, evaluate, and apply information that helps them to function effectively as individuals and to participate fully in society.
>
> A basic component of all media programs is the human interchange among the media staff . . . between media person and student. Media personnel strive to build bridges between content and context. They apply to the achievement of learning objectives and a knowledge of the potential of various information sources—verbal, symbolic, pictorial, and environmental—as well as an understanding of different teaching and learning modes. This concept of program focuses on human behaviors and interactions, with staff members supporting students and teachers and all other users in utilization of media to achieve learning goals. [1]

This human interchange, the ability to build bridges between content and context, as it applies to the achievement of learning objectives, and a knowledge of the potential of various information sources, is the key to effective implementation of reference service.

It would be difficult to separate the reference function from the myriad duties performed by the school librarian. The traditional role of the study hall monitor and "keeper of the books" is, I hope, an image of the past. The era of technological development is upon us. But, have we overlooked the fundamental element of librarianship, the human interchange? I submit that school librarians may have wrapped themselves in the security blanket of selection policy statements and numerous dicta from school boards of education and administrators concerning daily protocol, and have paid scant attention to the significance of the explosion of information and students' right to access.

It is not my intention to level a broad-based criticism upon all librarians. However, through my own experiences as well as my investigation of the literature, I have observed the following five practices occurring all too frequently:

- inconsistent service
- questions of professional ethics
- censorship
- ineffective reference interviews
- inadequate professional preparation

Without a service code or policy statement serving as a guideline, students and faculty/administrators may receive varying degrees of adequate reference service, dependent upon the mood or inclination of the librarian. Our levels of reference service too often reflect personal preference and convenience, rather than students' needs or the achievement of educational objectives.

INCONSISTENT SERVICE

Using James Wyer's three levels of service as examples it is apparent that the quality and degree of service can differ drastically:

Conservative—Directing a library user to an information source that might fulfill the need, but not consulting the source for or with the user except to give instruction in its use.

Moderate service—Sometimes directing the user to a source, sometimes consulting it for or with the user.

Liberal service—Undertaking the patron's information search, even using the resources of other libraries if necessary.[2]

Whether we choose one or any combination of the three levels of reference service described by Wyer, the user has the right to *expect* and receive a consistent, identifiable quality and quantity of service, which reflects the philosophy of the educational program.

PROFESSIONAL ETHICS

The question of professional ethics is a critical issue challenging the profession during the '80s. Bernard Vavrek has addressed two types of ethics:

> The first of which is directly related to policies or attitudes of reference service in relation to inquiries which are symptomatic of current social change. The second type . . . is associated with the quality of individualized reference service, that is, the one-to-one service provided by the reference librarian on behalf of the library inquirer.[3]

Questions dealing with sensitive social issues and personal decision-making must be addressed on a daily basis. The student is often at the mercy of the librarian's value judgement. While no code of conduct should be so rigid as to deny an opportunity to utilize professional judgement, a mutually agreed upon set of principles or guidelines *can* be of assistance, providing a "constructive method of dealing with reference inquiries with sensitivity."[4]

CENSORSHIP

School librarians are sorely tempted to behave in a prescriptive, rather than a descriptive fashion, prejudging what is "best" for the student. The American Library Association holds that it is the parents, and only the parents, who may restrict their children, and only their children, from access to library materials and services. This principle of intellectual freedom provides the right of unrestricted access to all information and ideas regardless of the medium of communication used. It is in relation to intellectual freedom that libraries have a special role " . . . the responsibility to provide, through their institutions, all points of view on all questions and issues of our times, and to make these ideas and opinions available to anyone who needs or wants them, regardless of age, race, religion, national origins, or social or political views."[5]

REFERENCE INTERVIEWS

The reference interview is a particularly important opportunity for positive human interchange.

To want to help and to try to establish a rapport with the young person are the prime requisites of a good interview . . . The interview enables librarians to link their knowledge of materials to the needs of individuals. By doing so they expand those individuals' knowledge of libraries and library research far beyond the rudimentary principles laid down in orientation talks.[6]

To be receptive to the student and his question is only the beginning. It is equally important to refrain from prejudgement, on the basis of the student's manner, mode of dress, or length of hair. A strong desire to interrupt the student will certainly be a temptation. It is vitally important to listen to the one who has initiated the question, before proceeding to narrow the generalized inquiry in search of some specific fact. Some hesitance on the part of the librarian to ask questions for fear such inquiries might be interpreted as invasions of privacy can only be overcome through honest endeavor.

PROFESSIONAL PREPARATION

The information function of the media center, according to the 1975 guidelines, "relates especially to providing sources and services appropriate to user needs and devising delivery systems of materials, tools, and human resources to provide for maximum access to information in all of its forms."[7] Are school librarians prepared to accept this responsibility? Some critics of the education of school librarians decry the increasing curriculum demands of state certification requirements "linking much of the curriculum for school librarians to the field of education rather than librarianship."[8]

> Unlike most other types of library managers, media center professionals have little control over their priorities, . . . or even methods of operation. The way they allocate their time, practice special skills, and employ special knowledge is determined frequently by administrators who may or may not understand the professional responsibilities of librarians, or who may not be aware of the full potential of the media center services in helping them meet their educational objectives.[9]

In spite of these constraints, it is evident that most administrators are supportive of school librarians, but are not very cognizant of their responsibilities. Reflecting upon my list of criticisms, a reference service policy would provide a vehicle for clarification of staff responsibilities, as well as a means of communicating the role of the librarian to administrators and faculty.

FOOTNOTES

1. *Media Programs: District and School*, American Association of School Librarians, American Library Association and Association for Educational Communications and Technology. Chicago/Washington, DC, 1975.
2. James Rettig, "A Theoretical Model and Definition of the Reference Process," *RQ*, Fall 1978, pp. 19–28.
3. Bernard Vavrek, "Ethics for Reference Librarians," *RQ*, Fall 1972, pp. 56–58.
4. Ibid.
5. *Intellectual Freedom Manual*, Office for Intellectual Freedom, American Library Association. Chicago, 1974.
6. Kathryn Secton, "The Reference Interview and the Young Adult," *Top of the News*, June 1974, pp. 415–419.
7. *Media Programs*, op. cit.
8. Charlotte Mugnier, "Views on School Librarianship and Library Education," *School Library Journal*, December 1979, pp. 19–22.
9. Ibid.

Reference Policies and
Procedures for
Academic Libraries

INTRODUCTION

Purpose of the Policy Manual

UNIVERSITY OF MASSACHUSETTS
(Amherst, Massachusetts)

PURPOSE OF THE REFERENCE SERVICE MANUAL

General Statement. The purpose of the *Reference Service Manual* is to state guidelines for providing reference service in order to insure a uniform standard of service of the highest possible quality consistent with available resources. This statement will express the understanding between the library administration and the Reference Department concerning the manner in which the Department's responsibilities are carried out.

Uses. The manual will be used for orienting new staff members, as well as a source of information in case reference librarians have questions concerning departmental policy.

Availability to Readers. The manual may be made available to any library user if he or she has a question concerning the service policy of the Department. It will serve as a basis for a briefer statement which will be published and distributed to library users.

Annual Review of Contents. The contents of the manual will be reviewed annually by the Reference Department staff and the library administration to insure that policy and practice are in conformity and that changes are made as needed.

MCGILL UNIVERSITY
(Montreal, Canada)

The purpose of the *Reference Service Manual* is to provide the Reference Staff with a handy compendium of information concerning policies and procedures in order to insure a uniform standard of service of the highest possible quality consistent with available resources.

The manual is designed both to orient new staff members and to be an information resource for experienced reference librarians.

The manual may be made available to any library user if he or she has a question concerning the service policy of the Department.

The contents of the manual will be reviewed annually by the Assistant Head of the reference Department for currency and accuracy and completeness. Individual changes are made throughout the year as the need for them arises.

THE UNIVERSITY OF TEXAS AT AUSTIN
(Austin, Texas)

Purpose of Guidelines. The purpose of these guidelines is to describe the levels and forms of reference and information services that are offered by the General Libraries. These guidelines are intended to insure the development and implementation of a uniform standard of the highest quality in all public service units, despite the diverse size, resources, staff, and clientele of the various units. They are also a source of information concerning library policy and procedures. They are to be used in conjunction with the *Reference Collections Policy* and other related policies and publications of the General Libraries.

Use of Guidelines. These guidelines are for the use of staff members[1] of the General Libraries who provide reference and information services.

Public Service Units. The public service units that are covered by these guidelines are Perry-Castaneda Library, the Undergraduate Library, the Branch Libraries (including Architecture and Planning, Art, Biology, Chemistry, Classics, Communication, Engineering, Geology, Library School, Music, Pharmacy, Physics-Mathematics-Astronomy, and Social Work), and the Special Collections (including the Benson Latin American Collection, the Barker Texas History Center, the Middle East Collection and the Asian Collection).

Review of Guidelines for Reference and Information Services. The *Guidelines for Reference and Information Services* are reviewed annually by the Reference Services Committee to incorporate the latest library policies and to reflect current practices and procedures of the units providing reference and information services.

---

1. Throughout the document, the term "staff members" is used to refer to all reference and information service personnel. When a statement is intended to apply only to professional librarians, the term "librarian" is used.

Statement of Objectives

UNIVERSITY OF ALBERTA
(Edmonton, Alberta, Canada)

The *function* of the Reference Services is primarily:
1. To provide a specialized reference service to graduate students and faculty within the Humanities and Social Sciences, excluding Law and Education.
2. To provide a general reference service (of an inter-disciplinary nature), to all students and faculty.

Reference Services rely heavily on the resources of its bibliography collection and the Union Catalogue in order to fulfill these functions.

ARIZONA STATE UNIVERSITY
(Tempe, Arizona)

REFERENCE SERVICE ORGANIZATIONAL GOALS

Goal #1: To Provide Effective Direct Reference Service
Definition: Direct reference service is person-to-person aid in the

reference room or group instruction by a reference librarian. It is the prime function of the reference department.

Implementation of Goal #1
Attention must be paid to A) Staff, and B) Organizational arrangements.

Goal #2: To Provide Effective Indirect Reference Service
Definition: Indirect reference service includes behind-the-scenes work, such as making decisions on the cataloging of materials, book selection, weeding the reference collection, the preparation of bibliographies, and consultation with faculty members.

Implementation of Goal #2
In implementing goal #2, care must be taken to maintain the proper balance between direct and indirect service. Reference librarians average about 17–18 hours per week (including weekends) at the reference desk. Plans to increase direct service should not add more than four hours a week; close to 50% of our time must be saved for indirect service.

Should the work load increase enough to require more man-hours at the reference desk, staff should be added so as to permit the same balance between direct and indirect service.

UNIVERSITY OF ILLINOIS
AT URBANA-CHAMPAIGN
(Urbana, Illinois)

Ref/Info Service Goal. To meet the info/research needs and instruct UIUC library users (faculty, students, staff & *all* other patrons) accurately, efficiently, & pleasantly, whether the questions are received in person or by phone. Always be APPROACHABLE, smile, make patron comfortable.

LOUISIANA STATE UNIVERSITY
(Baton Rouge, Louisiana)

INTRODUCTION

Think of yourselves as information specialists, or to be more precise, specialists in locating information. Think of a request as valid whether it originates with an LSU patron, or with the patron of another library . . . and whether the material requested for an LSU patron is available from this library, or must be borrowed from another.

The Reference Services Division should be reaching out into the academic community to demonstrate that we can satisfy the appetite for information.

UNIVERSITY OF MASSACHUSETTS
(Amherst, Massachusetts)

GOALS OF REFERENCE SERVICE

General Statement. The two major goals of the Reference Department are: (a) to facilitate access to library collections through direct personal service to the library's users; and (b) to support the University's instructional program through providing formal and informal library and bibliographic instruction.

Basic Philosophy. As a general rule, because of the size of the library's clientele and the large number of highly specialized (and changing) interests among them, assistance to readers, apart from "ready reference" kinds of inquiries, must ordinarily take the form of providing guidance in the pursuit of information rather than providing the information itself. The individual librarian must exercise his or her judgment in determining the application of this policy in specific situations. The objective situation—i.e., the needs of the user, the amount of time available, and the knowledge upon which the staff member can call—must be the determining factor and not favoritism to any one reader or group of readers.

MCGILL UNIVERSITY
(Montreal, Canada)

OBJECTIVES

Within the limits of the library's policies and its budgetary constraints the Department works towards the following objectives:

1. To maintain in the department an up-to-date, relevant and readily accessible working collection of reference materials which relates primarily to the University's programs in the humanities and social sciences.
2. To give appropriate reference assistance to the library's clientele.
3. To provide instruction by the most effective methods, in the use of our resources and those of the library as a whole, with suitable coordination and cooperation with other library units.
4. To promote an increased awareness of library resources available to the McGill community.
5. To facilitate access to materials not available in the library needed by members of the University, by loan and photocopy from other libraries and documentation centres.
6. To make copies of documents for the library's staff and clientele.
7. To provide the clientele of other libraries with access to our materials by loan or photocopy through interlibrary loan.
8. To create an environment for and a tradition of good service within the Department and to promote the effective utilization of the manpower and materials at our disposal.
9. To cooperate with other library units by providing them with information about user needs derived from ongoing contact with our readers.

MICHIGAN STATE UNIVERSITY
(East Lansing, Michigan)

The goal of the General Readers' Services Department staff is to participate in providing collections and to provide a full range of reference, information, circulation, and related services in support of the curricular, research, and general information needs of M.S.U.

students, faculty and staff working primarily in the humanities and social sciences; and, in addition, to assist in fulfilling the Libraries' obligations in local, state, regional and national information programs.

In pursuing this goal, the staff directs its efforts towards the achievement of these nine continuing objectives:

1. Undergraduate users will have available information services and resources in sufficient copies to satisfy most of their needs.
2. Graduate, faculty, and staff users will have available information services and resources to satisfy a high percentage of their needs.
3. Users will be able to locate and retrieve needed information or known items quickly and easily.
4. Users will be provided with access to information resources not available in the University Libraries.
5. Users will learn to use the University Libraries and information sources effectively and efficiently.
6. Users will be provided with improved space and equipment for the effective use of information resources.
7. Users will be aware of the University Libraries' resources and services.
8. Appropriate resources and services will be made available beyond the primary user community.
9. Staff will communicate with other library units to improve services for users.

NORTHWESTERN UNIVERSITY
(Evanston, Illinois)

REFERENCE DEPARTMENT

The goals of the Reference Department are: (1) to provide information about the Library and its holdings, and about the University; (2) to answer questions through use of reference books; (3) in helping to carry out the Library's goals of closer coordination with the University's academic programs and better communication with the faculty, to assist and guide students and faculty in their research and to provide instruction to individuals and to groups in the use of the Library; (4)

and to meet the above objectives, to collect and maintain the best possible selection of reference materials.

The primary focus of the reference collection in the main library is on the social sciences and humanities. Although the main reference service points for students and faculty of the Technological Institute, the School of Music, the professional schools and several other schools and departments are the branch libraries devoted to their disciplines, the services of the Reference Department are available to all members of the University community.

SAN DIEGO STATE UNIVERSITY
(San Diego, California)

GENERAL GOAL

The main objective of the Library's program is the continuing development of the library as an educational resource which implements the educational objectives of the University. The reference librarians and staff undertake all functions necessary to support the Library's program in the subject areas of social sciences (including education) and humanities.

OBJECTIVES OF REFERENCE SERVICE

1. All library patrons, regardless of status, are assisted in their search for information. In helping patrons, the reference librarians emphasize the understanding of the need of the user, the exact information he wants, his level of knowledge and interest, etc.
2. Users at all levels are guided in the use of our resources by personal or group instruction in basic, research and bibliographic problems, tours, exhibits, etc., and by coordinating the skills of non-professionals, general reference librarians, and subject specialists.
3. Within the framework of subject specialization, information is provided, or instruction may be given, if the latter seems more appropriate for the patron's need. In order to best use the re-

sources of all reference librarians, referrals are made to the appropriate subject specialist, whenever the need is indicated.

4. The most effective of conventional and innovative methods in providing services is used, whether it be in the form of literature searches, preparation of bibliographies and indexes, or current awareness programs.

UNIVERSITY OF TOLEDO
(Toledo, Ohio)

REFERENCE DEPARTMENT GOALS

1. To facilitate access to the library collections and to the content of those collections by:
   a. Providing direct personal service for the library users' reference needs;
   b. Acting as a communication resource and facilitator between the inquirer and the reference sources;
   c. Supplying aid in the formulation of user search strategies.
2. To support the University's instructional programs through library instruction, guidance, and assistance with research and library information needs.
3. To promote and encourage effective and independent use of the library.

UNIVERSITY OF WESTERN ONTARIO
(London, Ontario)

SELF-STUDY: OBJECTIVES

A recent document in RQ titled "A Commitment to Information Services: Development Guidelines" provides the general frame of reference for the direction of the Department's individual goals. These objectives only amplify the role of the Reference Department and in no way take away from the participation in the Objectives of the Library System or from the standards for Public Service.

In the introductory paragraphs the following appeared:

Since all functions of the library or information center should be viewed in ultimate terms, as facilitating the transfer of information, the distinguishing feature of reference service is that it specifically ensures the optimum uses of information resources through substantive interaction with the users on the direct and indirect levels cited below.

This paragraph may be considered as a statement of the *primary* objective for the Reference Department. All activities of the staff should be evaluated on the degree to which each activity supports this function. Building on this statement, a more detailed statement for the Department would appear as follows:

1. to maintain and develop the present levels of direct service to users at the designated assistance desks
2. to maintain a staff which has both the subject knowledge and competence, and the necessary interpersonal skills to provide the level of reference and information service required
3a. to maintain an orientation program for new library users on campus
3b. to develop a program of bibliographic instruction
4. to develop and maintain a strong reference collection
5. to provide informed and evaluative comments or feedback to:
    - the appropriate groups within Public Services
    - the Processing Division
    - the Collections Development Division
    - the Office of the Chief Librarian and the associated departments therein.

TYPES OF SERVICE

General Statement

UNIVERSITY OF BRITISH COLUMBIA
(Vancouver, British Columbia)

PURPOSE OF THE LIBRARY

The Library constitutes a vital instructional and research arm of the University of British Columbia and exists primarily to contribute to the University's teaching and research functions. Consistent with its primary function and within the limits of its resources, the Library also seeks to support teaching, research, and private study conducted elsewhere in the Province of British Columbia.

In its service to the community at large the Library can most effectively serve to supplement the resources and services of other academic, public and special libraries in the Province. Under certain conditions it can also make its collections and services available to individuals and organizations outside the University on a more direct basis.

GEORGIA INSTITUTE OF TECHNOLOGY
(Atlanta, Georgia)

Reference services and bibliographic verification, as distinguished from literature searching, are free to Georgia Tech faculty, staff, and students. They are likewise free to other academic and public libraries. These same services are available on a fee basis to libraries and research units in business, industry, government agencies, and to individuals, including Georgia Tech personnel acting in a private capacity. Many reference and bibliographic services to these latter groups are handled without charge. They are usually quick answers to reference questions and verification problems. Reference service requiring more extensive search and verification, or a considerable amount of professional time, may be subject to service charges. The unit within the Library charged specifically with fee-based service to off-campus users is the Information Exchange Center. However, personnel in other units are encouraged to assist any user unless services to fee-based users conflict with priorities to Georgia Tech users. If conflicts arise, the unit department head will decide if the user should be referred to the IEC. In any unit, fees are charged for services where extensive staff time is devoted to fee-based users. These fees are at the discretion of the librarian performing the service and are based on professional time and judgment. Please refer to the Library's current fee schedule for rates.

UNIVERSITY OF ILLINOIS
AT URBANA-CHAMPAIGN
(Urbana, Illinois)

SCOPE AND RESPONSIBILITIES

The Reference Department functions as the central information agency for the entire library system. In addition to responding to reference desk and telephone questions, the Reference Department is responsible for conducting computerized literature searching of data bases available through BRS and the New York Times Information Bank. The Reference Collection comprises approximately 20,000 volumes and includes general and research-oriented dictionaries, encyclopedias, biographies, catalogs, indexes, directories, yearbooks, almanacs, guidebooks and manuals, statistical sources, and other similar types of reference publications. Ready reference service and extensive assistance with research-related queries from these materials and other library resources, including instruction in their use, are available from professional staff. Information relating to the main card catalog, public shelflist, and the serial record is provided through the Reference Desk when the Information Desk is closed.

MIAMI UNIVERSITY
(Oxford, Ohio)

UNIVERSITY LIBRARIES—GENERAL

The King Library serves as the main library on the Oxford Campus. King contains seating for more than 2,000 and shelving for 600,000 volumes. Special facilities include private studies for faculty and graduate students, small group study rooms, a microform reading area, facilities for visually handicapped students, and a Media Department with an audio collection and listening equipment.

Library hours for all units are established at the beginning of the fall semester and are posted on the main door of King, in the *Student,* and in the *Miamian.* Vacation and summer hours are also listed in the same sources prior to the beginning of such periods.

The new Science Library in the west wing of Hughes Laboratories consolidates the collections formerly housed in the third floor of King, in Chemistry, in Geology, and in Physics-Mathematics libraries. The Science Library has seating for 700 and shelving for 200,000 volumes. All materials classified 500, 600, Q, R, S, and T are shelved in Science. These collections include books, periodicals, microforms, and maps.

Branch libraries serve the faculty and students in Art and Architecture (Alumni Hall), Music (Center for Performing Arts), and Hoyt Library.

STATE UNIVERSITY OF NEW YORK
COLLEGE AT POTSDAM
(Potsdam, New York)

Services available from the library include reference/information desk assistance and research guides/bibliographies designed to meet the specific needs of a course. Consider whether any aspects of your courses would benefit from one or more sessions on the SOURCES AND METHODS for doing LIBRARY RESEARCH. If many students will be doing a similar type of library research, a group introduction to specialized research tools and procedures may be advisable. Students engaged in independent study or writing research papers can also be referred to the library liaison who will make arrangements for individual help. All students and faculty are encouraged to use the Reference Department's Information Desk on an *ad hoc* basis for help in library research.

List of Services

UNIVERSITY OF ALBERTA
(Edmonton, Alberta, Canada)

The following *types of service* are provided by Humanities and Social Sciences, Reference:
1. Catalogue information and interpretation.
2. Quick reference information on a person-to-person basis or by telephone. This service is limited to the Humanities and Social Sciences and to questions of an inter-disciplinary nature. With the exception of higher education, questions relating to medicine, general science, law and education are referred to the respective library.
3. Information about bibliographical and research resources in the Humanities and Social Sciences.
4. Suggestions on sources and locations of materials for research reports, term papers and class assignments. For graduate students and faculty, this service is extended beyond the walls of this library via interlibrary loan.
5. Instruction, formal and informal, in the use of the library and the various indexes, abstracts, bibliographies and union lists within the Reference Services and the Bibliography Room.

6. Verification of Interlibrary Loan requests in the Humanities and Social Sciences.
7. Assistance to faculty and students in compiling literature searches—as time permits.
8. Assistance to faculty, students and outside clients in further searches via commercially developed on-line data bases.

BALL STATE UNIVERSITY
(Muncie, Indiana)

SERVICES

Reference Service provides direct personal assistance to all users who are searching for information in the Library. Service includes aid in using the card catalog, reference works, and indexes. The reference collection is cataloged and cards appear in the main card catalog. As a rule reference books do not circulate. Books on Reference Reserve are charged for Reference Area Use Only at the Reference counter for two hours, with renewal possible. All materials charged should be returned to this counter.

UNIVERSITY OF BRITISH COLUMBIA
(Vancouver, British Columbia)

REFERENCE SERVICES [FOR FACULTY]

A wide variety of services is available from reference divisions and major branch libraries. Local conditions may influence the way in which more specialized reference services can be provided, especially in the smaller branches. Among those which most divisions offer are the following:

Answers to factual queries. A phone call to the appropriate division may quickly provide you with an answer.

Brief selective bibliographies compiled at your request.

Assistance in the preparation of research papers. This may take the form of assisting with literature searches, verifying reference or facts, and assistance with bibliographical questions.

Monthly computer printouts of new acquisitions in your subject area. This is an in house service of the UBC Library called SDI (Selective Dissemination of Information) offered without charge to UBC faculty members. Consult with a reference librarian in your field; she/he will prepare an interest profile for you based on the Library of Congress classification scheme. You will then receive a monthly printout of newly catalogued books in your field.

On-line searches of computer bibliographic data bases. The Library has contracts with a number of public and commercial agencies allowing us to access their computerized bibliographic files. Journal and report literature in most fields is well covered by these data bases; moreover, on-line searching often provides a more thorough coverage of the literature than is possible through printed indexes. Searches are offered to faculty members on a partial cost recovery basis; since each search is unique, costs vary. For detailed information, contact the appropriate reference librarian, who can inform you if data bases are available in your field and provide a cost estimate.

Informal interest profiles may also be arranged for individual faculty members so that reference staff can pass on information from sources not covered by the computerized services.

UNIVERSITY OF NORTH CAROLINA
(Greensboro, North Carolina)

DAILY REFERENCE SERVICES AND RESPONSIBILITIES

A. General reference questions (how to find a periodical, biographical information, book reviews, addresses, statistics, pronunciations, definitions, etc.).
B. Location questions (Where is [are] the card catalog, *Readers' Guide,* Reserve Room, restrooms, pencil sharpener, periodicals, call numbers, photocopy machines, etc.?).

C. Search questions (evolving from general reference questions: fifteen minutes or more).
D. Instructions in how to approach research in a specific area or on a particular topic and how to use individual reference tools (pointing out limitations, explaining arrangement and abbreviations, indicating how to get to materials mentioned in a reference work—Periodicals, documents, ERIC, etc.).
E. Telephone calls which fall into categories A or C (The clientele served is the same as that stated above.).

NORTHWESTERN UNIVERSITY
(Evanston, Illinois)

REFERENCE DEPARTMENT

1. Instruction in and general information on the use of the Library and its resources, especially the Reference Department.
2. Assistance in finding the answer to specific reference questions.
3. Instruction in the use of bibliographic and other resources of the Reference Department.
4. Aid in the preparation of bibliographies.
5. Instruction in the use of the card catalog.
6. Verification of Library holdings and referral with an Infopass to institutions which have materials this Library lacks.
7. Orientation to the Library through tours, bibliographic lectures, etc. (by appointment).
8. Instruction and aid in research methods and/or sources for reports, term papers, theses, and dissertations.
9. Compilation and publication of various bibliographical aids.
10. Conduct of on-line computer-assisted bibliographic research, by appointment and for a fee.

THE UNIVERSITY OF TEXAS AT AUSTIN
(Austin, Texas)

SERVICES

A. Reference and information services in the public service units of the General Libraries serve the present information needs of the academic community at The University of Texas at Austin and anticipate future needs. New reference and information services are not implemented unless adequate funding is available.

B. A publication describing reference and information services is available at public service units.

C. Reference and information services are available to individuals who come to the library and to those who request assistance over the telephone or through correspondence. Although telephone and correspondence reference services are an integral part of reference and information services, priority is always given to users who come to the library.

D. Reference and information services are publicized utilizing all necessary forms of communication media.

E. Reference and information services are reviewed periodically.

LIBRARY USERS

General Statement

ARIZONA STATE UNIVERSITY
(Tempe, Arizona)

Goal: To Provide Other Services to the Academic Community as Required
Definition: The University requires the reference librarians to check theses and dissertations for format, the bibliographical style, and to edit a biennial bibliography of faculty publications. Other "one-time" tasks are required occasionally.

Implementation of Goal
As a service organization, the University Library is obligated to perform assignments within its area of competence, although we may question the appropriateness of the thesis checking. As long as we have these jobs, the work should be shared by all members of the reference staff, all of whom should make an effort to become qualified to perform them.

UNIVERSITY OF BRITISH COLUMBIA
(Vancouver, British Columbia)

ACCESS TO LIBRARY FACILITIES AND COLLECTIONS

Access to library buildings and collections will be available to all who require it, whether or not they are members of the University community. Access does not include the right to borrow materials for outside use. It should be understood, as well, that priority will be given to UBC patrons if funding or space is inadequate.

UNIVERSITY OF ILLINOIS
AT URBANA-CHAMPAIGN
(Urbana, Illinois)

GUIDELINES FOR OFFERING REFERENCE ASSISTANCE

Ancient Proverb: "Give me a fish, and I will eat for today; teach me to fish, and I will eat for the rest of my life."

The major emphasis in assistance of patrons is instructional. However, reference personnel will not only assist the patron in use of research tools and other resources but will, at times, retrieve information for the patron. Reference personnel must use their own judgment in offering the type of assistance needed by library users. Patrons should be served, according to their information needs, rather than their status. All library users should have equal access to information offered by reference personnel.

MCGILL UNIVERSITY
(Montreal, Canada)

POLICY

The principles underlying our policy are that we are pleased to give whatever assistance we can provide and that our prime responsibility is to the members of the McGill University community.

The quantity of assistance given must be governed by common sense, taking into consideration the number of readers requiring assistance as well as any other special conditions currently prevailing.

See chart. [The chart has eight categories from McGill Administrative Officers at the top to Undergraduates "not covered in" other categories. For each type of users the type of reference service is indicated. The Administrative Officers, for example, should receive "maximum service." In the latter group, primarily students not in McGill, the service is "basic assistance, but not at the expense of neglecting service to readers with higher priority."—Editor]

THE UNIVERSITY OF TEXAS AT AUSTIN
(Austin, Texas)

LIBRARY USERS

All activities involving direct service to library users have priority. Supporting activities, although essential to the maintenance of quality service, are secondary. No discrimination is made between University and non-University users when giving routine reference and information services. In the case of a time-consuming inquiry or of a request for special services, the question of the user's affiliation may have to be made. These inquiries are referred to the staff member in charge of the unit. For categories of library users see following list.

Categories of Users: Non-Resident

ARIZONA STATE UNIVERSITY
(Tempe, Arizona)

Goal: To Provide Service to the Community Outside the University
Definition: This category includes private individuals, organizations, and businesses in the Phoenix metropolitan area.

Implementation of this Goal
As a tax-supported institution with the largest library in the area, Arizona State University has an obligation to respond to the needs of the community, provided that the response does not interfere with the primary goal of service to the University itself. Accordingly, reference librarians offer service to all patrons, regardless of lack of affiliation with the University. Occasionally, we will perform more extensive services, such as bibliographical searches, for a state agency.

UNIVERSITY OF BRITISH COLUMBIA
(Vancouver, British Columbia)

CAN I USE THE LIBRARY—I'M NOT CONNECTED WITH U.B.C.?

Yes! While the Library's first concern is to provide adequate collections and services to students, faculty, and staff at UBC, we also attempt to make our collections and services available to anyone who needs them, particularly to people who cannot find elsewhere the specialized material they require.

Anyone who comes into the Library may use the library materials in any of the campus branches. *You may browse, read, look things up, listen to records, consult clipping files. *You may photocopy material at the normal rates. Use either the self-service machines (5¢ a copy) or the copy service (10¢ a copy) on the ground floor in the Main Library. *You may use the reference collections and services, ask questions, get help. (The Library reserves the right, however, to charge for extensive reference service at the rate of $20/hour.)

CAN I TAKE BOOKS HOME?

Sometimes. First you'll need a library card. With a card you may borrow most of the circulating books in the library for two weeks.

CAN ANYONE GET A CARD?

Almost.

Undergraduate students from other universities and colleges and high school students are *not* eligible for cards. Since their needs often conflict with those of UBC undergraduates we have to restrict this group to be fair to our own students. Their libraries should be able to provide the books they need and, if necessary, may borrow from UBC for their students through interlibrary loan.

Faculty, professional staff, and *graduate students* from other universities and colleges in British Columbia are eligible for complimentary cards.

Visiting faculty members from universities and colleges outside of BC may apply for complimentary cards for the duration of their visit to UBC.

Centre for *Continuing Education* students enrolled in non-credit courses may purchase cards for $5 for the duration of their courses.

Senior citizen cards are available for $5/year.

All *other* cards are $25/full year (September 1 to August 31); $10/ summer (May 1–August 31).

HOW DO I GET A CARD?

Go to the Circulation Division in the Main Library, just to the right of the main door. You will receive a card.

BUT I JUST NEED A FEW BOOKS, $25 IS A LOT:

Try interlibrary loan. If you have a card for a public library, a university, or a community college in British Columbia, ask *that library's* interlibrary loan department to borrow the book for you. You'll still get the book for two weeks and you won't need to buy a UBC card.

MAY I BORROW RECORDS?

Yes. But you will need a separate card from the Wilson Recordings Collections.

Wilson cards costs $25/year; $5/year for senior citizens. Only four single records or two sets may be borrowed at one time and must be returned before more records are borrowed.

WHAT ABOUT ORGANIZATIONS?

Institutional Borrower's Cards are available to business and industrial firms, private and public corporations, and government departments (but *not* schools) expecting to use the Library's collections or requiring a photocopy account.

Please send a staff member (anyone on your staff may use the card) to the Library to locate and retrieve materials. Short training sessions are available to assist such staff members in learning to use the Library.

Borrowing regulations *including the restrictions on journals* and other high use materials are the same as for other B card holders. Fees are also the same: $25/year (September 1 to August 31). Additional cards may be purchased for $5/year/card.

GEORGIA INSTITUTE OF TECHNOLOGY
(Atlanta, Georgia)

POLICY FOR OFF-CAMPUS USERS

The Georgia Tech Library through the years has provided off-campus users free access to its resources and also has given reference assistance to these individuals at no cost. These services have often been given at the expense of Georgia Tech because current funding does not provide sufficient manpower or resources for everyone. Unfortunately, it is no longer possible to continue this practice, and the Library has structured a fee system for off-campus users. This policy will enable the Library to continue service to outside users, and to maintain and build its collection for the benefit to all.

Reciprocal library services among academic and public libraries are not affected by this policy; however, as the Library attempts to support research and development throughout the state by continuing its role as an information source, special funds are necessary. Consequently, the Institute encourages those individuals and organizations who regularly use the Library facilities to contribute to the Library for the maintenance and enrichment of the collection.

Georgia Tech will continue to operate an open-door/open-access library but it will place restrictions on loan and reference services to off-campus users. The Director of Libraries will be responsible for the determination of fees, and for granting service privileges to off-campus users.

General user categories have been established which indicate both eligibility and the service fees applicable, which are as follows:

Off-Campus Users Eligible for Free Loan and Reference Services

Several groups of off-campus users are exempt from fees including: (1) families of Georgia Tech employees; (2) faculty members from other institutions; (3) non-enrolled Tech students (e.g., co-ops); (4) local high school students in need of scientific and engineering materials unavailable in their own school libraries, and who have a letter of request from their school principal; and, (5) students from the University Center and University System institutions. These five groups will continue to have free access to all resources and will receive reference assistance when needed. A person in these groups may obtain a non-transferable Borrower's Card upon presentation of proper identification, completion of an application form, and approval of the Director of Libraries.

Off-Campus Users Eligible for Free Loan Service

1. An active member of the Georgia Tech National Alumni Association may obtain a free, non-transferable Borrower's Card upon presentation of a current alumnus card, completion of an application form, and approval of the Director of Libraries. Reference and other services are available according to the fee schedule for those services.
2. A current employee of the State of Georgia may obtain a free non-transferable Borrower's Card upon presentation of current identifying credentials, completion of an application form, and approval of the Director of Libraries. Reference and other services are available according to the fee schedule for those services.

Off-Campus Users Subject to Fees for Loan and Other Services

1. An individual employee of a business or industrial firm (excluding information brokers), a local or federal goverment agency, or a civic, trade, or professional organization may obtain a non-transferable Borrower's Card upon presentation of a request from an official of the organization, completion of an application form, payment a $10.00 fee, and approval of the Director of Libraries. The Borrower's Card entitles the holder to five loans (books or items). It may be renewed for another five loans for an additional $10.00. The Borrower's Card expires at the end of each fiscal year (June 30) regardless of the number of times used, and no portion of the card fee is refundable. Reference and other services are available according to the fee schedule for those services.
2. Information Brokers, free-lance librarians, information specialists, and others engaged in bibliographic consultation may obtain a non-transferable Borrower's Card upon presentation of current identifying credentials, completion of an application

form, payment of an annual $1,000.00 library use fee, payment of a $10.00 Borrower's card fee, and approval of the Director of Libraries. The Borrower's Card entitles the holder to five loans (books or items), and may be renewed for another five loans for an additional $5.00. The Borrower's Card expires at the end of each fiscal year (June 30), regardless of the number of times used and no portion of the card fee is refundable. Borrowed items may not be transferred to a broker's client. Reference and other services are available according to the fee schedule for those services.

3. Any individual (not covered in the preceding sections) with a legitimate need may make application for a Borrower's Card to the Director of Libraries who will determine the nature and extent of library services for which the individual may be eligible.

UNIVERSITY OF MASSACHUSETTS
(Amherst, Massachusetts)

SERVICE TO NON-UNIVERSITY USERS

General Statement. No discrimination is made between University and non-University users when giving routine reference service. In the case of a time-consuming inquiry or in the case of special services the question of the user's affiliation may arise and some distinctions may have to be made. Guidelines for making these are given below. In applying the guidelines the reference librarian must use his or her own judgement, although senior staff members may be consulted.

Guidelines for Providing Special Services. Time-consuming Inquiries—As a general rule, if a library user *not affiliated* with the University as a member of the student body or faculty or staff (or not a Commonwealth official) has access to a library intended to serve his needs which is adequate for his purpose, he should be referred to that library for assistance. In cases where the University Library has special resources in staff or materials and the needs of the user seem to warrant it, assistance beyond the routine may be given.

UNIVERSITY OF NORTH CAROLINA
(Greensboro, North Carolina)

The Reference Staff feel the students and faculty of the University of North Carolina at Greensboro are their primary responsibility in answering all types of questions, in teaching the use of the Library and its resources, and in providing individual conferences. When services to these two groups are not impaired, the Staff feel they can serve other groups also: towns-people, students from other colleges in Greensboro, secondary school students, businesses, and special visitors, all of whom have exhausted other available resources.

NORTHWESTERN UNIVERSITY
(Evanston, Illinois)

POLICY FOR SERVICE TO NON-NORTHWESTERN USERS

In order to fulfill the Library's primary obligation to Northwestern-affiliated users, it is necessary to limit services available to non-Northwestern users. The Library's policy for guest borrowers already indicates that "Library services and facilities for non-Northwestern readers are limited to personal consultation of the collection in accordance with established library regulations, and do not ordinarily include reference or public services excepting on an occasional basis to be determined by the Assistant University Librarian for Public Services."

In keeping with the above policy only the following reference services will be provided for telephone and in-person queries:

1. Holdings: No more than three titles will be checked in the Library's catalog.
2. Information and Directions: Questions concerning the University and the Library.
3. Ready Reference: Simple questions which can be readily answered by one source.

Limited help with substantive reference questions may be given as time allows. Visitors needing extensive reference help will be referred back to their own libraries. Reference staff will not instruct non-Northwestern users in the preparation of bibliographies or in research methods for the writing of term papers.

ON-SITE ACCESS PRIVILEGES FOR NON-NORTHWESTERN USERS

An Infopass or letter of introduction from another library entitles a person with no Northwestern affiliation to enter the Library once during hours of limited access. Individuals needing extended use of the Library should inquire at the Reference Desk for On-Site Access Privileges. An On-Site Access Privileges card (OSAP) is only granted for a short period of time, with a maximum of two weeks, for the use of materials that are unique to the Northwestern University Library in the Chicago metropolitan area. If the user's needs are not adequately documented on their Infopass, they may be asked to have an Application for On-Site Access Privileges Card filled out by their referring library, listing the specific materials which they need to use at Northwestern and certifying that these materials are not available elsewhere in the Chicago metropolitan area. On-Site Access Privileges Cards will be granted only on the basis of unique information need and not on the basis of convenience of location or hours of service. OSAPS are not issued during Northwestern's reading and exam weeks. Persons needing to use the Library for periods more extended than two weeks will be referred to the Library Privileges Office to inquire about purchasing library cards.

Categories of Users: Handicapped

COLORADO STATE UNIVERSITY
(Fort Collins, Colorado)

POLICY

It is the mission of Colorado State University Libraries to provide equal access to information by all who request it. For those who are disabled, the Libraries can make special provisions which will permit the user to examine sources, complete assignments, and conduct research. Barriers are eliminated insofar as feasible within the present facilities. When obstacles do exist, retrieval of materials, catalog drawers, or equipment by staff members at the Loan and Reference Desks is considered necessary.

Subject and reference librarians, in their collection development responsibilities are sensitive to needs of patrons with disabilities and thus allocate funds for special materials when required or requested. Coordination and cooperation with the Office of Resources for Disabled Students and other agencies on campus are maintained for the maximum benefits to the disabled community.

KENT STATE UNIVERSITY
(Kent, Ohio)

HANDICAPPED STUDENTS

1. Room 818K is kept exclusively for the use of handicapped students. It is equipped with a Braille typewriter. The room is to be locked when not in use and the key is available from the Reference Desk.
2. When a student requests the key to Room 818K he is to sign for it at the Reference Desk. The key is to be returned to the Reference Desk and a record is kept there of the time the key was returned.
3. The key to Room 818K is available only during reference service hours.

STATE UNIVERSITY OF NEW YORK
COLLEGE AT POTSDAM
(Potsdam, New York)

HANDICAPPED SERVICES

A handicapped person is one with a permanent or temporary physical impairment that substantially limits one or more major activities:

It is the policy of the Federick W. Crumb Memorial Library to make its resources readily available to handicapped persons and to provide the facilities to implement this policy effectively.

Please feel free at any time to contact the Information Desk to inquire about the equipment, for assistance with library research, or suggestions/complaints about library service.

Information Desk:

1. Extraordinary personal service is available to handicapped individuals at the desk (e.g., paging books, interpretation of card catalog, assisting with copying, etc.). Special locations for use of personal equipment, use of elevator, use of large-type typewriter, may be arranged.

2. Library materials which normally do not circulate (e.g., micro-
    forms) may be loaned if necessary.

Staff will assist the handicapped person in the use of photo reproduction equipment which is available for public use; micro-copying,
which is done on request for any user, is already one of the services
provided by the Library. Rates for hard copies: 5¢/image; rates for
micro-copying: 10¢/image.

PRIORITIES

UNIVERSITY OF BRITISH COLUMBIA
(Vancouver, British Columbia)

SERVICE PRIORITIES

While direct access to collections and essential services will continue to be available to the outside community as long as funding permits, non-UBC patrons should be encouraged to explore the resources of their primary libraries first, and to use the UBC Library as a secondary resource.

The Library should also, as far as possible, protect on behalf of UBC students and faculty the core collection of heavily-used materials which the libraries of other institutions can reasonably be expected to provide for their own users. Payment of a fee for borrowing privileges will not, for example, entitle outside patrons to borrow materials that are in heavy demand on campus, such as reserve books and journals. On the other hand, relatively free access can be offered to the rarer and more specialized items in UBC's collections, since these may be available only at UBC.

The needs of the UBC community must also have priority in the use of library services. Payment of established charges for reference and other services will not ensure priority service for the outside patron. Special services to the outside community can only be extended when they do not interfere with normal services to UBC students and faculty.

Provision of Basic Reference Service

Together with access to collections and facilities, the Library will attempt to provide basic reference service to outside patrons. Basic reference service may be defined as assistance in gaining access to materials held in the UBC Library system. It is characterized by the following attributes:

   (a) Priority is given to patrons present in the Library and prepared to help themselves.

   (b) Somewhat lower priority is given to those who choose to telephone for assistance or information rather than come to the library in person. Circumstances from time to time in some library divisions may require stricter limitations on the extent of assistance that can be provided in response to telephoned requests from non-UBC patrons for reference assistance.

CASE WESTERN RESERVE UNIVERSITY
(Cleveland, Ohio)

SERVICE TO PATRONS—PRIORITY

1. Patron in person should be served before the telephone caller, provided he has been at the desk at the time of the call.
2. When the telephone rings during the service to a patron, the call will be taken, the caller will be put on hold ("Hold on, please") and the patron at the desk will get the requested assistance.
3. Several waiting patrons have to be screened:
   - those requesting directions only;
   - inquirers about location of material according to the call number;
   - those with request for brief factual information;
   - patrons with request for material on a specific topic or literature search.
4. The patron in need of longer assistance but having arrived at the desk earlier than the others, should be asked if he/she is willing to wait until the ones with simpler requests are served.
5. Whenever possible, help from Reference Office should be requested.
6. If both desks are staffed, Desk 2 attendant has to be available for back-up services.

UNIVERSITY OF ILLINOIS AT URBANA-CHAMPAIGN
(Urbana, Illinois)

PRIORITY IN HANDLING QUESTIONS

Providing quality and efficient service when the phone is ringing and several patrons are standing at the desk waiting for assistance has always been difficult in libraries. Professional judgment is important— you must decide what takes precedence. But to be fair, think of in-house users first, phone callers second. If it's busy in-house, answer the phone but take caller's name and phone number, and call back when you can with the answer to his/her question. Do not keep phone callers on the phone on hold for more than 2-3 minutes, and please do push the "on hold," don't let the caller listen to you help other patrons (that is rude to caller [noise] and doesn't help you maintain confidentiality that patrons should be assured).

Take in-house patrons in order and get them started, tell them you will return to ascertain if they are finding what they need—or encourage them to return to you if they do not find what is needed. Check on progress and help several users concurrently.

UNIVERSITY OF MASSACHUSETTS
(Amherst, Massachusetts)

PRIORITIES

General Statement

The Reference Department gives priority to all activities involving direct service to library users. Supporting activities, although essential to maintain the quality of these services, must take a second place. Among direct services, the order of priorities is: (1) service to the individual reader, (2) library instruction to groups, (3) computer literature searches, and (4) bibliographical verification of interlibrary loans.

Service to Individual Readers

First Priority. As a general rule, service to library users who come to the Reference area take priority over any other activity. Reference librarians should make a determined effort to schedule appointments, meetings, and supporting activities at times when it is expected that library use will be relatively light.

Scheduling During Busy Periods. When the University is in session, three Reference librarians will be scheduled for the desks from 10:30-3:30 on the days known to be busiest during the week (generally, Mon.-Thurs. and during peak periods, Fridays as well). One of the three librarians may make arrangements with the Desk 1 librarian to be on call rather than remain stationed at the desks should there be an unexpected decrease in desk activity on any given day. When exceptionally busy periods occur during the semester, however, one or more additional librarians will be scheduled for on call duty to assist the three librarians at the desks.

Telephone Calls. In accordance with the rule on first priority above, the user who comes to the Reference Desk takes priority over the person who calls on the telephone or who has left an inquiry at the desk. The one exception to this is in the case of librarian or reference assistant who is formally scheduled for telephone duty in the reference office.

Priorities among Waiting Readers. In cases where there are two or more library users waiting, help should be offered first to the person who has been waiting longest. If it appears that the answer to the inquiry will take a little time, the librarian may deal first with the questions which can be answered immediately, if this is agreeable to the persons waiting.

Pending Reference Inquiries. If the immediate needs of readers who are in the library or who are telephoning are being adequately taken care of, next priority should be accorded to following up inquiries not answered when they were taken while on desk or telephone duty. All such questions must be dealt with immediately by the person who accepted them unless other arrangements have been made, or service to users who are waiting interferes. The desk supervisor (The Assistant Head of the Department) will be responsible for seeing that librarians report on these questions promptly and in proper form.

Instructional Services

Library and bibliographic instruction has the second major priority among tasks performed by reference librarians. Reference Librarians are expected to be available to help the Instructional Services Librarian when they are not assisting individual readers; this assistance may take the form of actual instruction or the preparation of materials for instructional purposes.

Interlibrary Loan Verification

Although interlibrary loan is not administratively a part of the Reference Department, we have agreed to provide bibliographic support to the Interlibrary Loan Office. Interlibrary Loan requests waiting for verification take priority when the needs of individual readers and of library instruction have been satisfied.

Selection Officers

Members of the Reference Department staff who are also Selection Officers have special responsibilities involving the Bibliography Division. As a general rule, service to readers must take precedence if there is a conflict of priorities.

MCGILL UNIVERSITY
(Montreal, Canada)

REFERENCE DESK SERVICE POLICY

A basic policy of our reference service is that reference queries made in person have priority over those received by the telephone or by letter.

DESK POLICIES
General Guidelines for Desk Duty: Nature and Extent of Responsibility

ARIZONA STATE UNIVERSITY
(Tempe, Arizona)

ROLE OF THE REFERENCE LIBRARIANS

The reference librarians have a dual role, combining the duties of the subject specialist and the reference librarian. All share equally in providing service to students, faculty, and other patrons. The reference librarians must answer questions in all subject areas and therefore must possess a working knowledge of the basic tools in each field. In addition, they are asked to develop reference service in a particular subject, to develop their knowledge of that field and to make creative use of it.

Staff

1. Improvement of present staff is a responsibility of the group. Experienced staff members particularly must counsel inexperienced ones on deficiencies and help them to develop in effectiveness. Peer evaluation is a useful technique in staff development.

A portion of each reference meeting should be devoted to training in reference tools and techniques, each librarian taking his turn as instructor.

2. Selection of new staff members. Reference librarians must have the opportunity to study the credentials of applicants and to interview them. No one should be offered a position without the approval of present staff members.

Organizational Arrangements

Our objective to staff the reference desk so as to provide maximum service to the public. At peak hours, there are three librarians on duty. In order to expand service, several plans have been proposed: "Off-duty" librarians would be available at desks in the reference room, or librarians might maintain regular office hours in order to make themselves available to the public. Another proposal, the aim of which is to provide more effective service, is to staff an information desk with a well-trained clerk to answer directional and other routine questions.

CASE WESTERN RESERVE UNIVERSITY
(Cleveland, Ohio)

GENERAL REFERENCE DESK—1ST FLOOR

Opening

1. The staff member scheduled to the General Reference Desk at 8:30 a.m. should arrive a few minutes earlier so that reference services—in person and by telephone—can be initiated at 8:30 a.m. sharp.
2. It is his/her duty to unlock the desks and the telephones and to connect the recorder. The key to the Reference Office is kept at the Circulation Desk; the keys to the desks and the telephones are in the Reference Office.
3. The same staff member has to straighten up the reference department area whenever it is possible between questions from patrons:

- Quick reference publications and drawer material should be returned to shelves and drawers;
- Publications scattered on tables and carrels should be arranged into one pile on each table or carrel;
- Abstracts and indexes—Section II—should be reshelved;
- Telephone directories reshelved;
- College catalogs scattered in the reference area should be assembled and placed on a black truck for reshelving;
- The "College Blue Book" Table should be cleared of any material lying around and not belonging to the Table. Such publications have to be placed on a black truck for reshelving.

Leaving the Reference Desk

Before leaving the desk duty a staff member is responsible for the following:

1. All Quick Reference books used at or returned to the reference desk should be reshelved;
2. Desks and counters should be cleared of personal material;
3. Memos, flyers, notes placed either in box on Desk 1 or on the yellow pad on the shelf next to it;
4. Drawer material returned to the respective drawers;
5. Recording messages should be erased each time after taking care of them, or before leaving the desk.

Time Spent on One Question

1. Should depend on the number of patrons to be assisted at that particular time. However, it should not exceed 15 minutes. Research can be continued when off the desk-duty.
2. Use your common sense—be flexible.

Consultation with other staff members

1. General policy: never let a patron go away without some kind of information or advice unless you used all ways known to you and then after consulting with another staff member available at the time of inquiry.
2. Whenever you are in doubt about the correctness of your information seek another opinion.

3. Remember: each one of us might have some kind of information which might be useful for a particular patron.
4. Therefore: *No negative answer before consulting.*

COLORADO STATE UNIVERSITY
(Fort Collins, Colorado)

REFERENCE—SELECTED POLICIES AND PROCEDURES

Reference Desk Schedules. The Reference Librarian is responsible to the Associate Director of Libraries for the scheduling of staff members at the General Reference desk. The Associate Director of Libraries is responsible for the scheduling of staff members at the Science Reference Desk. Copies of the schedules should be deposited in the Associate Director's office and with the Director's secretary at the beginning of each term.

Patron Assistance. Reference questions should be referred to the staff member on duty at the appropriate reference desk by all library staff members in the Circulation and I.D. Departments and those other staff members working near the card catalog.

Patron Rapport and Referrals. Establishing rapport with the patron is basic to all librarian-patron relations. An adequate referral of patrons from one staff member to another, or from one service point to another, is as important as answering a question at the original source of inquiry.

Reference-Circulation Duties. A strict division of duties is important between the service points at the reference desks and the Circulation Department. Reference desk personnel are not to render circulation service nor are staff members at the Loan Desk to attempt reference service. However, the decision to circulate reference titles is the responsibility of staff members on duty at the reference desks.

Implementation. Interpretation and implementation of these policies and procedures is the responsibility of the Head of the Reference Department and/or the Associate Director of Libraries.

UNIVERSITY OF ILLINOIS
AT URBANA-CHAMPAIGN
(Urbana, Illinois)

SERVICES FOR LIBRARY STAFF

Library staff may contact the catalog Information Desk to verify locations and copy numbers in the shelflist for items which departmental libraries feel conflict with the LSC record. Reference desk personnel will assist departmental libraries in locating information in the Reference Room collection by assisting in the use of bibliographical tools.

A reference acquisitions list is complied at six month intervals and will include major reference titles purchased for departmental libraries and listings of these titles submitted to the Reference Department for inclusion for the acquisitions list.

Orientation and instruction on reference research resources and other relevant reference services are available to any individual staff member or group.

RESTRICTIONS ON REFERENCE SERVICE

The Reference Department does not compile or check bibliographies for individuals, faculty, or otherwise.

The staff does not do extensive bibliographical checking for departments (i.e., completion of order items for books to be requisitioned) or individuals, but rather assists staff and others in the use of bibliographical tools.

No searching is done for answers to puzzles, quizzes, TV contests, etc. Assistance is limited to individuals about where they might search for themselves.

Telephone reference assistance is primarily limited to ready reference types of requests. Extensive or in-depth reference questions should be asked at the Reference Desk in person.

Reference Room materials do not generally circulate to any borrower for use outside the room. A photocopy machine is available in the room.

INFORMATION DESK

The function of the Information Desk is to assist library users in the use of LCS and the card catalog; to refer reference questions to the

Reference Department or appropriate departmental libraries; to interpret library rules, regulations and procedures; to give directory information about the Library, campus and community; and answer inquiries about the location and holdings of serials.

When users in departmental libraries need information about a book from the main catalog, the staff of the Library should make the call to the Information Desk rather than asking the individual to do so. This procedure will save time, since the staff member will often be able to give the call number or appropriate bibliographic information to help answer the question.

LOUISIANA STATE UNIVERSITY
(Baton Rouge, Louisiana)

PUBLIC SERVICE POINTS—SCHEDULES AND RESPONSIBILITIES

1. The staffing of public service points, Interloan, Information, and Central Reference Desks, is the primary task of the Reference Services Division. "All other duties and assignments are secondary, and they should be accomplished during periods in which the staff member is not assigned to public desk duty." (9/27/79)

2. "Keep to a minimum the work that you bring to duty on the reference desk. No work should be done there that requires such concentration that you are not able to stay alert to the needs of patrons. In arranging schedules (an) attempt will be made to see that no librarian is on the reference desks for longer than two or three consecutive hours, except, of course, nights and weekends. This will enable each of us to give our entire attention to the task of providing conscientious and attentive reference service, while on the desk." (5/9/78)

3. Librarians should schedule around their assigned desk hours a 36 hour work week while school is in session. (1/17/80)

4. "Each of your schedules should reflect your non-service desk duties." (1/17/79) "You may find, for example, that you must schedule yourself for one or two late afternoons or very early mornings in order to have access to OCLC terminals for verification purposes." (1/17/80)

5. The service desk schedules are posted.

6. There are one or two librarians on duty in Central Reference each hour that the library is open, and one or two library assistants and/or trainees. (1/17/80)

7. "The first librarian listed each hour is to be considered the 'Duty Librarian.' That person is responsible for the Central Reference Desks during that period, and should be sure that the library assistants and trainees are backed up by adequate professional personnel, even if this means calling another librarian to the desk. Librarians who are not on desk duty are subject to being called in by the Duty Librarian. The Duty Librarian should station himself/herself at the first or second Reference Desk, and not at the third desk with back to the door. (1/17/79)

8. "Librarians have been assigned roughly 15 to 17 hours per week on desk at Central Reference, plus weekends. They may also be called upon for substitution and/or extra duty as explained above under "Service Desk Schedules." (1/17/79)

9. "Staff should remember that in all schedule conflicts between service desk staffing and any other activity (e.g. committee meetings, university business, coffee breaks, preferred lunch periods) the former must take precedence." (9/27/79)

10. "Reference Librarians who find it necessary to leave during assigned reference desk duty should secure replacement by other librarians. Under no circumstances should librarians create a substitution situation in which there is no librarian on duty at Central Reference." (9/27/79)

11. "Before leaving at the end of a period of desk assignment, each staff member should be sure that his or her replacement has arrived for duty." (9/27/79)

12. "Habitual tardiness for service desk duty is unacceptable behavior. And being on time for such assignment does not mean that the staff member is coming through the front door when due on the desk, or out of sight in an office. It means that the staff member is on the desk on time and ready to work." (9/27/79)

13. "If you are the last person on the reference desks, DO NOT LEAVE." (8/25/78)

14. "You should be always sensitive to the workload carried by the Information Desk." Only one person is scheduled at that desk, "and can ill afford to have the reference staff sending patrons for help with the card catalog. The card catalog, for our purposes, is part of the reference collection, and instruction in its use is part of the responsibility of the reference librarians." (5/9/78)

15. "Before referring a patron to the Louisiana Room, or some other area of the library, be sure through a thorough reference interview that you cannot satisfy the patron's need." (5/9/79)

UNIVERSITY OF MASSACHUSETTS
(Amherst, Massachusetts)

DESK SERVICE

General Statement and Instructions

Nature and Extent of Responsibilities of Librarians on Desk Duty.
1. *Priorities*—The primary responsibility of reference staff on desk duty is provision of direct personal service to readers who come to the Reference and Information Desk for assistance, or who call by telephone.
2. *Clipboard Messages*—Reference staff are responsible for reading the messages attached to the desk clipboard as soon as they come on duty. The purpose of the clipboard is to record information and special short-term instructions needed by staff on desk duty that day. Messages should be added to the clipboard by staff on desk duty as appropriate. Examples of such messages are: 1) notes concerning material placed on the reference hold shelf for use by readers returning later in the day; 2) notes concerning class assignments involving use of reference materials; 3) notes concerning procedures for answering a difficult question being asked repetitively at the desk.
3. *Reference Staff Vertical File*—This file is a collection of materials brought together to serve special informational needs of reference staff on desk duty. Examples of the kinds of materials found in this file are: brochures describing area library facilities and resources; statements concerning library policies and procedures; guides to the use of selected data bases; copies of campus and 5-College news publications relating to current events; information relating to special collections owned by the library, etc. Generally, because of the format or ephemeral nature of these materials, they are not suitable for cataloging and retaining on the reference shelves. A guide to the subject headings

used in the file is kept in a notebook shelved inside the vertical file.

4. *Approachability*—Reference staff on desk duty must be constantly aware of how approachable they appear to library users who are in need of assistance. Being approachable is a first step in encouraging users to seek assistance at the Desk. Users need to be educated to the fact that individual assistance is the primary responsibility of staff on desk duty, that reference librarians are interested in the problems that face library users, and are willing to help. Since the attitude and behavior of staff on duty go a long way toward creating an image of the Reference Department, Reference staff should strive to make that image a positive one.

5. *Activity During Slack Periods*—During slack periods at the desk, staff may work on other assignments, examine new reference materials, read professional literature, etc., as long as it does not interfere with the provision of desk service. They should walk the floor occasionally to see if they can be of assistance to readers working elsewhere in the reference area or at the public catalog. Staff must be careful not to become so engrossed in other work that they fail to see readers in need of assistance in the reference area or at the public catalog.

6. *Staffing Level and Mobility*—It is the policy of the Reference Department to staff the reference desk at all hours that the Library is open with the exception of late-night hours. Under normal circumstances, the staffing level should be such that at least one librarian is available to assist readers elsewhere in the room (at the public catalog, at the index tables, etc.) or to deal with requests that must be handled immediately away from the desk (for example, assistance in using reference tools shelved at a far end of the floor; microforms; etc.).

The "Reference Schedule" form will be used to announce the numbers and names of staff assigned to desk duty at particular times of the day. Occasionally, the designation "on call" will appear alongside one of the names on the desk schedule when, in the opinion of the Schedule Officer, this person's assistance will be needed for part, but probably not all, of the time period involved in a given shift. The purpose of the "on call" designation is to allow for flexibility in the use of staff time without impairing provision of desk service. A librarian scheduled as "on call" should report for desk duty as usual; but, should the level of activity at the desk not require his or her presence full-time, he or she may arrange with the Desk 1 librarian to work on other projects away from the desk during quiet periods (e.g., verification of interlibrary loans, or other work which can be done in the vicinity of, or in view of, the desk). The "on call" librarian is responsible for either being at his or her desk in the office or for keeping an eye on activity at the desk, returning whenever he or she observes that additional help is needed there, or whenever he or she is recalled by other librarians on desk duty.

7. *Leaving the Desk Uncovered*—Should it ever be necessary to leave the desk uncovered for more than a few minutes (to assist a reader in the Microforms Room, for example), the sign which reads "Reference Librarian will return shortly" should be placed in a visible location on the desk. A librarian's absence from the desk should never be so prolonged as to interfere with the rights of others who are waiting for service.

8. *Inaccurate Information*—If one reference librarian overhears a colleague giving inaccurate factual information to an inquirer in person or over the telephone, he or she will discreetly inform the colleague to insure that the inquirer receives the correct information.

MCGILL UNIVERSITY
(Montreal, Canada)

SUBJECT RESPONSIBILITIES

Reference librarians are expected to develop competence in the use of the reference resources of McLennan library. In addition to this general competence an attempt is made to secure expertise in the literature of each specific discipline and area for which the McLennan library is responsible. This is effected by selecting staff with differing subject and language backgrounds, and by assigning pertinent subject responsibilities to each one. Individual librarians develop their knowledge of the literature of their assigned subject responsibilities on the job.

A subject responsibility involves:

1. Familiarity with the curriculum and research interests of the

relevant departments through knowledge of the appropriate documentation, and through contact with faculty and students.

2. Thorough familiarity with the reference and bibliographic resources of the assigned disciplines and areas through study and experience in providing reference services. Duties are as follows:
   - Answers difficult questions and provides in-depth guidance to readers in the use of library resources in assigned subjects.
   - Compiles and updates bibliographies of reference resources for assigned subjects for the use of the library's clientele.
   - Gives bibliography seminars for graduate students and advanced undergraduates in assigned subjects.

3. Engaging in book selection and collection development for the McLennan Reference Collection as detailed below:
   - Surveys the reference collection in assigned subjects.
   - Makes recommendations for the purchase of both retrospective and current titles for the Reference Collection.
   - Suggests transfers from and retirements to the McLennan Stacks.

MICHIGAN STATE UNIVERSITY
(East Lansing, Michigan)

The following specific objectives have been identified as some short-term (one to two years) steps toward meeting the continuing objectives. The objectives are listed in order of their relative emphasis.

— to review and codify current selection policy.
— to study work loads of both full-time and shared professional staff to promote maximum utilization of each librarian's capabilities.
— to establish liaison with science academic units whose research and teaching needs are to be met from the Science Library's collection in order to encourage and facilitate faculty participation in the identification of the most useful library materials.
— to develop forms to facilitate patron recommendations of needed library materials.
— to attend subject seminars, departmental meetings, etc., to publicize the science library's services and collections.
— to provide staffing arrangements which facilitate personal or professional growth.

—to disseminate information to faculty and graduate students explaining the services and resources of the MSU science library particularly the data base service.

—to document need for professional personnel to maintain hours for maximum reference services.

—to increase communication within the public services sub-unit of the science library and with other units within the library system.

UNIVERSITY OF OKLAHOMA
(Norman, Oklahoma)

REFERENCE AREA AND REFERENCE SERVICE

The staff at the Reference Desk on the main floor provides assistance in using the Library's collection and services. They will help you use the Card Catalog, find articles in magazines, locate information in reference books, and assist you with papers or other research projects.

The reference collection includes encyclopedias, dictionaries, almanacs, biographical sources, college handbooks, a collection of phone books, and many other subject reference books.

An ID must be presented in order to obtain materials. In the case of "restricted" materials, which do not leave the building, the ID will be held until their return. All reserve materials should be returned at the north end of the desk only, as overdues are fined at the rate of twenty-five cents per hour for two-hour items or twenty cents per day for overnight items.

STATE UNIVERSITY OF NEW YORK
COLLEGE AT POTSDAM
(Potsdam, New York)

The principal responsibility of librarians assigned to the Reference Desk is to see that all questions asked are answered as fully and pertinently as possible, and that anyone who looks puzzled is approached with an offer of help.

Free time should be used to examine new reference books on the truck near the Reference Desk and to read material from the professional literature information baskets. Work from your own department should not be brought to the Reference Desk.

If you are at a loss as to where to look for an answer to a question, call on any available librarian for help. If an adequate answer has not been found, put a note on the permanent memo side of the reference notebook. If the resources of our library are not adequate to furnish the information wanted, consider a phone call to Clarkson or the Potsdam Public Library, or interlibrary loan. There are, of course, some questions which we are not equipped to answer and sometimes time limitations make interlibrary loan impracticable, but every reasonable effort should be made to get the user the information needed.

Although it is obviously not possible to be at the Reference Desk all of the time, every effort should be made to avoid becoming so involved in answering one user's question that others are denied service. If any librarian scheduled at the desk must be away from the desk for any lengthy period of time ask any librarian in the reference or card catalog areas to fill in, or call 2940 and ask for a librarian to help at reference. Reference clerks will help also, but remember they handle only routine business and should not attempt to answer reference questions of any sort.

If someone is needed to run errands, ring the bell at the reference desk. This will summon the student assistant or the reference clerk.

SAN DIEGO STATE UNIVERSITY
(San Diego, California)

ENVIRONMENT FOR REFERENCE SERVICE

1. The importance of general reference services requires that service points are located convenient to the focal point of activity in the library, the main card catalog.
2. Subject specialists' service points are located near relevant reference materials.
3. All reference service points are placed so that the necessary conversation between library users and reference librarians and staff is not disturbing to others.

4. Adequate physical facilities are provided for the convenient use of the reference collection.

THE UNIVERSITY OF TEXAS AT AUSTIN
(Austin, Texas)

ENVIRONMENT

The environment is arranged to help users feel at ease in requesting assistance and while using library resources.

A. Reference and information service points are easy to locate. Clearly worded signs, conspicuously posted, indicate where users are to go for assistance. Instructional signs are also used to explain the use of library tools.

B. Staffing patterns and hours of service for each public service unit of the General Libraries directly reflect, within budgetary limitations, the needs of the users. Whenever possible a librarian is available to assist users during all hours that a unit is open and a regular service schedule is maintained.

C. Whenever possible the reference area is arranged so that conversation between library users and staff members is private and does not disturb others.

D. Seating at tables or carrels is provided near the reference collection.

General Guidelines for Desk Duty: Guidelines for Handling General Inquiries

CASE WESTERN RESERVE UNIVERSITY
(Cleveland, Ohio)

HANDLING OF REQUESTS FOR BOOKS

1. Establish patron's familiarity with the use of the public catalog;
2. If he is familiar
   - refer him/her to the Author/Title Catalog when author and/or title is known;
   - refer to the Subject Catalog when books on a certain subject topic are requested and neither author nor titles are known;
3. If patron is not familiar with the Public Catalog—give personal assistance;
4. Ask the patron to return to the reference desk for assistance if he is not able to locate a publication in the Public Catalog when searching on his own;
5. Recheck the Public Catalog; however, establish first if patron does not mind your doing it. Explain that a librarian has certain

ways of approaching the search. If not found under author—try under title or a different spelling of the author's name.

6. When patron has call number and asks where it would be located in the stacks, explain the location chart next to the elevator;

7. If patron is not able to locate a book on the shelves and returns to the reference desk, advise him/her:
   - to check at the Circulation Desk to see if it has been taken out;
   - if no circulation record found, assist the patron: recheck the public catalog for mistakes in call number or location (library);
   - if both are correct, assist in locating the book on the shelves—there is always the possibility that it has been misshelved or, that the patron is not familiar with the classification system and looked in the wrong sequence.

8. Whenever an entry for a publication does not exist in the public catalog, or, the book is not found in the stacks:
   - use the OCLC terminal for establishing other locations;
   - if location found and the patron is member of CWRU, explain the ILL services and refer him/her to the ILL Office;
   - if not found on OCLC, establish accuracy of bibliographic information (BiP,NUC), ask the patron to show you the reference: it might be to an article in a periodical, to a chapter in a book, or, to a government document.

9. Whenever a specific publication requested by the patron cannot be located anywhere, advise him/her to search the catalog for another book on the same subject.

HANDLING OF REQUESTS FOR TOPICAL INFORMATION

1. *Reference Interview: clarify what the patron really wants*
   - rephrase in your own words the request and ask the patron if you understood him/her correctly;
   - establish how much information is needed;

2. Relate to the patron, get interested in his/her problem; a seemingly trivial question should be given the same attention as any other;

3. Review in your mind sources known to you, they should be the starting point in your search for answer;

4. Try those on QR first—if any available—then search under the same call number in the regular reference stacks;

5. Leave patron with the sources, then follow up: did he/she find the information or the material he/she needed?

REQUESTS FOR LITERATURE ON A PARTICULAR SUBJECT OR TOPIC

1. Reference Interview: clarify what the patron really wants. Establish:
   - academic level — if student
   - how much information needed
   - for what purpose (term-paper, talk, etc.)
   - what period has to be covered (how far back, present, etc.)
   - what sources needed (original, periodical articles, gov. documents, reviews, books);
2. Recommend the use of the Subject Catalog for monographs — if patron not familiar with the catalog, accompany and assist;
3. Recommend abstracts and indexes for periodical articles: general ones and in the specific field;
4. Assist in finding these publications in Section II and explain their uses;
5. Recommend indexes to bibliographies on the catalog cabinet next to the reference desks:
   - Council of Planning Librarians
   - Reader's Advisory Service;
6. Recommend Vertical Files material (list of subjects on the cabinet);
7. If a subject heading is not used in the Subject catalog, introduce patron to the Lib. of Congress Subject Headings List;
8. Follow up: did the patron find what he/she needed?
9. The General Reference Desk attendant is responsible for giving service in the Periodical area on nights and on week-ends only.

UNIVERSITY OF ILLINOIS AT URBANA-CHAMPAIGN
(Urbana, Illinois)

1. If the librarian does not have the necessary expertise on a subject or research question, be careful not to offer misleading,

incorrect, incomplete or erroneous information. Offer only information that you are certain of. Do not guess about possible locations of materials. In this system absolutely no generalizations can be made. Refer the patron to another librarian for further assistance if necessary. The patron can be asked to return at a more appropriate time when a specific librarian is available. If the patron cannot return at that time, note the patron's name, telephone number and request on the form provided, so that other librarians can complete the transaction and respond to the patron later. It is extremely important that reference personnel realize their own limitations and refer the patron to another librarian when necessary. One incorrect, incomplete, misleading or erroneous response can be detrimental to library service and may mean that a patron leaves with a negative attitude toward libraries and library personnel which can be carried over to other potential users. There will be times when it is essential to request advice, or consult with another librarian to make certain that all aspects of question negotiation are carried out and the search completed satisfactorily with all major resources covered.

2. All patrons should be encouraged to return for further assistance. This should be an automatic comment made to all patrons each time they are assisted. If possible, return to patrons assisted earlier to inquire if they need further assistance, as many are hesitant to return to request additional help. Active reference assistance is encouraged. Seek out those patrons who may need assistance but may be reluctant to ask, or who may be unaware of the reference service offered. Aggressive reference service makes for a positive attitude toward libraries and library personnel and is a mark of professionalism.

3. Learn from all reference librarians. Never be reluctant to take a problem or referral to another librarian as consultation and further knowledge will assist in improvement of skills and knowledge. If further assistance from someone else is needed, but no one is available at that time, inform the patron that he/she may request further information from another librarian(s). Give office hours and appropriate librarian's name to the patron.

4. Recognize the importance of all patron requests whether these are for directions, quick fact, in-depth or extended instruction.

Show each patron the utmost courtesy and give topnotch service no matter what the level or type of question. Answering any query involves more than subject expertise or instructional abilities. It involves professional image and attitude, empathy, skills in interpersonal communication and interviewing techniques. Each response a reference librarian makes (verbal and non-verbal) will affect the patron's attitude and perception of libraries and librarians and is a powerful stimulus to the motivation involved in the learning process. The communication process can be a forceful or detrimental factor in determining whether or not a patron learns to recognize and use the full repertoire of the library's research resources or never learns to use libraries effectively. Our purpose is to increase bibliographical sophistication and enjoyment of library services, programs, and resources.

5. The most common problem library personnel face is knowing *when* to refer a patron to another librarian or other resources. Librarians are not always aware of, or familiar with, additional and/or approriate information. Therefore, the best advice is, do not be afraid to admit you do not know everything. If possible refer the patron to another librarian immediately if uncertain, or ask another librarian for suggestions later to help improve your competencies in future encounters.

6. A problem all librarians face is the amount of time that should be spent with a patron. This is a decision that will have to be made frequently. Consideration should include how busy it is, the number of other patrons waiting for assistance, the number of library personnel available to help patrons, the nature of the patron's request, the patron's prior knowledge of library resources and use. If possible, never leave other patrons waiting for lengthy time periods. Get patrons started on their projects and then return to them as time permits.

7. Remember that many patrons will be hesitant to approach a reference desk and that most will not approach if librarians are engaged in casual conversations, telephone calls, and/or are engrossed in paper work. Library users will return to request further assistance if the librarian is courteous and helpful in the first encounter. Make it easy for the patron to approach. Seek out library users who might need help but will not ask. Library users appreciate assistance more if the librarian is willing to

leave the desk area to assist them, even for a minor request. Satisfied library users will return again and again, and the level of sophistication of their questions will increase if librarians are competent and approachable. This does not mean that there will be fewer directional or quick fact questions. Good service at reference and information desks will increase the number of users who in turn will become more adept at the question negotiation process and in their bibliographical abilities.

8. Library users need the librarians' full attention. The appropriate amount of time spent with them is always appreciated. Telephone calls, other patrons waiting for assistance at the desk, and librarians' involvement in other activities is irritating to the patron who wants the undivided attention of reference personnel. If possible do not let distractions interrupt the reference interview. However, if no one else is at the reference desk, it will be necessary to return to the desk to take incoming calls, even though the reference transaction is not completed.

9. Patrons frequently do not ask for what they actually need. If a patron asks for a specific reference title or a location of an item, do no just hand the item to the patron without further questioning. Find out as much as possible about the patron's topic and offer further assistance. Direct the search to the best possible sources. Many times an encyclopedia or almanac will provide information on the topic, but these sources may not be the best tools to use. At other times the patron may ask for one thing that will actually provide no helpful information on the topic at all. In such a case, investigate further, otherwise the patron will go away without the needed information.

10. Patrons should be encouraged to interrupt activities that librarians might be carrying out at a desk that do not involve assisting another patron. Library users should feel that the primary purpose of a reference librarian is to help them.

11. Bring to the attention of the head of the reference department problems that arise, questions, or suggestions and recommendations so that these can be reviewed, discussed, clarified, or resolved immediately.

12. Keep up with the literature of the field and with popular and current topics of interst. Browse through new reference and

general circulation books to improve knowledge and abilities as a reference librarian. Browsing assist one learn to anticipate needs of library users.

13. Record reference transactions that cannot be answered; but do not place this record keeping task ahead of the patron's needs.

UNIVERSITY OF MASSACHUSETTS
(Amherst, Massachusetts)

Handling General Inquiries.
1. *General Statement*—It is expected that judgment will be used in determining which questions can be handled to completion by the librarian and which ones are best answered by providing guidance in selecting sources to consult. In the first category are directions, general questions concerning library policies and services, information on library holdings and ready reference questions involving specific facts easily determined from standard sources.
2. *Direction*—In giving directions, explanations should be given when possible with reference to appropriate printed aids available at the Desk or near the public catalog (e.g., the stack directory, the directory of locations, the Campus Guide, etc.) so that the explanation will be as clear as possible and the reader can, if he wishes, find his own way the next time he has a similar question.
3. *Library Policies*—When the reader comes to the desk in person it may be preferable to make the inquiry for him if it is necessary to refer to another service point for full information.
4. *Library Holdings*—In giving information on library holdings the reference librarian should never give a negative answer without fully verifying the item requested and checking in all appropriate collections or sources. If the reader does not want to wait until this can be done or is satisfied with a less than complete search, be sure to indicate in your answer that it is possible that a more thorough search would locate the material wanted.

When it has been established that material needed by the reader is not available in the University Library system, suggestions should be made concerning other possible locations which may be appropriate, such as local libraries, bookstores, and libraries outside the Valley.

5. *Information Service*—Answers to other questions should be based on data in standard reference sources whenever possible. The printed information should be shown to the reader, or in the case of a telephone inquiry, the source of the information should be cited. It is not our policy to vouch for the accuracy of a particular answer or source, although we should be prepared to give some indication of its reliability. We will not normally cross-verify answers except in the case of obvious discrepancies.

In a second category are questions which require much longer, more detailed answers; e.g., questions concerning search strategy for information in a specific field, perhaps involving several forms of material (periodical articles, books, government documents, etc.) or questions which will require search through a number of specialized sources which are located some distance away from the Desk area. When these more complicated, time-consuming questions arise at the Desk, there are several possible procedures to follow: for example, (1) inform the reader courteously that his question will probably take considerable time to answer fully and ask if he or she is willing to come back later for an answer, or for individual help in locating the answer; the librarian should then record the question on a "Request for Information" form, (2) alert an "on call" librarian to assist at the Desk, (3) ask an "on call" librarian to assist with the question, (4) or give the reader a bibliography already prepared by a member of the Reference Department if there is one which is directly relevant.

- Amount of Service—The amount of service that can be given at any particular time will vary, depending on such factors as how busy it is at the desk, how many other reference librarians are available to help, etc. What is practical at one time may not be at another; it is important, however, that an effort be made to provide adequate service. Some guidelines that may be followed are given below:
  1. Always try to suggest some sources and specific headings (in the public catalog, an appropriate index or bibliography,

etc.) and encourage the reader to come back for further suggestions if the results are not satisfactory.

2. If the inquirer is beginning his or her search and is unfamiliar with the relevant sources you may want to set up an appointment with you or one of the other reference librarians for a conference on how to make full use of library resources in that field. Such a conference will enable a reference librarian to give much more assistance to an individual student than is possible on the spur of the moment at the busy reference desk.

3. If you are unfamiliar with what sources might be available and wish to investigate when you have more time, fill out a request for information form and arrange to report on the question later.

4. When likely sources of information are known but a search of them will be very time-consuming, or require specialized knowledge which you do not have, you should suggest that the inquirer do the search for himself, or employ a research assistant.

5. When the search appears to require a quick check of a large number of potential sources which would be difficult to explain to a reader, the reference librarian may, if the purpose of the question seems to justify it, invest a reasonable amount of time on the research.

THE UNIVERSITY OF TEXAS AT AUSTIN
(Austin, Texas)

SERVICES

A. Reference and information services in the public service units of the General Libraries serve the present information needs of the academic community at The University of Texas at Austin and anticipate future needs. New reference and information services are not implemented unless adequate funding is available.

B. A publication describing reference and information services is available at public service units.

C. Reference and information services are available to individuals who come to the library and to those who request assistance over the telephone or through correspondence. Although telephone and correspondence reference services are an integral part of reference and information services, priority is always given to users who come to the library.
D. Reference and information services are publicized utilizing all necessary forms of communication media.
E. Reference and information services are reviewed periodically.

REFERENCE AND INFORMATION SERVICES AT THE DESK

The units of the General Libraries which provide reference and information services vary in size from a unit with one staff member responsible for all activities, to a unit with many staff members whose only responsibility is to provide reference and information services. The diversity of these units makes it impossible to include the detail usually found in reference manuals. It is expected that each public service unit offering reference and information services will add the detail applicable to the unit.

A. Basic Services

The provision of basic services is common to all units but extended searching is dependent upon the public service staff and resources of a unit. Staff members consult other library staff, when necessary, for assistance in answering any question.

1. Directional and locational information are provided upon request; factual answers which can be found in the reference collection are supplied. Search questions are also accepted and are referred to a librarian. Assistance is given in locating library materials.
2. Informal instruction is provided when deemed necessary by the staff member. Informal instruction includes explaining to an individual the organization and use of the card catalog, indexes, abstracts, loose-leaf services, and other reference materials.
3. Individual instruction in library methodology and bibliographic research is provided when deemed necessary by the librarian, e.g., explaining the organization of the literature

of the field, suggesting subject headings to use in a literature search.

4. Bibliographic verification of materials is also provided. For those items not available on campus, assistance is given in obtaining them through Inter-Library Service, or referral to off-campus collections, or, on occasion, purchase by the library.

B. General Guidelines for Service Points

The first priority of staff members on desk duty is to provide reference and information service to users who come to the library.

1. Staff Attitude

Individual assistance is the primary responsibility of those on desk duty. This is reflected in the attitude and behavior of staff. Staff members appear alert, interested, and willing to help. They apply well-developed communication skills to ascertain the needs of users and are not judgmental regarding a request. Courtesy, patience, sensitivity, and tact are important in all interactions with library users. Staff members survey the reference area for users who appear to need assistance and offer to help them.

2. Staffing Level

Whenever possible at least one staff member is on-call and available to assist the person on desk duty. Because of budgetary restrictions this is often unobtainable.

3. High-Use Periods

When users are waiting for assistance, staff members offer help first to the individual who has been waiting the longest. If this inquiry will be time consuming to answer, staff members answer first the briefer questions of other users who are waiting, or seek assistance from other staff members.

4. Low-Use Periods

During low-use periods staff members on desk duty may work on other assignments, examine new reference materials, read professional and subject related literature, etc., as long as these activities do not interfere with the provision of desk service. Staff members must not become so engrossed in other work that they fail to see users in need of assistance.

5. Leaving the Desk

Absences fromthe desk or desk area are as brief as possible. If it is necessary to leave the desk for more than a few minutes and a replacement is not available, a sign stating that the person on desk duty will return shortly is placed in a visible position on the desk.

6. Messages for Desk Staff

Messages providing the answers to recurring questions, to difficult questions, or about materials being held for users, etc., are left for other staff members on desk duty.

7. Paging Users

Library users are not paged.

8. Personal Telephone Calls

Except for emergencies, staff members do not make or accept personal telephone calls while on desk duty.

9. Public Use of Library Telephones

Telephones at the reference and information desks are for official library use only. Users are referred to the nearest pay phone or the nearest PAX phone for campus calls.

General Guidelines for Desk Duty: Guidelines for Handling Problem Inquiries

UNIVERSITY OF ILLINOIS
AT URBANA-CHAMPAIGN
(Urbana, Illinois)

Contests—invite user courteously to come in for some assistance.
Legal information—explain sources we have, refer to Law Library (give hours professors are available)–but do *not* make legal interpretations–or medical ones–quote verbatim from sources if phone call, and give source title and date–absolutely *no* interpretation.

UNIVERSITY OF MASSACHUSETTS
(Amherst, Massachusetts)

HANDLING PROBLEM INQUIRIES

1. *Questions Received at Closing Time*—Whenever possible, handle questions received at closing time to completion even if it means working overtime. However, if the questions seem very involved,

or you have other commitments which prevent you from working overtime, ask the reader to return for assistance at a time when the Desk will be staffed by a reference librarian. Readers should be informed that the role of the student assistant who is on duty from 10:00–12:00 p.m. is to assist with routine directional and simple informational questions only. (Reference service hours are posted in a visible location at the Desk.) Fill out a "Request for Information" form, summarizing the main points of the inquiry, so that you or the librarian coming on duty in the morning will be able to handle the question to completion at the time agreed upon with the reader.

2. *Genealogical Questions*—are those which involve the tracing of lines or details of family history, and not just the identification of a person, or the finding of brief biographical information about a person, such as would be included in a "who's who" type directory.

   - The reference staff will assist in answering genealogical questions within the scope of the resources of the Library, in the same manner in which any other type of question is answered. "Normal" assistance is direction and instruction in the use of the card catalog and reference sources which explain techniques of genealogical research. General aid is also given in finding bibliographical guides to information. Librarians will not normally digest information for the reader or undertake elaborate searches for details in books of local history, genealogies, newspapers, microfilmed records, etc. An exception to this rule is a reasonable search of published materials relating to the University, when these sources may be expected to contain pertinent information. Questions involving reference materials kept in the University Archives Collection would be referred to the Archives Librarian for reply.
   - At times when there happens to be a person possessing expertise in genealogical research on the Library staff, a reference librarian may refer more involved genealogical questions to that person if such referrals are acceptable to that person and to his/her supervisor.
   - Inform the reader that agencies which may help in his genealogical research are listed in: e.g., the latest *Directory of Historical Societies and Agencies,* Ref. E 172 A51 and Lee Ash, comp., *Subject Collections: a guide to special book collections,* Ref. Z 688 A2A81.

3. *Questions Relating to Take-Home Exams, Contests, Puzzles, etc.*—
Challenging questions are sometimes posed by instructors as
part of take-home examinations or as "puzzles" intended to encourage students to learn how to use library resources.

Generally, the initial approach of the librarian should be the
same as it would be to any other question: i.e., to direct the
reader to probable sources of information, encouraging him to
return if those sources are unsatisfactory. However, when a
group is involved in pursuit of the same information, it becomes
difficult to provide individual assistance or even instruction in
search strategy. The reference staff must then judge the relative
importance or propriety of the question and act accordingly to
avoid time-consuming repetition of effort.

Establish as complete a picture as possible of sponsor, purpose,
and progress-to-date of the parties involved in finding the answer to the question, by interviewing the reader, other staff who
have been involved, and/or the sponsor by contracting him directly. In general, the less the purpose of the question has to do
with education or research (by admission of reader or sponsor)
the readier the reference staff should be to direct readers immediately to sources known to contain the answer, or even to
provide the answer. Considering the relative obscurity of some
questions, the library staff must not be expected to assume
responsibility for the correctness of the solutions found; it is not
part of our normal service to cross-verify answers, except in
obvious cases of contradictory information. The interpretation
of the questions and the acceptability of the response must
remain the responsibility of the reader.

Special arrangements made by an instructor prior, e.g., to a
take-home examination, should include a full explanation of his
purpose and the information sought, as well as a list of known
participants. Such arrangements will only be accepted as modifying normal reference service when their purpose is clearly
educational and a discussion with the sponsor shows that he has
carefully considered alternatives such as instruction by the
staff in the use of libraries or the strategy of a literature search.

THE UNIVERSITY OF TEXAS AT AUSTIN
(Austin, Texas)

SPECIAL INQUIRIES

Class Assignments

Staff members help users locate information for class assignemts. When a class assignment creates a problem, the head of the unit is responsible for seeing that the instructor is contacted about the present and possible future class assignments.

Interpretation of Material

Staff members do not interpret legal, medical, financial, or statistical information.

Recommendations of Books for Purchase by Individuals

Staff members refer users to standard reviews of the work in question and advise the user to examine the library copy, but they do not make recommendations.

Appraisal of Books and Artifacts

Staff members do not appraise items. Users are advised to consult a professional appraiser, but specific appraisers are not recommended.

Genealogical Questions

Genealogical searches are not undertaken. Card catalog assistance and the location of standard reference sources are offered. These questions are referred to the Texas State Library and Barker Texas History Center as appropriate.

Contests, Puzzles, etc.

Staff members suggest appropriate sources but do not locate the information.

General Guidelines
for Desk Duty:
Behavior and Attitudes

ARIZONA STATE UNIVERSITY
(Tempe, Arizona)

To Promote Effective Communications with the Faculty
Definition: The objective is to make faculty members aware of the services that the Reference Department provides and to encourage the use of these services. Although the reference librarians offer assistance in collection development, the primary goal is more effective use of the collections by the faculty and by the students.

Implementation of Goal:
A. Reference librarians assigned subject specialties should share, to some degree, the subject knowledge and interests of the faculty members they serve. This subject background need not necessarily be acquired from formal study of the discipline.
B. All reference librarians in a university library must display a helpful attitude and must demonstrate sympathy with academic objectives. Prompt responses to inquiries from professors are one way of conveying a positive and constructive approach to faculty-librarian relations.
C. Reference librarians should exercise the initiative in promot-

110

ing contact and communications with faculty members. They may do this in a variety of ways; the more effective methods involve a direct, personal offer of assistance to the professor in teaching his students the use of the library and in developing the collections.

CASE WESTERN RESERVE UNIVERSITY
(Cleveland, Ohio)

APPEARANCE AND ATTITUDE

1. Remember: the Reference Desk is like a stage; we are in the public eye most of the time. This fact should influence the appearance, attitude, and behavior of any staff member on duty;
2. The attitude at the desk should reflect approachability and encourage the patron to ask for information;
3. When not giving service, spot and assist patrons seemingly lost or obviously confused or in doubt in the reference department;
4. Lengthy social conversations either with patrons or with colleagues should be avoided;
5. When assisting a patron away from the desk, the position should be such that the desk and anyone waiting there could be seen;
6. When a question takes the attendant away from the desk for more than a few minutes:
   • alert another available staff member to watch the desk and the telephone, *or*
   • turn on the recorder and display the sign "Librarian will return . . ."

UNIVERSITY OF MASSACHUSETTS
(Amherst, Massachusetts)

APPROACHABILITY

Reference staff on desk duty must constantly aware of how approachable they appear to library users who are in need of assistance. Being approachable is a first step in encouraging users to seek assistance at the Desk. Users need to be educated to the fact that individual assistance is the primary responsibility of staff on desk duty, that reference librarians are interested in the problems that face library users, and are willing to help. Since the attitude and behavior of staff on duty go a long way toward creating an image of the Reference Department, Reference staff should strive to make that image a positive one.

THE UNIVERSITY OF TEXAS AT AUSTIN
(Austin, Texas)

STAFF ATTITUDE

Individual assistance is the primary responsibility of those on desk duty. This is reflected in the attitude and behavior of staff. Staff members appear alert, interested, and willing to help. They apply well-developed communication skills to ascertain the needs of users and are not judgmental regarding a request. Courtesy, patience, sensitivity, and tact are important in all interactions with library users. Staff members survey the reference area for users who appear to need assistance and offer to help them.

General Guidelines for Desk Duty: Recording Statistics and Questions

CASE WESTERN RESERVE UNIVERSITY
(Cleveland, Ohio)

STATISTICS

1. Statistics are being recorded every two months during the academic year. A statistics sheet will be at the reference desks (first and second floor). Any question is to be recorded—in person or over the telephone—and the status of the inquirer has to be established: undergraduate, graduate, faculty, others.

RECORDING OF REFERENCE QUESTIONS

1. Graduate Assistants and Trainees will record reference questions other than location of books and periodicals and directional ones, indicating the sources used in providing information.
2. All questions that have not been answered for one reason or other should be recorded by any staff member on desk-duty in the notebook provided for this purpose. These questions will be analyzed during staff meetings and possible sources will be discussed.

COLORADO STATE UNIVERSITY
(Fort Collins, Colorado)

REFERENCE QUESTION

For statistical purposes, a reference question is one which requires knowledge of library techniques, library holdings, and/or bibliographic tools to answer. In this context, a question relating to the location of an item in the Libraries, with no subsequent explanation concerning that item, shall not be counted as a reference question.

A sampling is made of all questions asked at the reference desks. A report each semester is made to the Associate Director of Libraries.

UNIVERSITY OF MASSACHUSETTS
(Amherst, Massachusetts)

RECORDING STATISTICS AND QUESTIONS

1. *Daily Statistics Report*—It is the policy of the Reference Department to keep statistics on inquiries received at the Desk in order to provide a factual base for review of reference service. One of the responsibilities of all librarians and reference assistants working with the public while on duty at the Desk or "on-call" is to keep an accurate record of contacts with inquirers.

   Record the number of contacts made with inquirers on the Reference Department's daily statistical report form, following instructions outlined in "The Daily Statistical Report Form: Instructions for Using, and Definition of Terms," a copy of which is filed in the Staff Vertical File, Reference Department folder. The Department secretary or the librarian assigned to Desk duty when the department opens for service is responsible for seeing that the form is placed at each desk station, properly dated, and ready for use. At the close of the day, completed forms are placed in the tray labeled "statistics." The statistics are compiled on a monthly basis and reported in the Department's monthly report. A file of these reports is kept in the Department office. From time to time, the Department will use sampling methods to collect data wanted for special purposes: e.g., for national reporting.

2. *Request for Information Sheet*—It is the responsibility of persons assigned Desk work to record questions they are unable to answer while on Desk duty. The purpose of recording these questions is threefold: (1) to have a record of unanswered questions to be worked on later, when there is more time to search and/or ask for assistance from others; (2) to record questions that could not be answered with the resources in the Library (specific titles and/or types of material which should be added to the collection to answer similar questions in the future should be noted on the form); (3) to compile a collection of questions useful for the training of new staff.

Record all necessary information on the *Request for Information* form following the instructions for using it on file in the Staff Vertical File in the Reference Department folder. These "Instructions" include a procedure on what to do with the completed form.

UNIVERSITY OF NORTH CAROLINA
(Greensboro, North Carolina)

RECORDS

1. Record search questions, indicating steps in search, whether with positive or negative results.
2. Use paper other than the search question form for temporary interstaff notes.
3. Record telephone questions *in detail*, whatever their nature.
4. Record all lectures and tours in the appropriate folder.

THE UNIVERSITY OF TEXAS AT AUSTIN
(Austin, Texas)

EVALUATION OF REFERENCE AND INFORMATION SERVICES

The measurement and evaluation of reference and information services is the responsibility of the reference librarians and the library administration.

Statistics

In order to have a basis for the review of reference and information services, each public service until keeps daily statistics on inquiries received. Each staff member scheduled for duty at reference and information service points has the responsibility for accurately recording these inquiries. Circulation questions (e.g., book renewals, interlibrary loan requests which do not require verification or other reference work, tracing of missing books) are excluded from reference statistics.

Definitions to Be Followed for Recording Statistics

Each question is counted once, regardless of the number of sources consulted. However, each question asked by a user is recorded if the user asks more than one question about more than one subject.

1. Direction Questions

   A DIRECTION question is one which is concerned with the physical location of rooms, offices, etc., and not related to interpretation, locations, use, or organization of information resources. (Sample direction questions: location of restrooms, pencil sharpeners, drinking fountains.)

2. Information Questions

   An INFORMATION question is one which concerns information resources[2] and/or their use. It is answered from personal knowledge of the staff member without his consulting any other information resources except the card catalog. (Sample information questions: library hours, location of a French dictionary, library holdings.)

3. General Reference Question

A GENERAL reference question is one which is answered through the use of information resources. The answering of a general reference question requires a specialized knowledge of information resources. The source of information used is more frequently one which is obvious to the staff member at the time inquiry is made. The general reference question requires less than fifteen minutes to answer. Bibliographies compiled exclusively through the use of the card catalog and/or pre-existing bibliography are counted as general reference questions.

4. Search Reference Question

A SEARCH reference question is one which requires more than fifteen minutes of time to answer.

5. Problem Question

A PROBLEM question is one which requires more than an hour of time to answer. The answering of such a question employs the specialized knowledge of a trained librarian, as well as an extensive use of library rosources which extends beyond the general reference collection. Unanswered questions on which the librarian has worked more than an hour should be recorded here.

6. Bibliography

A BIBLIOGRAPHY is a systematic list of writings relating to a given subject or author and is the original work of a reference staff member. It is compiled by using several library resources and requires at least an hour of work. Bibliographies should be prepared using the *Guidelines for Typed Bibliographies* (Policies and Guidelines No. 9). Regularly issued acquisitions lists and continuously issued bibliographies are not counted in this or any other category.

7. Correspondence

Letters requesting information which are answered by your unit should be listed as CORRESPONDENCE.

Monthly Summary of Reference Statistics

1. The subject content of all questions in the Search, Problem, and Correspondence categories are recorded and reported with the Monthly Summary. A copy of each bibliography prepared should also be forwarded with the Monthly Summary.

2. Monthly Summary sheets are sent to the Statistics Clerk by the fifth of the following month.

Special Surveys

Special surveys may be conducted periodically to determine the relevance and effectiveness of the reference and information services offered. Proposed surveys are submitted to the library administration for approval.

---

2. Throughout these definitions the phrase "information resources" is intended to be an all-inclusive term. It refers both to the personnel resources and to all of the bibliographic resources available in the general university, i.e., those in offices, departments, and laboratories as well as in the library system per se.

General Instructions for Information Assistants on Desk Duty

UNIVERSITY OF ILLINOIS
AT URBANA-CHAMPAIGN
(Urbana, Illinois)

In-person policies—Service to the public comes before any other work, such as filing, shelving, reading, studying (which we prefer you do not do) when you are scheduled at the desk. *Be alert to user needs,* even while doing other work such as shelving, etc. *Be ready to offer assistance even before it is requested. Explain* what you're doing, instruct while you help!

1. Remember you represent the library in a direct way—thus your manner, your concern for the user, and your prof's competence should reflect this. Do not mislead a patron into believing you are a librarian, if the question arises, but act like one at all times.
2. Use tact, flexibility, and good judgment in dealing with *all* the users. Be as *flexible* as you can. Go out of your way to help. If necessary, bend a rule rather than anger a patron unnecessarily—but use your best judgment before bending the rule.

3. Don't be afraid to leave the desk but don't leave it unstaffed for long periods of time either.
4. Offer to train new users on LCS if time permits.
5. Go with the patron *whenever possible*—do not point!!
6. *Use question negotiation skills* so you are sure you understand exactly what patron wants. Always recheck card catalog on LCS if patron says they cannot find an item—but do so without making patron feel stupid.
7. Always *ask* us if you have questions—don't be afraid—none of us know everything. Leave notes for us if you have a question about resources or the system, etc. that you cannot answer, or if you were unsure of whether you provided the best sources—this is good learning experience and helps us in training as well.
8. *Every library user should recieve the same courteous, accurate service as the next. Never* respond to rudeness or anger in a like manner. LISTEN and then do everything possible to help—if that doesn't work, give the angry, rude patron my name and number and ask that he/she contact me during the day, or MFC if serious!!

LOUISIANA STATE UNIVERSITY
(Baton Rouge, Louisiana)

STUDENT ASSISTANTS

One of the librarians "will be responsible for the scheduling of student assistants in Central Reference, and for assigning and supervising their work. Other staff members who wish to utilize the time of student assistants should give their projects to this librarian, who will work them into the students' schedules." (4/21/78)

LIBRARY ASSISTANTS

A library assistant is assigned for a few hours each week to help each librarian. Librarians should make certain that the hours and duties assigned to library assistants do not interfere with assigned service desk hours or other primary tasks assigned to the library assistants. (1/17/79) Exceptions to library assistant work schedules may be made only with the approval of the Head of the Division, or in the Head's absence, with the approval of the supervisor involved. (9/6/79)

TRAINEES

A librarian will be designated Trainer of Trainees. A trainee is assigned to each Interlibrary Loan Team. Other trainees are scheduled mostly for service desk duty, but may be called upon to help teams if needed, provided they are properly relieved from desk duty. A librarian will be responsible for scheduling trainees for weekend duty (Friday night through Sunday). (1/17/79)

UNIVERSITY OF MASSACHUSETTS
(Amherst, Massachusetts)

RESPONSIBILITIES FOR REFERENCE ASSISTANTS

General Statement

Reference assistants receive in-service training to prepare them for carrying out a variety of support duties essential to maintaining the quality of Reference Desk service. They are expected to provide back-up assistance for routine procedures, questions, and problems; for example, the BORF routine; searching for missing reference materials; helping readers to locate desired microforms, etc. They may also be called upon to help individual reference librarians by checking sources for answers to specific reference questions.

In addition, they may be called upon during peak service periods to assist more directly by helping to answer the telephone.

For a list of general support activities assigned to individual assistants and the names of the reference librarians with whom the assistants work on particular assignments, see the folder labeled "Reference Dept.," in the Reference Staff Vertical file.

Level of Responsibility

Reference assistants are expected to use independent judgment and make decisions within guidelines, but consult with reference librarians on difficult or unusual problems. Assistants are expected to refer to a librarian questions concerning areas in which they lack knowledge or may have only partial information.

Assistants share with other members of the Reference staff a responsibility for becoming familiar with the contents of this manual, giving special attention to the Introduction and section on Desk Service.

Special Public Service Assignments

1. Telephone duty—for staffing and services, see section on Desk Services, Telephone.
2. Microforms Room—for staffing and services, see sections on Desk Services, General Inquiries.

RESPONSIBILITIES OF STUDENT ASSISTANTS

General Statement

A mature student may be assigned to supervise the reference area on the Main Floor of the library during late night hours when no reference librarians are on duty.

The assistant will receive in-service training on how to handle inquiries, emergencies, and referrals. It is the policy of the Department to identify through signs those hours when a student assistant, rather than a reference librarian, is on duty.

Level of Responsibility

The student assistant is generally not expected to be able to answer questions except those concerning locations, library policies and services, and library holdings. The student should not give a negative answer without suggesting that the inquirer return or call at a time when a reference librarian is on duty, or leave an inquiry at the desk which can be followed up the next day.

NORTHWESTERN UNIVERSITY
(Evanston, Illinois)

SERVICES PROVIDED BY REFERENCE STUDENT ASSISTANTS

1. Answer basic directional questions concerning the library and specifically the Reference Department.
2. Answer basic informational questions about the library (e.g., library hours) and its holdings (e.g., titles recorded in the catalog).
3. Hand out books from the Reference Desk collection and accept rental fees for the use of the rental typewriter.

Telephone: Incoming Calls

CASE WESTERN RESERVE UNIVERSITY
(Cleveland, Ohio)

TELEPHONE REQUESTS

1. Identify the institution: "Freiberger Library. Reference. May I help you?"
2. If two lines ringing at the same time, answer one, put on hold, answer the next, put on hold saying "Hold on, please" or, whatever you feel appropriate, then return to the first call and take the question.
3. If several patrons are waiting, excuse yourself and proceed as indicated above.
4. Give the caller a choice:
   - waiting until you finish assisting the patron;
   - to call later (15 min., 30 min. or so)
   - you will return the call, in such take name and telephone number
5. Request to locate a publication in the Public Catalog:
   - take down as accurately as possible the information given over the phone
   - in case of any doubt ask the caller to spell the last name of the author and/or the first word of the title;
   - check the Catalog by author, if not found, by title;

124

- if entry found check the circulation files and report result to caller;
- if entry not found, inform caller about it and ask whether he wants you to check the OCLC terminal for locations in other libraries;
- if caller agrees, check on the OCLC terminal.

6. Whenever the caller asks to locate the publication on the shelves and to reserve it for him/her: exercise your judgment according to the situation and be flexible:
   - if no patrons are in sight, or, another staff member can take over, you are able to leave the desk. Ask caller to hold on explain the distances, or, take his/her telephone number to call him back;
   - if the situation is such that you cannot leave the desk, explain the situation to the caller and promise to give him the information later, once you are off the desk or, somebody else can be sent to the stacks. Take name and telephone number and be sure to call the person back, one way or the other.
   - when publication is found, put it under the caller's name on "Hold" shelves at the Circulation Department.
   - if publication is not found, try to reach the patron to inform about the result of your search.
8. Inform the attendant following you at the desk if you want to relate a message to the patron whom you where assisting.
9. Do not keep patron waiting for any answer for more than 3 minutes approximately. Ask telephone and name and return the call whenever you find the information.
10. Patrons cannot be paged—unless in cases of emergency.
11. Personal calls received at the desk should be kept as brief as possible.

TELEPHONE REQUESTS FOR PERIODICALS

1. Request for checking whether the library owns a particular *periodical* should be taken and answered at the General Reference Desk, unless the caller explicitly asks to be connected with Periodical Reference.
2. Request for checking whether a particular *issue* of a periodical is in the library, or, for verifying a citation in a periodical, should be transferred to the Periodical Reference.

UNIVERSITY OF ILLINOIS
AT URBANA-CHAMPAIGN
(Urbana, Illinois)

If a phone question requires *in-depth* lengthy research, ask if patron could come in for help. If not, fill out a search form and promise to get back to caller. Three to five sources can be checked, if larger lists of titles, ask caller to come in and you'll assist in person.

If you get a long distance call, try to answer it immediately. If you cannot, fill out search form and phone number of caller, so we can return call later. Refer these to us if we must call back.

When users call for information that is more readily available elsewhere, after helping the user, suggest that in the future the caller may wish to contact the appropriate source directly, e.g., an item located on LCS, caller should contact phone center.

Paging users—we do not have a paging system. If not busy and caller can identify (by description) person in Reference Room, look. If busy, and it's not an emergency, suggest caller come in and check.

If you must go to card catalog area, stacks, or another part of building, put phones on hold—the ringing disturbs other patrons. Likewise, do not let the phone ring for long periods of time.

Can hold items at desk for caller overnight but tell him material will be reshelved early next morning.

When transferring a user's call, explain why and to whom you are referring the call.

KENT STATE UNIVERSITY
(Kent, Ohio)

ANSWERING TELEPHONE QUESTIONS AT THE REFERENCE DESK

At a Readers' Services meeting these points were discussed and agreed upon as the proper procedure to follow in answering telephone questions:

1. As a general practice, call the person back rather than hold the line. Patrons who are in the Library should never be required to wait while a telephone question is being answered.

2. If the caller is a University student, ask him to come to the Library for reference assistance.
3. Questions from faculty members should be answered by telephone, but, again, the line should not be held.
4. Questions from persons outside the University community which can be answered quickly may be answered by telephone, but the person should be encouraged to come to the Library for assistance in solving more complicated problems.
5. Brief card catalog checks may be made for a telephone patron, but, if more than three items are to be checked, it is our policy to ask the patron to come in person or send an assistant to do the checking.

UNIVERSITY OF MASSACHUSETTS
(Amherst, Massachusetts)

TELEPHONE INQUIRIES

Incoming Calls

1. Who Answers the Telephone—The persons who are at the Desk are responsible for answering the telephone. The telephone will ring both in the reference area and in the reference office. If the phone rings more than three times, it should be answered in the reference office by reference staff working there (i.e., by the departmental secretary when she is on duty; by reference librarians, or a reference assistant when the secretary is absent).

The departmental secretary is responsible for answering routine questions relating to hours, library staff, and departments, referring all others to a reference librarian. The reference assistant is responsible for answering routine questions, referring all other questions as appropriate. Both follow instructions outlined in "Telephone Procedures for Reference Assistants", a copy of which is kept in a folder at the telephone desk.

The "Telephone Procedures for Reference Assistants" include instructions to always ask the advice of the reference librarian on duty when in doubt as to the best procedure for handling difficult or unusual inquiries. An assistant must not assume responsibility for answering questions concerning areas in which she lacks knowledge or may have only partial or incorrect information. If the response to an inquiry is to be in the negative (i.e., the library does not own the requested material), the assistant or reference librarian should offer to verify the item before giving a final answer to the reader.

Reference staff members working in the reference area are, of course, expected to come to the aid of those on desk duty whenever the need arises. When there is only one person at the desk, that person answers the phone even if he or she is speaking with a reader, since constant ringing will disturb the whole room. However, if the phone call interrupts service you are giving to a reader at the desk, ask the person on the phone if he can wait or if you can phone him back later with the answer to his question. Service to readers who have come to the desk for assistance is given priority over service to readers who are asking for assistance by phone.

2. *Service Standards*—The telephone is one of the most important means of providing and arranging for service to library users. Members of the Reference Department are responsible for maintaining the best possible standards of telephone service. Since the manner in which telephone inquiries are handled has a direct bearing on both the operation of the department and the public impression of the University Library, it is important that the telephone techniques outlined below be practiced.

DEVELOP A PLEASING TELEPHONE MANNER
—Make the caller's first impression a good one.

IDENTIFY THE DEPARTMENT
—So that the caller knows immediately he has reached the right department, answer the phone by saying, "University Library, Reference Department . . ."

GIVE PERSONAL SERVICE
—Treat callers as individuals. Take time to be polite.
—Do not leave a person holding the line for more than a few minutes while you search for an answer. If a search is going to take more than 2-3 minutes, arrange to call the

reader back if it is a local or WATS line call, or have him call back at a specific time. Tell him the information will be left with the librarian then on duty.

HANDLE CALLS TO COMPLETION (see also Checking Records below)
—Many callers do not know the person who can help them. You may have to transfer them to the right person. See the campus *Telephone Directory* for instructions on transferring (off-campus calls may be transferred through the University switchboard, but give the number to the caller in case you are cut off trying to transfer the call. On-campus calls cannot be transferred; give callers the correct number they should call direct).
—If you know that the information a caller wants is to be found in specialized sources and can be better provided by another department or branch library, make sure the caller knows whom he should consult and the type of service he can expect. In some cases it is best to refer the caller to a specific person by name and title.

LEAVE EFFECTIVE MESSAGES
—When the call is for someone in the department who cannot be reached immediately, always offer to take a message. Make it clear, concise, complete. Messages for staff members should be written on the appropriate forms and left in mailboxes.
—Get the details right even if you have to ask the caller to repeat or spell names.
—Use the Reference Department "Request for Information" forms to record answers to questions callers will be phoning back for at some specified time. Give these to the Desk 1 reference librarian so that they can be attached to the clipboard.

RECOGNIZE SERVICE PRIOITIES
—Answer all general information calls which can be answered in a few minutes without questioning the status of the caller. Whenever possible, answer the inquiry rather than switch the call to another extension.
—Complicated questions are often better answered if the caller is encouraged to come in person to the library. If this is not possible, a written reply may be preferable to a lengthy telephone conversation.
—When it is clear that the question being asked will take

more than a few minutes to answer, it may be necessary to take into account not only the nature and urgency of the request, but the status of the inquirer as it relates to the University. For example, if the caller is a member of the faculty or administration and needs information for official purposes, it will be more expedient for the librarian to make the extra effort than require the caller come to the library personally. (This may involve going to the stacks to check something known to be there.) Many factors enter into decisions concerning the amount of service that can be given to individuals, and judgment must be exercised.

3. Paging Readers—When phone requests to page readers are received, follow the procedure outlined in the Staff Vertical File under "Paging Patrons (Procedures)."

4. Checking Records—The Reference Department receives a number of phone requests each day for catalog information. Answer all public catalog questions from the branch libraries. During the day you may refer Central Serials Record and Bindery questions from the branch libraries to the appropriate department; at other times, the reference staff must answer these inquiries.

    Do not refer callers from outside the Library system to the Technical Services Departments. Consult the records yourself. When a list of items or a complex subject inquiry must be checked, encourage the caller to come to the library in person or to send in a written request for information. See section on Bibliographic Services.

5. Circulation Information—If a caller inquires about whether a specific book for which he has obtained the call number is actually in the library, inform him courteously that it is not possible to look on the shelves, and offer to refer him to the Loan Services Department (or appropriate branch library) which will check to see if there is a record that the book has been checked out.

6. Questions about Library Policies—Answer questions concerning general library policies if the inquirer simply wants to know

what the policy is. However, if the question concerns interpretation of policy, or an individual problem affected by a policy, refer
the inquirer to the service desk or department responsible for
carrying out that policy.

Example: Questions concerning renewal of books charged out
from Loan Services. —If the inquirer wants to know what the
policy is, inform him that "books may be renewed in person or by
phone at the library from which they were borrowed if they have
not been requested by another reader." (Refer to the Reference
Staff Vertical File as necessary for exact wording of general
library policy statements). However, if the inquirer wants to
renew his books by phone, or to discuss an individual problem
affected by this policy, refer him to the Loan Services Department. Before making this referral, find out if the books were
borrowed from the stacks and if the patron has the call numbers
for any books he wishes to renew. (The Loan Services Desk will
need to have the call numbers in order to check their records.)

7. Personal Calls—You may arrange to be called on Department
   lines, but keep personal calls to the minimum, in number and
   length. Try to arrange to be called on the unlisted numbers
   during regular working hours so as not to interfere with calls for
   reference service.

   Transfer or refer calls for other members of the library staff to
   the correct department and give the number to the caller for
   future use. If the person called is not listed in the staff card file,
   and his/her department is not known, check the University
   telephone directory. As a last resort, transfer or refer the call to
   the main office of the library.

8. Emergency and Nuisance Calls—In an emergency situation,
   such as a bomb threat, try to obtain as much information as
   possible from the caller and write it down. Notify the Campus
   Police at once (Ext. 5-3111). (See emergency instructions kept
   on clipboard at reference desk.)

   Nuisance calls should be dealt with as quickly and unemotionally as possible. If they persist, notify the University operator.

MCGILL UNIVERSITY
(Montreal, Canada)

PREFACE

A basic policy of our reference service is that reference queries made
in person have priority over those received by the telephone.

POLICY

In the interest of good public relations—*take down and answer all
initial requests* (except Category 8, below). In the interest of accurate
reference service—attempt quick verification (BIP, FB) when time
permits.

No matter what the category of the enquirer, we answer all questions relating to McGill publications. No matter what the category of
the enquirer, we refer government document enquiries to the McLennan
Government Documents Department. Exceptions would be quick-
reference questions that we or any library reference department
could answer with such basic tools as the *Canada Year Book* or the
Canadian Almanac.

Judgement should always be exercised as to what constitutes a
reasonable telephone request. For example, if a branch librarian
asks us to check in the catalogue a list of a dozen books or periodicals,
we would suggest that the list be sent to us to be checked.

The Reference Department does not supply cataloguing information (L.C. call numbers, subject headings, etc.). If such information
were requested we would ask the librarian to come in person.

Judgement should always be exercised as to the status of the
enquirer as he relates to McGill, and the nature and urgency of his
request.

The following list of categories is a guideline to the priorities given
to those who request information by telephone. [Here follows five
pages of categories and types of reference service for each—Editor]

TELEPHONE PROCEDURES AND PRACTICES

Incoming Calls

Reference librarians are scheduled on telephone duty for approximately 2 hours per day. prime responsibility is to obtain a written record of every call which comes through on lines—*4943* or *4944*

Telephone Signals:

Buzz and Light Flashing Slowly —INCOMING CALL
Light Flashing Quickly   —HOLD CALL
        (Press HOLD for call to be held;
        two calls may be held at once)
Steady Light   —CALL WAS ANSWERED
I/C   —Intercom
        (Press HOLD, then press I/C and
        SIGNAL)
(N.B. Always press button before lifting receiver)

Some Telephone Practices:
1. A ringing telephone should be answered as quickly as possible, not only for the sake of the caller, but also to avoid disturbance to readers in the library.
2. Librarians should answer the phone by saying "Reference Service, McLennan Library"
3. Whenever possible, Reference Staff already engaged on one line when another starts ringing should use "Will you hold the line, please?" in preference to letting the phone ring.
4. If readers needing help in the Department are being kept waiting because of a lengthy phone call (happens frequently Saturdays, nights) ask the caller to ring back later.
5. Establish the caller's identity and affiliation.
6. Do not accept WCB's without taking phone numbers, unless the caller really does not have a phone.
7. Indicate priority and urgent questions as such.
8. Find out what sources have already been checked and note exact *years* as well as names of tools, e.g., Ulrich—which edition? N.S.T. what years and latest month checked?
9. Referrals: • If the question clearly belongs to another library or department tell the client and ask him to re-dial the appropriate number. (see telephone referral Guidelines)
      • Straightforward "DYH because we want to borrow" requests from campus or city libraries should be transferred to the interlibrary loans assistant in charge of city lending.
10. The librarian on telephone duty is expected to put down all the necessary information and pass on the request to the Desk.

11. If the question is particularly complicated, the Librarian who took the original request may decide to handle it entirely himself. If this is the case a clear note should be left on the telephone slip indicating "Leave For KW", etc.
12. The slips should not be accumulated before they are sent out to the Reference Desk.
13. Spare time while on telephone desk duty may be devoted to other duties, such as examining the new reference tools and writing answers to reference letters.

see also LONG DISTANCE PHONE CALLS

Telephone Slips in Process

When the telephone slips are sent to the Reference Desk to be researched, the librarians on desk duty or those specifically assigned to the question are ultimately responsible for completion of these requests. Assistance may be obtained from any staff member. It is most important that information on the slips is very clear as to what has been done and by whom, so that work on the question can be pursued efficiently.

Answers to requests should be communicated to the client as soon as possible. If more than one day is required to answer the question, the enquirer should be notified by an interim telephone call. Unfinished requests are kept on the NEW REQUESTS clipboard. Slips awaiting information from outside of the Reference Department, and slips completed, but awaiting successful contact with the enquirer, are kept on the PENDING clipboard.

1. The senior librarians
   • Check clipboards at least twice daily, or whenever they are scheduled for desk duty.
   • Clear off "Pendings" by contacting the department or person from whom further information is needed and by phoning, or asking the librarian on telephone desk duty to phone, answers to clients who have been unavailable.
   • Make timely "interim" phone calls.
   • When necessary, split the questions up and ask colleagues to take their share.
2. Telephone slips should not be removed from the clipboard for lengthy periods. When long-term or out of reference area work is needed to answer the questions, xerox the slip note the xerox

copy as "being worked on by _____ (Name), and _____ (date) and leave the copy on the "Pending"clipboard, taking the original slip with you to work on.

3. Telephone slips should not be spread in gay profusion all over the Reference desk, or scattered like rosepetals throughout the library. They should be either completed or put back on the clipboards or replaced with a xerox copy as noted above, as quickly as possible.

4. Before ticking as "finished" (in right hand upper corner of slip) a telephone which is unsolved or dubious, consult with the librarian who took the original request.

5. Outgoing Calls: for the most part, the Reference librarian who researches the request will communicate the answer to the requestor. For convenience, however, the librarian on telephone duty may be asked to return the call. Regardless of who in fact, completes the transaction, the slip should be ticked in the upper hand corner. The form may then be put into the slot for completed request forms at the Reference Desk. From here it will become part of our statistics. (Completed telephone slips are kept in the bottom drawer of the filing cabinet in the Asst. Head's office for aproximately 3 months.)

For Telephone Replies by long distance, see "LONG DISTANCE TELEPHONE CALLS"

"Finished" Telephone Slips

"Finished" telephone slips are examined daily by the librarians responsible for checking. The purposes of slip checking are:

1. To serve as a training device for the librarian who worked on the question by indicating any possible short cuts to the answer.

2. To serve as a training device for all reference staff by bringing to their attention new tools used to obtain the answer, or imaginative uses of old tools for the same purpose.

3. To ensure that questions are indeed completely answered or, in the case of a negative result, that all reasonable possibilities have been exhausted.

THE UNIVERSITY OF TEXAS AT AUSTIN
(Austin, Texas)

TELEPHONE REFERENCE SERVICE

Telephone reference service is an integral part of reference and information services. Priority, however, is given to users who come to the library for assistance.

Training

The unit head is responsible for assigning and training staff members to answer the telephone. Staff members who answer the telephone are courteous and efficient and are familiar with the General Libraries' *Guidelines for Telephone Use* (Policies and Guidelines No. 12).

Priorities

General information calls which can be answered quickly are responded to as they are received. When telephone calls come at a busy time, or when questions will take more than a few minutes to answer, staff members take down the question and the name and telephone number of the caller. Staff members give their name and inform the individual that the call will be returned, giving an approximate time. For out-of-state telephone calls, the individual is asked to call back, or the staff member and out-of-state caller may agree that the staff member will return the call "collect."

Types of Questions Not Answered

Whenever appropriate, a caller is urged to come to the library for in-person assistance rather than telephone assistance. Information pertaining to the selection of term paper topics and the identification of taxonomic classifications are not provided over the telephone. Only general information about computer-based searches is given over the telephone. Statistical, medical, financial, and legal information are not given over the telephone.

Long Distance Calls

If any inquiry received by long distance cannot be answered immediately, arrangements are made to respond at a later time. Long distance calls within the state of Texas are returned on the TEX-AN network. For out-of-state telephone calls, the individual is asked to call back. The name and telephone number of the staff member handling the inquiry as well as an approximate time to call back are given. In the event that it is difficult to estimate the time needed to prepare a response, the staff member and out-of-state caller may agree that the staff member will return the call "collect."

Paging Users

Library users are not paged.

Personal Telephone Calls

Except for emergencies, staff members do not make or accept personal telephone calls while on desk duty.

Public Use of Library Telephones

Telephones at the reference and information desks are for official library use only. Users are referred to the nearest pay phone or the nearest PAX phone for campus calls.

Telephone: Outgoing Calls

CASE WESTERN RESERVE UNIVERSITY
(Cleveland, Ohio)

OUTGOING CALLS

1. Patrons should be advised to use official telephone in the lobby.
2. Personal calls should be reserved for breaks or lunch periods, unless emergency exists.

UNIVERSITY OF MASSACHUSETTS
(Amherst, Massachusetts)

OUTGOING CALLS

1. General Guidelines—When placing official calls, always identify yourself as a member of the Reference Department of the University Library.

2. Long Distance Calls—There are no restrictions on calls to campus

or local numbers, other than need and brevity. However, long distance calls to areas not covered by a University WATS line must be reported to the head of the department.

If any inquiry comes to us by a long distance telephone call outside our WATS area and it is necessary to call back with the requested information, be sure that the inquirer will accept a collect call. Such calls should not be charged to the University.

3. Calling Local Libraries—Typical out-going calls are those made to libraries in the local area to obtain information about their holdings or the use of their facilities by University readers. We do not ordinarily call long distance for such information.

The 5-College libraries Reference Departments will provide card catalog information by phone to individual readers and will handle reference inquiries made by reference librarians.

4. Reader Use of Telephone—Telephones at the Reference Desk are available for official library business only. Readers should use the public pay phones, or the free campus phones for all calls.

As always, there are exceptions. The phone may be used by the public when:

- Questions of library policies or operations are involved. Example: A research assistant wants to call a professor concerning an interlibrary loan he was sent to inquire about.

- An emergency situation occurs. Common sense is the best guideline here. Try to have the reader use one of the phones in the Reference Office for such calls, not the phones at the Reference Desk.

5. Personal Calls—Staff members making personal calls should use the public pay phones or free campus phones whenever possible. If the call must be made from the Reference Department, use a phone in the Reference Office, preferably the instrument with the unlisted number. University WATS lines should not be used for making personal calls.

Circulation of Materials

UNIVERSITY OF ILLINOIS
AT URBANA-CHAMPAIGN
(Urbana, Illinois)

CHECK OUT POLICIES

Reference materials are non-circulated. If necessary, ask patron to check with librarians during 8–10 p.m. Never check out documents to a user, unless you have permission from librarians or documents personnel first.

KENT STATE UNIVERSITY
(Kent, Ohio)

CIRCULATION OF READY REFERENCE MATERIALS

As of January 5, 1976, all Ready Reference materials will remain in the Library at all times and circulate only for two-hour periods from the reference desks. They will *not* circulate overnight.

These materials have been designated as "Ready Reference" because of their heavy use by students and librarians. Therefore, it is essential that they be in the Reference Center *all* hours the Library is open. This non-circulating policy will insure that Ready Reference materials will be available when the Library opens in the morning and until it closes in the evening.

Older editions of most Ready Reference materials can be circulated and copy machines are readily available.

Ready Reference materials will *not* leave the Library for any reason, including for photocopying to other departments outside the Library. All patrons are asked to use the copying machines available in the Library. Arrangements can also be made in the Microform Center for copying.

UNIVERSITY OF MASSACHUSETTS
(Amherst, Massachusetts)

CIRCULATION FUNCTIONS OF REFERENCE STAFF

Pamphlet File.
Pamphlet file materials may circulate for two weeks. All authorized University Library borrowers have the same borrowing privileges. Pamphlets are charged out from and returned to the Reference Desk. Material may be renewed if not in demand by other library users. There are no fines for overdue Pamphlet File materials. Procedures for charging them out are on file in the Reference Circulation Policy Manual.

Microforms.
Microforms (with the exception of a few heavily used titles) may circulate to authorized University Library borrowers for a period of one week. The circulation record will be kept in the Microforms Room. Loan Services problems (recalls, fines, etc.) will be handled by the Loan Services department. A copy of the charge slip will be sent to Loan Services with a request for action. See the reference Circulation Policy Manual.

Educational Tests.
Educational tests circulate for use outside the Library for three

days. All authorized University Library borrowers have the same privileges. Procedures for charging out tests are found in the Reference Circulation Policy Manual.

Stack Reference Books.
Non-circulating books in the stacks and books from the Oriental Reference Collection are charged out from and returned to the Loan Services Desk.

Government Documents.
Government Documents will circulate from the Loan Services Desk during those hours when the Documents Department is not staffed. Circulation problems (recalls, fines, etc.) will be handled by the Loan Services Department. A copy of the charge slip will be sent to that Department with a request for action.

Unprocessed Materials.
Unprocessed materials may circulate for use outside the building only if authorized by the appropriate department head (e.g., Head of Serials Dept.). These materials should be signed out from and returned to the Reference Desk. Unprocessed materials may be charged out for in-building use following procedures on file in the Reference staff vertical file under "In-Process Materials."

Reference Books
1. Circulation for Use Outside the Library—In general, reference materials are not circulated outside the Library building so that they will be accessible to as many users as possible for the whole period the Library is open. Many reference tools, such as periodical indexes and the latest editions of standard encyclopedias and almanacs, are in such constant demand that they cannot be taken from the building without causing severe inconvenience to other library users. In most cases, the reference needs of the majority must take priority over the needs of a single individual.

   However, since some reference materials are in much less demand than others, reasonable requests to borrow less heavily used titles for brief periods of time will be granted to any eligible borrower. Borrowers must present a valid library identification card at the Reference Desk. (A request will be considered "reasonable" if the needs of the requestor are best served by using the volume outside the building, and it is the judgment of the reference librarian on duty that the removal of that volume from Reference for a brief period of time will not seriously inconvenience other library users.) Whenever there is doubt as to the advisability of loaning a reference volume, the request can be referred to a senior reference librarian for a decision. A reference volume will not be lent if there is a duplicate copy available for circulation elsewhere in the library system.

Examples of situations in which a reference volume might be lent for use outside the Library are given below. In general, the length of the loan period is based on the needs of the requestor, and the judgment of the reference librarian as to the possible use of the materials by others.

a. Books from the Central Reference Collection

- An hour or two, if a student would like to borrow a specific atlas for use in a classroom demonstration.
- Overnight (at 9:00 p.m.), due back an hour after the library opens the following day when a reader needs to use a reference book after the library has closed.
- Several hours, if a reader needs to take a volume elsewhere on campus for photoduplication, or to an office where an adding machine or other equipment is available to facilitate use of data contained in the reference work.
- Several days (during intersession, for example) when no demand for a particular volume is expected.

Procedures for charging reference books for out-of-building use are found in the Reference Collection Policy Manual.

2. In-Building Use—In general, reference books should be used in the room in which they are shelved so that they can always be located quickly when needed by others. Reference books are reshelved periodically throughout the day to help insure efficient use of the collection.

Readers who have a special reason for wanting to take reference books to another floor of the building for use should sign these books out from and return them to the Reference Desk. If reference material is to be left at the Copy Center for photo-copying, a circulation slip should be completed and left in the reference circulation file until the item is returned.

Procedures for charging reference books for use on another floor are found in the Reference Circulation Policy Manual.

3. "Desk" Books—Unlike reference books shelved in other locations, books shelved behind the reference desk in the "ready reference collection" must be signed for by the borrower for use on the Main floor. Each borrower must write his signature, ID number (or address), the date and time on the card provided, but he is not required to show identification (unless he is not a student or the book is being loaned for use *outside* the building) since all library users regardless of status are free to use reference materials in the building. The purpose of signing for "desk" books is simply to help control their use, since they are often in heavier demand than other reference books, and it is helpful to the librarian on duty to know which of these books are in use at any given time.

4. Renewals, Recalls, Fines—Reference material may be renewed if an extended loan period is not likely to inconvenience other users. Reference books signed out for more than a few hours are subject to immediate recall by phone if needed urgently by someone else regardless of the hour due. There are no fines for overdue reference materials.

MCGILL UNIVERSITY
(Montreal, Canada)

CIRCULATION OF REFERENCE BOOKS

1. Reference books generally do not circulate. Readers are expected to use reference books in the Reference reading area. Special circumstances are outlined below.
2. Reference books circulating to McLennan Library staff within the building, e.g., to Rare Books or Serial Departments, may be signed out at the Reference Desk on green L.C. call cards and

placed in the box on the Ref. desk labeled "Circulating Reference Books."

3. Books in the reference collection fall into two categories:
   I. Reference Books: Books which because of their nature are used for factual and consultation purposes. These only circulate in special circumstances and for a very limited period.
   II. Books which, because of shelving requirements, must perforce live on the main floor (such as Library Science Z's or Printing monographs).

These two categories are treated differently:

Reference Books

- Have reader fill out, in full, two charge cards per volume including call number, accession number, volume, author, title, borrower's name, address, and phone no.
- Determine a reasonable loan period (overnight, 48 hours, etc.) and indicate this on both cards where it says "date due." Sign and date bottom of both cards and ask reader to take book and one of the charge cards to the Circulation desk to have loan processed. Ask borrower to bring book back to Ref. desk after it has been returned and cleared by Circulation so Reference records can be cleared.
- Deposit other charge card in box labeled "Circulating Reference Books."
- Assist. Head will check the circulating books file and telephone for recall when necessary.
- Circulation will keep records in their one day file and will desensitize and resensitize books as they are loaned and returned. They will not follow up overdues.

Non-Reference Books Shelved in Reference

- Have reader fill out in full two charge cards per volume including call number, accession number, volume, author, title, borrower's name, address, and phone no.
- Write "treat as stack book" on lower portion of cards and sign and date both. Ask reader to take book and one of the charge cards to Circulation desk to have loan processed.
- Deposit other charge card in box labeled "Circulating Reference Books."

- Circulation will process book like any other stack book loan including overdues, fines, etc.
- When book is returned, Reference shelver will pick it up from sorting shelves behind Circulation. Circulation will have left charge card visible in volume so reference shelver can pull card from "Circulating Reference Books" box.

4. Special Circumstances

It is difficult to define what special circumstances may arise but a few examples might serve as guidelines. (If in doubt refer problem to the Assist. Head or Head of the Ref. Dept.)

Examples

- Professor or student needs a Reference Book to illustrate a point at seminar or lecture.
- The Principal or a VIP needs a Reference Book for limited period (and a xerox substitute not practical); e.g., the last time the Selection Committee for a new Principal met they needed our *Who's Who in Canada* for a day.
- Burney project staff may borrow books on genealogy or heraldry for a few days if necessary as they are little used.
- Calendar needed for student/advisor conferences.
- Author bibliography (maximum loan period one week).

NOTE: Policies and decisions concerning the circulation of Reference Books shelved in the General Stacks come under the Circulation Department.

UNIVERSITY OF NORTH CAROLINA
(Greensboro, North Carolina)

RECORD ANY LENDINGS

a. Lending of reference books is rare and is done only in special circumstances for UNCG students and faculty. Materials may be checked out for
   1. classroom use, provided they are checked out shortly before the class meets and are returned shortly thereafter.

2. overnight from the time the Reference Department closes until 9:00 a.m. the following morning.
3. over a week-end or holiday when the library is closed, provided the times mentioned in (2.) are followed.
4. urgent needs of faculty or administrative offices.
5. certain interlibrary loan requests for reference materials. (Each request is reviewed individually.)

b. College catalogs may be checked out in special cases. See appropriate section under "Special Collections."
c. Annual reports of corporations, maps, and art catalogs circulate. See appropriate sections under "Special Collections."

NORTHWESTERN UNIVERSITY
(Evanston, Illinois)

USE OF REFERENCE BOOKS IN THE REFERENCE ROOM

In the case where a reference book which is already in use is requested by another user, the following policies obtain:

1. Any reference book is recallable after two hours for the use of another Northwestern-affiliated patron.

2. Preference will always be given to those affiliated with Northwestern over those having no Northwestern affiliation in the use of Reference books.

LENDING REFERENCE MATERIALS FOR USE OUTSIDE ROOM

Policy for Use Within Building, Including Deering

Normally reference materials must be used within the Reference Department. Although staff members should discourage the removal of reference materials, exceptions to this rule may be made as follows by reference librarians:

1. Library staff members may borrow some reference materials for use within the building for one working day. Materials must be retrievable at all times for use by another user. Lesser used materials may be borrowed for longer periods of time, at the discretion of the reference librarians.

2. Northwestern students, faculty, staff, guest borrowers who hold a current guest borrower's card, and, for exceptionally pressing reasons, other users, may under one of the following circumstances borrow materials for use within the building for no longer than four hours:
   - Need for xerox copies from Copy Center, or when copy machines in Reference are out of order. (Materials should be returned to Reference within 30 minutes.)
   - For use with other materials which are non-circulating or otherwise difficult to bring to the Reference Department.

The above points are intended only as a guideline to the outer limits of what is permissible. In each case the reference librarian must use his or her own judgement based on the reason expressed for borrowing materials, the qualifications of the user, and the nature of the materials to be borrowed. Reference librarians are encouraged when in doubt about a specific request to consult with another reference librarian.

Procedure for Use Within Building

1. Fill out white in-building call slip. If borrower is a student or faculty member, have him fill in his name and user number in the space indicated. If the borrower is a library staff member, ask him to substitute his department for user number.

   If the borrower is not from Northwestern, ask him to write down his name, address, and telephone number. Ask to see some identification to confirm name and address. Non-Northwestern users should be allowed to remove materials from the room only under exceptional circumstances.
2. Write in date and time material is due back on the bottom of the call slip and initial.
3. Put call slip in the wooden box on the reference desk, or if loaned for more than one day to a library staff member, file in the binder/missing charge tray.
4. If an item is not returned on time, give slip to the Library Assistant and ask him/her to telephone, requesting return of the material. Problems should be referred to the Department Head.

Policy and Procedures for Use Outside Building

The Head or Assistant Head of the Reference Department may approve the loan of material outside the building. Loans may be made for library staff or faculty members who wish to demonstrate the use of requested materials to a class. The loan period may not exceed four hours when the Library is open. Faculty and library staff members, under very special circumstances, may borrow Reference materials when the Library is closed, i.e., within one-half hour of closing and due back the following day within one-half hour of opening. Anyone not returning material on time should be denied borrowing privileges in future.

Reference Librarians should refer to the Head of Reference only those cases which they recommend as exceptions or those cases where the user becomes extremely irate because he cannot borrow materials. Standard Register Keypunch forms should be used on the circulation of reference books outside the building.

SAN DIEGO STATE UNIVERSITY
(San Diego, California)

RESOURCES FOR REFERENCE SERVICE

1. Provision is made to maintain in the main reference area a working collection of materials to accompany all levels of instruction and research needs primarily in the social sciences and humanities. All reference materials are examined regularly for usefulness and currency.
2. Every effort is made to facilitate the access to needed materials in other library departments, campus information centers, community, regional, state, and national resources.

THE UNIVERSITY OF TEXAS AT AUSTIN
(Austin, Texas)

CIRCULATION OF REFERENCE MATERIALS

Reference materials are for library use only. Permission to borrow them is given only at the discretion of the unit head.

Inquiries for "In-Process" Materials

UNIVERSITY OF MASSACHUSETTS
(Amherst, Massachusetts)

Types of Inquiries. There are several types of inquiries for "in-process" materials: (1) inquiries regarding order slips which have been filed in the public catalog; (2) requests for materials (especially serials) which are in the process of being prepared for binding; (3) requests for University of Massachusetts theses and dissertations which have been received but not yet cataloged by the Library; (4) new serial titles not yet cataloged.

BORF Routine. The Book Order Request Form (BORF) was designed as a means of notifying the library user of the availability of a book which is on order. Upon receiving such an inquiry, the reference librarian should query the computerized Book Order System (BOS) on the department's terminal, and record the status of the order on the Book Order Request Form. If the book has been received, and if the reader has an immediate need for it, the librarian should follow the procedures agreed upon with the Technical Services Division to secure the book and have it processed on a "rush" basis. (Detailed procedures for BORF and BOS are outlined in the "Terminal Operating Information and Operating Instructions" notebook in the Reference Desk 3 center drawer.)

Bindery Materials. The following material may be retrieved for a reader's use:
1. Material which has been prepared for the bindery, but has not been boxed.
2. Material which has been returned from the bindery, but is still in End Processing.
3. Serials which are being held for missing issues. These may be charged out for use in the Library.
4. Duplicate subscriptions (i.e., "bindery copies" of popular magazines). These should be used only when the Periodical Room copy is for some reason unavailable. They must be used in the Serials secion when it is open. See the "In-Process Materials" folder of the Staff Verticle File for details of procedures to be followed when that section is closed.

If the reader requests that binding be delayed, the established procedure agreed upon with the Technical Services Division should be followed. If material is held temporarily at the Reference Desk, care must be taken to assure that it is returned to the proper shelf or area after use.

Theses and Dissertations. Senior honors theses, master's theses, and doctoral dissertations which are in process may be retrieved for a reader's use. See "Notes on Handling and Status of Dissertations and Theses" in the "Theses and Dissertations" folder of the Staff Vertical File for details for procedure.

New Serial Titles. New serial titles, not yet cataloged: These must be used in the Serials section when that section is open. See the "In-Process Materials" folder of the Staff Vertical File for details of procedure to be followed when that section is closed.

Departmental Cooperation. In all of the above situations, nothing should be done which would unnecessarily disrupt the work flow of the Technical Services Division. Material should not be removed from the Division without notifying the proper personnel, or leaving the appropriate records. Procedures to be followed when borrowing books from Acquisitions for reader use in the reading area are outlined in the "In-Process Materials" folder of the Staff Vertical File.

Obtaining In-Process Materials. A reasonable effort should be made to locate in the Technical Services area "in-process" material needed by a reader. If you cannot readily find it, make a record of the request and follow it up the next working day.

Records in Technical Services Area. A reasonable effort should be made to locate records kept in the Technical Services area (such as the shelflist and the central serial record) any information needed to help a reader. If you cannot readily find it, make a record of the request and follow it up the next working day.

Use of Technical Services Area. When using the Technical Services area for locating "in-process" material or for consulting records, be sure to leave all doors locked behind you when leaving. Check the identification of any person whom you do not know who is in the area outside normal working hours.

THE UNIVERSITY OF TEXAS AT AUSTIN
(Austin, Texas)

IN-PROCESS MATERIALS

Staff members contact the appropriate Bibliographic Control section for information about in-process materials. Users are not referred to Bibliographic Control departments. When these areas are closed, questions are deferred until the next working day. Users are contacted as soon as the information is located.

Referrals

CASE WESTERN RESERVE UNIVERSITY
(Cleveland, Ohio)

REFERRALS TO OTHER LIBRARIES AND SERVICES

1. Cleveland Public Library contact:
   a) establish if the book is available at CPL on OCLC:
   b) get information on a topic if we do not have the necessary sources;
   c) fill out the yellow card and place it into the box provided for it;
   d) whenever other patrons are waiting for the service, recommend that the one concerned call the CPL himself. If he is willing to do it, provide him with the telephone number and the yellow card.
2. Whenever material is requested that falls into the category held by Sears, SASS, Music or Health Sciences Library, or, a Public Library, refer the patron to these libraries. However, if it is a specific title they want, it is advisable to call ahead to make sure the item is available.
3. For special services or other libraries, consult the *Information Manual* in the top desk drawer.

UNIVERSITY OF ILLINOIS
AT URBANA-CHAMPAIGN
(Urbana, Illinois)

If the Reference Department does not have the information needed by a patron, or is unable to find it, referrals to librarians, other libraries, or other agencies may be beneficial. It may be necessary to ask the patron to return at a time when a librarian with special subject expertise is available. If it is necessary to refer a patron to other library personnel, make certain the patron knows which library, the contact hours, and the person's name to contact. If a research request is a complex one that will involve other libraries, it may be best to ask the patron to visit other libraries as well. In this case, be sure to give the patron the hours of the library to which he/she is referred. It may be beneficial to call the other library before referral to ensure that the appropriate item is there and appropriate reference personnel are available.

The most common problem library personnel face is knowing *when* to refer a patron to another librarian or other resources. Librarians are not always aware of, or familiar with, additional and/or appropriate information. Therefore, the best advice is, do not be afraid to admit you do not know everything. If possible refer the patron to another librarian immediately if uncertain, or ask another librarian for suggestions later to help improve your competencies in future reference encounters.

Be familiar with other libraries and when to refer to these units or to ILL. Do not make referrals arbitrarily—users should feel you have done everything possible to help them. Before making a referral at night, call the appropriate library to be certain that the source needed is there, or that appropriate professional help is available. If not, fill out a referral form and point out that patron is more apt to find a professional between 8 a.m. and 5 p.m. in most department libraries—or leave a search question for reference librarians to work on the next day.

UNIVERSITY OF MASSACHUSETTS
(Amherst, Massachusetts)

REFERRALS

A. General Statement—A reasonable effort must be made to answer every reference question. When the librarian receiving the question has been unable to answer a question satisfactorily after having consulted the known sources or has reason to believe that the question cannot be answered by sources in the University Library, he or she should refer the reader to another source of information.

B. Referring Questions to Colleagues—The librarian on duty should ask colleagues for advice and/or assistance as necessary, but should not refer readers to the latter without first notifying them of the problem, and telling them what sources have already been checked. Verbal communication is best, but if this is impossible, leave them a short note so that they will be aware of the problem when the reader returns. Reference librarians should keep in mind the specialized knowledge held by colleagues in other departments of the library (such as Cataloging, Bibliography, etc.), and should call on them for help in appropriate circumstances.

C. Referrals to Other Libraries or Services—In general, do not refer a reader to a colleague in another department, another library, or to a service without calling ahead to make sure they can be of assistance. This is a courtesy to both the library user and the person or institution to which he is being referred. It is helpful to the branch librarians if readers referred to them bring along a "Request for Information" form on which the inquiry and list of sources already checked are recorded.

D. Unanswered Questions—Incompletely answered questions, or those for which information does not appear to be available, should be recorded on "Request for Information" forms and discussed with other staff members on duty before consulting with senior members of the department. (The purpose of the "Request for Information" form is outlined in Section on Desk Services: Recording Statistics and Questions). The person who received the question originally is responsible for seeing that the question is handled promptly to completion.

All reference librarians should follow through on these questions whenever possible, since they are a useful stimulus to education in the use of less frequently consulted reference materials.

MCGILL UNIVERSITY
(Montreal, Canada)

Among the Reference Department's responsibilities is that of serving as liaison between readers and other departments and libraries. The Reference Staff must be aware of other departments' and libraries' general service policies, act in accordance with them, and take care never to infringe on areas proper to other departments and libraries. If it is necessary to refer a visitor to another McGill Library, the reference librarian assisting him is responsible to ascertain if he will be welcome.

UNIVERSITY OF TEXAS AT AUSTIN
(Austin, Texas)

REFERRALS

Staff members recognize their own limitations and ask colleagues within the unit for advice and assistance as necessary. They also refer users to others who are better qualified to serve particular needs. Staff members confirm that other units, libraries, or special collections can be of assistance before referring users to them. Referrals to other libraries or agencies off campus are made whenever appropriate. Staff members can always call the Perry-Castaneda Reference Department for assistance, particularly at night and on weekends when librarians are not available in many units.

INTERLIBRARY LOAN

General

BALL STATE UNIVERSITY
(Muncie, Indiana)

GENERAL INFORMATION

Library materials not owned by Ball State Library may be obtained through Interlibrary Loan Service. Interlibray Loan means a loan from one library to another library. Such loan procedures are regulated by a National Interlibrary Loan Code. Most libraries loan materials for use by graduate students and faculty only, however, a cooperative agreement among several Indiana state-owned libraries make borrowing for undergraduates possible, if these libraries own the materials needed.

REQUESTING

Interlibrary loan request forms are on the counter at Interlibrary Loan Service and may be filled out and left at the counter any time that the Bracken Library is open. Giving all the information requested on the form is important for prompt borrowing.

USE OF BORROWED MATERIALS

The lending library sets the loan period and any restrictions on the use of the materials. The average use period is two weeks. The length of time between the requesting and the receiving depends upon where the requested material can be located and upon mail service.

PERIODICAL ARTICLES

Copies of articles from a periodical not owned by Ball State Library System often can be obtained only if the requestor is willing to pay for service and copying charges prescribed by the library where the periodical is located.

PHOTOCOPIED MATERIALS

The copyright law of the United States (Title 17, United States Code) governs the making of photocopies or other reproductions of copyrighted material.

UNIVERSITY OF BRITISH COLUMBIA
(Vancouver, British Columbia)

INTERLIBRARY LOAN SERVICE

Materials not available on this campus may often be borrowed from other libraries through interlibrary loan. While it is recommended that candidates for advanced degrees undertake research in areas where UBC's library collections are strong, the terms of the Interlibrary Loan Code allow us to supplement our own resources by borrowing from other libraries for faculty and students.

Exceptions generally include: books currently in print, reference books, materials in constant use in the lending library, exceptionally rare or fragile items, and works which are difficult or expensive to ship. Periodicals and dissertations are usually not available for loan, but may be purchased in photocopies on microfilm or microfiche.

The following policies are, for the most part, those set out in the International Interlibrary Loan Code. This code was designed to protect large lending libraries from overuse and unreasonable demands by smaller libraries.

Who May Use the Interlibrary Loan Service?

In accordance with the national policy, materials may be borrowed for the use of faculty, graduate students, and authorized research personnel. Undergraduates may use the service for material available in Canada but should be aware that interlibrary loan takes time. For more information, please visit the Interlibrary Loan Office near the Main Library subject catalogue, or phone the staff at x2274.

Applications

Interlibrary loan request forms are available at the Interlibrary Loan Office and at all reference desks in the Main and branch libraries. Your requests should be typed or legibly printed, and should include full bibliographical data as well as a published source of reference. Members of the reference departments will assist you in every way possible with identification of materials needed for research.

Terms of Loan

The loan period and conditions of use are determined by the library from which the material was borrowed. Please pick up and return items personally at the main Interlibrary Loan Office or the appropriate branch library.

CASE WESTERN RESERVE UNIVERSITY
(Cleveland, Ohio)

INTERLIBRARY LOAN

1. Whenever a requested publication is not owned by the CWRU Libraries, advise the patron to request it on Interlibrary Loan provided he/she is a member of CWRU.

Explain:

Faculty, students & staff of the Medical School and the Univ. Hospitals have to contact the Health Sciences or the Allen Memorial Library;

_____ of the Sciences, Technology & Business, the Sears Library;

_____ of the Law School-the Law Library;

_____ of the Library School-the Library School Library.

2. Inform the patron that the ILL Office hours are from 8:30–5:30 p.m. Monday–Friday only. Previous arrangement with the ILL Librarian is requested to get the material on weekends or in the evenings.

3. Whenever a patron appears in the evening or on a weekend with an ILL request form signed by the librarian of his library, make sure that the book is being held at the Circulation Desk. If so:

   • check if the form is duly filled out: requester's name, call number, author, and title, etc.;
   • indicate the date due-4 weeks-in the upper right corner
   • sign in the same space;
   • keep the white and yellow forms, place the pink form into the book;
   • leave the retained forms on the ILL Librarian's or the assistant's desk

4. In the evenings and on weekends the filled-out forms should be checked if properly filled out and placed into an "ILL" folder (Desk I upper drawer). Whenever possible, they should be taken to the ILL Office the same day.

KENT STATE UNIVERSITY
(Kent, Ohio)

INTERLIBRARY LOAN POLICIES AND PROCEDURES

Purpose

The Interlibrary Loan service is intended to provide Kent State

University faculty and graduate students with access to materials not to be found in the Kent State University Libraries. Undergraduate students are restricted from using this service, however, the Interlibrary Loan Librarian may make such exceptions as are deemed necessary. Kent State University Libraries subscribe to the National Interlibrary Loan Code and will encourage Library clients to conduct transactions in accordance with the code.

Method of Use

The Library user must fill out all required forms before the desired item(s) will be ordered by the Interlibrary Loan staff. The staff shall determine the most appropriate library from which to borrow and the most expeditious manner in which to make the request.

Charges

There is no charge for Interlibrary Loan service. However, if the lending library charges for photocopies, that charge will be passed on to the Kent State University Library client. Likewise, although the Interlibrary Loan staff will make a reasonable attempt to borrow from non-charging libraries, all other charges, should they be incurred, will be passed on to the requester.

Interlibrary Loan Overdues

Any Kent State University Interlibrary Loan user who keeps borrowed materials thirty days beyond the due date will be invoiced for the cost of the materials plus a surcharge of $10.00. Further, should such persons repetitively abuse the Interlibrary Loan service, they will lose the privilege of using the service.

The following are, in descending priority order, the types of libraries which the Kent State University Interlibrary Loan will serve:

1. KSU Regional Campus Libraries
2. NEOMAL members
3. IULC members
4. Other Ohio academic and research libraries (e.g., Columbus, Cincinnati; Akron and Youngstown Public Libraries)
5. Ohio special libraries
6. Academic libraries outside Ohio

7. Special libraries outside Ohio
8. Ohio public libraries
9. Public libraries outside Ohio

When the ILL unit cannot accommodate outside requests within four working days, those requests will be answered in the negative, more specifically those requests in categories nine through five above.

Effective beginning Fall Semester, 1979, each graduate student and faculty member may order through ILL, three microfilmed dissertations per twelve month period. The cost will be paid by the library and the dissertations will belong to the library.

Photocopies obtained on ILL for which the library is not invoiced will be provided free to the requester. Those which are invoiced must be paid by the requester at the time of, or prior to, his receipt of the copies.

ELIGIBILITY FOR INTERLIBRARY LOAN SERVICES

General Policy Statements

National Interlibrary Loan Code, 1968
III.1 . . . . Requests for individuals with academic affiliations should be limited to those materials needed for faculty and staff research, and the thesis and dissertation research of graduate students.

OCLC Interlibrary Loan Code
The OCLC Interlibrary Loan Code does not include any stipulation on the eligibility of individuals for interlibrary loan services.

NEOMAL
The NEOMAL draft agreement does not include any restrictions on eligibility.

Classes of Patrons Who Are Eligible for Services

1. Kent State University faculty, including part-time faculty and spouses of faculty members. Spouses are not eligible for financial support for purchase of xeroxed or microfilmed materials. Faculty members at the Regional Campuses should ask their regional campus library for interlibrary loan services.
2. Kent State University graduate students.

3. Kent State University undergraduate students (within the limits of the separate statement "Interlibrary Loan Services to Undergraduate Students"). Only currently enrolled Kent campus students are eligible, regional campus students should ask their regional campus library for interlibrary loan service.
4. Kent State University staff members.

Restrictions on Interlibrary Loan

The following are not usually available for interlibrary loan:
1. Items owed by the Kent State University Libraries.
2. Rare, hard to pack, or fragile material.
3. Reference books.
4. Moderately priced U.S. books in print. (These will be purchased by the K.S.U. Library instead.)
5. Entire issues or volumes of periodicals. Photocopies of articles may be requested. The copies will be mailed to you as soon as they are received.
6. Ph.D. dissertations already reproduced on microfilm. These must be purchased instead. Consult *Dissertation Abstracts* for order number and price. The Interlibrary Loan Service will order these dissertations upon request.
7. Materials for class use.
8. A large percentage of books needed for one thesis, or a large number of books from any one library.

Photocopies and Microforms

Interlibrary loan service is normally provided free of charge. This library will absorb charges for photocopied periodical articles and microformed books, theses, or dissertations, up to $10 per quarter or $30 per year, for each person requesting materials. Items ordered in excess of the financial limits must be paid by the person requesting the item. Xeroxed periodical articles are retained by the requestor. Microfilmed books, theses, and dissertations will be retained in the library collections.

Special Requests

Exceptional circumstances may justify rush requests or other adjustments to meet unusual needs. Please consult the I.L.L. staff in case of special problems, or if any questions arise.

LOUISIANA STATE UNIVERSITY
(Baton Rouge, Louisiana)

INTERLIBRARY LOAN

Definition

Interlibrary Loans are transactions in which library materials are made available by one library to another.

Patron requests

1. It must be determined that the demand for materials requested via Interloan cannot be satisfied by other library holdings and that "indeed the material sought is needed." 8/11/78
2. LSU should "not own the material requested." 5/11/78
3. Patrons must fill out request forms "completely and legibly. Incomplete forms will not be processed by the ILL office." 1/11/78
4. All requests should be verified. "Until an OCLC terminal can be installed at Central Reference, requests to be OCLC verified will have to be held until it is convenient with Technical Services to use a terminal." 8/11/78
5. Librarians should "determine, if possible, the best *three* libraries from which the ILL office should attempt to borrow the material. If all three attempts fail, the request will be returned to the originating librarian for consultation with the patron before going on in an attempt to borrow from other libraries." 8/11/78
6. "Place the request in the box labeled 'Patron Requests' in yellow." A Library Assistant "will pick up these requests daily and deliver to the ILL office." 8/11/78
7. "It should be repeated here that all patron requests must bear the initials of a librarian before they are processed. In doing so, the librarian certifies that the material is not owned by LSU. The librarian further certifies that the information on the request form is accurate, complete, legible, and verified. Requests that do not meet these criteria will be returned to the originating librarian. Requests that are not initialled will be placed on reference desk #2." 11/6/78
8. "OCLC will begin charging 90¢ per request initiated on the ILL Subsystem 1 July 1979. I should like to have the option of ordering any request this way, but cannot do such unless the

patron agrees to pay the fee. Hereafter please ask each patron whether he or she is willing to pay $1.00 extra for this faster service. 6/25/79

Patron Request Problems

Periodically, each librarian will be given "neat little stacks of problem Interloan patron requests." For one reason or another it will be necessary for the librarian to recontact the patron to determine whether the material is still needed. Obviously we don't want to spend an extraordinary amount of time attempting to borrow material for a graduate student who has received his degree and already gone into the world to make his fortune, or for a faculty person who has gone on to his reward or another university.

When you contact a patron, please do not leave the impression that you are questioning his judgement in ordering the material in the first place. Simply explain our problem in locating this material, and several weeks or months having passed, you are calling to inquire whether the material is still needed. You might also explain, in the event that the material is still needed, that given the difficulty already encountered, it might be some time before we can locate it." 8/23/78

Library Requests

Three teams are designated to process all incoming ILL requests. Each team consist of one librarian, one trainee and student assistants.

"Library requests will be assigned to teams. Each team librarian will receive requests in batches that are consecutively numbered, together with a checklist of numbers. Each team is responsible for the following:

1. To determine *beyond doubt* whether LSU owns the material requested, reverifying if in doubt about borrowing library's accuracy.
2. If material is available for lending, place material and requests on book truck labeled "INTERLOAN." Suzanne will deliver the material to the ILL office each morning, and return the booktruck to Central Reference.
3. If the material is not available, requests should be placed on the same truck, together with clear notations as to why it is unavailable. Each checklist should be placed on the truck when all items have been dealt with.

The name of the game is quality control. Accuracy must come before speed—but not much before." 8/11/78

UNIVERSITY OF MASSACHUSETTS
(Amherst, Massachusetts)

INTERLIBRARY LOAN SERVICE

General Statement

Although the Interlibrary Loan Office is not administratively a part of the Reference Department, the two units cooperate closely. Requests for interlibrary loans are accepted at the reference desk, and materials on loan from other institutions are provided to readers by reference desk staff when the Interlibrary Loan Office is closed. In addition, the reference libraries are responsible for assisting with bibliographic verification of interlibrary loan requests as stated in the policy on departmental priorities.

In general, our interlibrary loan policies are governed by the American Library Associations' 1968 *National Interlibrary Loan Code* and by the regulations of lending libraries. By special agreement with Amherst, Hampshire, Mt. Holyoke, and Smith Colleges and Forbes Public Library, we are able to make major exceptions to the *Code* on a local level. Some minor exceptions are made through cooperative programs with other libraries, notably the Boston Consortium Libraries (Boston College, Boston Public, Boston University, Brandeis, M.I.T., Northeastern, State Library, Tufts, and Wellesley); and the NELINET Libraries (Universities of Maine, New Hampshire, Vermont, Connecticut, and Rhode Island). Other exceptions to the *Code* and all exceptions to the policies stated below are made by the Interlibrary Loan Librarian.

Borrowing Policies

A. Full Borrowing Privileges—the following have full borrowing privileges:
- faculty
- staff
- graduate students

B. Undergraduates—may borrow within the 5-College area.
C. Honors theses and Independent Study—Seniors writing honors theses may be granted limited borrowing privileges beyond the 5-College area, as some institutions are willing to lend to undergraduates. Honor students who inquire about interlibrary loan should be referred to the Interlibrary Loan Librarian.
D. Visiting Faculty and Unaffiliated Scholars—Visiting faculty who are attending short-term institutes at the University may borrow within the 5-College area only. Other visiting faculty members should be referred to the Interlibrary Loan Librarian. Scholars or researchers who are not affiliated with the University but who live in Amherst (e.g., authors preparing manuscripts for publications, doctoral candidates writing dissertations for other universities) should be referred to the Interlibrary Loan Librarian.
E. Borrowers Not Eligible—The following are not eligible to borrow materials on interlibrary loan:
  • Dependents and family of members of the University community.
  • Alumni.
  • Non-University readers who have been granted special borrowing privileges by Loan and Reserve Services, except as described in D.

Types of Materials

A. Materials Requested—In addition to materials normally available according to the provisions of the *National Interlibrary Loan Code* or according to the agreements with the 5-College or NELINET libraries, the Interlibrary Loan Office will request:
  • Materials missing from the University Library.
  • Materials in circulation at the University Library, unless the due date is near, which are available in the 5-College area; such material will not be requested beyond the area.
  • Photocopies of pages missing from University Library materials; one copy of such material will be supplied free of charge to the reader.
B. Materials not Requested—In addition to materials not normally available according to the provisions of the *Code*, the Interlibrary Loan Office will *not* request:
  • Materials on Reserve at the University Library (exceptions may be made for researchers who are not enrolled in the course for which the material is on Reserve).

- Microfilm or photocopies to be purchased from University Microfilms.

Form of Request

A. Requests must be submitted on the form provided by the Interlibrary Loan Office and turned in at the reference desk at the main library, or at the Morrill or Physical Sciences Library.
B. The Reference librarian who accepts the request should initial it and make sure that the citation is complete and legible; he or she should also ascertain the patron's deadline, if any, and willingness to pay for photocopies if necessary.
C. A reference librarian or the Interlibrary Loan staff may refuse to accept a request because of insufficient bibliographical information or failure to comply with borrowing restrictions.
D. Graduate students who are beginning thesis research and who expect to make numerous interlibrary loan requests, should be referred to the Interlibrary Loan Library for orientation to standard verification sources.

Use of Interlibrary Loan Materials

Interlibrary Loan materials must be picked up and returned to the main library. Materials which are restricted by the lending library to use in the building are not sent to branches for use there; such restricted materials may not be kept in carrels, but must be returned to the Interlibrary Loan Office or Reference Desk after each use.

Each reader must comply with all regulations and restrictions placed on materials by the lending library. Renewals should be requested only rarely, and readers should be aware that many libraries do not permit renewals. Renewals on materials from the Valley libraries are more easily available.

Items on Interlibrary Loan may be recalled at any time by the lending library.

The user is financially responsible for the replacement or repair of materials lost or damaged during his use of them. Failure to return materials borrowed through Interlibrary Loan and/or failure to pay replacement charges will result in the suspension of the patron's borrowing privileges at the University Library.

Photocopy Charges

The reader must pay any charges for photocopies supplied by lending libraries, unless he has indicated on his request form that he is unwilling to do so. The reader is responsible for payment of such charges even if the material has arrived after his deadline. The reader may set a price limit for photocopy charges, but may not cancel a photoduplication request once it has been sent to another library. Failure to pay photocopy charges will result in collection through the Treasurer's Office and in suspension of the patron's Interlibrary Loan privileges.

Hand-Carried Loans

The Interlibrary Loan Office will not permit hand-carried loans to readers from other libraries, nor will it hold materials while awaiting a formal request from the patron's own library.

If a reader has ALA interlibrary loan forms which have been signed by the Interlibrary Loan Librarian at his own library, the Interlibrary Loan Office will accept the forms and forward the requested materials to the reader's library through the mail.

Night and Weekend Procedures

For details of procedures to be followed by reference desk staff on nights and weekends when the Interlibrary Loan Office is closed, consult the "ILL" folder in the Staff Vertical File.

Lending Policy

For the University Library's policies on loans to other institutions, consult the ILL folder in the Staff Vertical File.

Boston Library Consortium Cards

A. General Statement—Consortium arrangements include issuance of Consortium borrowing cards to faculty and graduate students of member institutions. Applications for BLC cards are made at the home library. At the University of Massachusetts/Amherst, such applications are made at the Reference Desk, and Consortium borrowing cards are issued to eligible persons by the Reference Department.

B. Procedures—Instructions concerning the screening of applicants for Boston Library Consortium cards, completion of application forms, and issuance of the cards are on file in the Reference Staff Verticle File, in the folder labeled "Boston Consortium Libraries."

MIAMI UNIVERSITY
(Oxford, Ohio)

INTERLIBRARY LOANS

Before attempts are made to borrow research materials from other institutions, the reference librarians and the Interlibrary Loan Librarian try to meet the needs of the user from our collection. If books, articles, and other materials which are not owned by Miami are needed, the librarian serving the specific academic department should be consulted for assistance.

UNIVERSITY OF NORTH CAROLINA
(Greensboro, North Carolina)

INTERLIBRARY BORROWING

"The purpose of interlibrary loans is to make available, for research, materials not owned by a given library, in the belief that the furtherance of knowledge is in the general interest....Requests for individuals with academic affiliations should be limited to those materials needed for faculty and staff research, and the thesis and dissertation research of graduate students."

A.L.A. National Interlibrary Loan Code, 1968

I. Interlibrary Loan requests are accepted from UNC-G faculty, faculty spouces, and graduate students for materials needed for research purposes. Occasionally Interlibrary Loan privileges are extended to undergraduates (see Section VII). Requests for Interlibrary Loan are *not* processed for faculty and students of other colleges and universities or for the general public.

II. Materials usually available through Interlibrary Loan include:

A. Books. Many libraries are willing to lend their books which are not otherwise easily available to the requesting library (because they are out of print or prohibitively expensive).

These books usually include monographs in series. A few libraries now charge for book loans; the borrower is notified if his request must be sent to one of these libraries. The request will not be sent unless the borrower is willing to pay the fee.

B. Microforms. These include books, journals, newspapers, and even manuscripts which are on microfilm; sometimes other microforms are lent as well.

C. Dissertations and theses which have *not* been made available on microform. Colleges and universities which cooperate with University Microfilms, Inc., usually do not lend dissertations. University Microfilms order forms and information concerning the policies of universities can be obtained in the Reference Room. Abstracts of dissertations available from University Microfilms can be found in *Dissertation Abstracts International*, which is located in the Reference Room.

III. Materials usually *not* available through Interlibrary Loan include:

A. Journals. Most libraries furnish photocopies of articles in lieu of lending the journal. If the borrower is willing to purchase a copy, he should so indicate on the request form, stating the maximum amount he is willing to pay. This information eliminates the need for added correspondence and speeds up the receipt of materials. The Reference Department can usually furnish the approximate costs of copies from a particular library.

B. United States books in print of moderate cost.

C. Rare materials. (Sometimes these are available in microform.)

D. Basic reference materials.

E. Genealogical, heraldic, and similar materials.

F. Bulky or fragile materials which are difficult to pack.

IV. When requesting materials through Interlibrary Loan, it is necessary to follow the procedure listed below:

A. Before requesting an item through Interlibrary Loan, check the holdings of the Walter Clinton Jackson Library. Material is frequently available in the library and can be identified and located by the use of indexes and catalogs. Ask at the Reference Desk for assistance in properly identifying material. Items owned by Jackson Library will not be requested on loan unless they are missing.

B. Submit requests on Interlibrary Loan request forms, which are available at the Reference Desk. Items requested should be identified and described completely according to standard bibliographic practice. A complete source of reference (where the articles or books were cited) must be provided for each request. Requests are *not* accepted by *telephone*.

C. Await notification by telephone or campus mail of the arrival of the requested material. Often rush requests can be obtained quickly; however, it should be remembered that a period of two to three weeks is needed for items to come through the mail and for large libraries to respond to requests.

D. No item will be released to a borrower until any charges due have been paid;

V. Upon receipt of the requested material, the borrower assumes the following responsibilities:

A. Borrower returns material no later than the date due and should observe all the instructions given on the pink slip on the book.

B. Renewals should be requested only in the most unusual circumstances, at least four days prior to the date due. There is no single policy covering renewals. Check with the library assistant in charge of Interlibrary Loans for each request. (Some materials arrive at UNC-G with the notice "No Renewal." Other materials usually are renewable unless there is another request for them.) No renewals will be requested on or after the book's due date.

VI. Interlibrary Loan practices are governed by conditions set forth in the American Library Association's National Interlibrary Loan Code, 1968. Compliance with the described procedures is necessary and must be required of all borrowers.

VII. Interlibrary Loan privileges are extended *within North Carolina* to students in the Honors Program, seniors involved an independent study, and undergraduates enrolled in 500-level courses who are expected to do graduate level work. All such students wishing to apply for Interlibrary Loan must have a statement from the professor for whom they are doing their work.

VIII. Other cooperative agreements:

    A. Intercampus cards are issued to faculty and graduate students; undergraduate students with other Interlibrary Loan privileges are *not* eligible for intercampus cards. Upon presentation of this card at the circulation desks of the other fifteen constituents of the University of North Carolina and of Duke University, the holder may check out books unavailable at UNC-G which are needed for course work or research.

    B. Faculty and graduate students, upon presentation of the UNC-G I.D., are eligible to check out materials from the main Library, Law Library, and Babcock Library (business), of Wake Forest University. The Library of Bowman Gray School of Medicine does not participate in this agreement.

    C. All UNC-G students and faculty may personally borrow specific titles not owned by Jackson Library from the libraries of Guilford College, Greensboro College, and Bennett College. Students must present a form signed by a UNC-G Reference Librarian and the UNC-G I.D. at the library from which the material is to be borrowed; these forms may be obtained in the Reference Department. Faculty members need only show their I.D.

    D. The Greensboro Public Library honors the UNC-G I.D. in allowing faculty and students to check out materials.

NORTHWESTERN UNIVERSITY
(Evanston, Illinois)

INTERLIBRARY LOAN

Reference books may be sent out on interlibrary loan with the approval of the Head or Assistant Head of the Reference Department. Items will be lent only if it appears that they are not likely to be found in very many other U.S. libraries and if there seems to be no ongoing need for the material by Northwestern faculty and students.

UNIVERSITY OF OKLAHOMA
(Norman, Oklahoma)

INTERLIBRARY LOAN POLICIES

The Interlibrary loan policies of the University of Oklahoma are determined by the *National Interlibrary Loan Code* and the *Oklahoma State Interlibrary Loan Code*. In accordance with these codes, requests to borrow material, or purchase photocopies, must be limited to items which are not owned by the OU Libraries and which cannot be readily obtained at moderate cost.

Research topics should be selected according to the resources on hand and should not require extensive borrowing from other libraries. If a large number of items which are located in another library are needed, you should make arrangements to use them at that library. No more than ten requests per week can be processed for any one individual or group project. If a large number of requests is to be placed, the individual or group placing the requests will be required to perform some of the beginning tasks necessary to send an interlibrary loan request. These steps are usually handled by the Interlibrary Loan staff, but we will be glad to show you how to do them. Please contact the office for such projects. (325-6422).

American books in print cannot usually be borrowed unless available within the state.

Since August 1977 the University of Oklahoma Libraries has been a member of The Center for Research Libraries (CRL), a non-profit organization operated and maintained by the member institutions. Faculty, students, and staff of the University of Oklahoma may request materials from CRL's more than 3 million volume colllection. For further information on the holdings of CRL ask your area librarian or the Interlibrary Loan Office. A CRL catalog, handbook and other literature is available for study in the ILL Office.

INTERLIBRARY LOAN PROCEDURES FOR REQUESTING A LOAN

1. To request desired materials, first determine that the item is NOT owned by OU libraries.
2. Get the proper request form from the Information Desk at Bizzell Library. (Books and theses on green form; periodicals on yellow form; dissertations on white form).
3. Fill it out in detail, giving *full* bibliographical information,

including full name of author, full title, date, page numbers, and place of publication. Requests will not be taken over the telephone.

4. The source of your reference *must* be furnished in detail. (example: Readers' Guide, Vol. 25, p. 333) Your request can be processed much faster if you will also provide verification information from the National Union Catalog, Union List of Serials, New Serials Titles, etc. (Verification is also required for items submitted in large projects.) The more complete your information, the faster your request can be processed.

5. If time is a limiting factor, be certain to specify the latest date you can still use the item. Three to six weeks is a working estimate of the time between the date of your request and the receipt of materials available in out-of-state libraries. When a search is necessary it may be much longer before materials arrive. Items from the OU Medical Center and Oklahoma State University usually take one week.

6. There is usually no charge for borrowing; however, some institutions do charge for lending materials through interlibrary loan.

STATE UNIVERSITY OF NEW YORK
COLLEGE AT POTSDAM
(Potsdam, New York)

INTERLIBRARY LOAN

Interlibrary Loan is a service provided to assist library users in obtaining books or periodical articles needed for research and not available in their own libraries. The NYSILL (New York State Interlibrary Loan) system, of which Crumb Library is a member, provides through State Library and 12 contracting or referral libraries, materials not owned in our regional NCRRR System (North Country Reference and Research Resources Council). We are now also doing ILL via OCLC.

All Interlibrary Loan transactions must conform to established codes and to whatever restrictions are imposed by the library lending the material, and violation of these requirements could result in withdrawal of service from the offending library. It is therefore important for borrowers to understand the limitations of Interlibrary Loan, and to be willing to cooperate.

To realize maximum benefit from Interlibrary Loan, it is necessary that patrons provide *complete* bibliographic information and accurate verification (source of information) for the materials requested. State Library will not accept unverified request. There are several categories ineligible for referrals to the various contracting libraries, such as fiction, juvenile books, textbooks, genealogy, and, unfortunately, books recently published. Most materials, including xerox copies of articles up to 24 pages, are provided without charge. If we need to request materials from libraries outside the NYSILL system, however, there may be charges, subject to approval of the borrower. No charges if borrowed from another SUNY Library.

Despite all of the above, Crumb Library has been successful in getting most of the materials requested. Unfilled requests usually fall into one of three categories: esoteric or ineligible material; not available in the referral library; or insufficient time allowed by patron to secure material.

Request forms are available at the Information Desk at Crumb Memorial Library, and a librarian will be available to help in filling out the request and in answering any questions concerning the services.

UNIVERSITY OF SOUTH CAROLINA
(Columbia, South Carolina)

INTERLIBRARY LOANS

Faculty and graduate students may borrow books or purchase photocopied materials from other libraries through the interlibrary loan service in the Reference Department Office. A leaflet giving more detailed information is available in that office.

THE UNIVERSITY OF TEXAS AT AUSTIN
(Austin, Texas)

INTER-LIBRARY SERVICE

On request, Inter-Library Service borrows, or obtains photocopies of material which is not available on campus. The brochure, *Inter-Library Service*, available for public distribution, gives more information. Questions regarding Inter-Library Service should be referred to the Inter-Library Service Librarian.

Photocopy

UNIVERSITY OF BRITISH COLUMBIA
(Vancouver, British Columbia)

PHOTOCOPY FACILITIES

Currently there are over 20 coin-operated machines in the Main and branch libraries. The Main Library's photocopiers are located inside the stack entries on levels 3, 5, and 6, and in the Fine Arts and Asian Studies Divisions. The following branches also have machines: Sedgewick, Woodward, Law, MacMillan, Social Work, Biomedical Branch, Music, and the Curriculum Laboratory. The cost of photocopies made on most of these machines is five cents per exposure.

In addition to the coin-operated machines, staff are on duty in the Library Copy Service at the rear of the Main Library's entrance hall to do copying for you. They provide this service between 9 a.m. and 5 p.m., Monday to Saturday, at the cost of 10 cents per exposure. Map Division staff operate an oversize copier; 11" × 17" prints are 25 cents, 18" × 24" prints are 50 cents.

The Government Publications and Microforms Division has microprinters which will provide paper copies from microforms at a cost of 25 cents per print (self-service), 30 cents (staff service). This division also has a microfiche duplicator. Duplicate fiche can be made for 15 cents an exposure.

LOUISIANA STATE UNIVERSITY
(Baton Rouge, Louisiana)

PATRONS AND CHARGES

In taking patron requests for material to be copied at other libraries, you should be aware that certain libraries charge more than others for Xerox.

Examples of libraries that charge above average are: Minimums: Princeton, $5.00; Columbia, $5.00; Yale, $8.00; Cornell, $5.00; UCLA, $7.00; Harvard, $8.00; Toronto,$12.00; British Columbia, $8.00; Berkeley, $5.00; NY Historical Society, $5.00; University of Pennsylvania (Law), $3.00; Public Library of Cincinnati and Hamilton County, Cincinnati, Ohio, $5.00 loan and copy minimum to 25 pages; L. C., $5.00; National Ag. Library, under 10 pages, $2.00.

We are receiving more and more notifications from libraries that are starting to charge fees for loaning books to other libraries. Columbia University now charges $10 to loan a book and $5 just to look and see if they have it. For example, the university system of Iowa has announced a $5 charge to loan a book outside the state, as has the Cleveland Public Library.

In addition, systems of loaning like the OCLC Interlibrary Loan Subsystem charge fees that must be passed onto the patron.

Because of these trends I believe that it is absolutely necessary that we caution our patrons about such charges, and extract from them a maximum amount that they are willing to pay for a transaction.

Hereafter, please explain to all ILL patrons that fees for photocopy and borrowed material vary according to lending library and/or method used in borrowing. If the patron does not indicate a maximum acceptable charge, we shall assume that there is no limit.

ILL REPRODUCTIONS

The two following types of requests should be referred directly to the Photoduplications Department for reply, quotations, to be filled, etc.

1. Requests from outside the United States, except Canada, for reproductions of any library materials.
2. Requests for reproduction of LSU theses. Do not send estimates to borrowing libraries. If not on the shelf for loan, transfer directly to Photoduplications.

UNIVERSITY OF OKLAHOMA
(Norman, Oklahoma)

MICROFILM AND PHOTOCOPY

If photocopy or microfilm copies will be acceptable in lieu of a loan, or if you wish photocopy or microfilm only, please indicate the maximum cost acceptable to you. *You are responsible for the cost of photocopy and microfilm* (other than those available from University Microfilms). Whenever possible we will try to obtain free copies, but any costs incurred are the responsibility of the requesting patron. Funds for covering these costs will have to be provided by each person or through his/her department's research fund. Please discuss possible cost for *each* photocopy or microfilm request with the Interlibrary Loan staff; charges vary from library to library. We will be glad to help you with any problems you may have in making your requests.

Interlibrary loan is an agreement between libraries which may be rescinded by any library at any time. The *lending* library sets the rules for loans. If "For Use In Library Only" or other restrictions are specified by the lending library, they must be honored. The loan period is ordinarily for two weeks from the date of receipt. Renewals are to be requested only in unusual cases and must be made through the Interlibrary Loan office *at least five days before the due date.* Oklahoma State University does not allow renewals under any circumstances as they allow a one month loan period. Books requested at one time will probably arrive at one time. Please space your requests so as to be able to use all the material when it arrives. Failure to return borrowed material on time may result in the cancellation of interlibrary loan privileges.

The Interlibrary Loan department hopes we can expand the research materials available to you. Just fill out an interlibrary loan form at the Information Desk.

COPYRIGHT LAW

The Federal Copyright Law 94-553, enacted January 1, 1978, has resulted in a limitation on the number of copies of articles each library may request from relatively recent issues of periodicals—those published within five years prior to the date of the request. In most cases this will not affect our ability to request the material you need; but the Interlibrary Loan department reserves the right to refuse to accept requests which in our opinion would be in violation of copyright law.

BIBLIOGRAPHIC SERVICES

GEORGIA INSTITUTE OF TECHNOLOGY
(Atlanta, Georgia)

LITERATURE SEARCHES AND OTHER REFERENCE SERVICES

A literature search usually consists of a custom tailored list of information sources pertinent to a user's subject. It can be retrospective, current awareness, or a combination of the two. Both manual and computerized searching are available and may be combined, as needed, to cover a topic and the time span of interest.

Literature searches are performed in the two Public Service divisions of the Library, the Bibliographic Services Division and the Users Services Division.

In the Bibliographic Services Division literature search service is offered to Georgia Tech users by the Reference Department and to off-campus users by the Information Exchange Center. Personnel in the other units of the Division, the Special Collections Department and the Architecture Library, conduct literature searches when their expertise is needed. If a literature search request is received directly by either of these two units it should be coordinated, from the beginning, with the Reference Department if the requester is a Georgia Tech user, or with the Information Exchange Center if the requester is an off-campus user. This will insure that standard searching and billing procedures are followed.

In the Reference Department searches are provided for Georgia Tech faculty, research personnel, and students when they are engaged in instruction or research that is funded by the Institute.

A search is initiated by completing a request form available in the Reference department. After a librarian has reviewed the request and prepared a preliminary search strategy, a personal interview with the user is then requested to clarify concepts and finalize details. This consultation is imperative for a successful search.

Manual searching, while occasionally undertaken free of charge for faculty and research personnel, requires a substantial professional staff time investment. Manual searching is not available for students, nor can it be substituted for computer searching for faculty and research personnel. When offered at all, it will be at the discretion of the head of the Reference Department. The user should be aware that this type of searching takes considerably longer than computer searching. In lieu of manual searching, reference librarians will suggest appropriate sources and provide instruction on how it is done.

UNIVERSITY OF ILLINOIS
AT URBANA-CHAMPAIGN
(Urbana, Illinois)

We do not do bibliographies for library users—faculty or student— we will assist in direction and guidance to appropriate sources on topics. Published bibliographies should be noted if available.

UNIVERSITY OF MASSACHUSETTS
(Amherst, Massachusetts)

BIBLIOGRAPHIC SERVICES

Reference Initiated

When time and resources are available, the head of the Reference Department may authorize the preparation of bibliographies by staff members when the results of such bibliographic endeavors would contribute significantly to the work of the department.

User Requests

A. Preparation of Bibliographies—Due to the heavy demand of desk and ancillary duties, staff members are unable to undertake the preparation of bibliographies on behalf of individual faculty members or students.

Bibliographies may be prepared for University administrators and staff in the performance of their official duties. The provision of this service is at the discretion of the head of the department.

B. Checking Bibliographies—Library users requesting that bibliographies and extensive reading lists be checked against the library's holdings should be referred to the Bibliography Division for assistance.

Staff members whose duties regularly include book selection in conjunction with the Bibliography Division will handle requests for the checking of book lists within the guidelines provided by the Bibliography Division.

Current Awareness

At present, there are insufficient time and resources available for the preparation and dissemination of a "current awaeness" bibliographic service to the University community; however, library users will be given assistance and suggestions regarding other "current awareness" services which are available.

Computer Literature Searches

The Computer Search Service within the Reference Department does computerized literature searches in over sixty data bases in the social, physical, and biological sciences and in business and the humanities. Questions concerning the Service should be directed to the computer searches. A list of librarians trained in computer literature searching arranged by subject fields is located in the Staff Vertical File under "Computer Search Service." This is useful in making referrals when inquiries are received at the Reference desk. A detailed Policy Statement, located at the Computer Search Service desk in the Reference Office and in the Staff Vertical File under "Computer Search Service," outlines the responsibilities of the computer searchers, the Coordinator of the Service, and the Associate Director for Public Services.

MCGILL UNIVERSITY
(Montreal, Canada)

Bibliographies should not be undertaken without the permission of the Head of the Department or her assistant.

UNIVERSITY OF NORTH CAROLINA
(Greensboro, North Carolina)

—to provide bibliographic aides such as briefly annotated subject guides and assistance in identifying, locating, and using information resources including those not available in the University libraries.

THE UNIVERSITY OF TEXAS AT AUSTIN
(Austin, Texas)

BIBLIOGRAPHIC SERVICES

The compilation of bibliographies by staff members is encouraged; however, precedence is given to direct service to users. The *Guidelines for Typed Bibliographies* (Policies and Guidelines No. 9) is followed when preparing any bibliography. Guidelines for the preparation of specific bibliographic series are available in each unit.

General Bibliographies

Bibliographies which meet the needs of users are prepared for public distribution. Approval for the preparation of a bibliography is given by the librarian in charge of the unit and/or the librarian to whom the staff member reports.

Selected Reference Sources

Subject-oriented annotated lists of reference sources are issued as part of the *Selected Reference Sources* series and are available for public distribution. Librarians wishing to prepare bibliographies for this series should contact the Assistant Director for Public Services, the editor of the series, to discuss scope, anticipated use, distribution, etc. Bibliographies to be issued in the series are sent to the Assistant Director for Public Services for publication.

Selected New Reference Books

This monthly publication informs staff members about new reference books. The unit head assigns the responsibility for selecting the books and preparing the annotations. Contributions are due in the office of the Assistant Director for Public Services by the 25th of each month.

Bibliographies for Individuals and University of Texas Administrators and Staff

Although staff members do not prepare bibliographies for individuals, they do assist users in compiling their bibliographies. Exceptions may be made to prepare bibliographies needed by University of Texas administrators and staff in the performance of their official duties.

Recent Acquisitions

Recent acquisitions are called to the attention of users by a display of book jackets, by a lists of current acquisitions, with a shelf of recently received books, or by other appropriate means. At the discretion of the staff, individuals are informed about specific titles when available for use.

CORRESPONDENCE

UNIVERSITY OF MASSACHUSETTS
(Amherst, Massachusetts)

REFERENCE CORRESPONDENCE

Incoming Inquiries

A. Who Drafts Replies—Incoming inquiries to the Reference Department are referred by the head of the Department to an appropriately qualified librarian for reply. The departmental secretary keeps a record of these referrals which is cancelled when the reply is typed.

B. Signature—A letter replying to a reference question is signed by the individual librarian answering the inquiry. Official letters, i.e., correspondence having to do with the policies and procedures of the Department, are signed by the head of the Department.

C. Copies—Letters are typed in duplicate so that one copy may be retained in the departmental correspondence file.

D. Policy for Handling Requests—Not all inquiries asking for general information ought to be answered by the Reference Department. In general, our policy is not to provide information for the general public that can be obtained from local libraries unless the questions can be answered quickly and briefly. Nor will we complete homework assignments for students. However, replies to inquiries we do not answer should suggest a more appropriate local source of information.

The Reference Department will attempt to answer letter as fully as possible when they come from inquirers who are considered primary library users; i.e., members of the University community, particularly the staff, alumni, trustees, state government officials, librarians and faculty from the Massachusetts state colleges, and people from the local area.

The Reference Department will answer inquiries concerning subject on which the Library has unique or unusual resources, as well an inquiries concerning the Commonwealth of Massachusetts, whenever we are able to supply the information requested.

E. Promptness in Answering—Replies should be mailed back to inquirers no later than one week after receipt. When suitable, we should invite the inquirer to come here to use the Library in person, in the event that we have neither staff nor time to answer his inquiry fully.

F. Requests for Holdings Information—Specific, easily answered requests to check library records and report holdings (e.g., what title does the Library own relating to a particular, narrowly defined subject) will be referred to a reference librarian for reply. However, questions concerning holdings in broad categories should be directed to the Chief Bibliographer.

G. Information about the University—Except for inquiries that should go to a known office (e.g., requests for catalogs to Admissions), letters requesting information about the University will be forwarded to the Archives for direct reply or referral to the appropriate office.

H. Surveys—Letters requesting information about the Library will be referred to the appropriate unit head for reply. A copy of any completed questionnaire relating to the Reference Department will be sent to the Associate Director for Public Services for his information.

I. Supplying Photocopies—The Library will not normally supply more than 10 free pages of photocopied material as part of a reply to a reference inquiry by letter. If more copying is necessary, bibliographical information concerning the source should be supplied to the inquirer, with the suggestion that he request the material through interlibrary loan, or come to the Library to use the material here.

Outgoing Inquiries

A. Letters of Introduction

- Purpose—Letters of introduction are written upon request for students, faculty, and staff under the following circumstances: (1) when the resources of this Library have been exhausted and Interlibrary Loan is not feasible as an alternative means of obtaining needed material; (2) when the requestor will be residing temporarily outside the 5-College area and is able to express a reasonable need to visit another library while on leave. It should be emphasized to all persons requesting letters of introduction that these letters do not guarantee admission to another library; they are merely requests on our part, and the reader can be refused admission to the other library. For this reason, readers who request letters of introduction should always be informed of their interlibrary loan and Boston Consortium Library privileges and encouraged to take advantage of these services whenever appropriate.
- Format of Letter—For readers visiting libraries beyond the 5-College area, an individually typed letter is necessary. Letters should indicate what subject the reader will be investigating and the fact that the materials in this area have already been used and more information is needed.
- Policies of Other Libraries—Leaflets describing use of certain libraries by visiting readers (e.g., Harvard, Yale) are filed in the staff vertical file. Consult these for information on policies affecting visitors, such as restricted stack access.
- Application Form—Readers requesting letters of introduction should be given an Application for a Letter of Introduction. The Librarian accepting the application should initial it and give it to the Departmental secretary for typing.

B. Requests for Information—The Reference Department will write letters to other organizations for readers to obtain information not available here. This is a service that should be provided sparingly when it is felt that the information can be more easily obtained by the Reference Department than by an individual correspondent. In most cases, the individual library user should be informed of the address and/or telephone number of the source which might have the information and be encouraged to secure the data himself.

MCGILL UNIVERSITY
(Montreal, Canada)

POLICY FOR REFERENCE QUERIES RECEIVED BY MAIL

The Reference Department receives a number of queries by mail from persons not directly connected with McGill University. These enquiries arrive from individuals ranging from grade school children to university professors and bibliographers and come from countries throughout the world.

Letters are stamped and dated received by the Department secretary. She passes them to the Department head who logs them in and assigns them to staff who answer them in accordance to the criteria listed below. Draft answers are returned to the department head who O.K.'s and signs all letters. Letters are typed and sent out by the secretary who also maintains a file of answered letters by name of requestor.

1. The Reference staff do not undertake genealogical queries. Genealogical requests if they refer to Canadian families are referred to the staff of the Gagnon Room in the Montreal Civic Library.
2. Questions relating to McGill University or to persons connected with the University or to publications issued by or about this University are answered as fully as required.
3. Questions relating to Rare Books and Special Collections, the University Archives or Special Libraries of this University, e.g., Blacker, are referred directly to the appropriate library or department for response.
4. Questions relating to specific materials held by McGill (e.g., a query by a bibliographer concerning the editions held of a certain author's works) are always fully answered.

5. Questions not covered by the above categories but of a nature for which the McLennan's collections are a logical source, and for which less than one hour's work is necessary, are answered.

6. Questions which would take more than an hour to answer are returned with a statement that we do not have sufficient staff to undertake them. Where possible information is provided to the enquirer giving him the name of the most appropriate library in his region to which he should refer his question.

7. When suitable and consistent with this Library's policies we would invite the enquirer to come and use our Library in person.

8. We will provide up to 10 exposures of xeroxing free of charge as part of a reply to a reference query by letter. If more copying is necessary we request payment in advance and only send the material after receiving the money.

THE UNIVERSITY OF TEXAS AT AUSTIN
(Austin, Texas)

CORRESPONDENCE REFERENCE SERVICE

Correspondence is an integral part of reference and information services and every effort is made to answer written requests for information within a week of receipt.

Routing Incoming Correspondence

1. All units of the General Libraries route letters to the appropriate library unit for reply.

2. The unit head is responsible for correspondence reference service. The responsibility for answering letters may be delegated. The unit head answers all letters concerning unit policy and approves all outgoing replies prepared by other staff members.

3. Referral form letters are used when sending an inquiry to another unit on campus for the information requested. One copy of the form letter is sent to the inquirer; one copy of the form letter and the original letter requesting information are sent to the unit receiving the referral and one copy of the form letter is retained as a record of the referral.

Types of Questions Answered

1. Letters requesting information about University of Texas at Austin theses and dissertations are answered in detail. If an answer requires a list of more than twelve thesis/dissertation titles, the reply suggests that a request be sent to Inter-Library Service. This unit is responsible for photocopying the catalog cards.
2. Letters requesting information about publications written by UT Austin faculty or staff members, sponsored by UT Austin departments or institutes, or published by campus bureaus are answered as completely as possible.
3. Letters requesting broad subject information require only a brief indication of sources with an invitation to visit the General Libraries for personal assistance or with a referral to a library near the correspondent.
4. The Perry-Castaneda Library uses form letters to answer requests for genealogical searches or extension Loan Library information packets.

Photocopying

A maximum of eight pages is photoduplicated from hard copy without charge when answering a letter. If photocopying exceeds eight pages, the citations and a copy of the Photoduplication Price List are sent to the inquirer. The inquirer is instructed to send the request for photoduplication to Inter-Library Service.

Record of Correspondence

A record is maintained of letters received and the name of the individual who is responsible for answering the letter. A copy of the reply is retained in the unit.

ORIENTATION AND INSTRUCTION

ARIZONA STATE UNIVERSITY
(Tempe, Arizona)

Goal: To Provide Appropriate Library Instruction to Library Users:

Definition. Instruction ranges from tours of the Library to a library use course and specialized instruction in resources for graduate students.

Implementation of this Goal:

Subject specialists should offer orientations to students in their fields of interest. They should also prepare *Know Your Library* guides or other appropriate bibliographies designed to inform users of the resources of the Library. One reference librarian, designated as the orientation librarian, provides instruction to undergraduates (with the assistance of the subject specialists), manages the freshman library project, and coordinates staff effort in teaching the library use course.

UNIVERSITY OF BRITISH COLUMBIA
(Vancouver, British Columbia)

ORIENTATION AND LIBRARY INSTRUCTION

New faculty members in need of library orientation are invited to contact the reference division or branch library responsible for their subject areas. The staff in the Information and Orientation Division can provide general orientation to the Main Library building and instruction in the intricacies of the Main catalogues.

Students at all levels are offered a variety of opportunities to learn about the UBC libraries. Faculty members can assist their students by making them aware of these programs and by taking advantage of the subject-related instruction offered by most campus libraries.

1. *Orientation Tours,* including basic information on the whole Library system, are offered in the Main Library and in Sedgewick Library at the beginning of each session.
2. *Instruction for First Year Students* is given in cooperation with English 100 instructors, who are invited to bring students to the Library for one class period during the winter session. The classes consist of an introduction to the resources and service of the Library and instruction in basic research techniques.
3. *Term Paper Clinics* are held in Sedgewick Library in both fall and spring terms. During the clinics, students from the School of Librarianship under the supervision of the Sedgewick librarians work with individual students on research procedures related to specific assignments. For more information, contact any of the Sedgewick reference librarians.
4. *Course Related Instruction* covers more specialized materials and bibliographic procedures. Librarians are available to advise and lecture to classes. For more information, contact the approriate reference division or branch library.
5. *Self-Help Aids and Publications* allow students to learn about the campus libraries at their own speed. In each library, instructional signs are displayed, particularly in the catalogue area, and a variety of publications explaining resources, services, and physical layout can be picked up.

If you have any questions about library instruction, or if you wish to arrange a class tour not described above, please call the Information and Orientation Division.

COLORADO STATE UNIVERSITY
(Fort Collins, Colorado)

LIBRARY INSTRUCTION

Instruction in the use of the libraries on the undergraduate level is the responsibility of the Reference Department; on the graduate and faculty level, of the subject librarians. However, because the total instructional program calls for cooperation and occasional sharing of these responsibilities between reference staff and subject librarians, an Assistant Reference Librarian assumes responsibility for coordinating the instruction and orientation programs.

GEORGIA INSTITUTE OF TECHNOLOGY
(Atlanta, Georgia)

DEPARTMENT OF LIBRARY INSTRUCTION

Within the Users Service Division searches are performed by instructors in the Department of Library Instruction. As a part of the Library's teaching program instructors conduct classroom demonstrations of online searching for ICS 2250 and ICS 4250. Both manual and computer search techniques are used to illustrate to students how information and bibliographic resources relate to their academic work and their subject fields of specialization.

Literature searching may also be used in other instructional activities with special interest groups requesting this kind of service. This searching will normally be provided by staff in the Department of Library Instruction but on occasion personnel from the Bibliographic Services Division may be asked to participate. If a request from a special interest group is received by Bibliographic Services personnel it should be cleared by the unit department head with the Associate Director for Public Services. Every effort is made by the Library to respond to this kind of informational need not only from the point of view of good public relations but also as a professional contribution in this area of librarianship. Fees for these services are charged as required.

UNIVERSITY OF ILLINOIS
AT URBANA-CHAMPAIGN
(Urbana, Illinois)

SPECIAL SERVICES—TOURS AND INSTRUCTION

The Reference Department librarians conduct orientation tours and instructional sessions for faculty and students in subject related or research methodologies courses, students in English Language for foreign students, and any other areas requested. Individuals may receive the same type of assistance through making an individual appointment. Schedules may be arranged by contacting the head of the Department or individual reference librarians by a call or personal visit in advance of the orientation or instruction needed.

LOUISIANA STATE UNIVERSITY
(Baton Rouge, Louisiana)

TOURS

1. Scheduling and arranging for tours will be assigned to a librarian with assistance from the library assistant at the Information Desk. Other staff who are contacted directly for tours should be sure there is no conflict with tours scheduled by this librarian and should give this librarian information concerning tours scheduled. She will also assign staff with needed expertise to conduct tours.
2. The responsibility for conducting tours of the Middleton Room is that of our department. All personnel in Central Reference and the Information Desk should have sufficient familiarity with that room to enable them to conduct tours.

UNIVERSITY OF MASSACHUSETTS
(Amherst, Massachusetts)

ORIENTATION—ORIENTATION ACTIVITIES INCLUDE

1. *Guided tours* of the building for freshmen, transfer, and foreign students, interested members of the university community, and visitors to the university campus.
2. *Preparation of publications* describing the layout of the library buildings and the service points within them (such as the Library Brochure, the Library Handbook, the Self-Guided Walking Tour).
3. *Preparation of Non-print media* which may complement or offer an alternative to tours and publications.

> *Instruction*—Instruction in the use of library records, bibliographic tools, and other sources in the reference collection should be a routine part of reference service. Encourage the reader to follow your steps as you seek out the information or sources, but never force instruction on a reader who asks a simple question which can be answered by reference to one or two sources.
>
> Reference librarians should be alert to the kinds of questions that indicate a need for instruction in techniques of library research; in general these questions will fall into three main categories—occasions when an inquirer is looking for material for a paper, speech, or other project, is investigating a topic exhaustively, or seems unfamiliar with the use of a particular reference tool and indicates an interest in learning how to use it effectively.
>
> Reference librarians should also be alert to questions indicative of class assignments where formal library instruction for the entire class might be more fruitful than answering individual questions at the reference desk. If possible, attempt to determine the nature of the assignment, the due date, and the name of the instructor. This information should be referred to the reference librarian in charge of instruction, who will judge whether the instructor should be contacted.

ORIENTATION AND INSTRUCTION

General Statement

An Instructional Services Librarian in the Reference Department is responsible for planning and developing programs of orientation and instruction in the use of library resources, and for coordinating library instruction offered within the University Library system.

Within the constraints of availability of staff, library instruction receives high priority in the activities of the Department, second only to service to the individual reader at the Reference Desk.

Responsibilities of Reference Librarians

The Instructional Services Librarian may call upon reference librarians (and, in appropriate circumstances and with the permission of the relevant supervisor, upon other members of the library staff) for assistance in orientation and instruction activities.

Instruction—Instructional activities include:
- Course-related sessions for undergraduate or graduate classes.
- Assignment-related sessions for students in such programs as Rhetoric, Nursing, and Business.
- Subject- or discipline-oriented workshops or mini-courses.
- Preparation of publications related to the above activities, such as the library information series, guide to HRAF Microfiles, Information Sources in Exercise Science, etc.
- Preparation of nonprint media which support instructional activities.

Policy and Procedures

A. Orientation—Reference librarians should be sufficiently familiar with the route of the standard tour of the building to be able to conduct a group through it expeditiously. Although building tours are offered at regularly scheduled times (e.g., several times daily the first week of the semester, during freshman orientation in summer and winter, weekly through the rest of the year) and inquirers should be so informed, requests for individual tours at other times should be honored, either by appointment with the librarian receiving the inquiry or by referral to the Instructional Services Librarian.

Requests for group visits should be referred to the Instructional Services Librarian, who maintains a master calendar for scheduling purposes and will honor such requests at his/her discretion.

Suggestions for improvement of printed directional information should be routed to the Instructional Services Librarian.

B. Instruction—Faculty-initiated requests for library instruction for their classes should ordinarily be routed to the Instructional Services Librarian.

Joint programs may be planned with librarians in other departments who have special subject responsibilities, to be held in whatever location is most convenient; these sessions are often most useful in multi-disciplinary programs.

Preliminary information (name, phone number, and department of the requestor, class size, preferred time and date) may be recorded on the *Request for Class Instruction* forms, kept at the Reference Desks. After completion of the class, a brief summary of the major elements in the presentation should be recorded on the form.

Requests from faculty members who are associated with the specialties of librarians in rhetoric, business, government documents, education, and health sciences should be referred directly to those librarians. Requests from faculty members in the sciences should be referred to the appropriate branch librarians. The librarians concerned will then notify the Instructional Services Librarian of the arrangements which are made and consult with him/her about the presentation.

Assisting Users at the Card Catalog

A. Responsibility—One of the chief responsibilities of the Reference Department is instruction in the use of the public card catalog. Since an understanding of the catalog is a key to self-sufficiency in library use, the librarian should always accompany to the catalog, the reader who may have a question concerning it.

B. Kinds of Problems—Readers are sometimes unable to find specific entries in the catalog because:

- their information is incomplete or
- they don't understand the Library's filing system
- they have confused the author-title and subject catalogs
- they may not have used the correct subject heading (the librarian may take this opportunity to introduce the Library of Congress *Guide to Subject Headings* and other ways of identifying subject entries.)
- the cards for which they are searching have been misfiled (a search under title as well as under author is wise)
- the Library does not own the book
- the item wanted is owned by the Library, but is not represented in the catalog (e.g., some microforms, documents, maps)

C. Retrace Steps and Verify—Because of these problems, the librarian should retrace at the catalog, the steps taken by the reader who reports that the library does not own a particular item, and if sufficient information is presented, should always verify the item before informing a reader that the Library does not own it.

If time does not allow for verification and the reader is interested in further information, a "Request for Information" form may be completed.

D. Offering Assistance—If readers appear to be having difficulty at the catalog, ask them if they need help. Each librarian should use his own judgement in identifying such a situation. Since the Library does not have a separate catalog information desk, floor walking should always include the public catalog area.

UNIVERSITY OF NORTH CAROLINA
(Greensboro, North Carolina)

INSTRUCTIONAL SERVICES

A. Orientation lectures are given for various groups—freshmen, transfer students, graduate students, and new faculty members. These lectures are primarily to acquaint the audience with the kinds of materials available in the library, including special collections—ERIC, Documents, etc., and with the location and arrangements of materials available in this particular library.

B. Since English 101 is the only required course at UNC-G, all sections of that course attend a library lecture as one of the class sessions. The lectures acquaint the freshmen with the facilities and procedures of the Library and introduce to them some basic reference materials necessary for doing research in English and other subjects.

C. Upon request, any classes—undergraduate or graduate—will be given specialized instructions in the library or the classroom during their specialized instructions in the library or the classroom during their regular meeting time; however, the Staff is especially interested in assisting classes of bibliography and methodology or design and philosophy of research. Individual staff members have compiled various types of lists for several courses.

LIBRARY TOURS

Scope

Jackson Library will give guided library tours of the type and to the groups listed below.
1. General orientation tours for all persons at UNC-G.
2. Subject lecture/tours for classes at UNC-G.
3. Local high school groups, with an assignment, that have exhausted the resources of the public library.
4. High school seniors from other states.
5. Senior high school groups that are affiliated with a library, e.g., media center helpers, library clubs.

Any groups that do not meet the above criteria will be encouraged to take the self-guided cassette tour which is available at the circulation desk.

Procedure

1. Requests for library tours will be referred to the librarian designated as Coordinator of Library Tours. If she/he is not avail-

able, the request will be referred to another librarian. If neither is available, the Library Assistant/Library Technical Assistant will take a message and the Coordinator will contact the requestor.

2. The Coordinator/Library Technical Assistant will determine the need for the tour, the level of the students, i.e. undergraduate, graduate, etc. She/he will obtain the preferred date for the tour and at least two alternate dates. She/he will inform the requestor that a librarian will call back within two working days, Monday through Friday, and confirm the date.

3. The Coordinator will discuss with a "subject specialist" the most "convenient" date for the tour. After a decision is made, the tour will be recorded on the calendar. The librarian who will give the tour will telephone the requestor and confirm the date, discuss subject coverage, level of students, etc.

Policy

1. Tours for undergraduate students will be scheduled only if the professor will be present or if attendance is mandatory. The librarian can not be responsible for taking attendance.

2. Only three tours will be scheduled per day. No tours will be scheduled on Friday except when that is the only day on which the class is scheduled.

3. Only one tour will be scheduled for each time period.

4. A notice of two weeks will be required for all tours.

5. When practicable, the number of night tours will be limited to two per week. No librarian will be asked to give more than one night tour per week.

6. All absences from work, e.g., vacations, appointments, meetings, compensatory time off, during the first six weeks of each semester will be cleared with the Tour Coordinator and the calendar.

THE UNIVERSITY OF TEXAS AT AUSTIN
(Austin, Texas)

USER EDUCATION SERVICE

The detailed user education program is described in *A Comprehen-*

sive Program of User Education for the General Libraries, The University of Texas at Austin, December 1976. The need for assistance to individuals or to classes in these areas should be referred to the librarian in charge of the unit.

INFORMAL INSTRUCTION

In general, users receive instruction in the use of library resources when they are searching a topic or when they express an interest in learning.

AIDS AND GUIDES TO LIBRARY RESOURCES

Publications such as the *Library Directory* (a campus map with library hours), the *Handbook for Faculty and Graduate Students*, unit brochures, self-guided or walking tours, and bookmarks are available to assist users in locating resources in the General Libraries. Brochures on special resources, such as HRAF, are available.

UNIVERSITY OF TOLEDO
(Toledo, Ohio)

BIBLIOGRAPHIC INSTRUCTION PROGRAM: GOALS

Because the collection, evaluation, and synthesis of information are essential to the learning experience in every discipline, a student cannot operate effectively without a knowledge of the processes underlying identification and use of appropriate information sources. Hence bibliographic instruction ought to be a component of the educational process in all subject areas and at all levels. The library, because of its resources and personnel, is the logical body to develop and coordinate programs which improve bibliographic skill.

Within this context, our goals are to:

1. provide instruction for students in the skills necessary to find, analyze, evaluate, and synthesize information, thereby promoting user confidence and independence;

2. deliver instruction through a variety of means, including signage, printed guides, reference services, group presentations, and course-integrated instruction;
3. coordinate bibliographic instruction to students, combining instruction in basic skills early in a student's career with reinforcement and more sophisticated training at advanced levels;
4. promote faculty participation in bibliographic instruction programs;
6. devise methods for evaluating overall program quality as well as particular activities;
7. assure professional growth of faculty members involved with bibliographic instruction.

ETHICS OF REFERENCE SERVICE

UNIVERSITY OF MASSACHUSETTS
(Amherst, Massachussetts)

ETHICS OF REFERENCE SERVICE

The needs of library users must always be taken seriously and treated with utmost respect. Under no circumstances should there be any discussion of an individual or a group of users, or of any transactions between user and reference librarian, outside of a professional context.

THE UNIVERSITY OF TEXAS AT AUSTIN
(Austin, Texas)

ETHICS OF REFERENCE AND INFORMATION SERVICES

The needs of library users are taken seriously and treated with respect. Under no circumstances is there any discussion outside of a professional context about an individual or a group of users or about any transaction between user and staff member. The "Statement on Professional Ethics, 1975" issued by the American Library Association is a standard to be followed.

STATEMENT ON PROFESSIONAL ETHICS, 1975[3]

INTRODUCTION

The American Library Association has a special concern for the free flow of information and ideas. Its views have been set forth in such policy statements as the *Library Bill of Rights* and the *Freedom to Read Statement* where it has said clearly that in addition to the generally accepted legal and ethical principles and the respect for intellectual freedom which should guide the action of every citizen, membership in the library profession carries with it special obligations and responsibilities.

Every citizen has the right as an individual to take part in public debate or to engage in social and political activity. The only restrictions on these activities are those imposed by specific and well-publicized laws and regulations which are generally applicable. However, since personal views and activities may be interpreted as representative of the institution in which a librarian is employed, proper precaution should be taken to distinguish between private actions and those one is authorized to take in the name of the institution.

The statement which follows sets forth certain ethical norms which, while not exclusive to, are basic to librarianship. It will be augmented by explanatory interpretations and additional statements as they may be needed.

THE STATEMENT

A Librarian

Has a special responsibility to maintain the principles of the *Library Bill of Rights*.

Should learn and faithfully execute the policies of the institution of which one is a part and should endeavor to change those which conflict with the spirit of the *Library Bill of Rights*.

Must protect the essential confidential relationship which exists between a library user and the library.

---

3. *American Libraries*, April 1975, p. 231.

Must avoid any possibility of personal financial gain at the expense of the employing institution.

Has an obligation to insure equality of opportunity and fair judgment of competence in actions dealing with staff appointments, retentions, and promotions.

Has an obligation when making appraisals of the qualifications of any individual to report the facts clearly, accurately, and without prejudice, according to generally accepted guidelines concerning the disclosing of personal information.

Reference Policies and Procedures for Public Libraries

INTRODUCTION

Purpose of the Policy Statement

ANN ARBOR PUBLIC LIBRARY
(Ann Arbor, Michigan)

PURPOSES OF THIS POLICY STATEMENT

1. To describe the services and resources which are offered by the Department; the extent to which they are provided; any priorities or limitations; and to whom and by whom such services are offered.
2. To serve as a basis for consistent action on the part of the staff.

BIRMINGHAM PUBLIC LIBRARY
(Birmingham, Alabama)

The Reference Service Policy is designed to guide reference service throughout the library system. The Reference Policy is the basis for setting procedures, and will furnish guidelines when questions arise concerning the kind of reference services the Library provides. Another purpose of this policy is to set standards for service and ensure continuity in the reference service provided by the Library, despite changes in staff.

The Reference Service Policy will be revised every two years by a Reference Service Policy Committee, appointed by the Associate Director of the Central Library.

DUNEDIN PUBLIC LIBRARY
(Dunedin, Florida)

The purpose of the policy manual is twofold. It serves as a guide to those who serve at the information desk and to those who are being trained. It sets standards and guidelines for services reflecting a suggested level of performance. It details for the patron, to whom it is available, which services and resources are offered, the extent to which they are provided, the limitations on their provisions and to whom and by whom such services are provided.

INGLEWOOD PUBLIC LIBRARY
(Inglewood, California)

It has long been recognized that a comprehensive manual on reference service would be beneficial in training new librarians as well as familiarizing all staff with the functions of our reference service and the duties of the reference service staff. However, it was not until a move to a new library imposed new demands on the reference service that the need for a manual became imperative.

Thus, it is hoped the following information will clarify for all staff the function and scope of our reference service as well as define the duties of all reference service personnel. Additionally, it will aid administrators and city officials in understanding the function of reference service and enable other library administrators to make comparative evaluations of their own operations. A manual of this nature may also provide useful information for case studies in library school courses.

THE NEW YORK PUBLIC LIBRARY, THE RESEARCH LIBRARIES
(New York, New York)

The following standards are set forth to guide research librarians in their work with the public. Good service, however, depends on a high quality of performance of the entire staff at all levels and in all types of work.

THE FREE LIBRARY OF PHILADELPHIA
(Philadelphia, Pennsylvania)

A library is judged, among other things, on the speed, the skill, and the manner with which it assists readers and gives them the information they require. The following statement is an effort to encourage the sort of professional action that will produce a favorable public judgment. It confronts the realities and the potential for reference work in a large urban system and is intended to give purpose and direction to future service.

PROVIDENCE PUBLIC LIBRARY
(Providence, Rhode Island)

The Service Code of the Providence Public Library is designed to provide the library staff with a philosophic framework of library service to the public—those general service principles upon which all library activities are based.

Our library's objectives are expanded upon in greater detail in the "Materials Selection Policy." This Service Code is an attempt to pull together methods of achieving the library's objectives through patterns of service which utilize the abilities of each staff member to the fullest.

Implicit in this document is a belief in the capability of all staff members to make judgments in their own areas of competence and to translate the ideals set forth here into workable procedures that fit concrete situations. However, specific guidelines have been suggested for certain areas where experience has shown a need for more precise direction and where certain policies or procedures have proved to be the most realistic means for providing efficient and consistent library service.

Nature of Reference Service

THE BERKELEY PUBLIC LIBRARY
(Berkeley, California)

Reference Service in a city with the varied composition of Berkeley is challenging, stimulating, and demanding. Above all, it requires flexibility to meet the changing needs of the wide spectrum of this community.

The Berkeley Public Library regards as valid every reference question asked by any patron. All questions will be given equal consideration, and each will be answered as accurately and completely as possible within a reasonable time limit. Full library service will be available to all patrons, and no questions asked by a patron will be considered unanswerable. Our primary objective is to give as much assistance as is practicable, drawing on the expertise of others and using the resources of such cooperative library agencies as the Bay Area Library Information Service (BALIS), the Bay Area Reference Center (BARC), and the California State Library when necessary.

BIRMINGHAM PUBLIC LIBRARY
(Birmingham, Alabama)

The nature of reference service is supplying information. Reference service may be defined as the direct personal aid, usually but not necessarily within a library, to persons in search of information for whatever purpose, and also various library activities especially aimed at making information as easily available as possible. Direct personal aid in supplying information includes answering questions, providing guidance in beginning research, and providing instruction in library use. Indirect functions of reference service are selection and acquisition of materials, organization of materials, and evaluation of services.

Good reference service involves identifying a person's information need and proceeding to fulfill it; using the resources available in the Library system; and including referral to resources in other libraries or agencies, if necessary.

PUBLIC LIBRARY OF CHARLOTTE & MECKLENBURG COUNTY, INC.
(Charlotte, North Carolina)

The Main Library Public Services librarians try to meet the needs of every citizen of the community for information, research, reading advice, or learning materials. Whether from the Library's own resources, the use of other libraries, or referral to an appropriate agency, the public service librarians seek to guide people to the answers they need. The function involves service in person and by telephone, and by letter if necessary. It includes instruction in library and bibliographic skills, service to groups as well as individuals, devising appealing exhibits, conducting library tours, cooperation and sharing with other libraries and learning institutions in the area, and articulation with local economic, social and cultural programs.

DUNEDIN PUBLIC LIBRARY
(Dunedin, Florida)

The Information Services Department of the library is that part which addresses itself to aiding readers find information. The service is both advisory and selective; it utilizes services within and outside the library. It is concerned with:

1. Information searching
2. Bibliographic preparation
3. Instruction in the use of the library
4. Internal development and improvement
   - Staff
   - Collection

Information services are developed to meet current needs, to improve present services, and to anticipate needs and demands.

The reference staff endeavors to bring practice up to these standards of principle.

INGLEWOOD PUBLIC LIBRARY
(Inglewood, California)

A library's reference service operates to meet the informational needs of its public and to assist the public in the use of the library's resources. There are two types of reference service: direct service and instructional service. Although the debate continues as to which of these is preferable, most libraries utilize both types of service to meet the requirements of each particular situation.

Direct service consists of providing the patron with the information requested, without any attempt to teach the patron to utilize the library's resources independently. Telephone inquiries are of necessity handled by direct service. With in-person requests many types of questions are more readily answered directly, although the patron may be directed to a particular reference book, index, or the public card catalog for information. However, once the reference librarian directs the patron to the source of information the librarian is responsible for insuring the patron knows how to use the reference source and is able to retrieve the information needed. This is where instructional service is employed.

Instructional service attempts to teach the library patron independent use of the various library resources such as the public card catalog, periodicals indexes, and business services. This service has as its objective the emancipation of the patron from dependence upon a reference service for all except the most complex queries, and consequently is greatly favored by libraries with severely limited staff. Although teaching the patron to use the various reference tools requires more time initially, in the long run it reduces the public's demands upon the reference staff for assistance.

KINGSPORT PUBLIC LIBRARY
(Kingsport, Tennessee)

The purpose of this policy is to present written guidelines for the provision of reference service at the Kingsport Public Library, in order to insure a uniform standard of reference service of the highest possible quality consistent with all the available resources. This policy expresses the understanding among the Reference Department staff and the Library Director concerning the manner in which the Department's responsibilities should be carried out. The policies stated herein should not be regarded as rigid rules or strict limitations, but rather as guideposts for reference work and personal conduct before the public. Each of the following policy statements must be interpreted with good judgement and a friendly desire to give the best possible reference service.

This policy is intended for use with both current staff members, who may from time to time have questions concerning departmental policy, and new staff members, who need to become quickly oriented with the same. This Service Policy should also be made available to library patrons upon demand, whenever questions arise concerning the types and/or quality of reference service available at the Kingsport Public Library.

The Reference Service Policy should be reviewed each year by the Reference Department staff and the Library Director in order to insure that policy and practice are in conformity and that necessary changes are made as required.

THE FREE LIBRARY OF PHILADELPHIA
(Philadelphia, Pennsylvania)

The reference and information function is one of the most important aspects of the Free Library's service. The delivery of information to the public through the reference process is supported by the library's selection, acquisitions, cataloging, and programming activities.

The term reference and information encompasses all of those activities by which the library assists people to acquire information which they are unable to acquire on their own. The reference transaction defines the basic units of reference and reader advisory service. It embodies all activities, techniques and procedures related to the request for information by a library patron and its provision by the librarian either in person, over the telephone or teletype or in writing. The reference worker provides pertinent information or reader guidance but does not interpret the facts or draw conclusions based on personal convictions.

Reference and reader advisory service, as herein defined, shall be restricted only the the limitations imposed by the nature of the resources themselves. Resources—which include staff, materials, equipment and facilities—may vary from one period of time to another and limitations shall be detailed as necessary in a statement of guidelines, which shall be revised periodically to reflect changing conditions, and changing objectives affected by circumstances—without losing sight of major goals.

PROVIDENCE PUBLIC LIBRARY
(Providence, Rhode Island)

Libraries in a democracy exist to encourage freedom of thought through open access to information and ideas. "Access" here implies more than "availability"; it indicates "usability" and it is the primary responsibility of the staff to bring the library's resources and potential users together through a variety of techniques and levels of activity. As our world grows increasingly complex, the challenge becomes one not merely of acquiring information in its many forms, but of making it available in a meaningful way to a public that uses us for a variety of purposes.

Statement of Objectives

ANN ARBOR PUBLIC LIBRARY
(Ann Arbor, Michigan)

DEPARTMENTAL OBJECTIVES

1. To provide personal assistance to library users in making the best practical use of library resources.
2. To select, acquire and organize sources of information to meet the needs of library users and prospective users.
3. To educate library users on the various methods of gaining access to sources of information, both inside the library and beyond it.
4. To plan and provide public programs of interest to the community.
5. To cooperate with other community agencies and organizations in their efforts to serve the community.

BIRMINGHAM PUBLIC LIBRARY
(Birmingham, Alabama)

1. To provide direct personal aid to persons seeking information regardless of their race, sex, nationality, religious background,

education, or the nature of information they require.

2. To give first priority to direct reference work (e.g., serving the public), and second priority to indirect reference work.

3. To service the information needs of persons who call the Library or come into the Library, with priority given to groups such as branch and extension libraries; City of Birmingham and Jefferson County governments; Birmingham and Jefferson County users.

4. To assess the information needs of non-users of the Library, and to promote means for supplying reference services and for fulfilling information needs of these non-users.

5. To provide the most efficient reference service through direct provision of information or through provision of instruction in sources to each person to the degree that he or she individually requires. This means that patrons will have the opportunity to receive instruction in the use of sources and facilities, but will not be denied information on the basis of whether or not they learn or accept instruction. However, the Library will encourage patrons who will need to use reference tools time and again, to learn the use of these tools.

6. To provide such service that each patron leaves feeling his visit (or telephone call) to the Library has been worthwhile.

CHICAGO PUBLIC LIBRARY
(Chicago, Illinois)

To meet the information needs of Chicago Public Library users accurately, efficiently, and pleasantly, whether the questions are received in person, by telephone, by letter, or through the Illinois Library and information network (ILLINET).

DUNEDIN PUBLIC LIBRARY
(Dunedin, Florida)

The objective of Information Services is to provide effective communication of information to help patrons by locating resources, furnishing materials and aiding in their use to solve problems, answer questions and get services they need. In its best and widest sense for quality library service the department is charged with the responsibility of selecting an adequate, suitable and up-to-date collection of reference and non-fiction materials arranged and maintained for easy and convenient use in a wide variety of subject fields for people of all ages, educational backgrounds and personal and professional needs. The ultimate objective is to provide an end product in terms of information sought by the patron.

INGLEWOOD PUBLIC LIBRARY
(Inglewood, California)

In all cases, the reference librarian should strive to provide the best materials for the particular inquirer, and this should also be a major goal of all reference service. However, in addition to a library's public there are other factors affecting the type and quality of reference service a library is able to give.

These factors, or limitations, include the size of the physical plant, the size, scope, and quality of the collection, staff, and budget. Most libraries follow the basic principles of reference service; however, each must make adaptations for its own unique situation. The type of reference service discussed here is that service which is actually provided by the Inglewood Public Library.

KINGSPORT PUBLIC LIBRARY
(Kingsport, Tennessee)

GOALS OF THE REFERENCE DEPARTMENT

The Reference Department subscribes to the basic goals of the Kingsport Public Library to acquire bibliographic materials related to the educational, recreational, and cultural needs and interests of the greater Kingsport community; to organize these materials in a comprehensible and accessible fashion and display them; and to make these materials easily available to partrons, all in a safe and physically attractive environment. The main goals of the Reference Department are: (1) to faciliate access to the Library's collections and to the informational content of those collections through direct, personal service to patrons; (2) to provide a Reference collection and services adequate to meet anticipated demands; (3) to provide available, trained, and capable staff to assist patrons in a polite and helpful manner; and (4) to insure adequate time for staff development in the areas of library reference services and bibliographic tools, in order to maintain a high quality of reference service.

LOUISVILLE FREE PUBLIC LIBRARY
(Louisville, Kentucky)

GOAL

In the interest of maximum service to the community the overriding goal of the reference and information function of Louisville Free Public Library is to provide accurately, efficiently, and pleasantly, the assistance and information products that are required and requested by users, whether in person, by telephone or in writing.

SCOPE OF REFERENCE SERVICE

All information requests are to be handled. If information is available, it is provided to users without making a judgment on its moral or aesthetic worth.

NEW CASTLE COUNTY
DEPARTMENT OF LIBRARIES
(Wilmington, Delaware)

1. To develop a geography of public library information services in New Castle County; i.e., a reliable picture of who goes where for

what information and library materials and the kind of response they get.

- To identify geographical concentrations of usage by subject.
- To identify concentrations of subject usage in particular libraries.
- To evaluate the mobility of library users by subject.
- To evaluate the effectiveness and potential effectiveness of particular libraries to provide resource level services in particular subject concentrations and/or serve a general resource function.
- To identify subject areas which are not being adequately served in order to seek ways to provide the service.

2. To develop a management tool to help each library evaluate and develop information services and support funding requests.
   - To develop data to optimize scheduling and personnel utilization.
   - To identify areas for in-service training.
   - To identify both absolute and quantitative gaps in the collection.
   - To evaluate the effect of space utilization and organization on information services.

3. To identify levels of service and develop standards, guidelines and contract specifications and identify the cost of providing service at various levels.
   - To determine the costs of various levels of service.
   - To develop data to be used with A Commitment to Information Services in developing local guidelines.
   - To develop descriptions of levels of service and measures for the development of any referral allotments or contracts.

ORLANDO PUBLIC LIBRARY
(Orlando, Florida)

The reference philosophy of the Orlando Public Library System is: (1) To provide the best possible library and information services meeting the educational, informational, recreational, and cultural needs of the residents of its service area; (2) To anticipate these needs when possible; (3) To efficiently process, store and retrieve information upon request, in the manner most meaningful and useful to the patron.

THE FREE LIBRARY OF PHILADELPHIA
(Philadelphia, Pennsylvania)

The public library's clientele is the public-at-large. The library's role is to try to meet the general and special, cultural, educational, vocational and informational needs of all segments of the public regardless of age, race, sex or physical condition.

Since reference and reader advisory services are basic and vital aspects of library service, it is important that they receive the highest priority at all levels of library operation. For only such priority will ensure that reference service is provided in the most effective manner possible for a large and varied clientele.

PROVIDENCE PUBLIC LIBRARY
(Providence, Rhode Island)

Libraries *are* difficult to use. Perhaps this is the most important concept to be grasped by a library staff. All library planning and activity, then, must be directed toward usability. The layout of the physical structure, the hours of service offered, the informational signs and literature, the organization of the collection, the out-reach programs, and especially the direct service function of the staff focus on this goal. The educated and experienced individual and the individual with limited background need, in varying degrees, help in finding their way through the intellectual world of print, film, and recorded sound. This guidance will very often stimulate and prepare the user to progress further under his own initiative, but there are also those who will always be in need of human mediation between themselves and the library's materials. Determining and providing the level of help required by each individual are integral parts of the librarian's public service skills.

SAN DIEGO PUBLIC LIBRARY
(San Diego, California)

It is the objective of this library to provide accurate, prompt and courteous information and reference assistance in response to requests from all persons. This service is given impartially to all and with as much expertise as training and professional guidance make possible.

TYPES OF SERVICE

General Statement

ANN ARBOR PUBLIC LIBRARY
(Ann Arbor, Michigan)

REFERENCE AND INFORMATION DESK SERVICE—
THE REFERENCE DESK STAFF

1. Provides information in the form of short answers to specific questions and guidance in locating material for patrons who appear in person, call on the telephone, or request information through correspondence.
2. Assists patrons in the use of the library and teaches research methodology, when appropriate. This includes providing help in developing a research strategy and advice on whether a trip to the library would be worthwhile for individuals who telephone.
3. Provides bibliographic verification of items both in the library and not owned by the library and will assist patrons in obtaining materials through interlibrary loan, when appropriate.
4. Refers library users to other departments, agencies and libraries in pursuit of needed information.

5. Engages in individual projects while on desk duty.
6. Is responsible for the loan of items from the art rental collection.

BIRMINGHAM PUBLIC LIBRARY
(Birmingham, Alabama)

TYPES OF REFERENCE SERVICE

The Library offers many types of Reference Services. Some services, particularly in providing information over the telephone, may be limited. For example, staff cannot identify or estimate the value of rare or used books, coins, stamps, or other items. Also, limited staff time does not permit searching such things as genealogical or historical records in microform, or unlimited staff photo copy service. Some Reference Services offered by the Library are listed below.

1. Information service, viz., answers to specific questions.
2. Instruction in the use of the Library, i.e., how to use the COM, periodical indexes, bibliographies. This includes orientation of groups and instruction on methodology and bibliography (i.e., how to do a literature search, how to cite a publication or article).
3. Assistance in locating library materials, including location information and reserves of up to three titles over the telephone.
4. Provision of bibliographic information that can be verified with standard tools, such as *Books in Print,* the *National Union Catalog, CBI,* etc.
5. Instruction in the use of microform, audio-visual, and photocopy equipment.
6. Provision of specific information from Birmingham City and Suburban directories to local callers.
7. Assistance in the use of particular materials, including price guides to books, coins, stamps, etc.
8. Referral to other agencies, suppliers, or brokers for information.
9. Interlibrary loan services to obtain materials not in the Library.
10. Photocopies without charge to City and County government offices and departments.

DUNEDIN PUBLIC LIBRARY
(Dunedin, Florida)

A. Information services utilize reference resources through personal interaction with users on both direct and indirect levels. The services range from answering apparently simple questions to supplying information based on a bibiographic search combining the staffs' competence in information handling techniques with competence in the subject of inquiry.

B. List of Services
  1. Information Services Desk
     - Information services—answers to specific questions, statistics, biographies, etc.
     - Instruction in the use of the library—how to use the card catalog, periodical indexes, bibliographies
     - Answering inquiries from other libraries
  2. Bibliographic Service
     - Bibliographies
     - Demand bibliographies
     - Current awareness services
  3. Correspondence—answering inquiries from individuals
  4. Document Service
  5. Orientation and Instructional Service

THE FREE LIBRARY OF PHILADELPHIA
(Philadelphia, Pennsylvania)

The reference and reader advisory function of the modern public library may be described as personalized aid or guidance provided to users in the pursuit of desired information. Its aim is optimum access to and use of existing resources within and beyond the Free Library system. The assistance provided may take a variety of forms depending upon the particular needs of the individual inquirer. Among these are: location of specific facts; reading guidance, selection of materials to meet a particular interest or need; aid in identifying the best sources of information for a given purpose; instruction in the use of the library or a particular tool; development of bibliographies, indexes and other aids promoting access to information; seeking an answer from or referral to other agencies or information sources outside the library.

Branch and Regional Services

PUBLIC LIBRARY OF CHARLOTTE & MECKLENBURG COUNTY, INC.
(Charlotte, North Carolina)

COOPERATING WITH THE BRANCHES

When a Branch Librarian receives a request which turns out to be a reference question, she may call or send the question to the Reference Desk at Main, giving the Reference Librarian (who will treat it the same as any other reference question) as much information relative to the question as possible.

The Reference Librarian on duty will check the Main Library's shelves for materials specifically requested over the telephone for a branch patron who will come to the Main Library to get the material if it is found to be in. The Reference Librarian will reverse this procedure when a Main patron will go to a branch when the material can be located at a branch.

In all cases when material is sent to a branch, it is checked out from the Main Library to the individual patron and not to the branch.

CHICAGO PUBLIC LIBRARY
(Chicago, Illinois)

SERVICE TO BRANCH AND REGIONAL LIBRARIES

Reference Service

When staff of affiliate libraries call or visit The Chicago Public Library, the guidelines for "Service to the Public" (I.E.) apply.

Affiliate libraries should continue to contact the subject divisions for answer to information questions when appropriate. If the question cannot be answered over the telephone, the affiliate library should fill out an Information Request form and forward the request to the Bibliographic and Interlibrary Loan Center. It is the responsibility of the affiliate library to list all sources that have already been searched. Full bibliographic information is necessary. If a subject division has been called, this should be noted on the request, and all sources checked by the division should be listed.

The Bibliographic and Interlibrary Loan Center staff will search further in The Chicago Public Library collection, if necessary. If the request has not been filled, it will then be referred to the appropriate Research and Reference Center. Each of the R & R Centers handling the request will respond directly to the affiliate library. In some instances the request may be further forwarded to a Special Resource Center.

DENVER PUBLIC LIBRARY
(Denver, Colorado)

REFERENCE SERVICES

Reference work is accomplished in all agencies of the Library. While subject deparments of the Main Building accomplish both general and specialized reference and research, it is expected that complex reference requests at smaller branches be referred to the larger branch libraries or to the Main Building subject departments, and that materials will be borrowed from DPL agencies or other outside systems to meet specific requests.

Bookmobiles and satellite libraies provide a minimum of reference services because of the nature of their collections.

Reference functions for which agencies are responsible include the following:

Providing readers assistance services;

Assisting readers in the pursuit of self-directed educational programs (On Your Own);

Answering reference questions;

Borrowing materials from other libraries through Interlibrary Loan;

Referring reference requests to other agencies when unable to provide the information;

Maintaining and organizing pamphlet files, clipping files, "Looked-up" files, and other information files as authorized;

Participating in the preparation of bibliographies including those retrieved through Metro Retrieval Network (Computer Data Bases).

DUNEDIN PUBLIC LIBRARY
(Dunedin, Florida)

Branch staff may feel free to call Reference occasionally when assistance is needed—*after checking with the person in charge at the branch.*

INGLEWOOD PUBLIC LIBRARY
(Inglewood, California)

ORGANIZATION

Branch libraries are maintained to provide a first level of library service to a community. Although the branch library collection is tailored to meet the needs of the surounding community, it will generally be duplicated in the holdings of the main library. A branch library is organized under the direction of a branch librarian with one additional librarian and several clerical assistants. As staffing is limited, many areas of responsibility are not maintained within strict limits but tend to overlap. A high degree of cooperation among the staff is necesary for the smooth functioning of a branch library.

The librarian on duty, whether this is the branch librarian or an assistant, is responsible for the reference function at the branch library. In the absence of a librarian, which does occur occasionally during lunch hours and emergencies, the Circulation Supervisor or next highest clerical person on duty is responsible for assisting the patrons with their requests as much as possible. If additional service is required, the person on duty will contact the reference desk at the main library for assistance. The reference librarian at the main library will then either provide the information requested over the telephone or advise the patron to come to the main library reference desk for futher assistance.

DUTIES

The branch librarian is responsible for the overall operation of the branch library as well as reference service. When another librarian is assigned to the branch library, the librarian is primarily responsible for reference service and supervision of the library in the absence of the branch librarian. As branch libraries do not have Information Assistants, their general function is performed by both librarians and clerical staff at the branch library. The librarians have more responsibility for answering directional questions, completing title searches, answering the telephones, etc., than their counterparts at the main library.

Another service shared by the librarians and clerical staff is the readers' advisory service. Due to the intimacy of a branch library, the clerical staff, especially the Circulation Supervisor, has regular contact with the patrons and comes to know their reading interests. Increasingly, the clerical staff will assist the patrons with their reading selections, especially in the area of fiction and new books on the best-seller lists.

Branch library reference service (assisting patrons in their requests for information and their use of the library's resources) is similar to that provided at the main library, with the major limitation being the limited collection and resources of a branch library. As a result of these limitations the branch librarian will, at times, call on the reference service at the main library to assist in answering a patron's inquiry.

Also, in a branch library the separation of adult and children's services is not as clearly defined as at the main library. Although children's librarians do serve in branch libraries on a regular basis (several times a week), there are no children's librarians assigned to the branch libraries on a full-time basis. Consequently, branch librarians will frequently provide reference service and reading guidance to children as well as adults.

MEMPHIS PUBLIC LIBRARY
(Memphis, Tennessee)

REFERENCE QUESTIONS REFERRED FROM A BRANCH TO A MAIN LIBRARY DEPARTMENT

    a. Research questions which cannot be handled in the branch are referred directly to the deparment.

    b. Let the patron at the branch talk to the assistant in the department so that there can be a thorough, direct interview.

BOOK TITLES REQUESTED BY A PATRON IN A BRANCH LIBRARY

    a. If the book is needed immediately and the patron is willing to pick the book up, contact the Branch Office to see if the title is in the library.

    b. If the patron does not wish to go to another branch where the book has been located, or if the book cannot be located on the shelf anywhere, the patron should fill out a reserve card in his branch. The reserve will be requested by telephoning the Branch Office. The Branch Office will then borrow the titles from whatever branch or department has the titles available, and materials will be delivered by van to the branches.

    c. If the material is not on the shelf at any of its locations the Branch Office will reserve it at a location if the requesting agency desires.

LIBRARY USERS

General Statement

THE BERKELEY PUBLIC LIBRARY
(Berkeley, California)

IDENTIFICATION REQUIREMENT

1. *Identification* is required to use:
   Reference Desk materials (from behind Desk area)
   Magazine Storage materials
   Supp. Ref/Ref Cal books
   Playboy microfilm
2. *Library Card* or other acceptable identification is clipped to the book card or slip, and put in the middle lower shelf list drawer marked "Library cards."
3. *Leaving* of keys, books, knives, sweaters as I.D. is to be discouraged. Accept only from new patrons, who don't know the system. They should be told to bring a library card or proper I.D. next time. If such an item is left, patron should fill out name and address on a library use slip.
4. For *emergencies* (no I.D., no nothing) and for specific books marked

234

"For use behind the Desk only," patron may be seated at the small table behind the desk.

5. *Acceptable Identification*
   Library Card (BPL or other California Library)
   Driver's license
   School I.D. card
   Other I.D. with name and address of patron
6. *Take out* of Reference materials under special circumstances. *Must* be approved by Supervising Librarian of Reference Division Patron must leave two good I.D.'s or deposit.

THE DAYTON AND MONTGOMERY COUNTY PUBLIC LIBRARY
(Dayton, Ohio)

Reference services are available on an equal basis to all without regard to race, color, creed, sex, or age.

DUNEDIN PUBLIC LIBRARY
(Dunedin, Florida)

Library users are all people seeking information whether in person or by telephone. No effort is made to determine whether they are entitled to library cards before service is given except to decide whether or not informational material will be checked out or interlibrary loan requested.

Information Services will be revised at regular intervals to identify those individuals who are or are not being served and to determine how individuals not utilizing such services can be reached.

KINGSPORT PUBLIC LIBRARY
(Kingsport, Tennesse)

BASIC PHILOSOPHY OF DIRECT PERSONAL SERVICE

All patrons and inquiries should be treated equally. The needs of each library patron should always be taken seriously and treated with the utmost respect and confidentiality. Discussion of any individual group of individuals, or their inquiries, outside the professional context is strictly prohibited.

As a general rule, because of the size and diversity of the Library's clientele and the limited number of staff in the Reference Department, assistance to patrons, apart from "ready reference" types of inquiries (which include directions, general questions concerning library policies and services, information on library holdings, and reference inquiries involving specific facts easily determined from standard sources), should ordinarily take the form of providing guidance in the pursuit of information, rather than the provision of the information itself. Each staff member on duty at the Reference Desk must exercise his or her own judgement in determining the application of this policy statement in specific situations, being careful to weigh such factors as the needs of the individual user, the amount of time available, and the knowledge upon which the staff member can draw. It should be remembered that such instruction of library patrons as to the means of pursuit (versus the actual provision) of information has the additional benefit of training patrons in research methods which can be reapplied independently in future situations.

LOUISVILLE FREE PUBLIC LIBRARY
(Louisville, Kentucky)

Service is provided to everyone. Valid card holders have no priority. Personal inquiries from staff members are to be treated as for non-staff users. However, staff members on duty should be careful not to impose their work on the reference staff because of the convenience.

NEW ORLEANS PUBLIC LIBRARY
(New Orleans, Louisiana)

The Periodical Back Issue Request Card may be used by Orleans Parish residents who have forgotten their library cards and who only wish to use periodicals. Circulation Division staff will request to see identification to verify the person's name and parish residency. The patron's name and current date is filled in and "Resident" is checked by the Circulation Division staff member, so that a refund will not be issued.

THE FREE LIBRARY OF PHILADELPHIA
(Philadelphia, Pennsylvania)

The Free Library functions as the resource and information center for the people of Philadelphia. Further, under the Pennsylvania Code, the Free Library bears additional responsibility within the state both as a district library and as a regional resource center charged with servicing in-depth collections in the assigned subject areas. Finally, as a major public library, the Free Library also recognizes responsibility on the national level for providing access to unique informational resources such as local history materials and specialized research collections.

The Free Library recognizes that there will be a diversity of interests and needs represented by its present and potential clientele. As an institution composed of multiple service units extending over a large geographical area, the Library will vary its informational service in keeping with the nature of the individual community served. However, the Library understands that it must avoid quick and easy generalizations about these communities, which are frequently in a state of flux.

As an institution dedicated to public service, the Free Library broadens and adapts its reference services to reflect areas of present social concern—such as employment, housing, education, mental health, and consumer affairs—and attempts to anticipate significant future concerns.

While the Library does not engage in social casework, it functions properly as an information and referral link between a person with a problem and the social agency which can help him. It is necessary to underscore that the service provided by the Library is "information" not counseling.

Categories of Users: Non-Residents

NEW ORLEANS PUBLIC LIBRARY
(New Orleans, Louisiana)

A Louisiana resident who does not have or does not wish to buy a non-resident borrower's card, may buy a permit at the Circulation Desk to use back issues of Central Library periodicals. The Periodical Back Issue Request Card costs $.50, is good only for the day it is purchased, and entitles the holder to a maximum of five filled periodical volume requests. If none of the holder's requests are filled, they may get a refund on the day of purchase from the Circulation Desk. If more than five periodical volumes are needed, additional permits may be purchased at the Circulation Desk. To use the permit, the patron's name and date purchased are written and "$.50 pd." checked by Circulation Division staff member. The patron presents the permit to the Periodical Desk staff member along with the requests for periodical volumes. When the volumes are received from the basement, the Periodical Desk staff member counts the volumes and checks the appropriate blocks in ink on the permit. (For example, if the patron requested three periodical volumes but only two were located, blocks 1 and 2 are checked). Depending on which comes first, the permit is void when all five blocks are checked or the library closes for the day. Permit holders who present unchecked permits on the day of purchase to the Circulation Desk are entitled to full refunds.

239

OUT OF STATE

Out-of-state visitors to Central Library are usually pemitted to use bound periodicals on the premises. They are given a Periodical Back Issue Request Card, free of charge, at the discretion of the Head of Circulation. The card is filled in with patron's name and current date and "Resident" is checked by a Circulation Division staff member, so that a refund will not be issued. A resident of another Louisiana parish is required to purchase either a nonresident card or a Periodical Back Issue Request Card.

THE FREE LIBRARY OF PHILADELPHIA
(Philadelphia, Pennsylvania)

OTHER OUT-OF-TOWN REQUESTS

A letter from a person out of the Philadelphia Library District and not a holder of a FLP borrower's card should be especially examined for the appropriateness of the work requested. When Philadelphia information or information only available in FLP is requested, an effort should be made to answer the question or describe the resources available, provided this does not conflict with other stated policy. In other instances, a polite referral to other resources or networks should be indicated in a reply that notes the unfortunate limits to our ability to perform the work requests.

Categories of Users: Handicapped

THE FREE LIBRARY OF PHILADELPHIA
(Philadelphia, Pennsylvania)

Reference service for deaf patrons is available through a TDD (tele-communication device for the deaf) located in the General Information Department. The level of reference service which can be provided to deaf patrons via TDD closely approximates the telephone reference service provided hearing patrons.

PRIORITIES

CHICAGO PUBLIC LIBRARY
(Chicago, Illinois)

No user should expect to monopolize a staff member's time. If a user has a complex question and needs to be introduced to many sources, staff should help begin the search, help other waiting users, then check on the progress. Sometimes it is necessary to help several users concurrently.

DUNEDIN PUBLIC LIBRARY
(Dunedin, Florida)

Priority is given to requests from City officials. They are handled by the Head of Information Services unless delegated.

Courteous, prompt, efficient service on the Information Desk is the primary priority of every reference staff member, whatever his other responsibilities.

INGLEWOOD PUBLIC LIBRARY
(Inglewood, California)

While on desk duty, service to the public takes precedence over any other duties, and service to the patron in the library takes precedence

242

over telephone inquiries. Frequently, it is not sufficient for the reference librarian to wait for a patron to request assistance. Since many patrons are reluctant to request aid, it is the responsibility of the reference librarian to anticipate public needs and offer service when it appears needed.

KINGSPORT PUBLIC LIBRARY
(Kingsport, Tennessee)

The Reference Department gives top priority to all activities involving direct personal service to library patrons, either to an individual patron or to a group of patrons. Supporting activities, although essential to maintain the quality of these services, must take second place. Priorities for direct personal services from highest to lowest include:

1. Direct personal service to library *patrons who come to the Reference area* takes priority over all other reference activity. Reference Department staff should make a determined effort to schedule all appointments, meetings, and supportive activities at times when reference use is relatively light and/or when other staff members are available in sufficient numbers to handle demand. Patrons in the Reference area are served on a first-come, first-served basis.
2. Telephone inquiries.
3. Pending reference inquiries, i.e., inquiries not answered when they were taken at the desk or over the phone, for whatever reason, should be answered by the person who accepted them whenever possible, unless other arrangements have been made.
4. Library orientation and bibliographic instruction (Library tours are available only to groups of patrons or group leaders).

KNOXVILLE-KNOX COUNTY PUBLIC LIBRARY
(Knoxville, Tennessee)

LML Reference is forced to limit questions and title searches to no more than *three* at a time per patron. If branches have time, they may make exceptions to this rule.

ORLANDO PUBLIC LIBRARY
(Orlando, Florida)

A. Provide service on a "first-come, first-served" basis, whether for telephone or walk-in patrons.
B. Provide service to patrons without bias and without imposing value judgements as to the importance of their questions or needs.

PROVIDENCE PUBLIC LIBRARY
(Providence, Rhode Island)

Fact finding, research, and reading guidance requests come to service personnel in a number of ways. In the course of a day, staff members will receive inquiries directly from users in person, by telephone, and sometimes by mail. In addition, other requests will be referred from the PPL Systems Office, from other departments or agencies, and in writing from other libraries.

No arbitrary order of service can be established for handling these different request categories. Such variables as the anticipated length of time needed to complete the question, the number of staff members available at the time, the work load of the department or branch, and any deadline indicated by the patron or referring agency will all help to determine in what order requests will be served. In making the decision it must be remembered that all requests are equal in importance and that direct patron service must take priority over the numerous support activities—those routine tasks so important to the effective functioning of each department and branch.

DESK POLICIES

General Guidelines for Desk Duty: Nature and Extent of Responsibilities

ANN ARBOR PUBLIC LIBRARY
(Ann Arbor, Michigan)

GENERAL GUIDELINES FOR DESK DUTY

1. Helping the library users who appear *in person* is the highest priority for all desk personnel.
2. Staff members assigned to desk duty should report promptly to the desk and "cover" that desk as closely as possible until they are relieved by the next person. This means that if it becomes necessary to leave the desk for any length of time—either to help a patron with a question, or for a coffee break, or for whatever reason—other departmental staff members are informed of the absence and suitable arrangements are made. (Coffee breaks taken while on desk assignment should be taken

at quieter times and with the agreement of other staff members also on the desk.)

3. In situations where a staff member is not satisfied with his or her response to a patron's question, referral to or consultation with other staff members is desirable. Information Desk staff, in particular, should refer patrons to the Reference Desk, or to other departments, whenever it is appropriate.
4. Staff members should be prepared to help each other in the handling of difficult patrons if necessary.
5. Personnel at both desks are responsible for picking up their respective areas at the end of each shift as follows: Reference Desk: Reference Department study tables and carrells, index table, and quiet room; Information Desk: Study tables and carrells on rest of second floor, consumer table, business table, microfilm area, telephone book collection, and the card catalog.
6. The Reference Department cannot be responsible for patrons' personal belongings. Lockers are available on the first floor.

PUBLIC LIBRARY OF CHARLOTTE & MECKLENBURG COUNTY, INC.
(Charlotte, North Carolina)

Long conversations and taking undue time with any one patron when others are waiting must be avoided. Staff conversation must cease when a patron comes near.

The senior Reference Librarian on duty is "In Charge" of the Library at all hours when the Public Service Head, the Assistant Director, or Director is not present.

The Reference Librarian(s) on duty assume responsibility, with the Security Guard, for reasonable order in the Library, employing reasonableness, restraint, firmness, common sense, and compassion.

PROVIDING INFORMATION ON THE MESSAGE RECORDER

The Head of Reference is responsible for composing and recording messages concerning the Library's hours. The Head of Reference keeps a file of messages and obtains a substitute recorder when he will be away at times the message is to be changed.

Messages are changed when hours change, and when holidays will be observed by the Library.

The Reference Librarian on duty in the evening until 9 p.m. (6 p.m. on Saturdays) is responsible for checking the recorder immediately before leaving to see that the machine is turned on and gives the correct message.

CLEVELAND PUBLIC LIBRARY
(Cleveland, Ohio)

AWARENESS

1. If you are at the service desk, give the patron your prompt attention. This overrides any conversation you may be having with subordinates, co-workers, or superiors.

2. If you are busy with a patron try to see that the next person waiting is referred to another staff member; if no one is available, ask him to wait a few moments. Often it is important to get something into the hands of each one and to return to them as needed. The patron is always first, not another staff member or other work.

3. If a patron is wandering around the room, offer assistance. Judgment is necessary here; some parons want to browse and do not want to be interrupted or bothered. Others may be hesitant about approaching our somewhat formidable-looking desks. Remember to get up and help.

4. Consider that the patron may be new to the Library or is not skillful in using it.
   - Show where books are on the shelf; do not point.
   - Help, explain, suggest (catalog, forms, arrangements). We all need to help make the Library usable.
   - Follow-up to make sure patron is getting what he needs.
   - Remember that some kind of a brief reference interview may need to be conducted to enable you to meet the patron's needs.
   - Try to see that no patron is referred more than once. It is helpful to telephone ahead to make sure the department has the required material. It often will help if the patron has a name of a staff member.
   - Try to explain in lay, not library, terms. We are so accustomed

to our own language that we fail to notice that it is puzzling.
- Insofar as possible, give the patron the benefit of the doubt, e.g., credit for good intentions, honesty, etc.

ACTUAL SERVICE

1. Good judgement is basic to supplying kind, depth, and quantity of information.
2. Actual staff time available per question will probably not exceed 10 minutes; 5 when very busy. At less crowded times patrons can obviously be granted more time. On the other hand, we need not let a patron's demands become excessive.

INGLEWOOD PUBLIC LIBRARY
(Inglewood, California)

REFERENCE ACTIVITIES

In the previous discussion of descriptions, a summary of the duties required was included with each position in an effort to delineate further the respective positions. Those duties identify various end results which the person filling the position is responsible for achieving. Here the focus is on the activities or methods by which the end results are to be achieved. Activities are listed for the four positions previously identified.: Head—Reference and Information Services, Reference Librarian II, Reference Librarian I, and Reference Clerk.

There are both public activities and non-public activities. The non-public activities are further identified according to the positions they comprise. Public activities are performed by the librarian at the reference desk regardless of the position filled by that person within the Library system.

Non-public activities are those tasks performed by the Reference and Information Services staffs when functioning in their respective positions within the library system and not staffing a public desk. These are generally referred to as "off-desk" activities.

General reference activities. The following activities will be performed by all librarians while serving at the reference desk.

1. Answer telephone.
2. Assist and instruct the public in the use of periodical indexes.
3. Assist and instruct the public in the use of special reference services—business, consumer, etc.
4. Assist and instruct the public in the use of the public card catalog, both author-title and subject.
5. Assist the public in the use of reference materials.
6. Assist the public in the use of specialized library equipment.
7. Explain Library policies and procedures to the public.
8. File reference services.
9. Give directional information as required.
10. Identify library materials from telephone requests.
11. Observe, report on, or correct stack conditions and materials.
12. Perform readers' advisory service.
13. Provide reference service to telephone inquiries.
14. Receive, edit, and complete materials requests.
15. Report any malfunctioning equipment to the Library Administrative Office.
16. Review new reference books.
17. Supervise the closing of the library.

Specific activities—Head—Reference and Information Services. The following activities are performed by the Head—Reference and Information Services as an integral part of this position.
1. Attend meetings and conferences.
2. Conduct and arrange library tours.
3. Confer with Library staff/City employees.
4. Confer with representatives of organizations (including vendors).
5. Coordinate adult book selection.
6. Coordinate reference service with other divisions.
7. Give talks and demonstrations.
8. Perform activities related to professional affiliations.
9. Plan overall operation of the Reference and Information Services.
10. Prepare and review the Reference and Information Services budget.
11. Prepare studies and reports.
12. Read correspondence.
13. Read professional literature.
14. Review and initiate correspondence.
15. Review and select reference materials.

16. Select, evaluate, and counsel personnel.
17. Supervise and train reference librarians, Reference Clerks, Librarian trainees, and Information Assistants.
18. Supervise preparation of schedules and payroll.
19. Visit libraries, schools, and other facilities.

The Reference Service is a public service established to meet public needs. Generally, these consist of information requests, interpretation of library resources, and instruction in the use of the Library's resources. Although requests for directional information will usually be answered by Information Assistants, it is not unlikely some of these queries will be directed at the reference librarian. Consequently, reference librarians should be familiar with the physical structure of the building, including the location of other divisions, public restrooms, public telephones, conference and study rooms, typing rooms, etc.

KINGSPORT PUBLIC LIBRARY
(Kingsport, Tennessee)

AREAS OF RESPONSIBILITY

The areas of Reference responsibility are divided below into three broad types according to the qualifications required and/or the functions served. These divisions in no way prescribe priority or importance. The first of these, *Professional,* represents those areas for which formal library science training is considered essential for proper completion and the highest possible quality. The second, *Supportive,* lists those areas which are not purely reference in nature and require no formal library science training, but which, nonetheless, support vital library goals and fall under the auspices of the Reference Department. The last area, *General,* represents areas of service which are performed daily or several times daily and which vary greatly as to the degree of training required.

Professional

Supervision of the Reference Department

Supervision of the Reference area
Selection and development of the Reference collections, including the
    Association File
    College Catalogs
    Microforms
    Periodicals
    Reference book collection
    Telephone directories
    Vertical file materials
    Bibliographic instuction
Interlibrary loans
Preparation of monthly and annual reports

Supportive

    Audiovisual previews
    Circulation of films
    Daily operation and maintenance of the copying machine
    Duplicate exchange
    Local newspapers
    Periodical issue requests
    Preparation of bindery materials and maintenance of bindery records
    Preparation of monthly and annual film reports
    Service of the Palmer Room during unstaffed hours

General

    Filing of vertical file materials
    Filing of the various updating materials in the Reference collection
    General upkeep of the Reference area
    Provision of direct, personal service to patrons

LOUISVILLE FREE PUBLIC LIBRARY
(Louisville, Kentucky)

When questions are asked of the staff, a serious effort should be made to produce the answer. If a question cannot be answered, other appropriate staff member should be consulted. Those that remain unanswered through this method should be recorded, including name and phone number of patron, and taken up with one's supervisor.

Questions that cannot be answered at branches should be referred to the Main Library's Ready Reference and Information Desk or the appropriate subject section.

ORLANDO PUBLIC LIBRARY
(Orlando, Florida)

RESPONSIBILITIES

Administration and Management

1. Maintain the Orlando Public Library as the resource center for the system.
2. Provide sufficient staff and materials to meet reference and circulation demands.
3. Provide training of reference staff* in the use of materials and equipment.
4. Provide the staff with current information about library services and programs.
5. Provide procedural guidelines for the reference staff to follow in the areas of reserves, circulation, interlibrary loans, security, and emergencies, and to inform them of changes in procedures prior to the effective date of the change.
6. Establish and utilize all means of communication available to further cooperation and understanding among departments and community libraries.

Reference Staff

1. Know the resources of your own department or library in depth, and maintain awareness of the total system's resources and services. Keep abreast of current events on local, national, and international levels.
2. Maintain a professional, yet accessible, image. Be courteous to patrons and staff alike. In keeping with this philosophy, accept

---

*The terms "staff" or "reference staff" refer to those staff members who are either reference librarians or other staff filling the reference function in public service work.

only library business phone calls and scan only relevant reading materials while at a public service desk.
3. Keep accurate data on information and reference questions in the manner determined by the administration.
4. Follow the guidelines for reference service with the understanding that each librarian, using his/her judgment, will make occasional exceptions to the policy when necessary.

THE FREE LIBRARY OF PHILADELPHIA
(Philadelphia, Pennsylvania)

A high level of professional competence is expected of all staff in providing accurate and complete responses to inquiries. A cheerful and courteous manner should be employed in dispensing information and reference service.

In view of shared responsibilities among departments, regionals, and branches working under pressure and peak periods and the problems of communication in a large and complex organization, the following guidelines are set forth for relative uniformity in performing fair and equitable service to our patrons. These guidelines have been adopted as a result of the examination of solutions to practical problems based on experience of reference workers in the Free Library of Philadelphia as well as in other public libraries. Although guides are set for general practice and limits of service are established, the nature of public library reference work is such that all aspects cannot be covered in a directive. Application of rules, such as the amount of time spent on a single question, depends upon the nature of the question, the needs of the reader, and, above all, the judgment of the librarian.

The single most important factor in the delivery of reference and reader advisory service is the staff responsible for providing it. The reference/information librarian must be the link between library resources and library users. This transfer funcion requires that the librarian have knowledge about library materials, possess skill in their use and be able to communicate effectively with people.

Reference and reader advisory services hold equal professional importance with other duties performed by the professional staff. The nature of the reference service may vary with the type of library agency but staff must be provided throughout the library system to meet reference and reader advisory needs. Work of a clerical nature should be reduced to a minimum so that the reference librarian can best perform professional assignments.

Reference staff should have the opportunity to develop their professional skills through the process of continuing education. This may include on-the-job training, in-service workshops, staff meetings, formal academic instruction, and participation in activities sponsored by professional associations. Most of such training should be directed toward specific aspects of reference and information services. It must also be fully understood that individual reference librarians are expected to take an active responsibility for their own professional growth.

Every effort should be made to keep effective reference workers in the field and reward them in proportion to their skills.

ST. LOUIS PUBLIC LIBRARY
(St. Louis, Missouri)

GUIDELINES FOR IN-PERSON REFERENCE SERVICE

Service to individuals who are physically present in the library MUST take precedence over other library-related matters, within every library department. In providing good service to these patrons, various techniques may be used:

Make yourself available to the patron.

1. Do NOT bury yourself in books
2. Look around and see if someone needs assistance
3. Walk through department when patrons are in the vicinity
4. Do not appear formidable, uninterested, or too busy to be interrupted

If telephone rings during person-to-person reference or service encounter, excuse yourself from the patron, respond to caller by announcing department and asking if patron would like to call back later, be called later, or wait (if you know it will only be a short time) as you are helping someone.

If patron appears while you are engaged in telephone conversation, acknowledge his presence with a nod or hand signal. End phone conversation as quickly as you can or inform the caller you will return the call.

Be available *whenever* patron needs assistance.

The key to successful reference work is the reference interview. In-person interviews are easier to conduct than those over the phone since you can also rely on the interviewee's countenance as a measure of the communication. The purpose of the reference interview is TO DEFINE THE PATRON'S INFORMATION NEED IN TERMS OF OUR RESOURCES or OBTAIN ENOUGH INFORMATION TO MAKE A REFERRAL TO THE APPROPRIATE DEPARTMENT, SERVICE OR OUTSIDE AGENCY.

In order to do this effectively, the interviewer should:
1. *Listen* carefully and attentively
2. Provide a relaxed atmosphere for open communication
3. Know the resources of the library
4. Know the resource potentials of staff members
5. Know the resources of his department
6. Know the services of the library and his department
7. Adopt an open mind
8. Always be courteous and respectful
9. Know that each patron feels his request is legitimate and important—even though it may not seem so to the interviewer

The limit of reference service will vary. STLPL's main functions are guidance, direction, and instruction. The amount of time necessary to perform these functions will depend on and vary according to:
1. Library and educational background and experience of patron
2. Patron's time limit
3. Patron's ability to comprehend instructions
4. Complexity of materials to be used
5. Number of patrons needing assistance
6. Number of available staff to help patrons

Suggestions to expedite service:
1. Do not engage in superfluous conversations with patrons—stick to the point
2. Instruct the patron to the point he may work independently and mention that you will give further aid if and when needed
3. Know your resources and their contents—physical locations also, so as not to waste time searching

---

SAN DIEGO PUBLIC LIBRARY
(San Diego, California)

POLICY

Information given is always based on accurate printed sources or learned from a reliable authority. The opinion of staff, even when requested, is not given as fact.

Sources of information include the entire book and non-book resources of this library as well as the resources of the community, both its institutions and its people, made available through the knowledge and experience of the staff.

The staff at reference desks are welcoming and accessible and make every effort to communicate readily with people of all ages and social groups.

MEANS

The Information/Directory Service Desk. This central service desk area in the lobby has four distinct functions. It serves 1) as a central information desk where library users stop for directions; 2) as a general reference service giving answers quickly reachable in a small collection of basic reference tools; 3) as a directory answering service for those needing information from the extensive directory collection; and 4) as staff assistance point at the main card catalog.

The Section Reference Desks. Whether the request comes in by phone, mail, or over the desk, there is a serious effort made to find what is asked for in a most direct way. A telephone call to a known authority is preferable to an extended search. There is a conscious effort made to meet people's needs which involve the ability to listen and to interpret what is being asked. Help in this search for information or materials is provided in a way most useful to the questioner, either a precise quick answer from a specific source, or extensive guidance in the use of the library or one or more bibliographic tools.

General Guidelines for Desk Duty: Guidelines for Handling General Inquiries

THE BERKELEY PUBLIC LIBRARY
(Berkeley, California)

GENERAL REFERENCE SERVICE

Reference Interview. Try to determine exactly what the patron wants to know before starting to search. In many cases the original question is too general and must be refined by additional questioning of the patron. Determine patron's time frame and depth of information needed. Establish rapport with patron, restate the question in other words to encourage the patron to supply any pertinent information lacking or unclear in the original question.

Verification of Reference Questions. In answering reference questions, always verify answers and cite a source. Never answer off the top of your head.

Cooperative Reference work. If stumped—ASK another Staff

member. Sometimes our best resource is the pooled knowledge of Reference Staff members.

Desk Procedures. Please clear your desk area of materials used before going off desk.

BIRMINGHAM PUBLIC LIBRARY
(Birmingham, Alabama)

REFERENCE SERVICE INSTRUCTIONS

Each public service librarian shares an equal responsibility to supply library users with the information they are seeking. It is the responsibility of the staff in charge at any given time to see that information needs are fulfilled.

The Policy is intended to provide standard service throughout the Library, so that a patron going from one department to another has a reasonable idea of what to expect in terms of types of service and attitudes of the staff.

Because Library users who have come in person to the Library have expended a special time, effort, and interest in seeking information, it is the policy of the Library to aid these persons first and to give them priority over Library users who telephone for information or, of course, those who write for information.

Guidelines for Handling Inquiries in Person

Some general guidelines for assisting people who have come to the Library are as follows:

1. When the desk is open, staff at the Information Desk on the first floor will ask patrons who come into the Library if they would like assistance. Ask once to help a patron who comes into your department.
2. Generally, each staff member will handle reference service to patrons who approach him or her. However, before determining that the Library does not have the information the user requires, a staff member will consult with another staff member on the request.

3. A staff member should not refer a patron to another department or extension before checking sources in his or her own department; *OR* before determining that there is a particular source, tool, or section of the Library which will probably satisfy the patron, *OR* which will provide more efficient service.
4. If information is not available in the Birmingham Public Library, the inquiry can be handled through acquisition of needed material, referral to Interlibrary Loans, or by referral to other organizations, libraries, or agencies.

PUBLIC LIBRARY OF CHARLOTTE & MECKLENBURG COUNTY, INC.
(Charlotte, North Carolina)

ASSUMING RESPONSIBILITY IN REFERENCE DUTIES

The Reference Librarian taking the request normally does the searching and answering. Although he does take into consideration the special knowledge of all the other librarians, he does not seek undue help from his cohorts. If at the end of the day a question remains unanswered and the Reference Librarian will not be present the next day, or in other instances where the Librarian taking the question is prevented from concluding the search, he may ask another Reference Librarian to answer the query, relating research he has already made.

Patrons may be directed to the card catalog and to given areas of shelving *only* as an interim measure until the Reference Librarian can give personal assistance.

Questions are answered as completely as possible (sources and dates given especially in regard to statistics and biographical data) without overwhelming the patron with material.

CHICAGO PUBLIC LIBRARY
(Chicago, Illinois)

SERVICE TO THE PUBLIC

General Policies

In order to give the most accurate and authoritative answers, staff members should always quote from published sources and should never make personal recommendations, evaluations, or interpretations. The title and date of the source used should always be cited.

If a question cannot be answered, other appropriate staff members should be consulted. When the Library's resources have been exhausted, the user should be referred to another information source or library.

Users of The Chicago Public Library have the right to expect that any transactions with the Library will be kept confidential.

In-Person Policies

Service to the public comes before any other work, such as filing, etc., when staff is stationed at a public service desk. Staff should be alert to the needs of users even while doing other work and be ready to offer asistance even before it is requested. Users of The Chicago Public Library should be made to feel welcome. Eye contact with a smile can help convey a friendly attitude indicating the staff's desire to assist. Staff should always help users in the order of their arrival. One way to do this is to ask, "Who's next?"

Users whose questions or projects involve research should be introduced to library resources which could be helpful to them. It is best to take a user to these sources and explain their use slowly and patiently.

Indentification—Everyone is welcome to use the materials of The Chicago Public Library. However, for security reasons, and so that the whereabouts of key materials can be determined immediately when necessary, library users may sometimes be required to provide valid identification.

THE DAYTON AND MONTGOMERY COUNTY PUBLIC LIBRARY
(Dayton, Ohio)

Up to one hour may ordinarily be spent on a reference question. If the situation warrants, the reference librarian may spend more time on the question during special off-desk hours. Remember that there is usually an answer to questions or a solution to problems. Check all sources thoroughly and always be sure to consult a senior librarian or the division head before admitting defeat. Do not ever tell a patron "No" without asking others for help and suggestions.

In this same vein, the reference librarian should be aware of the material in other divisions. It is sometimes necessary to refer one question to all three subject divisions. The reference worksheet makes provisions for this sort of situation; so do not overlook the possibility of making a referral.

Be sure to give the source in answering reference questions. It is not the library or the librarian that should be quoted but the original source with complete citation that constitutes the authority for the answer.

DUNEDIN PUBLIC LIBRARY
(Dunedin, Florida)

Prompt reporting at the Information Desk for duty is essential. All personal needs should be taken care of before reporting. The staff member being relieved relays any matters of importance and points out patrons who may need further help, what resources have been consulted, etc. Any materials being held at the desk will be explained. Current school assignments are relayed.

The reference staff member will entertain all questions coming to him and make a whole-hearted attempt to satisfy fully with the most accurate information possible. If time does not permit a complete solution, he will follow through within 24 hours with the information telephoned to the patron or the patron requested to return to the Library for the information or materials. If an answer cannot be found the patron is to be so advised with suggestions as to where it might be found; another library, be specific; interlibrary loan, offer to make one if the patron holds a library card; Federal Information Bureau; County Court Houses; etc.

If the desk in not busy the carousels can be checked for misplaced periodicals, new periodicals can be checked for articles of current interest for the vertical file and to spot trends and to fill in retrospec- tive gaps. Bibliographies and gift books can be checked against the library's holdings. Verification of titles can be made. However, the patron must never be ignored or sacrificed for any reason.

While working on a question away from the Information Desk, the staff member is alert to notice patrons who may be waiting at the desk for help.

If the workload on the floor becomes too heavy, another staff member should be telephoned for temporary assistance.

If the reference staff member on the desk is unable to determine a source or location for information and thinks there may be an answer in the Library or in the community she should contact the Head of Information Services first. If the Head of Information Services is not available, the Assistant Reference Librarian should be consulted, then other reference staff members. The patron's name and tele- phone number should be recorded if there is the slightest doubt more information could be helpful. The telephone number should be re- peated to the patron to insure its correctness. If the patron seems uncertain about the information, if the reference staff member does not understand the question or know the field of inquiry, the Head of Information Services, then her assistant, then other reference staff members should be consulted. Again, if any doubt remains, the patron's name and telephone number should be recorded.

A notebook is kept in the Information Desk for notations about needed materials or subject areas not adequately covered. The refer- ence staff member should be diligent in noting needs, reading the notes of other staff members, and sharing information on sources the others may not have thought of.

Knowledge of current events, national as well as local, is an obliga- tion of the Reference Staff.

The Reference Staff is expected to be familiar with cataloging procedures and variations.

The Reference Staff is urged when possible to guide patrons to materials rather than give oral direction.

Forms and instructions for their use are available at the Circula- tion Desk for patrons making a strong objection to specific materials included in or excluded from the collections. These forms are for persons with the serious intent of reversing a library decision.

When the staff member on the desk is relieved from duty, he should check to be sure that reference books not in use have been returned to their shelves and that other materials not in use have been placed for re-shelving. The reference area should be tidy.

INGLEWOOD PUBLIC LIBRARY
(Inglewood, California)

A large part of reference service consists of interpreting the library's resources to the user. This includes the general collection as well as the reference works. The depth to which a reference librarian will be able to interpret the Library's holdings in any specific subject area will depend upon the librarian's knowledge of the subject. The more knowledgeable a librarian is in a subject area the more extensive the assistance should be. However, the librarian should use discretion when interpreting the meaning of a work to the patron.

Interpreting the collection, in this respect, means advising the user of the Library's holdings in a subject area and assessing an individual work in relationship to the other works available in the same area. This will include directing the patron to the most appropriate format for the information he seeks, whether this is a monograph, periodical, encyclopedia, etc.; assessing the difficulty and comprehensiveness of a work and comparing it to other works on the same subject for ease of use and information provided; and determining the location within the collection of a specific type of information.

When information is provided on any subject, including the most common knowledge, the reference source for this information should always be cited. The reference librarian should never provide information "off the top of his head" without citing an authority.

Consistency in answers is also important. While many factors may affect the amount of information required to answer a patron's inquiry, every effort should be made to be as consistent as possible in the quality and quantity of the service given. Understandably, during busy periods the reference librarian will not be able to spend as much time with each patron, and the information given may not be as extensive as it might be at another time. However, the information should be accurate and the appropriate sources cited. It is also helpful for the reference librarian to suggest the patron return at a less busy time for additional information.

Of course, any business not included at the end of a reference librarian's tour of duty at the reference desk is passed on to the librarian coming on to serve at the desk. The patron should never be abandoned in the midst of a search for information because the reference librarian is going off duty. If there is to be a change of librarians assisting a patron, the patron should be advised of this by the first librarian.

In answering a patron's request for information as many resources within the Library as needed should be utilized, as should resources within the larger community when necessary.

THE NEW YORK PUBLIC LIBRARY, THE RESEARCH LIBRARIES
(New York, New York)

WORK WITH READERS

The librarian is expected to treat all readers with courtesy and to acknowledge their presence pleasantly and as promptly as possible. Readers with diverse interests and uneven levels of skill in using the collections bring their questions to the librarian. Attention is given to the question and not to the manner in which it is expressed. Neither the reader's nor the librarian's personal opinions and beliefs should influence the quality of service given.

A staff member answers questions about library services or, when necessary or advisable, directs readers to other units for further assistance. Care should be exercised in referring readers from one building to another. The Library often has printed forms, e.g., the address and hours of opening of the Annex, The Performing Arts Research Center, and the Schomburg Center, to supplement a verbal reply. (See Research Libraries Technical Memorandum No. 10, "Referral of Readers from One Building to Another Building.") Care should be exercised also in referring readers from one division to another.

In response to a request for ready-reference information, the librarian directs the reader to materials at hand that are likely to contain the information needed. When the information is not available on shelves nearby, the librarian suggests bibliographical aids that are likely to lead to the desired answer. The aids might consist of card and printed catalogs, periodical indexes, abstracting services, bibliographies, or special files of information. To help the reader in the use of The Research Libraries' catalogs and other aids, the librarian suggests subject headings, gives examples of pertinent entries and explains the arrangement of some of the more difficult sources of information. If the reader reports that he is having difficulty in his search, the librarian gives further assistance. When the librarian cannot provide other suggestions for supplying the desired information, he consults with a more experienced librarian or supervisor.

The extent of assistance given to an individual reader is a matter of judgment and is dependent upon the time the librarian can spend without being unfair to other readers or staff members. The Library's main endeavor is to provide and direct readers to sources of information and only incidentally to provide the information itself.

Since The Research Libraries are part of a network, formally or informally organized, of sources of information linking the city, state and nation, it is the librarian's responsibility to direct readers to sources outside the Library when its holdings have not met their requirements.

Service to readers is usually anonymous. Since each staff member works only part of the time the Library is open, searching for a particular staff member upon the request of a reader takes time that could be better spent with readers. A librarian may regret having given his name when he is asked over the telephone or in a letter to perform a service that is beyond the call of duty. If a reader wishes to make a complaint, however, the staff member gives his name in accordance with the procedure contained in Research Libraries Technical Memorandum No. 4, "Complaints of Readers."

THE FREE LIBRARY OF PHILADELPHIA
(Philadelphia, Pennsylvania)

RESOURCES: ENVIRONMENT

The reference transaction should be conducted in an atmosphere of quiet, convenience, and comfort so that the maximum interplay between the reader, the librarian, and the resources can take place. Reference interviews, whether in person or on the telephone, should be conducted with as few distractions as possible.

Proper attention should be paid to the optimum use of lighting; ventilation and temperature and lighting should be easily controlled. Sufficient space should be provided for laying out materials pertinent to the reference interview; convenient and ample shelving for books and periodicals most used in answering reference questions should also be provided. Furniture should be arranged in an attractive and functional manner. Ample storage space should be set aside for non-book materials and equipment which can serve to answer reference questions.

The telephone system should facilitate rather than complicate reference transactions. Telecommunications equipment should make effective contact between all parts of the system possible and provide proper facilities for transferring calls from one agency to another. Telephones and computer terminals should be located where they will cause a minimum of distraction to patrons.

These factors are to be considered not only in planning new agencies but also in reconstructing and rehabilitating older ones. The ideal may be impossible to achieve immediately but adaptation and replanning of present facilities should bring them closer to the desired standards.

ORLANDO PUBLIC LIBRARY
(Orlando, Florida)

TYPES OF SERVICE PROVIDED BY REFERENCE STAFF

Information, direction, location

Give patrons clear instructions as to location of departments and facilities. Accompany patron to specific location in department or library when possible and provide as much assistance as needed in locating appropriate materials.

Reference Services

Utilize all possible sources, including staff, other libraries and collections within the system, outside resources and agencies—via telephone, interlibrary loan, TWX, or other forms of communication. Always identify yourself by name and department or library when referring a question. Encourage direct dialogue between patron and other staff member when appropriate.

Walk-in Service

Respond as soon as possible with the answer and/or suggested sources. When materials on subject are located in more than one area of library, refer patrons to all other departments involved, beginning with the one containing the most material. Provide as much assistance to walk-in patrons as to phone patrons.

Unanswered Questions

Staff should record question, patron's name and phone number, and sources checked. Note if information will be useful if supplied at a later date. Department heads will review these unanswered questions to consider further sources and to evaluate for retention. The questions retained will be reviewed periodically as new tools and resources become available. Records of unanswered questions are useful in demonstrating tools with which staff are unfamiliar and in revealing deficiencies in the collection.

Readers Advisory Service

Staff should apply their familiarity with materials in their subject areas to aid patrons in selection of materials most suitable to their needs.

SAN DIEGO PUBLIC LIBRARY
(San Diego, California)

LENGTH OF SEARCH

The search for the answer to a question ceases when the answer is found or the resources of the library have been exhausted. The Main Building Subject Department Head, or designee—usually the subject specialist, or division head—will determine whether the resources of the library have been exhausted.

If the patron wishes the library to search further, the Subject Department head will initiate such action as is necessary through Interlibrary Loan and the Bibliographical Center or by referral to other libraries or outside agencies.

General Guidelines for Desk Duty: Guidelines for Handling Problem Inquiries— School Questions

ANN ARBOR PUBLIC LIBRARY
(Ann Arbor, Michigan)

Students are included in the kinds of users served by the Department, but extensive help on homework assignments will not be provided while other library users are waiting for service.

Because homework assignments are usually made for the very purpose of teaching students the process of finding information, the Department sees as its primary role the instruction in the use of library tools and methodology, rather than the provision of the "answers."

THE BERKELEY PUBLIC LIBRARY
(Berkeley, California)

Homework questions. Reference Staff will guide patron to sources of information. By telephone, may be answered if very brief—otherwise suggest that patron come to the library.

PUBLIC LIBRARY OF CHARLOTTE & MECKLENBURG COUNTY, INC.
(Charlotte, North Carolina)

Homework should not be done for students over the telephone but simple, short answers that may be read quickly from sources at hand may be given for non-research questions.

CHICAGO PUBLIC LIBRARY
(Chicago, Illinois)

Students should receive the same service as anyone else according to the general guidelines for service. If there seems to be a problem about a class assignment, the school name should be taken together with the instructor's name and assignment. The person in charge will follow up on it in order to establish a communications link with the instructor.

THE DAYTON AND MONTGOMERY COUNTY PUBLIC LIBRARY
(Dayton, Ohio)

School assignments are made to help the student learn. The student should be invited to come into the library or make use of the nearest branch if the question is one which will involve more than a simple, quickly determined fact. See the policy on telephone questions in general.

In the case of fact questions such as the names of officers, spelling a word, date of an event, etc., we will answer the question unless it appears that the assignment was given specifically to train the student to use reference materials. Explanation should be made to the student or parent who calls that the major purpose of school assignments is training in the use of the library. Information furnished directly by a librarian benefits the student only if the student learns where such information is available. No learning takes place when a question for a student is answered by telephone without the student's use of the reference books.

In the case of mass assignments or other circumstances which warrant, form 3420 may be used. These forms are to be used only in those cases in which the branch librarians, division head, or any senior staff member on duty is positive that all resources have been exhausted and the situation is one which calls for use of the notification. In some cases a direct visit or telephone call to the teacher might be the best way to handle mass assignments.

Under no circumstances should the patron be told bluntly or hastily that we do not answer school questions but instead an explanation should be given.

DENVER PUBLIC LIBRARY
(Denver, Colorado)

STUDENT ASSIGNMENTS

Student assignments often present considerable difficulty due to a lack of material of the proper level, lack of material on the subject assigned, or lack of sufficient quantities of material to supply the demand from students. If the librarian is unable to find proper material, the division head, subject specialist, or branch head should fill out Form DPL 41 so that the student may give it to his instructor.

The Young Adult and/or Children's Coordinator(s) should be notified whenever it appears to agency personnel that an *"en masse"* assignment has been made. The Coordinators are authorized to notify the approriate school authorities of this breach of DPL/DPS Council policy so that an amicable solution can be effected.

For a student request, the DPL does not locate the same material in several forms, e.g., newspaper, book, periodical, encyclopedia, pamphlet and microform.

KNOXVILLE-KNOX COUNTY PUBLIC LIBRARY
(Knoxville, Tennessee)

School homework questions *are* answered over the telephone—as many as three quick answer questions. Do not do extensive research for school assignments or read long passages over the telephone.

LOUISVILLE FREE PUBLIC LIBRARY
(Louisville, Kentucky)

When students approach the library for assistance, they should be accorded the same service as everyone else.

MEMPHIS PUBLIC LIBRARY
(Memphis, Tennessee)

Answer student questions on the telephone and in the library but whenever possible, instruct the student in the use of library materials, so that the student will become familiar with the library and learn to use his own library skills in doing school work.

THE NEW YORK PUBLIC LIBRARY,
THE RESEARCH LIBRARIES
(New York, New York)

Do not help a student below the college level.

ORLANDO PUBLIC LIBRARY
(Orlando, FLorida)

Staff does not collect non-circulating material for term papers, or other school assignments.

THE FREE LIBRARY OF PHILADELPHIA
(Philadelphia, Pennsylvania)

School questions should be answered by telephone if they can be answered quickly from a known source, without a lengthy search. If a school question does not fall into the "ready reference" category, the student or his parent should be told to come to the library, where the librarian will point out likely sources and help with their use.

General Guidelines for Desk Duty: Guidelines for Handling Problem Inquiries — Puzzle, Contest, Quiz Questions

PUBLIC LIBRARY OF CHARLOTTE & MECKLENBURG COUNTY, INC.
(Charlotte, North Carolina)

Contest questions are not answered but the patron is directed to sources from which he may seek his answer.

CHICAGO PUBLIC LIBRARY
(Chicago, Illinois)

Contests. The Library invites users to search their own answers because of the volume of questions of this type and the chance for misinterpretation.

THE DAYTON AND MONTGOMERY COUNTY
PUBLIC LIBRARY
(Dayton, Ohio)

Quiz Programs. If the reference librarian can find the answer immediately, it will be given to the person over the telephone. Otherwise, the patron should be invited to come to the library where the books which are available may be used. We will not tie up telephone lines answering quiz questions, but will make every effort to preserve the good will of the quiz public.

DENVER PUBLIC LIBRARY
(Denver, Colorado)

Contest Questions. Simple, factual contest questions are answered as are other questions. Some contest questions are tricky and might have more than one answer which seems to be correct. The library takes no responsibility to guarantee that this is the correct answer. The staff should refuse to conduct lengthy searches, interpret contest rules or do work which should be done by patrons, such as writing paragraphs. Patrons should always be invited to do their own searching.

DUNEDIN PUBLIC LIBRARY
(Dunedin, Florida)

Questions for exams, quizzes and puzzles are not answered directly. Information is given as to likely sources for the answers.

KNOXVILLE-KNOX COUNTY PUBLIC LIBRARY
(Knoxville, Tennessee)

Do not knowingly work on contest questions or crossword puzzles.

LOUISVILLE FREE PUBLIC LIBRARY
(Louisville, Kentucky)

Known Contest Questions. If these questions fall within the scope of the library's holdings and can be answered as a quick fact, they may be answered by phone. If not, the user should be invited to search the answers so he may take the responsibility of misinterpretation.

THE NEW YORK PUBLIC LIBRARY,
THE RESEARCH LIBRARIES
(New York, New York)

Do not help with a contest question.

ORLANDO PUBLIC LIBRARY
(Orlando, Florida)

Staff does not knowingly do research on contest questions.

THE FREE LIBRARY OF PHILADELPHIA
(Philadelphia, Pennsylvania)

Puzzle Questions should be answered by telephone if they can be answered quickly from a known source, without a lengthy search. If the question does not fall into the "ready reference" category, the patron should be told to come to the library, where the librarian will point out likely sources and help with their use. It is recommended that the answer to a puzzle question, as soon as it is found, be posted near the telephone on the department's public service desk.

General Guidelines for Desk Duty: Guidelines for Handling Problem Inquiries— Legal and Medical Questions

THE BERKELEY PUBLIC LIBRARY
(Berkeley, California)

Medical questions. Factual information can be provided from medical dictionaries and books, but questions that involve interpretation and opinion cannot be answered.

Legal questions. Citations from codes can be given, and other legal resources may be suggested, but legal advice and/or explanations cannot be offered.

PUBLIC LIBRARY OF CHARLOTTE & MECKLENBURG COUNTY, INC.
(Charlotte, North Carolina)

Medical and legal questions may not be answered, though definitions and direct quotations may be read, *never* interpreted. The Library seeks to maintain good laymen's libraries in both fields and these materials should be pointed out to the patron in the Library, but conclusions must not be drawn nor opinions stated, nor advice given, except advising the patron to consult a doctor or lawyer.

CHICAGO PUBLIC LIBRARY
(Chicago, Illinois)

Legal Information. If a user calls with a specific citation, a law, if not lengthy, will be read over the telephone. Legal searches or interpretations will not be made. If additional information is needed, the user should consult the Library's holdings or be referred to another source.

Medical Information. Brief definitions and descriptions can be given from published sources such as medical and/or drug dictionaries. These sources should be quoted verbatim with absolutely no interpretation on the librarian's part. If more information is required, users should examine the Library's collection or be referred to another source.

DENVER PUBLIC LIBRARY
(Denver, Colorado)

Medical and Legal Questions. The Library does not attempt to answer medical or legal questions which seek to obtain advice in the areas of law, medicine, copyrights, and patents. Material and guidance are made available to the patron when possible. The patron may be referred to the Colorado Supreme Court Library or the Denver General Hospital Library or the University of Colorado Medical Center Library.

DUNEDIN PUBLIC LIBRARY
(Dunedin, Florida)

The Reference Staff must not interpret legal or medical materials.

INGLEWOOD PUBLIC LIBRARY
(Inglewood, California)

Although every effort should be made to answer all questions, there are some areas which are better left to the experts in the field. Generally, these are considered to be questions requesting legal, medical, or consumer advice. Under no circumstances should a reference librarian offer advice in these areas no matter how commonplace the knowledge seems to be. The patron should be directed to the appropriate reference sources and assistance in the use of these, if necessary, until the needed information is secured. If this is not available within the Library's collection, the patron should be directed to a more specialized library in the area or advised to consult a professional in the field, e.g., a lawyer or doctor. Again, no recommendation for a specific person should be given in this referral, but rather, a general suggestion should be made.

LOUISVILLE FREE PUBLIC LIBRARY
(Louisville, Kentucky)

Legal Information. If information can be found in printed sources, it is provided. However, complicated legal searches will not be made nor will interpretations of legal matters be given.

Two referral sources are: Lawyers Reference Service—fees are charged for time spent with a lawyer; and Louisville Legal Aid Society—this agency provides many types of legal services to persons whose income is below the federally set poverty line.

Medical Information. Brief definitions and descriptions can be given from published sources such as medical and/or drug dictionaries. These sources should be quoted verbatim with absolutely no interpretation on the librarian's part. If more information is required, users should examine the library's collection or be referred to another source.

MEMPHIS PUBLIC LIBRARY
(Memphis, Tennessee)

Medical and legal questions. The patron can be told if the branch or department has information available, but the patron should come to the library to use the materials himself.
Guide but do not try to interpret medical or legal answers.

THE NEW YORK PUBLIC LIBRARY, THE RESEARCH LIBRARIES
(New York, New York)

Staff members are not expected:
—to provide medical information for the treatment of an ailment or disease.
—to give legal interpretations.

ORLANDO PUBLIC LIBRARY
(Orlando, Florida)

LIMITATIONS OF SERVICE

The staff does not answer questions which require a value judgement or interpretation by reference staff. Because of possible misinterpretation of material by either patron or staff, information should not be given over the telephone from law books, medical books, consumer reports, or similar types of materials.

THE FREE LIBRARY OF PHILADELPHIA
(Philadelphia, Pennsylvania)

Legal questions. The most a librarian may legally do for a patron is to show the patron the text of a requested law or give him a book dealing with the subject in question. Law should not be interpreted to the reader either on the telephone or in the library. It is best in this type of question to encourage the patron to come to the library and examine the law. The librarian may also suggest the service of the Charles Klein Law Library at Temple University and the Theodore F. Jenkins Law Library. For legal services, the Lawyer Reference Service will answer simple questions over the telephone and set up appointments with lawyers when needed. Community Legal Services offers free legal services to people who are eligible because of low income.

Medical information. The most a librarian should do for a patron who wants medical information is to answer questions requiring a simple definition. For the patron who is in the library and is looking for medical information, the librarian may give him any available general information dealing with his problem. The librarian should not give medical advice or give information over the telephone about dosage or prescription of drugs. For more technical medical questions when necessary material is not available, the patron may be referred to the College of Physicians of Philadelphia Library. The Health and Welfare Council provides information and referral sevice. Patrons can be referred to Philadelphia City Health Centers 2, 3, 4, 5, 6, 10 and Fairmount to join the Family Medical Care Program. The Philadelphia County Medical Society will provide names of primary care physicians and refer callers to organizations for names of specialists. Patrons calling for emergency medical advice should be referred to the nearest hospital, the police or the Poison Information Center. These telephone numbers should be posted prominently in every branch and Central public service department.

ST. LOUIS PUBLIC LIBRARY
(St. Louis, Missouri)

Medical advice is not given. Statements are not made to indicate whether or not a disease may be fatal. Information about drugs from the *Physicians Desk Reference* will not be made, except when the exact name of the drug is known. Identification will not be made from a physical description alone.

The librarian does not interpret bills, laws, or statistics.

SAN DIEGO PUBLIC LIBRARY
(San Diego, California)

There is no attempt to interpret information of any kind which requires the specialized skill of a professional person. Reference assistance in fields such as law and medicine is given to the extent that sources of information are suggested when such sources are available.

General Guidelines for Desk Duty: Guidelines for Handling Problem Inquiries — Personal Recommendations and Appraisals

ANN ARBOR PUBLIC LIBRARY
(Ann Arbor, Michigan)

Book recommendations. While the Department cannot recommend to patrons specific titles for purchase, guidance in locating reviews, selected lists and other means of evaluation will be provided.

CHICAGO PUBLIC LIBRARY
(Chicago, Illinois)

Appraisals. Although appraisals cannot be made, Library staff can provide current market value information from printed sources when available, if the user has specific information. Staff must be sure to qualify their quotations by pointing out that value information is dependent on condition of the item and other factors.

DUNEDIN PUBLIC LIBRARY
(Dunedin, Florida)

Encyclopedia and Dictionary Evaluation. Enquiring patrons are shown or read specific reviews of the works in question. It is often helpful for a librarian to indicate from professional experience the strong or weak points of a particular title.

Old Books for Evaluation or Sale. Patrons who have books for sale are asked to contact a used book dealer. The patron is shown how to use the Used Book Price Guide, Bookman's Price Index, Van Allen Bradley, etc., to determine a value for himself. It would be extremely unusual for the Dunedin Public Library to purchase a book from a patron.

KINGSPORT PUBLIC LIBRARY
(Kingsport, Tennessee)

RECOMMENDATIONS OF REFERENCE BOOKS TO PATRONS

Caution should be exercised by all staff members whenever patrons ask for recommendations of reference and/or subscription books. Opinions may be given on the reputation of a *specific* work, only if the staff member is familiar enough with that work to do so, and only if the staff member supports the opinion with reviews or comments from standard reference sources, such as *Booklist, Choice,* etc. It is the responsibility of the Reference Department to make readily available current reviewing sources, especially for items of proven high demand, such as dictionairies and encyclopedias. Patrons should always be urged to inspect an actual copy of a work in order to insure that the work meets their own individual needs and expectations.

Specific answers to specific questions about reference and/or subscription books should be provided to patrons in the library or over the phone, if the answers can be found in printed sources. Prices should *not* be quoted for subscription books, since these vary widely, depending upon bindings, time payments, editions, etc. More accurate price information can be provided by the subscription agents, a list of which should be maintained by the Library.

LOUISVILLE FREE PUBLIC LIBRARY
(Louisville, Kentucky)

Book Appraisals. The library is not equipped with experts for making appraisals of used and rare books or book collections. Single titles with full information can be checked through American Book Prices Current for auction prices. But because of the influencing factors such as exact date of publication, condition and edition, users are invited to bring the book(s) (or their listing of same) to the library in order to search standard or special sources for possible listings for their titles. Users are also provided commercial directories of used-book dealers.

Appraisals are also not made on books given to the library. The user indicates the value to him if an acknowledgement for tax purposes is desired.

Encyclopedias—Evaluation. No recommendations or personal opinions regarding encyclopedias are given to the public. Reviews and authoritative sources which discuss encyclopedias are given to user to read.

MEMPHIS PUBLIC LIBRARY
(Memphis, Tennessee)

Appraisals (Example: book values, art values). Refer the patron to materials within the collection and/or agencies which do make appraisals.

NEW ORLEANS PUBLIC LIBRARY
(New Orleans, Louisiana)

Recommendations. Personal opinion or recommendations (such as to encyclopedias, book stores, binderies, doctors, lawyers, etc.) are not given to patrons. Sources such as "Consumers' Reports," "Subscription Books Bulletin," "Directory of Medical Specialists," etc., are given to the patron for his own evaluation. Staff should refer the patron to the "Yellow Pages" of the phone directory except for items which they know to be exclusively available at one source.

THE NEW YORK PUBLIC LIBRARY,
THE RESEARCH LIBRARIES
(New York, New York)

Do not give a personal appraisal of the monetary value of a reader's personal material or authenticate a book, manuscript, or drawing, etc. An attempt is made, if requested, to guide the reader in the identification and authentication of material through the consultation of printed sources of information.

THE FREE LIBRARY OF PHILADELPHIA
(Philadelphia, Pennsylvania)

Encyclopedias and dictionaries. Staff members are frequently asked to recommend a specific encyclopedia or dictionary for purchase. Patrons should be directed to *Encyclopedia Buying Guide, Dictionary Buying Guide, Booklist* and other reputable reviewing media. Patrons should be encouraged to come to the library to examine encyclopedias and dictionaries under consideration. Because librarians have experience in working with these reference tools, they may discuss them with patrons, but should refrain from making specific recommendations.

ST. LOUIS PUBLIC LIBRARY
(St. Louis, Missouri)

The Librarian:
—Does not give appraisals.
—Does not quote prices on old books, although indication of whether or not such an item has appeared on the market in the past will be given.
—Will not attempt to search for information concerning incompletely described volumes.
—Will not act as an agency of information concerning patrons involved in trading, buying, or selling of items.

SAN DIEGO PUBLIC LIBRARY
(San Diego, California)

Appraisal of old books, manuscripts, paintings, antiques, etc., is the field of dealers and experts. The library provides resources such as published listings of prices paid at auction and reference works in these subject fields along with assistance in their use.

General Guidelines for Desk Duty: Guidelines for Handling Problem Inquiries— Genealogical Questions

ANN ARBOR PUBLIC LIBRARY
(Ann Arbor, Michigan)

Genealogical questions. The Department maintains a basic collection of local history and general genealogical materials. Staff members will provide general assistance in the methodology of genealogical research, guidance in locating items in the collection, and help in using the resources of interlibrary loan, but cannot engage in genealogical research for individuals. Because of the special research techniques required and the complexity of these questions, the burden for solving an individual's genealogical problems is his/her responsibility. Individuals will be referred to such specialized collections as the Bentley Historical Library, the State Library of Michigan and the Burton Historical Collection of the Detroit Public Library when the library's resources are exhausted.

DUNEDIN PUBLIC LIBRARY
(Dunedin, Florida)

Genealogical questions are answered in the areas of what is available in this library or on inter-library loan and on how to use our volumes. In the future we hope to have volunteers and workshops to provide more help. The Head of Information Services is available to help with genealogical questions.

KINGSPORT PUBLIC LIBRARY
(Kingsport, Tennessee)

Genealogical Research. The Kingsport Public Library, through its Palmer Regional History Collection, serves library patrons by its efforts to be a local and regional, historical and genealogical research collection. Because of the present limits of both space and staff, however, the Palmer Collection cannot serve as a complete depository for regional history and genealogy, nor can it fully support all levels of research. Instead, the Palmer Regional History Collection must be viewed as a vital part of a greater network of area history and genealogy depositories, which by means of coordinated services and collection development can provide a high level of service to patrons.

The staff of the Kingsport Public Library should assist users of the Palmer Collection in identifying publications and sources which relate to the subject areas of their research chiefly by explaining the use of indexes and other bibliographic guides. The staff of the library should *not* undertake research in family history or heraldry, since to do such work satisfactorily would require more time and staff than are currently available. Library staff should not normally digest information for the patron or undertake elaborate searches for details in books about local history, genealogies, newspapers, microfilmed records, etc. These types of searches usually require the services of a professional genealogist or heraldic researcher and are normally undertaken by these persons for a fee.

KNOXVILLE-KNOX COUNTY PUBLIC LIBRARY
(Knoxville, Tennessee)

If a question concerning local history or genealogy cannot be answered easily, the patron should be referred to the McClung Room. Similarly, a question about children's literature should be referred to the Children's Room.

NEW ORLEANS PUBLIC LIBRARY
(New Orleans, Louisiana)

Specialized research such as genealogical research is to be done by patrons. Leaflets, brochures, and booklists on appropriate topics which have been prepared by N.O.P.L. staff should be offered as guides to patrons.

THE FREE LIBRARY OF PHILADELPHIA
(Philadelphia, Pennsylvania)

Genealogical questions. The Library does not undertake family history searches. Librarians can instruct patrons in the use of reference works in genealogy and local history. Correspondence in this subject area should be limited in replies to factual information queries related to Philadelphia area history and located in basic sources. Patrons may be referred to other sources of data (Federal Records Centers, genealogical societies, state vital records sources, etc.) as appropriate.

ST. LOUIS PUBLIC LIBRARY
(St. Louis, Missouri)

Genealogies will not be read, although an indication of whether or not a requested one appears in an index will be given. Only three items per call will be checked in the "names" section of current city and surburban directories.

General Guidelines for Desk Duty: Guidelines for Handling Problem Inquiries— Consumer Information

THE BERKELEY PUBLIC LIBRARY
(Berkeley, California)

Consumer information. The Reference Staff can provide published material on various products or indicate to the patron where the information may be found. Recommendations and/or value judgements cannot be made for any item. Product ratings are not given over the telephone. The Consumer Index may be checked and the patron told if recent articles are available on the subject. The exception: brief ratings may be given on the telephone for handicapped or elderly patrons.

PUBLIC LIBRARY OF CHARLOTTE
& MECKLENBURG COUNTY, INC.
(Charlotte, North Carolina)

Consumer information sources are given to the patron in the Library but may not be quoted by telephone because of our being, incorrectly, cited for advertising.

CHICAGO PUBLIC LIBRARY
(Chicago, Illinois)

Consumer Information. Product ratings and evaluations will be given when a current printed source is readily available for direct quotation within the general time parameters. Otherwise, if the user calls, staff will check briefly to see if information is available and give the citation to the caller.

DENVER PUBLIC LIBRARY
(Denver, Colorado)

Consumer Questions. The library provides material for patron's use in making his own evaluation of books or other products. The librarian may read specific information requested from the various consumer guides, but will make no recommendations.

LOUISVILLE FREE PUBLIC LIBRARY
(Louisville, Kentucky)

Consumer information. Product ratings and evaluations may be given by phone when a current printed source is readily available and if the answer required is not too lengthy. Otherwise a citation is given.

THE FREE LIBRARY OF PHILADELPHIA
(Philadelphia, Pennsylvania)

Consumer reporting services. In answering these requests by telephone, staff members should tell patrons if a product has been covered by one of the consumer service magazines. If time permits, librarians may read briefly from these magazines, specifying models and stating sources. Interpretations of the articles should not be given, and patrons should be encouraged to come to the library to read the material themselves.

General Guidelines for Desk Duty: Behavior and Attitudes

ANN ARBOR PUBLIC LIBRARY
(Ann Arbor, Michigan)

Staff members on desk duty should always try to maintain an approachable manner, in spite of whatever desk work they may have, and always be prepared to go with the patron to the card catalog and/or shelves at the slightest indication of need on the patron's part.

BIRMINGHAM PUBLIC LIBRARY
(Birmingham, Alabama)

General attitudes and approaches to providing reference service in person and over the telephone are outlined below. Specific guidelines for handling inquiries in person, inquiries over the telephone, and inquiries by mail, follow.

1. Be approachable and ask patrons if they would like assistance, especially if you are not on telephone duty.
2. Give prompt, courteous, and unbiased assistance to all patrons. In order to maintain fairness in reference service, staff should not offer their personal opinions on social issues, politics, religion, etc., to Library users.
3. Refrain from discussing questions in derogatory terms with the persons who ask them, or with other persons.
4. Treat all questions seriously and assume that all questions have answers.
5. Conduct a reference interview, but do not quiz Library users to the extent of invading their privacy.
6. Record all statistics or measures of reference service at the request and discretion of the Head of the Department.
7. Direct dissatisfied users to the Head of the Department.

CLEVELAND PUBLIC LIBRARY
(Cleveland, Ohio)

GUIDELINES FOR QUALITY REFERENCE SERVICE

Good Manners—
1. Pleasant attitudes; a smile never hurts and may be all you have time for.
2. Friendly, interested manner; the patron is a person with a problem and you are his ally not his adversary.
3. Sometimes goodwill can be conveyed by a tone of voice or a manner of speaking.
4. Do not hesitate to give the patron your name unless he is offensive in some way. A name and a face help to make the institution less impersonal. We can build goodwill on the basis of your ability.

DUNEDIN PUBLIC LIBRARY
(Dunedin, Florida)

The staff member is also alert to offer assistance to patrons who may need help but have not requested it. This is done in such a manner that the patron feels free to continue browsing if he likes or to come to the desk for aid later. One might say, "If I can be of any help, please let me know" or, more simply, "May I help you?" The patron must never feel stupid or inadequate. Libraries *are* difficult to use. Sympathize with his confusion at the numbering system and explain briefly.

The physical attitude of the staff at the Information Desk is important. One should glance up frequently, notice patrons as they walk in, smile, contact the patron by eye, lean forward, appear willing and ready to leave the desk. One should not appear preoccupied. The patron should not be interrupting the staff. Remember that the staff's primary purpose on the desk is to serve the patron.

There are times when individual patrons are irritating, inconsiderate or rude. There are also times when staff members are upset by professional or personal problems and feel their blood presure rising. The patron is not obliged to be polite. A professional attitude requires the staff member to remain polite no matter how antagonistic the patron becomes. The Director should be summoned if a situation seems to be getting out of control.

INGLEWOOD PUBLIC LIBRARY
(Inglewood, California)

Attentiveness to the public is of utmost importance, and any work of a personal or distracting nature should be avoided while serving at the reference desk. This would include reading, knitting, doing homework, etc. Personal phone calls should not be made from the reference desk, and personal calls received should be kept to a minimum. When working with the public it is helpful to remember to always be courteous, polite, and sensitive to each patron's request and the problem the patron may have had in formulating an inquiry.

KINGSPORT PUBLIC LIBRARY
(Kingsport, Tennessee)

APPROACHABILITY AND STAFFING LEVEL

It is the policy of the Kingsport Public Library to staff the Reference Desk with at least one librarian during all hours which the Library is open. Determined efforts should be made to schedule an adequate number of library staff members at the Reference Desk during those periods of identifiable high use in order to sufficiently handle the anticipated demand.

Staff members on duty at the Reference Desk should be constantly aware of how approachable they appear to library patrons. Being approachable is the first step in encouraging users to seek assistance at the Reference Desk. Patrons need to be educated to the fact that individual assistance is the primary responsibility of the staff member(s) on duty at the Reference Desk. During periods when reference use is light, staff members on duty at the Reference Desk may work on other assignments, examine new reference materials, read professional literature, etc., as long as such activities are job-oriented and do not interfere with the provision of direct personal service to patrons. Staff members must be careful not to become so engrossed in other work that they fail to notice patrons who are in need of assistance in the Reference area. Staff members on duty at the Reference Desk should periodically walk through the Reference area in order to insure their visibility and approachability to any patrons who might be in need of assistance.

Staff members on duty at the Reference Desk should make every effort to demonstrate an amiable interest in patron inquiries and a definitive willingness to assist patrons in seeking solutions to their informational problems. Since the attitude and behavior of each individual staff member goes a long way toward creating an image of the whole Reference Department, each staff member should strive to insure that the image which he or she projects is a positive one.

MEMPHIS PUBLIC LIBRARY
(Memphis, Tennessee)

GENERAL ETIQUETTE

A. Be polite, interested, helpful and prompt.

B. Being neat and well-groomed will create a good impression.

C. Watch to see if the patron appears to need help and then ask if you may be of assistance.

D. If the patron asks for guidance in using a library tool, do not just point. Take the patron to the library aid and provide any assistance needed in using the source.

E. When on the reference desk, do not appear so busy that the patron is unwilling to ask for assistance.

F. Do not chat with other staff or patrons while waiting on a patron or while a patron is waiting for help.

PROVIDENCE PUBLIC LIBRARY
(Providence, Rhode Island)

Libraries and many librarians make some people feel uncomfortable. This emotional response in people of all ages and backgrounds can be a serious barrier to usability. Lack of familiarity with libraries and their function, feelings of personal insecurity in strange places, doubts that the request merits "serious" attention, and awe of the librarian can manifest themselves in a number of ways including a reluctance to seek help and a difficulty in articulating the specific need. Again the staff member at point of contact is alert to these factors and uses his skills to make the individual more comfortable — and thus the library more usable.

People are human, and since moods and personalities vary, there will undoubtedly be times when individual patrons are irritating, inconsiderate, or rude. There are indeed also times when individual staff members are harrassed by professional or personal problems and feel their emotions reaching the pressure point. It is obvious, of course, that while the patron is obliged to be polite only by the rules of natural courtesy—which he may not choose to follow—the staff member is obliged to maintain his professional attitude as an employee of a public service institution. Difficulties will arise, of course, and while it may not be possible to remain warm and friendly to an antagonistic patron, politeness is still in order. Too, the staff member realizes that, as in any human relationship, a number of factors are influencing both the patron's attitude and staff member's response, and a sincere attempt at communication and understanding may alleviate, if not eliminate, the problem. Often the aid of another staff member can reduce tensions in a situation which seems to be getting out of control.

Library service is public service in the finest sense of the word. As libraries and library systems expand, as technological developments extend the capabilities for and techniques of providing information, it is still the personal service the individual receives that determines his ultimate satisfaction. Some people use the library because they want to and some because they have to; many do not use it at all. An essential part of usability, then, is a warm, inviting atmosphere that will influence as many people as possible to use the library because they *want* to. Without this, the most complete, well-organized collections will remain unused despite all the outreach programs devised and promotional efforts expended. Employees in libraries large and small create that atmosphere through the friendly, helpful, concerned attitude with which they meet their public.

When staff is limited, phones ringing, patrons clamoring at the desk, and interlibrary requests piling up, the only-human staff member feels a tremendous frustration. Imbued with a desire to serve and to serve well, and unable to do so at the moment, he curses the promotional efforts and outreach programs that may have created these demands, the administration or supervisory staff responsible for personnel shortages, the public competing for his attention and his colleagues out working on special projects.

What may be forgotten here is that patrons *are* people and people are accustomed to waiting when they know there is a good reason. These same individuals wait patiently for an appointment with their doctor, for servicemen to do home repairs, and in almost any social or government agency they have had occasion to use. In other words, they *will* understand; the in-building patron will obviously be aware of the problem, and the telephone caller will understand and accept an explanation of an anticipated delay in completing his question.

General Guidelines for Desk Duty: Recording Statistics and Questions

ANN ARBOR PUBLIC LIBRARY
(Ann Arbor, Michigan)

Personnel are responsible for counting the number of questions received at their respective desks. All questions, regardless of their nature, are to be counted.

BIRMINGHAM PUBLIC LIBRARY
(Birmingham, Alabama)

DEFINITIONS

A reference transaction is defined as an information contact which involves the knowledge, use, recommendation, interpretation, or instruction in the use of one or more information sources by a member of the Library staff. Information sources include printed and non-printed materials, machine-readable data bases (including computer-assisted instruction), catalogs and other holdings records, and, through communication or referral, other libraries and institutions, and persons both inside and outside the Library. A contact that includes both reference and directional service should be reported as one reference transaction. When a staff member utilizes information gained from previous use of information sources to answer a question, report as a reference transaction even if the source is not consulted again during the transaction. Duration should not be an element in determining whether a transaction is reference or directional.

A *directional transaction* is defined as an information contact which facilitates the use of the Library in which the contact occurs and which does NOT involve the knowledge, use, recommendation, interpretation, or instruction in the use of any information sources other than those which describe that Library, such as schedules, floor plans, handbooks, policy statements. Examples of directional transactions include giving directions for locating, within the Library, staff, patrons, or physical features; lending pencils, etc.; and giving assistance of a non-bibliographic nature with machines.

PUBLIC LIBRARY OF CHARLOTTE & MECKLENBURG COUNTY, INC.
(Charlotte, North Carolina)

THREE TYPES OF QUESTIONS RECORDED STATISTICALLY

—The Ready Reference question, which is a request for information found without too much effort.

—The Reader's Advisory question, in which serious effort is extended to a patron to suggest or select books for reading or study.

—The Research question, requiring a great amount of time and effort to answer, involving the consultation and comparing of many sources, and possible combinations of materials in order to derive a satisfactory answer. The time consumed by the staff member(s) may vary from five minutes to several hours, even extend over several days, or a longer period of time.

DUNEDIN PUBLIC LIBRARY
(Dunedin, Florida)

RECORDING STATISTICS AND QUESTIONS

On the Information Desk is a daily calendar on which reference and directional statistics are noted. These are helpful for many purposes including scheduling and staffing. The staff must try to record every encounter in the following manner in order to protect the integrity of the report.

Clarification of Definitions and Instructions

An information contact is an encounter in person, by telephone, mail, or other means between a member of the reference/information staff and a user, in which information is sought or provided.

Report the Total Reference Transactions per Typical Day
A Reference Transaction is an information contact which involves the use, recommendations, interpretation, or instruction in the use of one or more information sources, or knowledge of such sources, by a member of the reference/information staff. Information sources include:
- print and nonprint materials;
- library bibliographic records, excluding circulation records;
- other libraries and institutions; and
- persons both inside and outside the library.

A question answered through utilization of information gained from previous consultation of such sources is considered a reference transaction even if the source is not consulted again.

Report the Total Directional Transactions per Typical Day.
A Directional Transaction is an informational contact which facilitates the use of the library in which the contact occurs, and its environs, and which may involve the use of sources describing that library, such as schedules, floor plans, handbooks, and policy statements. Examples of directional transactions are: (1) directions for locating facilities such as restrooms and telephones; (2) directions for locating library staff and users; (3) directions for locating materials for which the user has a call number; (4) supplying materials such as paper and pencils; and (5) assisting users with the operation of machines.

Instructions. The staff members should report each contact separately, whether or not the user has already consulted either that staff member or another on the same information need. A contact which includes both reference and directional service is one reference transaction.

The use of sources defines the nature of the transaction. Primarily the distinction lies in whether or not bibliographic information is used by the staff to answer the question. Secondarily, a source need not be bibliographic; for example, if the reference staff member uses a personal or institutional expert to assist the user, the transaction is a reference function.

The answer to a reference question has two parts: 1) identification of the source and 2) location of that source. Identification of the source and location of the source are about always based on bibliographic knowledge. Length of time is not an element in determining whether the transaction is reference or directional. A transaction that is both reference and directional is reported as the reference transaction.

The purpose of the statistical reports is to help in the conceptualization of reference work in an effort to make informed decisions on resources and their use for public service. They are used for evaluation, policy decisions, budget decisions, staffing, and scheduling.

LOUISVILLE FREE PUBLIC LIBRARY
(Louisville, Kentucky)

REPORTING STATISTICS

All main and branch library personnel whose assigned duties include provision of reference/information service should report all contacts. A staff member should report each contact separately, whether or not the user has already consulted either that staff member or another on the same information need. A contact which includes both reference and directional service is one reference transaction. Duration should not be an element in determining whether a transaction is reference or directional.

Interdepartmental requests are to be included.

Each transaction is to be recorded by a talley mark according to whether received by telephone, in person, or by mail.

MEMPHIS PUBLIC LIBRARY
(Memphis, Tennessee)

1. Information sheets are kept to record all questions.
2. The sheets must be dated and marked with the Department/ Branch name. The time period and asssstant's name are optional.
3. All reference questions should be written down.
4. Telephone requests:
   - Differentiate between telephone requests and in-person requests by putting a "T" beside the question.
   - Telephone calls will either involve information, i.e., reference questions, or miscellaneous questions. Information calls will be indicated with the "T" by the recorded question and miscellaneous questions by using a telephone miscellaneous section.

   The following diagram is a suggested form for "in-library" and "telephone" miscellaneous and periodical requests:

Misc.		Periodical requests	
T.	Lib.	T.	Lib.
𝚑𝚑𝚑 ///		/// 𝚑𝚑𝚑 //	

   - Do not keep a separate tally that simply indicates that the telephone rang.
5. Record each book requested either by author and title (particularly those not owned), or by call number. If books on a subject are requested, do not record each title provided, but simply the subject.
6. Requests for non-book materials are recorded by title, author, call number, composer, artist, etc.
7. If the material is not owned in the Department/Branch, or a question cannot be answered, indicate this with a zero.
8. If the material requested is not owned, but is on order, mark with a zero. The material is not yet available to the patron, therefore the request has not been filled.
9. If the requested material is owned but unavailable, mark with a dash ($-$).
10. If the material requested is available or the question is answered, mark with a (✔).
11. Periodical Request
    - Periodical requests are simply tallied.

- *Titles* of periodicals that are not owned or not within the time period the periodicals are held should be written down and marked with a zero.
- If a specific issue of a periodical subscribed to is not owned, the title does not need to be recorded but be sure it is included in the periodical tally.

THE FREE LIBRARY OF PHILADELPHIA
(Philadelphia, Pennsylvania)

REFERENCE TRANSACTIONS

All public service agencies of the Free Library must gather and report statistics of the use made of the staff's professional knowledge by the patron. These statistics of professional reference and information services are to be recorded on "Reference and Directional Transactions Record" (Form 20-L-122). The enquiries on this form should be reviewed regularly by the agency or department head and may be reviewed periodically by the appropriate Coordinator, Chief, or other administrative staff.

1. The reasons for keeping a record of reference transactions are:
   - The record is a good indication of the kinds of information people are seeking.
   - It is a quantitative measure of the reference transactions taking place in a department or agency.
   - It can be an aid in determining staff and schedule needs.
   - It can be used as a source of information for the Library's Public Relations Officer and other staff members when representing Free Library services and accomplishments to supporters and public.
   - It can be used as an in-service training guide. Discussion of individual transactions can help the staff increase its knowledge of sources and improve reference techniques.
2. The reference transaction is an encounter in person, by telephone, mail, or other means, between a member of the reference staff and a user. It involves the use, recommendations, interpretation, or instruction in the use of one or more information

sources, or knowledge of such sources by a member of the reference staff. These information sources include:

- Print and nonprint materials.
- Machine-readable data bases.
- Library bibliographic records.
- Persons both inside and outside the library.

NOTE: A question answered through the utilization of information gained from previous consultation of such sources is considered a reference transaction even if the source is not consulted again. This is particularly true in the area of Readers' Advisory transactions.

3. Here are some examples of "borderline" enquiries that are considered to be reference transactions by the ALA Committee on Statistics for Reference Service (see "National Reporting on Reference Transactions, 1976-78," *RQ*, Spring 1977):

   - "How can I find magazine articles on the current space flight to Mars?" This is a reference transaction even if the answer merely indicates a location, such as "over there on the table by the wall." (The librarian has professional knowledge that these particular magazines contain the required information.)
   - "How do I find out what the word 'Zeitgeist' means?" This is a reference transaction if a particular dictionary is pointed out to the patron.
   - "Where are the anthropology books?" Considered a reference transaction unless anthropology is named on a directory or floor plan of the library. (Admittedly, this stretches the point a bit, but the idea is that the librarian made use of professional knowledge of the library's subject classification scheme.)
   - "Do you have a list of recommended novels for young adults?" Considered reference (bibliographic) even if the patron is merely handed a mimeographed list prepared by the library.
   - "I don't find this book in the card catalog. Could you check to see if it is on order?" Professional (bibliographic) if the library's on-order file has to be checked.
   - "Does the library have Rand reports?" Professional unless Rand reports are named on a directory or floor plan of the library. (However, helping a patron finding a book for which he *already* has the call number is directional, not reference.)

DIRECTIONAL TRANSACTIONS

All public service agencies of the Free Library must gather and report statistics for directional (non-professional) transactions. These directional statistics are to be tabulated on the lower part of the "Reference and Directional Transactions Record" (Form 20-L-122). Directional transactions are important as a general measure of library activity or traffic. The following are examples of directional items that should be tabulated:

1. Questions as to the location of physical facilities (restrooms, telephones, copying machines).
2. Questions as to the whereabouts of particular individuals, rooms, or departments.
3. Book location discussions *if* the patron already has a call number that appears to be complete.
4. Requests for pencils, paper, paper clips, or what have you.
5. Provision of aid in the use of ordinary copying or viewing equipment.
6. Requests for information about hours of opening or address of agency.

Of course, it will not always be crystal clear as to whether a particular question is of a reference or directional nature. Common sense must be used.

Making and Reporting Records of Transactions

A. If a reference enquiry is received by telephone, mark a "t" before the question, in the far left margin. This is essential for statistical purposes.
B. If the answer to the patron's question is not found, this may be indicated by circling the number of the question.
C. Probably the most convenient way to record directional statistics is by using simple tabulation marks in groups of five (/////).
D. At the end of each month, the total number of professional services including directional transactions is reported on the General Statistics form (20-L-86). The number of telephone requests included in the grand total is also reported on 20-L-86.

Reading Services to Children and Young Adults

A. The children's department in each agency keeps separate transaction sheets, unless there is no children's library to do so. It is important to report all transactions regardless of the age of the requestor.

B. Where one professional librarian handles all three age levels, a "j" or "y" should be placed by each question asked by a juvenile or young adult patron.

SAN DIEGO PUBLIC LIBRARY
(San Diego, California)

Assistance to readers in their use of library materials is the most important part of library service, but this work is not shown by circulation statistics. In order to compare the work load between different branches and especially between the various sections of the Central Library, it is necessary to keep an accurate record of the number of reference questions asked daily. Since these statistics are used in justifying the need for additional help due to increased work, as well as in reports of the work of the library, it is important that they be kept as accurately as possible.

DEFINITION OF QUESTION TYPES

Information. A transaction in which directions to library materials and services are given. There is no attempt to evaluate the material or provide explanation or assistance in its use. *Count these.*

Traffic questions generally refer to matters concerned with the public's needs and comfort, i.e., toilets, public phones, drinking fountains, stairs, elevators, clocks, change, and such. *Do not count traffic questions.*

Reference. A transaction in which library resources have been made available for references, research, and advisory service through direct assistance of a staff member. Include also any question which requires the evaluation of a book, pamphlet, or document for a reader, or recommends any of these to a reader.

Research. An unusual or especially difficult question which involves prolonged search for library materials which cannot be located by the use of library tools or indexes. Research questions are usually unique and do not recur. Since search for the answer may take a long time, even days, and may involve several librarians and different sections of the library, supervisors are responsible for evaluating these questions and deciding how much time can be spent on a particular question.

COUNTING

Materials asked for are reflected in other statistics. Please count only the question or questions asked. A request for 6 college catalogs, 3 rolls of film, etc., is counted as one transaction. The number of items appear as your *materials used* count.

General Instructions for Information Assistants on Desk Duty

CLEVELAND PUBLIC LIBRARY
(Cleveland, Ohio)

Each department will have a variety of professional and non-professional staff at the service desk.

   a. Non-professional staff must have a clear picture of the limitations and/or areas of their competence. They must be encouraged to ask questions of and to refer questions to the professional staff. Ability here must be judged by the staff member's recognition of limitations. It is never a disgrace not to know.

   b. The professional staff must learn that much information can be supplied by pre-professional and clerical assistants and that their ability to provide such information is a matter of pride in an individual job.

   c. We all need to avoid a haughty or superior manner. At the same time we do not need to minimize our abilities. An air of confidence and goodwill are easily imparted to the patron.

INGLEWOOD PUBLIC LIBRARY
(Inglewood, California)

Specific activities—Reference Clerk. These activities comprise the off-desk work of a Senior Library Clerk whose on-desk time is spent as an Information Assistant.

1. Answer telephone.
2. Attend meetings.
3. Compile statistics on public information files.
4. Confer with Library staff/City employees.
5. Coordinate and schedule non-professional personnel.
6. Maintain and operate photocopiers, including making service requests and changing paper and masters.
7. Maintain public information files, including requesting or ordering, receiving, classifying, processing, editing, routing, and filing of pamphlets, college catalogs, commercial catalogs, occupations materials, annual reports, travel materials, geographical and topographical maps, organizations information, California cities and counties materials, and telephone directories.
8. Maintain reference office files and perform related clerical work.
9. Maintain the Library Service Collection.
10. Observe, report on, or correct stack conditions.
11. Perform bibliographic checking.
12. Prepare payroll information.
13. Receive, edit, and complete book requests.
14. Receive, process, and route mail.
15. Request Reference and Information Services supplies.
16. Route materials.
17. Supervise and train temporary personnel.
18. Survey the reference area to determine maintenance requirements.
19. Train Information Assistants on public desk duties and public information files.
20. Train personnel in telephone usage.
21. Type correspondence, memos, schedules, time-sheets, reports, etc.

ORLANDO PUBLIC LIBRARY
(Orlando, Florida)

NON-REFERENCE STAFF

1. Direct patrons to the reference staff for any information other than the location of departments or facilities, or sections of Dewey numbers. Urge patrons to speak to a reference staff member if they do not find the material needed.
2. Avoid interferring with patron access to materials or equipment.

THE FREE LIBRARY OF PHILADELPHIA
(Philadelphia, Pennsylvania)

Library assistants and clerical staff have been assigned to most public service agencies. They constitute an important staff resource and should, depending on their specific assignments, play an important part in reference and information services. They should be trained to take part in reference and information activities to the limits described in their job specifications.

Telephone: Incoming Calls— General Guidelines

ANN ARBOR PUBLIC LIBRARY
(Ann Arbor, Michigan)

TELEPHONE CALLS

a. Telephone reference service should be used for short, factual information questions which do not require extensive reading or interpretation on the library staff member's part. If the caller has a number of items to be answered or checked (e.g., titles in card catalog, zip code numbers, addresses), a limit will be placed at three at a time. Time limitations for staff work on telephone questions will be at the discretion of the staff member and dependent on the appropriateness of the question for telephone service and the busyness of the library at the time. At no time will the Reference Department engage in extended research for telephone callers.

b. Telephone callers may be asked to leave their names and numbers for return calls by staff members when the source of an answer is not immediately obvious to the staff member or when the library is busy and the answer cannot be quickly provided.

c. Circulating materials located through a search for a telephone caller will be held at the request of the caller at the Reference Desk for a period of not longer than three days.

d. No legal, medical or drug questions will be answered by telephone except in cases where simple, short definitions or descriptions are requested from identified sources without interpretation by the staff member.

e. No homework, puzzle, or contest questions will be answered over the telephone when they can be identified as such.

f. No consumer evaluations will be read over the phone, but the presence of such evaluations will be located and identified.

g. City directories will be used to answer questions only when the *name* of person is given by the caller.

h. The telephone book collection is maintained by the Reference Department as a supplement to services provided by the phone company. While the department will supply information from the books, requests for phone numbers which can be answered by the phone company will not be provided.

i. Bus, airline, and railway schedules will not be read over the telephone.

j. Reserves on library materials will not be taken by telephone.

k. Patrons should use the public pay telephones, but may be allowed to use library telephones in cases of emergency.

ATLANTA PUBLIC LIBRARY
(Atlanta, Georgia)

STATEMENT OF PHILOSOPHY OF TELEPHONE REFERRAL REFERENCE WORK

It is our intention to aid the public by providing accurate information in the most efficient manner possible, and we will make an attempt to answer all reasonable requests.

Minimum Standards

The following are minimum standards for doing telephone referral reference work in the subject departments of the Atlanta Public Library.

1. "Ready Reference" questions have a search limit of five mi-

nutes. An inquiry which cannot be answered in that time is to be referred to the appropriate subject department.

2. All sources checked are to be noted in writing on the Information Request Form. This is a courtesy to other staff members who may work on questions. Also, when calling patrons back, one can readily tell them where the library has checked. Jotting down sources searched also covers the librarian as having done an adequate and accurate job.

3. No single librarian is to decide an answer to a question cannot be found. In other words, if you have searched a question thoroughly you are not authorized to call a patron back to tell him the information is unavailable until you have had another librarian concur withyou. All signatures must appear on the slip of any unanswered question before the patron is called back. All librarians working on questions are to put their names on the Information Request Form.

4. Questions are to be checked each half hour in the routing bins in TRR. When a question is picked up from the bin, the time it was picked up is to be recorded on the TRR Referral Sheet.

5. Staff members of the subject departments should be able to tell patrons who have called back the status of questions at all times. This may be accomplished in several ways such as having a centrally located place where questions are held or by having a sign up sheet to show who is responsible for each question.

6. Patrons are to be contacted within twenty-four hours from the time their questions come in no matter what the status of the questions. Staff members working in TRR may tell patrons that an attempt will be made to call them back within 24 hours whether an answer to a question has been found or not. For this reason it is wise to find out as many telephone numbers as possible from the patron. If a department has been unable to begin working on a question within the 24 hour period the department is obligated to call the patron to report the status of his request.

7. Patrons are to be called back 3 times a day (morning, afternoon, and evening) for three days or at least nine times when a question has been asnwered. If the department is unable to reach them at the end of this time the question may be considered completed.

OR

Patrons should be asked what time of day would be most convenient for a call back (morning, afternoon, evening). If the deparment is not able to reach the patron with one call, the question is filed and held for 3 days. If the question was not answered and the patron wishes to come in for further searching, it is held so that all can see what sources were checked and avoid duplication of effort.

8. The length of search for any one question is not to exceed one hour. For our purposes and for the purposes of simplicity we may tell patrons that searching for longer than one hour constitutes research. If a further search is feasible the librarian should always be prepared to tell patrons what further sources may be checked if they wish to come to the library to continue the search themselves.

9. Each department is to have at least one person assigned to work on reference questions for eight hours of the day. This eight-hour responsibility may be divided by each department as it sees fit. The answering of questions is not to be the responsibility of the person who is staffing the public service desk.

10. From 6:00 to 9:00 p.m. all departments will be notified by TRR staff members when there are questions to be picked up in the TRR routing bins.

11. When the librarian has exhausted library sources (and only then) in searching for the answer to a question, and if he thinks a local outside source might be able to answer the question, he should call the outside source rather than refer the patron to it. We are here to provide the best service possible to patrons and if this means phoning local sources for them, then we should do it. The exception to this rule would be when a patron wants information that might be of a confidential nature. After exhausting library sources, the librarian should then call the patron back to ask if it would be all right to call outside sources for them. The patron may have reasons for not having the library call and the patron's wishes should be followed at all times. (Question: Are we going too far here? Could we not give the patron the source for futher information and let him call?)

12. Because the Children's Department takes questions from patrons over the telephone, departments may also call them when they have questions that may possibly be answered by sources in the Children's Department.

13. It is preferable for each department to search its own collection for answer to questions. There are times when an answer to a question may be found in several departments. When the li-

brarian has searched his department and thinks another department may find the answer, the librarian should then send the question to the other department rather than search it himself. The patron should be called at this point and informed that an initial search has failed and another department is taking over.

THE BERKELEY PUBLIC LIBRARY
(Berkeley, California)

TELEPHONE REFERENCE

If busy, use your judgement and limit the number of questions per telephone call. General guideline is a time limit of *5 minutes* per call.

Telephone reference service will be limited to specific requests for information, as opposed to subjective or evaluative information. If an answer is not immediately available, the Reference Staff will call the patron back later, ask the patron to call back at a specified time, or, if the question involves extensive research, ask the patron to come to the Library.

BIRMINGHAM PUBLIC LIBRARY
(Birmingham, Alabama)

GUIDELINES FOR HANDLING INQUIRIES OVER THE TELEPHONE

Incoming and outgoing calls are always secondary to helping people who are already at the Library. Some policies for answering questions over the telephone are listed below.

1. Answer questions while the caller is on the line, but do not tie up the telephone for more than two minutes. Call-backs should be taken after that amount of time.

2. Calls which need to be directed to another department should be properly transferred to that department. A caller should not be transferred more than once. If in doubt about where a call should go, take a call-back.

PUBLIC LIBRARY OF CHARLOTTE & MECKLENBURG COUNTY, INC.
(Charlotte, North Carolina)

Desk questions usually take precedence over telephone questions, since the individual has taken the time to come to the Library. The question, name, and telephone number of the telephone inquirer are taken and held until desk questions have been answered, unless the telephone question can be answered very quickly from a source at hand.

DAYTON PUBLIC LIBRARY
(Dayton, Ohio)

TELEPHONE QUESTIONS

It is important to be courteous and friendly when answering the telephone, just as in answering questions in person. Always identify the agency. If the question seems to be such that it will require some time to complete it, be sure to get the patron's name, address, and telephone number. Try to get the patron to describe and limit the question or problem clearly enough so that you can find what is wanted, and yet not waste time looking for more than is needed. Be sure to reach a clear understanding as to who is to call whom, marking the work slip accordingly, and allowing a reasonable time for the work to be completed, or a "progress report" to be ready if the patron is going to be telephoned back. Most patrons are interested primarily in the answers to their questions. They will understand, if you explain rotation of work schedules, that someone else may work on their question, and have the answer when they telephone back, or come in, or are telephoned. In most cases of follow-up contact, encourage the patron to ask for the division involved instead of the individual assistant.

These general telephone practices should be followed as closely as possible:

- If it is clear at once that a question cannot be handled within three minutes, do not hold the line open. Get the patron's name, address, and telephone number and arrange to return the call.

- Do not attempt to read anything over the telephone which will take more than three minutes. In such cases, try politely to suggest to patrons that they come in, borrow the material from main or a branch if it can circulate; or copy it if it cannot. Mention the library's photocopy service if it is material which can be done on the phtocopying machine. Remember that bound newspapers and nearly all Dayton Room material cannot be copied satisfactorily. Photocopies from micro-films are available in Industry and Science Division.

- Certain kinds of questions present unusual problems if attempted over the telephone. Use your experience and good judgment in deciding when to urge politely that the patron come in and work with the material. It is nearly always unwise to attempt "object identification" by telephone—that is birds, animals, works of art, antiques, old Bibles, rare books, etc. Be sure to point out to the telephone patron that the library has many books and much reference material on such subjects, which we will be glad to put at the patron's service so that identification and evaluation can be made by the patron. Evaluations of commercial products appearing in *Consumers Reports*; or ratings of encyclopedias as given in the *General Encyclopedias in Print* or *Booklist* (ALA) may be given over the telephone, provided the source of authority for such evaluation is given. Frequently a patron will appreciate the suggestion that the patron come in and actually compare different encyclopedias which the library has.

DENVER PUBLIC LIBRARY
(Denver, Colorado)

TELEPHONE QUESTIONS

Telephone questions are answered at the time of the call if this can be accomplished quickly and there is no patron waiting at the desk for information. Otherwise, the telephone patron's name and telephone number are requested for a return call. If the answer will keep the telephone in use for an unreasonable time (more than 5 minutes), the patron should be asked to come in for the desired information.

KINGSPORT PUBLIC LIBRARY
(Kingsport, Tennessee)

TELEPHONE INQUIRIES

Since the telephone is one of the most important means of providing and arranging for service to library users, and since the manner in which telephone inquiries are handled has a direct bearing on both the operation of the Reference Department and the public's impression of the Library as a whole, it is absolutely essential that staff members on duty at the Reference Desk maintain the best possible standards of telephone service and practice the following guidelines each time they handle a reference inquiry over the telephone:

1. identify the Department and give your name;
2. develop a pleasing telephone manner and give personal service, treating all callers as individuals and taking time to be polite;
3. handle all calls to completion, either by acutally providing the answer to the patron, or by referring the patron to another, more appropriate source for the information;
4. whenever necessary, leave effective messages, giving the caller's complete name and phone number, and providing all the available details;
5. recognize all service priorities.

Patrons making such telephone inquiries should never be asked to hold the line for more than a few minutes. If the answer to a question cannot be found within this time frame, then the staff member should arrange to return the patron's call at another appropriate time or, if this is not possible or convenient, have the patron call back at a mutually agreed upon time.

Complicated or lengthy answers, which might confuse the patron or tie up the telephone line for more than a few minutes, should never be given over the phone. Instead, patrons should be encouraged to come to the Library for such answers. This procedure is to the definite advantage of both the patrons and the staff. If the patron cannot come to the Library, then a written reply should be preferrable to a lengthy telephone conversation.

In general, no more than three reference questions should be answered over the telephone at any one time, again due to the amount of time which the answers would tie up the line and impede the staff from serving those patrons in the Library. Whenever a caller has more than three questions, then he or she should be encouraged to come by the Library and seek instruction as to the proper bibliographic tools in which the answers might be found. This general rule of three applies to all types of telephone requests.

KNOXVILLE-KNOX COUNTY PUBLIC LIBRARY
(Knoxville, Tennessee)

If you are helping a patron in the library and receive a telephone request, take the caller's number and tell him you will call back when you have the information requested. The patron in the library should have first consideration.

LOUISVILLE FREE PUBLIC LIBRARY
(Louisville, Kentucky)

TELEPHONE SERVICE

Telephone service is provided as an added convenience to the community. Problems often arise through trying to provide service to in-house users and telephone callers simultaneously. Professional judgment and common sense must determine prioities. In order to be fair, each user should be handled in order, but with those within the library receiving preference.

If a user is being helped and the telephone rings, the librarians should excuse themselves momentarily to answer, and either put the call on hold or take a number to call back. This should be done politely in order to eliminate the disruptive ringing of the phone.

Answering the Telephone

The telephone should be answered by giving the name of the unit being called, except in the case of the Ready Reference and Bibliographic Center. (The answer should be "Reference and Information.") In each location the next sentence should be "May I help you?" If it is necessary to put a caller on hold, the caller should *always* be given an opportunity to speak.

Long Distance Calls

Long distance calls are to be handled in the same manner as any other phone request. If a return call is necessary, the user must assume the cost of the call.

Time Limit

Due to the volume of incoming calls and staff limitations, telephone reference service is usually limited to five minutes. This does not mean that the search effort for a question taken by phone must be limited to five minutes. If questions cannot be answered immediately, the name and phone number of the user are to be taken in order to be called back.

Questions with complicated answers are generally not to be handled by phone, but the material with the answer is cited for the patron's use when he/she is able to come in.

Transfers

No calls should be transferred unless the staff member is certain that the area to which the call is being transferred is the appropriate one. The staff member should take the responsibility of finding the appropriate area, if uncertain, and either call the user back or have the appropriate area call the user.

When a call is transferred, the caller should be told to where and why the call is being transferred. Request that the caller tell the new unit who transerred the call.

MEMPHIS PUBLIC LIBRARY
(Memphis, Tennessee)

TELEPHONE ETIQUETTE

A. Answer promptly. Your voice represents the library, so make it sound friendly.

B. Identify your library:
  - Main—"Public Library and Information Center; name of the department."
  - Branch—"Public Library and Information Center; name of the branch"; the information desk says only "Information Desk."
  - Business-Technology Department—"Cossitt-Goodwyn Business-Technology Library."

C. Always be courteous.

D. Offer to take a message if the person called is not available.

E. The assistant answering the telephone should see that the transferred call is received.

F. If the assistant is busy and a patron calls for information, explain that you are busy and that you will call the patron back as soon as possible.

G. Never attempt to remember telepone calls. Take messages and write them down.

H. Repeat the patron's name and telephone number to be sure they are recorded correctly.

I. The patron in the library should be given preferential treatment over the patron on the telephone.

The assistant will answer any reasonable questions by telephone. If the answer cannot be found, ask another staff member for assistance. Before telling the patron the answer cannot be found, consult with the department head or branch head for possible new approaches. If no answers can be found in the department or branch and there is the possibility that another department or branch may provide the answer, consult with this new searching agency.

A. Either turn the question over to the new searching agency or ask the agency to share in the search.

B. If the question is turned over to a new searching agency, this new agency should, if necessary, call the patron to conduct a reference interview.

C. The original searching agency should also call the patron to inform him that the question has been transferred.

D. If the first department or branch retains the question but another agency searches and finds additional information, be sure to acknowledge this searching agency when transmitting the answer to the patron.

Whenever possible, provide the telephone patron with the answer over the telephone without expecting the patron to come to the library. Some patrons prefer to do all library business by telephone.

If the answer to a telephone question seems too involved to relate easily over the telephone, explain this to the patron. Suggest that the patron come to the library where the assistant can have the materials held and will be more than willing to show the patron how to use the materials to find the answer. If the patron insists on an answer over the telephone give as complete an answer as is possible.

Never answer a reference question without having the source on hand to refer to and to use to verify the information. Always quote the source of information.

There is no limit on the number of sources checked to answer a question.

Checking the official catalog for a patron's book request:

• This service is used when the patron in the Main library asks if a branch has book titles which Main cannot provide.

• Call the official catalog.

• Before calling the official catalog for a book title be sure to verify the correct main entry and title of the book.

• To check to see what department at the Main library might have the needed title, use the public catalog.

There is no limit on materials requested.

If the search for the answer to a telephone question will take considerable time, contact the patron to tell him the assistant is continuing the search and will keep in touch with the patron.

There is no time limit placed on answering a question.

If a question asked by a patron in the library will take considerable time to answer, offer to take the patron's name and telephone number, saying the library will continue the search.

The patron will then not be inconvenienced by having to wait in the library for a long time before the answer is found and can be relayed to him.

If the patron asks for material and the department is not responsible for such information, the assistant should check to see where the information may be located before sending the patron searching in another department.

- Check the card catalog, particularly the circulation department staff and the people at the general information desk.
- Call the department which might be responsible for the information. This is particularly important for those departments which do not have easy access to the main card catalog.

If asked for material the branch or department does not own, check to see where the information may be located. Still count as information not owned on the statistics sheet.

- Check the main card catalog.
- Call the appropriate branch or department to check whether the information is available.

NEW ORLEANS PUBLIC LIBRARY
(New Orleans, Louisiana)

The first duty of staff at all desks is service to the patrons in the library. Patrons in the library should have preference over those who have phoned in for information. Staff working elsewhere are to be called back when a desk is busy.

When answering questions on the telephone, the following should be kept in mind:
  a. All answers are to read from a reliable source, and title of the source given by staff members.
  b. If question is considered research, patron is to be told to come into the library. Only "ready reference" questions are answered over telephone.
  c. Questions in these categories are not answered:
    - Legal questions
    - Medical questions
    - Contest questions involving judgment

   d. Usually no more than five titles (or authors) are to be checked, nor more than five questions answered for a patron on the phone.

   e. A telephone is not to be held for more than five minutes. If more time is required, the telephone number and name of the patron are to be taken and patron called back.

   f. Telephone checking in out-of-town telephone books will be done for individuals as well as firms. However, it will be limited to five addresses.

   g. Extensive translations of foreign language materials are not to be done by staff members. The Foreign Language Division staff will assist with limited translations. Patrons may be referred to foreign consuls, language schools in the area, and translators listed in the classified section of the telephone directory.

   h. Descriptions of heraldic designs, crests, flags, etc., are not given unless descriptions are written out in a book.

   i. Lists, poems, speeches, etc. are not to be typed and mailed to patrons.

   j. As with patrons in the library, personal opinions are never given over the phone. Recommendations or evaluations from quoted sources may be given.

   k. Patrons requesting answeres to grammar questions are to be given a rule of grammar which applies to that particular case, and are not to be given staff member's opinion of what is correct.

THE NEW YORK PUBLIC LIBRARY, THE RESEARCH LIBRARIES
(New York, New York)

TELEPHONE SERVICE

In most instances it is to be assumed that a reference call has been screened by the Telephone Reference Service of the Branch Libraries or that a reader has ben supplied with a unit's telephone number because of the nature of his request.

The most satisfying use of The Research Libraries' collections is made when readers consult and interpret material for themselves. A request for information over the telephone is justified when the need is immediate and the few minutes of time needed to provide an answer would not seem to warrant a special trip to the Library.

Many standards previously stated apply equally to telephone calls. The general rules of courtesy are observed.

Because of the volume of calls coming into The Research Libraries, no call for information should exceed five minutes. The same time limit applies to the reading of texts. To hold requests to this time limit, generally no more than three items are accepted for checking.

This limit on time per call also restricts the information that can be provided to ready reference material at hand. If the desired information is not immediately accessible, the caller is invited to come to the Library to undertake a search under the guidance of the staff. If the librarian knows the information is easily accessible, although not at hand, he may make arrangements with the caller to convey the information to him at a later time. Each unit formulates its policy for handling the return call. If a third call is necessary, it is made by the librarian.

A staff member does not let the telephone ring when he is busy, but answers the telephone and asks the caller if he will wait.

In answering the telephone, the librarian identifies the unit. If a transfer is necessary, the librarian makes clear the name of the unit to which transfer is being made and the reason why. A reference call is not transferred to the Central Serial Record or to any other non-public unit. The librarian makes the call and conveys the information later to the caller.

A librarian attempts to make a constructive reply to a request for information that is not within the Library's area of responsibility. For example, a child or his parent is referred to his school or branch library if he seeks assistance with a school assignment.

A librarian does not summarize evaluations of reference works or consumer goods to prospective purchasers, but encourages callers to consult printed evaluations in accessible libraries.

A librarian substantiates his answer to a ready-reference question. Reliance on personal knowledge and memory has often led to embarrassment for the staff member.

A librarian offers more extended service to librarians of other institutions who identify themselves and report the sources they have already checked.

A librarian is not expected to page readers as a part of telephone service; however, in cases of emergency, an effort is made to find a reader if his subject interest can be learned and his appearance described. The caller is asked to give a number for the reader to call instead of holding open a service line.

ORLANDO PUBLIC LIBRARY
(Orlando, Florida)

TELEPHONE SERVICE

Respond as soon as possible with the answer and/or suggested sources. Verify answer and cite the source used. Give date of source when relevant. Inform patron if enough material on subject is available in library to warrant a trip. Try to give patron an indication of when you will return the call if it is not possible to answer the question within a couple of minutes. In all cases, patron should be given a response within one day, whether question is fully answered or not.

THE FREE LIBRARY OF PHILADELPHIA
(Philadelphia, Pennsylvania)

In the interest of efficiency, all telephone calls should be kept as brief as possible—other calls may be waiting. Try to limit incoming telephone inquiries to five minutes or less. Discourage long and involved conversations as politely as possible.

Some questions, although properly answered by telephone, cannot be answered quickly because a search for material which will answer the question is necessary. Suggest that the patron call back later (indicate how much time will be needed) or offer to telephone the patron when the material is at hand. If a search of material is necessary, i.e., if it is necessary to scan many pages or volumes for the answer, the caller should be asked to come in to do the research in person. Also, long passages should not be read over the telephone. If a seemingly simple question turns out to be complex, the librarian should recommend that the patron visit the library.

It is desirable that the source of an answer be given.

When a question involves more than five minutes search or when the librarian is alone and busy, a call back, either by the librarian or by the patron, should be arranged for. Have a clear understanding about who is to call whom. If the library is to call back, be sure to make an accurate record of the name and telephone number of the person to be called. If the patron is to call the library, the librarian who handled the question should be certain that a message giving either the answer or a report of progress is on the telephone desk in ample time to be given to the caller. If the patron is outside the city, he or she will have to be asked to call back or to accept a collect call from the library.

When possible, especially at busy times, separation should be made of telephone service and "in person" service. The question in process, whether from a patron in person or on the telephone, has priority. If the reader in person is being helped and the telephone rings, the call must be answered, but the telephone caller should be courteously asked to wait until the initial question has been handled, unless the telephone question can be answered immediately (therefore, it is necessary to give the caller a chance to speak—the person on the telephone may merely wish to know what time the agency closes). If a telephone call is underway when a reader comes to the desk, the latter's presence should be acknowledged and the person should be asked to wait until the telephone question is completed. Good judgment and tact are especially important in this situation to insure that neither patron feels slighted.

In transferring a call to another agency or department, it is important to suggest that the patron let the second agency know what has already been done on the reference question involved. The patron should also be given the telephone number of the agency transferred to in case of cutoff or busy signal.

Patrons and staff may call any agency at any time during working hours to determine if a book is in.

Staff members may call any agency or department at any time during working hours. If a person receiving the call is too busy to be of service, a return call should be arranged. If the call is being made for a patron who is waiting in person, it may be wise to hold the phone instead of arranging a return call; good judgment must be used. If the person answering the telephone asks the caller to wait, the caller should always be given a chance to reply to that request.

Staff members working in branches during the morning should answer all telephone calls even though the branch is closed to the public. If a patron is calling with a request that can be easily and quickly satisfied, this should be done. For example, if a patron calls to find whether or not the branch owns a specific title and whether or not it is on the shelf, this search should be made. If the patron calls with a reference question and a professional librarian is on duty, the question should be answered if the source is known and a search can be completed quickly. If the question cannot be answered quickly or if there is no professional librarian on duty, the patron should be asked courteously to call back when the library is open or to call another agency that is known to be open. Good judgment on which questions to answer and tact in asking a patron to call back are both important factors in these situations.

PROVIDENCE PUBLIC LIBRARY
(Providence, Rhode Island)

A telephone patron is taking advantage of a heavily promoted service and also deserves prompt attention. Most problems arise when a telephone inquiry interrupts an over-the-desk question. Here, the individual who has come to the library and presented his request first usually merits first priority, since most telephone patrons expect and will be satisfied with a later call-back with the answer to their question. However, the type of inquiry—for instance, a fact quickly checked while the patron is on the phone vs. a subject search for the in-building patron—may influence the order served. There is no perfect solution to this problem; a staff member's judgement determines when and how he juggles both questions, at the same time ensuring that both patrons are served to their satisfaction.

ST. LOUIS PUBLIC LIBRARY
(St. Louis, Missouri)

INQUIRIES BY PHONE

All telephone reference service will consist of checking 3-5 sources located within your specific subject department. (This may vary with subject.) Room reference collections should be based on this premise. Exceptions are Documents and the limitations covered under Redi-Reference and Microfilm. If the information cannot be located in this manner, the question then becomes one of research, requiring the patron to come to the library.

Research will *not* be done for patrons; whether by phone or in person. Appropriate resources will be delivered as well as explanations given on how to use tools to locate those resources, when the patron is in the library.

Discretion should be used in differentiating the extent of reference service, based on:

- patron's ability to come to the library
  - —urgency of need to obtain information
  - —physical impediments
- use of information
  - —immediate, serious
  - —incidental, casual
- patron
  - —use your judgement as to legitimacy

1. Inquiries pursued are general ones within the subject areas of the reference divisions of the Main Library. A second type of question answered relates to library services and resources.
2. Due to the following conditions, certain limitations are placed upon the telephone service offered:
   - misinterpretation of information
   - inability to comply with the patron's time limitations
   - the complexity of research
   - lack of resources in Main Library
   - insufficient descriptive information given by patron concerning request
   - same information offered via other public telephone services
   - responses too lengthy, complicated or detailed to read over the telephone
   - lack of adequate staff
3. All information will be given from an authoritative source.
4. Reference inquiries are limited to a 3 to 5 minute search. Those requiring more time will be call backs. These call backs will be made by appropriate subject specialists after a reasonable search for the requested information.
5. A limit of three separate items per call will be searched; e.g., addresses, book titles, etc.

SAN DIEGO PUBLIC LIBRARY
(San Diego, California)

To be able to give reasonable service to all, the library suggests a limit of three items to be checked and reported by phone. This applies to book titles, stock quotations, addresses, statistics, etc.

Telephone: Incoming Calls— Paging Patrons

ANN ARBOR PUBLIC LIBRARY
(Ann Arbor, Michigan)

Patrons will be paged for telephone callers when possible to do so in an informal and discreet manner and when the call is of some urgency.

CHICAGO PUBLIC LIBRARY
(Chicago, Illinois)

PAGING USERS

If there is a need to contact an individual and the caller knows where the person is, the staff in that unit will try to find the person by description or will announce the call. The message will then be given to the person.

In cases of extreme emergency when a caller must contact a library user and has no idea where the person may be, the public address system (in those libraries have one) may be used. The call should be transferred to the guard station. The guard will make the announcement and ask the person to report to the guard station.

THE NEW YORK PUBLIC LIBRARY,
THE RESEARCH LIBRARIES
(New York, New York)

A librarian is not expected to page readers as a part of telephone service; however, in cases of emergency, an effort is made to find a reader if his subject interest can be learned and his appearance described. The caller is asked to give a number for the reader to call instead of holding open a service line.

Telephone: Incoming Calls— Checking Public Catalog and Circulation Inquiries

CHICAGO PUBLIC LIBRARY
(Chicago, Illinois)

Specific Titles. When a user telephones seeking specific titles, three may be checked at the time of the call. If it is necessary to check a distant stack area, the user should be told that the call will be returned in about 15 minutes. The shelves must be checked for all materials including reference materials. Unless that title is part of the separate, heavily used reference collection, it will be held on the unit's reserve shelf. Always state the library unit and address when inviting a user to pick up materials, as many are not aware of the location. If the material is reference only, it should be emphasized that the material must be used with the library.

When items requested are currently available, the material will be held until the end of the second working day after the request: i.e., if the call is taken on Monday, the item will be held until closing on Wednesday; if the call is taken on Friday, the item will be held until closing on Monday.

If material is not currently available, one reserve for a circulating title in the collection or on order may be taken by phone upon user request. Postage will be collected when the item is available.

Subject Request Up to three items on a specific subject can be gathered and held for user. Staff should always emphasize that these are not recommended sources, but only what is currently available.

THE DAYTON AND MONTGOMERY COUNTY PUBLIC LIBRARY
(Dayton, Ohio)

As a general rule, we do not look up more than three titles at a time on a telephone request. When circumstances indicate, a reasonable number of additional titles may be taken down, and the paton promised that as time permits, they will be checked, and he will be called back.

Wherever possible (and in the case of students, always), the patron should be tactfully encouraged to bring in his list so that he may be shown how to check it himself, or mail it for checking and return.

DUNEDIN PUBLIC LIBRARY
(Dunedin, Florida)

Checking the public catalog or shelf for materials at the telephone caller's request demands a call-back. The telephone line should not be tied up for that length of time. "Please give me your name and telephone number. I will call you right away with that information. Will you want to place a reserve on that material?" Try to determine this so that the material can be removed from the shelf at the same time it is checked. If the patron inquires whether the Library owns a certain material, he is also concerned about its present availability.

KINGSPORT PUBLIC LIBRARY
(Kingsport, Tennessee)

Telephone inquiries concerning the Library's *ownership* of particular titles are the responsibility of the staff members on duty at the Reference Desk. No more than three titles should ever be checked for any one caller at any one time.

Telephone inquiries concerning the *availability* of particular titles owned by the library are also the responsibility of the staff members on duty at the Reference Desk. The availability of no more than three titles per caller should ever be checked by the Reference staff. If a title is available within the Library, then staff members may hold that title on the reserve shelf behind the Circulation Desk for a period of no longer than four days. Staff members handling such requests should inform each caller of this policy, ask for instructions as how to proceed, and then request a telephone number where the patron can be reached as soon as the search is completed. Searches should take place as soon as both time and staff are available.

Callers inquiring as to the availability of materials on a particular subject should be encouraged to come to the Library, if, after making a routine search of the appropriate bibliographic tools, the staff member handling the request believes such materials are, indeed, available at the Library. Staff members should explain to such callers that it is to the caller's definite advantage to visit the Library, since they can better recognize the suitability of the Library's materials to their own particular needs and since the staff may not pull and/or hold more than three sources for any one patron. Callers should always be assured of personal assistance in finding materials when they do come to the Library. By requiring the patron to come to the Library, the staff hopes to insure that the patron's exact informational needs are served and that the patron becomes more familiar with some of the basics of the research process.

LOUISVILLE FREE PUBLIC LIBRARY
(Louisville, Kentucky)

Specific Titles. When a patron calls seeking specific titles, five per call may be checked to determine if the agency owns. The patrons must be asked if they wish to know if the books are on the shelf. If the agency does not own, further search of the system is to be made and the patron should receive a follow up.

When items are available, they may be held for pickup up to one week after the item is located.

If material is in circulation, the staff should offer an alternative title or offer to reserve the requested item.

THE FREE LIBRARY OF PHILADELPHIA
(Philadelphia, Pennsylvania)

As a general rule, not more than three single questions should be answered in the course of one telephone call (e.g., author-title searches in the public catalog or in a bibliography). Obviously, the ease or difficulty of a search affects the number of questions that can be answered within a given time; the decision of when to terminate a call will rest on a good judgment of the librarian. If it appears that the call is going to exceed a reasonable time span, the patron should be tactfully ask to call back later, or better, to visit the library. If the caller has an extensive list of questions that cannot be answered handily in one or two calls, a visit to the library is required.

If they wish, patrons may ascertain what agencies own a certain title by calling the Catalog Department directly, but it is important that callers have complete and correct call numbers (non-fiction) or author-title information (fiction). Patrons should be told to identify themselves as such, so that the Catalog Department will give names of owning agencies instead of numbers. Also, patrons should be told to check later with owning agencies to make sure that books are in. Both patrons and staff members may call the Catalog Department from 9 to 5, Monday through Friday. No more than six titles will be searched in any one call to the Catalog Department.

Telephone: Outgoing Calls— General Guidelines

BIRMINGHAM PUBLIC LIBRARY
(Birmingham, Alabama)

Outgoing calls should be kept as brief as possible. Call-backs should be limited to specific facts, short encyclopedic articles, quotations, and short lists. In some cases, a request may be answered better by photocopying and mailing the information free of charge. Anything of length or highly technical nature should not be read over the telephone.

DUNEDIN PUBLIC LIBRARY
(Dunedin, Florida)

Patrons should not use the library telephones. They are directed to pay telephones at the Publix and if front of Eckerds. If a call must be made, the staff member places the call and relays the message for the patron.

Circulation Function of Information Staff: Reference Books and Other Restricted Materials

ANN ARBOR PUBLIC LIBRARY
(Ann Arbor, Michigan)

Except in unusual circumstances to be determined by the Head of the Department, Reference materials do not circulate.

PUBLIC LIBRARY OF CHARLOTTE & MECKLENBURG COUNTY, INC.
(Charlotte, North Carolina)

The Head of the Division and/or designated Reference Librarian(s) assist in the previewing and selection of films. Selectors should keep aware of current and standard non-book materials in their respective areas and make suggestions to the Audiovisual Librarians.

MAKING DECISIONS ABOUT BINDING, DISCARDING, AND REPLACING BOOKS

Selectors are responsible, in their areas, to decide about the need for binding, discarding, or replacing books. Books which are in too poor condition to be bound and are out-of-print may be transferred to Stacks, as may also books which should not be discarded but may be out-of-date, older editions of a title, etc. The Reference Librarian is responsible for regularly checking Main Floor's shelves of books in his selection area for the purpose of weeding, binding, transferring, and generally keeping his area(s) from being overcrowded.

In cases of mutilated books, the librarian finding should refer book to the selector in the subject area. When a page or two is missing the librarian may note date and pages missing on the book pocket and return to the shelves. If pages are loose, it may be taken to Processing for repairs. When many pages are missing, replacement or transferral to basement Stacks (if o.p.) may be considered.

SELECTING BOOKS, PAMPHLETS, AND AUDIOVISUAL MATERIALS

Utilizing special talents and interests when possible, Reference Librarians are assigned specific subject areas for which they select books and pamphlets, maintain a balanced collection of standard and popular works in their fields, and make decisions as to eventual disposition of books. Pamphlet selections, except vocational materials, should be submitted to the Reference Librarian in charge of the Pamphlet File to avoid duplication. Vocational pamphlets are selected by the Young Adult Librarian.

Reference selectors route their order slips to the Head of Reference, who reviews and routes them to the Head of Public Services, who turns them in to the Head of Acquisitions.

A Reference Librarian is responsible for handling United States Government Documents. Other Reference Librarians are urged to make suggestions for selections, particularly in their subject areas.

The Local History Librarian is chiefly responsible for selecting State and local materials. In cooperation with the Head of the Reference Section, the Local History Librarian shall seek to acquire needed copies of Chamber of Commerce and similar publications for the Carolina Room and the Main Reference and lending collections.

A Reference Librarian is designated to select for and maintain a changing small collection especially for Young Adults. A Reference Librarian also maintains a section on the Main Floor of Large Print titles.

When a patron requests a book not held and is found not to be on order, the Reference Librarian takes the patron's name and address, makes a note of the author and title and as much bibliographical data as the patron can give, and assures the patron that the Library will consider but never promise purchase of the book. The request is given to the Reference Librarian in whose selection area the book falls. The selector makes his decision after reading reviews and fills out a reserve postal for the patron if the book is ordered or notifies the patron that the Library will not be getting the book, noting reasons. If the book is not a recent or popular work, it may be possible to obtain an Interlibrary Loan, and the patron is so advised.

The Reference Librarians at Main working as subject specialists select most of the books and related materials acquired by the Library. When it is recognized that some ten million separately identifiable publications are issued in the world annually, selection from this outpouring is understandably complicated to acquire, organize, and retrieve within the confines of the budget. A great boon was the extension in 1967 of IN-WATS, toll-free, by the North Carolina State Library to tie the resources of the State's libraries into an easy access communications network.

Lifelong learning, independent study, and innovative teaching methods have all had heavy impact on libraries. The Public Library usually does not acquire textbooks or basic readers used in schools, but provides supplementary materials across a wide spectrum and is the chief source of back files of magazines and serials as well as bibliographical tools. A dynamic business community is requiring an ever-increasing collection of books and services and the assistance of well-trained librarians. A *Statistical Record* of services and types of questions is maintained.

INGLEWOOD PUBLIC LIBRARY
(Inglewood, California)

RESOURCES

Reference Collection. The reference collection consists primarily of the basic reference tools: general encyclopedias, several special encyclopedias and dictionaries, almanacs, biographical dictionaries, directories and indexes, several foreign language dictionaries, atlases and gazetteers, etc.

Community Information Resources. Since the branch libraries do not have an Information Service to maintain information on community activities and resources, this is done by the reference librarian. This information constitutes an important resource. Information comes in from many sources within the community. A major source is the City of Inglewood, which provides both the main library and the branch libraries with information it wishes disseminated to the public.

Telephone Directories. Branch libraries have limited collections of telephone directories for the Southern California area. Inquiries for other areas are referred to the main library.

College Catalogs. This collection is also more limited. It is generally restricted to colleges, universities, and vocational schools in California and neighboring states. However, due to the large number of Black patrons served by the branch libraries, an exception is made to include catalogs from formerly all-Black schools regardless of their location witin the United States.

Information Files. The branch libraries also maintain information files of pamphlet material. These are considered an important resource for reference service. Although the files at the branch libraries are not as comprehensive as those at the main library, the same general areas are covered: subject material, California cities and counties (general and historical information), occupations or careers, travel (foreign, United States, California—maps and pamphlets). The one area not covered at the branch libraries is the annual reports. As at the main library, the material in the information files does circulate.

KINGSPORT PUBLIC LIBRARY
(Kingsport, Tennessee)

REFERENCE BOOKS SHELVED AT THE REFERENCE DESK

Reference books should be shelved at the Reference Desk only if such a procedure would: (1) assist staff members meet anticipated high demand; (2) minimize the possibility of theft; and/or (3) prevent excessive wear or damage to a book due to its unusual size or format. The catalog cards of all books to be shelved at the Reference Desk should be flagged with a cover slip instructing patrons to request the materials at the Reference Desk. Furthermore, book dummies, complete with the title and classification number and marked so as to refer patrons to the Reference Desk, should be placed on the Reference shelves in the normal shelving position for all such books.

NEW ORLEANS PUBLIC LIBRARY
(New Orleans, Louisiana)

Reference books are normally in open areas easily accessible to public and staff; ready reference books (marked with one or two red dots on the spine) are behind the service desks for staff use, but may be made available to the public for a limited time. To insure the return of ready reference books, a driver's licence, or similar *substantial* piece of i.d. may be held. In order to assure the return to the Central Library Public Services desk of "key" materials (e.g., heavily used reference books, vertical file material, periodicals) the following procedure is used: Staff at the desk may hold as security for the return of materials one or more pieces of patron i.d.

THE NEW YORK PUBLIC LIBRARY,
THE RESEARCH LIBRARIES
(New York, New York)

The Research Libraries collect, catalog, and house the materials of recorded knowledge so that they may serve readers today and in the future. The collections are not easy to use. They are vast in size, and are broken up into units located in four separate buildings. The scope of the material, encyclopedic in range and diverse in format, is reflected in the complexity of the catalogs. For these reasons, the role of the research librarian in interpreting the collections and the catalogs becomes especially important.

THE FREE LIBRARY OF PHILADELPHIA
(Philadelphia, Pennsylvania)

MATERIALS

All materials in Free Library collections are potentially useful sources of information to the public. Central, however, to the reference function is a core of traditional materials consisting of reference or informational tools. Included among them are handbooks, encyclopedias, dictionaries, indexes, bibliographies, and directories. These tools and others like them enable staff to provide a substantial portion of the information needed by the public. They should be carefully selected and adequately represented in all public service agencies. It is important that information sources be selected for all the various sectors of the public and that they be as comprehensive, timely and accurate as possible.

It is recognized that the Pennsylvania State Resource plan will also affect reference and informational responsibilities in the Central Library. Other Central Library resources reflect the diverse reference needs of the more immediate geographical area.

Popular and frequently consulted reference tools are widely distributed throughout the Free Library system. Extension agency reference collections are designed to meet the individual informational needs of the communities served. This includes reference sources in appropriate foreign languages. Information sources available in the branches should include tools useful in referring clients to the Regional Libraries, Central or resources outside the library.

Various reference tools that provide users with access to sources of information outside the Free Library are an essential part of the Central Library's resources. They vary from book catalogs of other libraries to computer terminals for extralibrary data banks. Every effort is made to develop the reference capability of the library through the extension of this type of resource.

PROVIDENCE PUBLIC LIBRARY
(Providence, Rhode Island)

Some questions are best answered by a non-library source. Although each department is constantly expanding and changing its available contacts, we have included the standard referral lists and directories so that all staff can be more generally aware of this important trend in library services.

1. Reference Department
   - *CCS Directory.* A listing of health, recreational, and welfare agencies issued by the Rhode Island Council for Community Services. It gives address, directors' names, types of services provided, hours, and other pertinent information. While it is not a complete listing, it comes very close to being so.
   - *Organization File.* A list of various organizations and clubs in Rhode Island. The information comes primarily from newspaper articles and includes names of officers. Clubs are filed alphabetically, with a subject index.
   - *Fugitive File.* Within this collection of answers to frequently asked questions there is a list of special libraries in the Providence area with hours, addresses, and telephone numbers.
   - *ARISE Directory.* A directory of Adult Referral and Information Services in Education, compiled and published by the Providence Adult Education Department. It lists adult education programs around the state, guidance services for adults, and adult recreational opportunities.
   - *Government Documents Location List.* A list indicating by U.S. government document number which libraries in the state own certain docutments.
   - *Single Parent Referral File.* A card file listing organizations and agencies offering service to single parents. (Also found in all branches.)
2. Reader's Advisor
   - *ARISE Directory.*
   - *Women's Index.* An index for and about women, which in-

cludes a file of local organizations for women, including the names of contact persons if such are available.

- *Guide for Senior Citizens.* Another direcory published by the Providence Adult Education Department, which lists opportunities and services for senior citizens in six major areas: 1) Planning and education; 2) Health; 3) Income; 4) Housing; 5) Services; 6) Recreation and Liesure.
- *Education File.* A list by subject and school of the various vocational, career, and adult education courses offered around the state.

3. Business, Industry and Science Department
   - *Snag File.* Contains names and addresses of agencies such as the local IRS office, the Real Estate Commission, etc.
   - *Vertical File.* Contains names and addresses of organizations dealing with specific subjects, such as recycling centers.
   - *Local Business File.* The department indexes major articles on local businesses from the *Providence Sunday Journal—* Business Section.

4. Art and Music Department
   - *Reference File.* Includes a list of local organizations in the arts and certain hard-to-find local experts.

5. Periodical Department
   - The department maintains holdings list for local public and academic libraries.

6. Systems Office
   - Specific titles not available in Rhode Island libraries can be located through the following tools:
     1. National Union Catalog (Catalog Department).
     2. NUC Register of Additional Locations (Catalog Department).
     3. Mansell-NUC pre-1956 Imprints (Warwick and some academic libraries via teletype).
     4. Library of Congress (teletype).
     5. OCLC (a computerized data network via teletype).

AT THE BRANCHES

Each branch has developed an area or areas of specialization especially suited to its neighborhood. These collections should be remembered when looking for materials with which to suplement those available at a particular branch or department.

1. Fox Point—Materials in Portuguese.
2. Olneyville—Materials in Polish.
3. Wanskuck—Juvenile books in Italian.

Circulation Function of Information Staff: Periodicals

PUBLIC LIBRARY OF CHARLOTTE
& MECKLENBURG COUNTY, INC.
(Charlotte, North Carolina)

FILLING MAGAZINE REQUESTS

A magazine holdings list is maintained at the Periodicals Desk.

Students will fill out completely the magazine request forms provided near the indexes. A limit of four magazines at one time for an individual student, and fewer when excessive demand compels further limitation, may be brought up by the Page (who checks cited page numbers, ascertaining that all pages are intact, and signs or initials the form, in order to determine persons responsible for any later mutilation).

Magazines are to be used on the Main Floor unless no desk space is available on the Main Floor. They should be returned to the Periodicals Desk.

An adult may request more than four magazines at a time, unless he makes the request at a very busy time, but page numbers for each magazine are still checked by the Page.

Magazines at Main may not be checked out. However, the Reference Librarian in charge may grant special permission for a bound or back magazine to be taken from the Library for a short period in order to be photocopied, or in rare instances, to be shown to a group of people at one time, when the group cannot come to the Library.

DUNEDIN PUBLIC LIBRARY
(Dunedin, Florida)

A list of periodical holdings is kept in the center drawer of the Information Desk. The key to the microfiche cabinet is in a pink plastic case in the upper right drawer. When fiche is removed from the cabinet a plastic card with a red heading is inserted in the empty spot. The fiche are later refiled.

NEW ORLEANS PUBLIC LIBRARY
(New Orleans, Louisiana)

USE OF BACK ISSUES OF PERIODICALS AND NEWSPAPERS— CENTRAL LIBRARY

Any patron requesting an issue of a bound, unbound, or microform periodical newspaper from the Periodicals Reference Desk must first present either an Orleans Parish library card, or a Periodical Back Issue Request Card to the attendant at the desk. No one need have a library card, however to use periodicals published by the U.S. Government Printing Office. A list of these is kept at the Periodical Desk. Since these are government document depository items, we are legally required to make them available to any member of the public requesting them. Out-of-state visitors are usually permitted to use back issues in the library. They are given an accommodation card, free of charge, at the discretion of the Head of the Circulation Division. This is not true for residents of other Louisiana parishes, who would be required to purchase the non-resident card or the Periodical Back Issue Request card. This Card costs 50¢ and is good for having up to 5 periodicals retrieved from the basement. Money may be refunded if none of the articles sought can be located.

Circulation Function of Information Staff: Circulation of Materials

BIRMINGHAM PUBLIC LIBRARY
(Birmingham, Alabama)

CIRCULATION OF REFEENCE BOOKS AND OTHER RESTRICTED MATERIALS

Reference books, periodicals, and microforms do not circulate. Exceptions to this policy are made by the Department Head. Some vertical file materials do circulate. These vertical file materials are checked out within the department, and their loan period is consistent with that of other library materials.

PUBLIC LIBRARY OF CHARLOTTE & MECKLENBURG COUNTY, INC.
(Charlotte, North Carolina)

CHECKING OUT REFERENCE MATERIALS

The Reference Librarian in charge may decide or confer with the Division Head in deciding whether a given Reference book may be checked out, usually for an overnight or brief period.

If there is not a circulating copy or back issue available, which will suffice for the patron's need, the request for any given Reference book will have to be decided on its own merit by the Reference Librarian or Division Head. Encyclopedias, unabridged dictionaries, current directories, such as *Thomas' Register,* current yearbooks, and the like are examples of materials rarely if ever checked out, while handbooks, some bibliographies, collections of paintings, and other materials treated as Reference might be checked out for a short period when the Reference Librarian considers the patron's need vital.

A special loan form is completed by the Reference Librarian in charge for reference materials approved for short-term loans. This form is signed by the borrower who then takes the form and the item to the Lending Desk for check out. At the top of the form is a space for indicating the exact time for the special loan such as "two hours," "one day," etc.

When patrons have decided which pamphlets, maps, pictures, etc., they wish to check out, the Reference Librarian fills out the special materials card.

When Reference material is taken from behind the Reference Desk to be used away from the Desk, the patron should sign a request form (filled out by the Reference Librarian).

GRANTING PERMISSION FOR CIRCULATING BOOKS TO BE RE-CHECKED

While books may not be renewed, they may be brought to the Library where a request for re-checking is made at the Reference Desk.

The patron may be allowed to re-check the book(s) at the discretion of the Reference Librarian, if the book is not on reserve, is not a current year's title, and is not in demand. The patron will be urged to re-check only two or three books on a given topic and not re-check a great number in one field.

Books may be re-checked only once. Six weeks is the limit for the keeping of a book by one person.

When the Reference Librarian does not grant permission for re-checking, the book(s) must remain on the Library's shelves 24 hours before the same person may again check out the book(s).

THE DAYTON AND MONTGOMERY COUNTY PUBLIC LIBRARY
(Dayton, Ohio)

Reference materials usually do not circulate; however, the division head, Officer-in-Charge, a senior librarian in the division, Assistant Director or Director may authorize the issuance of reference material for a short period when a definite need exists.

DUNEDIN PUBLIC LIBRARY
(Dunedin, Florida)

CIRCULATING FUNCTIONS OF INFORMATION STAFF

Reference books and materials are not circulated. The Directory of the Library or the Head of Information Services makes exception to this rule, notifying the rest of the reference staff.

Circulating materials are from time to time put on reserve because of demand. The book cards are pulled and filed in a special section of the circulation files labeled, "Class Project." The reference and adult services staff work together in decisions for reserves "For Library Use Only."

Authorization for extended use of any non-fiction library materials comes from the Director of the Library or from the Head of Information Services.

Vertical file materials are prepared for circulation at the Information Desk. The staff member makes the decision concerning the number of pieces of material on one subject that can be checked out. The basis for this judgement is made on the determination of number of pieces or copies in the folder, present demand for material in that subject area, anticipated demand, and availability of other materials in the library in the same subject area.

Microforms are never circulated.

Unprocessed materials are circulated only at the discretion of the Director of the Library or the Head of Information Services.

KINGSPORT PUBLIC LIBRARY
(Kingsport, Tennessee)

CIRCULATION OF REFERENCE MATERIALS

In general, Reference materials (meaning Reference books, bound volumes and loose issues of periodicals, telephone directories, etc.) do not circulate outside the Library building so that they will be accessible to as many users as possible for all the hours which the Library is open. Many reference tools, such as periodical indexes and the latest editions of standard encyclopedias and almanacs, are in such constant demand that they cannot be taken from the building without causing severe inconvenience to other library users. In almost all causes, the reference needs of the majority should take priority over the needs of an individual.

However, since some reference materials are in much less demand than others, reasonable requests to borrow less heavily used titles for brief periods of time should be granted to legitimate library card holders. A request should be considered "reasonable" if the needs of the requestor are best served by using the volume outside the building, and it is the judgement of the staff member on duty at the Reference Desk that the removal of that volume from the building for a brief period of time will not seriously inconvenience other library users or jeopardize the physical condition of the material. A reference volume should not be lent, if there is a duplicate copy available for circulation elsewhere in the Library.

The length of the loan period granted should be based on the needs of the library patron and the judgement of the Reference staff member as to the possible inconvenience to others. Such special loans may be granted either for a few hours during the day (not more than three) or for overnight (the loan commencing not more than one-half hour before closing time and ending not more than one hour after opening time the next working day). A staff member on duty at the Reference Desk is responsible for securing a valid library card number, signature, address and phone number on a 3×5 card or slip before the material(s) may leave the building. The borrower should be instructed as to the exact length of the loan and to the fact that all materials borrowed in this manner should be returned directly to the Reference Desk.

KNOXVILLE-KNOX COUNTY PUBLIC LIBRARY
(Knoxville, Tennessee)

Reference books are not circulated, except for older editions which may be checked out for a week or less depending upon the patron's needs.

ORLANDO PUBLIC LIBRARY
(Orlando, Florida)

Loans of reference materials may be made to patrons and to other libraries within the system when such a loan will not be a disservice to other patrons. They are made at the discretion of the senior librarian on duty in the department or library. Loan period should be kept to a minimum and should be followed up promptly when overdue. These patrons must have a valid Orlando Public Library card. Check patron's record with circulation department when possible.

Inquiries for "In-Process" Materials

BIRMINGHAM PUBLIC LIBRARY
(Birmingham, Alabama)

Reference materials which are "in-process" are not directly accessible to patrons. The staff member should check bindery lists, mending lists, etc., for periodicals and books being processed to inform the patron of their status. Patrons who wish to see Reference books located in the Catalog Department should be accompanied there by a staff member, and must wear a visitor's pass while in Technical Services areas.

DUNEDIN PUBLIC LIBRARY
(Dunedin, Florida)

Inquiries for "on-order" or "in-process" materials are handled at the

Information Desk. Information is contained in a 2-drawer file on the right hand desk. Reserves may be made on "on-order" or "in-process" materials. "00" is written on the reserve card in the space "call no." Reserves should not be made for books the library does not own or have on order. Those titles should be brought to the attention of the department head concerned with ordering that type of material.

Referrals

PUBLIC LIBRARY OF CHARLOTTE
& MECKLENBURG COUNTY, INC.
(Charlotte, North Carolina)

If an inquiry cannot be answered from the Library's sources, the Reference Librarian tries to suggest another agency, association, or individual who might be consulted.

CHICAGO PUBLIC LIBRARY
(Chicago, Illinois)

REFERRALS

When branch resources have been exhausted, the Central Library should be contacted. After all resources of a division have been exhausted or if it has been determined that a question does not fall within the subject scope of a division or overlaps subject scopes of several divisions, the librarian should suggest other resources within The Chicago Public Library. The resources include the other divisions, specialized collections (such as the Vivian G. Harsh Collection or the Fine Arts Division picture file) or special services (such as The Information Bank or Interlibrary Loan).

If still more material is needed, users may be referred to larger or more specialized libraries or services using the Illinois Regional Library Council's Infopass or Datapass programs. Librarians should be familiar with library resources within the Chicago area, rules concerning issuance of Infopass and Datapass, and tools useful in making these referrals (such as *Libraries and Information Centers in the Chicago Metropolitan Area, National Union Catalog, Union List of Serial Holdings in Illinois Special Libraries*, and *Union List of Serials*).

Sometimes, questions can be more readily or appropriately answered by another governmental agency, service agency, or independent organization. Librarians should be familiar with these alternatives so that appropriate referrals can be made. In general, referrals should not be made arbitrarily. Users should be made to feel that the librarian has done everything possible to help them. In many cases, a phone call should be made by the referring librarian to verify the appropriateness of the referral.

DENVER PUBLIC LIBRARY
(Denver, Colorado)

Referral of the patron's question, when necessary, is made as soon as the librarian becomes aware that the question cannot be answered in that agency. Branch libraries will refer questions which they cannot answer to a larger library or to the Main Library Subject Department.

Referrals to another library or outside agency are not made until the resources of the DPL are exhausted.

DUNEDIN PUBLIC LIBRARY
(Dunedin, Florida)

Referrals are made to persons and institutions outside the Dunedin

Public Library and the Interlibrary Loan System. A 3×5 file on the Information Desk contains "local sources" for information. These range in scope from local and federal governmental agencies to persons personally known who are knowledgeable in a particular field. It is courteous, when referring a patron to a person, to contact that person first to see if he is willing to help. Other reference staff members may know of authorities in certain fields. Never hesitate to inquire.

LOUISVILLE FREE PUBLIC LIBRARY
(Louisville, Kentucky)

When the library's sources have been exhausted, the user should be referred to other sources or agencies for assistance. A phone call may be made by the librarian to determine if the alternative is the correct one. In any case, the users should be made to feel that the librarians have done everything possible to help them. Librarians should be as familiar as possible with specialized alternative resources for information within the community.

SAN DIEGO PUBLIC LIBRARY
(San Diego, California)

When no satisfactory materials or information are found after reasonable search and there is an indication that further research will be productive, the query is referred to Serra Research Center along with a list of sources searched and some indication of when the information is needed.

INTERLIBRARY LOAN

General

ANN ARBOR PUBLIC LIBRARY
(Ann Arbor, Michigan)

The interlibrary loan program administered through the Department provides access to materials not available in the library's collection. Interlibrary loan requests are limited to three in-process for an individual at a time. It is usually a free service, but there may be a cost to the patron if there is a need to go outside the State Library System for an item.

THE BERKELEY PUBLIC LIBRARY
(Berkeley, California)

Fill out INTERLIBRARY LOAN REQUEST form as completely as possible and give to ILL Unit, General Services Office. If necessary, assist patron to locate or verify bibliographic information. *Sources:* Books in Print, Forthcoming Books, Cumulative Book Index, U.S. Catalog, and British, French, German or Spanish Books in Print, etc.

ILL search process: First BALIS libraries are searched, then California State Library, and subsequently libraries farther afield. ILL is now possible with U.C. Berkeley Library, after BALIS system and California State Library resources are exhausted.

Telephone ILL: If book is on the shelf, it can be sent to another BALIS library. Fill out BALIS TELEPHONE ILL REQUEST form, being sure to get patron's name, address, and telephone number. Put request form in book pocket and give ILL Unit.

PUBLIC LIBRARY OF CHARLOTTE & MECKLENBURG COUNTY, INC.
(Charlotte, North Carolina)

INTERLIBRARY LOAN AND PHOTOCOPY PROVISION

The Library adheres, with a few exceptions, to the latest edition of the ALA GENERAL INTERLIBRARY LOAN CODE and to the North Carolina State Library's SERVICES BETWEEN LIBRARIES. In general, the philosophy behind these two codes is that interlibrary loan is designed to complement the resources of other libraries and to help those engaged in serious study. Its purpose is to aid research, but not to provide materials readily accessible elsewhere. It is recommended, for example, that thesis or term paper topics be selected according to the resources on hand and should not require extensive borrowing from other libraries. If an individual needs to use a large number of items located in another library, he should make arrangements to use them at that library.

INTERLIBRARY BORROWING

Requests

Patrons may request books on interlibrary loan through the Main

Library's Information Desk, either in person or by telephone. All Reference Librarians should be acquainted well enough with interlibrary loan procedures and policies to take requests. Questions about unusual requests or problems which may arise should be referred to the Interlibrary Loan Librarian.

Ordinarily, a patron is limited to two interlibrary loan requests at one time, unless a total of three will satisfy the patron's needs. Requests for more than three may be taken, if the patron desires; but they will be sent to the lending library only after the first two have been received and are being used by the patron. These restrictions do not hold for requests of photocopied materials.

Qualifications of Patron

Before taking a request, make sure that the patron making the request meets the following requirements:

1. Patron must be a resident of Mecklenburg County. Non-residents and fee card holders should be referred to their local public libraries.
2. Patron should be a registered borrower of the Library. He may, however, register after the book has been borrowed.
3. Students
    - College students who are currently in residence should make requests through their college or university libraries.
    - High school students for assignment-related materials should make their requests through their high school libraries. School librarians will, in turn, make these requests through the Public Library. Requests for any non-assignment-related materials may be made through the Public Library and will be treated as any adult request. If possible, for requesting purposes, use an occupation other than student (e.g., grocery clerk, musician, lifeguard), or make the request in the student's parent's name.
    - College students not in residence (such as those working on theses and dissertations), correspondence students, and extension students may make their requests through the Public Library.

Restrictions on Type of Materials Requested

The Public Library will ordinarily not try to borrow the following types of materials for patrons. (If the patron insists, contact the Interlibrary Loan Librarian.)

1. Genealogical, heraldic, and similar materials. Almost no libraries, including our own, lend this type of material and we feel that it is a waste of our time and the lending library's time to ask for material that is almost certain to be non-circulating. We will be happy, however, to get *locations* for genealogical works through the State Library and the Library of Congress.
2. Current fiction, which we will purchase rather than borrow.
3. Titles which the Library owns or has ordered, but which are not currently on the shelves. Reserve these instead.
4. Periodicals. We can request a photocopy if the patron is willing to pay whatever the suppyling library charges.
5. Basic reference materials. Again, we should purchase these rather than try to borrow them.

Before taking a request, the Reference Librarian should make sure that the Library does not own the book and that is not on order. Tactfully, he should check the card catalog himself, before the patron leaves, if possible. (If not, the Reference Librarian should check as soon as the patron leaves and call him if we do have the book.)

Information Required for Request: Patron

In taking a request, the following information about the patron should be recorded on the blue interlibrary loan request cards: name, address, home telephone number, occupation or status, firm, and business telephone number. This information should be obtained as diplomatically as possible and without insistent interrogation, since some patrons resent having to supply so much personal information just to borrow a book. We do explain that the lending library may suddenly recall a book, and we need to know how to get in touch with a patron even after business hours. We therefore try not to take a request unless the patron leaves a telephone number, if not his own, that of a neighbor, friend, or relative, at a location where he can be reached. If the patron is unable or unwilling to give a telephone number at which he can be reached, his request will be taken with the understanding that he must use the book in the building. If there is a date after which the patron cannot use the requested book, this date should be indicated on the request card.

Information Required for Request: Book

In taking a request, as much information as the patron can furnish about the book and the *source of his knowledge* of the book should be recorded on the interlibrary loan card: author (first and last names), title, and at least the approximate date of publication. Additional information should include edition wanted, publisher and place of publication, although these last are not as important as the first three items mentioned.

The Reference Librarian taking the request should check BOOKS IN PRINT, and if the title is listed, should make a note of this fact (e.g., "BIP 71"), and of any additional bibliographic information. If the book is not in BIP, this fact should be noted also.

After following the above procedure, the Reference Librarian will *date and initial* the request and turn it over to the Interlibrary Loan Librarian, or in her absence, to the Head of Reference. The card does not have to be typed, but it should be legible.

Review of Request

The Interlibrary Loan Librarian will review the request, making sure that it conforms with our policies and that the information about the patron is complete. She will then recheck both the card catalog and the order file to be certain that we neither own nor have ordered the book, and also investigate the possibility of the book's being held by a branch, e.g., North Branch is a good source for books on the Negro. She will then consider whether or not the material should be purchased instead of, or in addition to, obtaining it through interlibrary loan. If the Interlibrary Loan Librarian thinks that the book should be considered for purchase, she will give the bibliographic information to the book selector in the given area, with the suggestion that it be considered for purchase. Since the time required to read reviews, make the decision, order, receive, and have the book processed may well exceed the time limit of the requester, the Interlibrary Loan Librarian will ordinarily follow through with the loan. If, however, the loan is not followed through and the book is instead ordered, the Interlibrary Loan Librarian should see that an on-order reservation card is made for the requester and should notify him that it will be some time before the book is available.

Books Received

When the book is received, the Interlibrary Loan Librarian will place it in the interlibrary loan drawer at the Reference Desk. For security reasons *the book is checked out from and returned to the Reference Desk.* To check out an interlibrary loan book, the patron should read and sign the white slip in the book. The Reference Librarian lending the book then initials and dates the white slip, clipping it with the other white (charge out) slips in the ILL drawer. The blue slip with the date due information remains in the book. Remind the patron that if he should desire to renew a book, he must notify us at least four days before the book is due back in our library. (The practice of renewal, however, should *not* be encouraged.)

When an ILL book is returned to the Reference desk, the Reference Librarian checking in the book pulls the corresponding white slip from the clip, initials the charge out slip and notes the date that the book is returned. The white slip is then inserted in the returned book, and the book left in the ILL drawer until it is picked up by the ILL Librarian or the Secretary.

INTERLIBRARY LENDING

Requests received From Other Libraries

We fill requests received from university, college, junior or community college, technical institute, public, school, and special libraries. If we own the material requested, if it is in, and if it circulates, it is mailed to the borrowing library. Types of material which we do *not* ordinarily lend, with few exceptions, include:
  1. Books on reserve or otherwise in demand (best sellers, etc.)
  2. Reference material, although this is sometimes lent at the discretion of the Reference Librarian in charge.
  3. Genealogical and rare books.
  4. Serial holdings.
  5. Films and records.
Requests for non-circulating materials and the period of their loan, if lent, are considered on the basis of local demand, requesting patrons' needs, format and condition of materials.

Requests for materials in microform and the period of loan are considered on the basis of local demand.

Period of Loan, Mailing, and Charges

Books are loaned for one month. If a book is not in demand here, it may be renewed for an additional two-week period. Most of our books are sent uninsured. They are simply placed in a jiffy bag, stapled, and mailed Library Rate.

The borrowing library is not asked to reimburse postal charges, or to pay charges for overdue books, but is requested to insure returns which were insured when lent. There is no charge for limited photocopies supplied to libraries in Metrolina or for fourteen pages or fewer to libraries outside Metrolina. For more than fourteen exposures, the charge is 10¢ per exposure, with a minimum charge of $1.50 (invoice mailed with the material).

There is a charge of 25¢ per print of 3 M microfilm (negative copy).

Requests Received in Person

Occasionally we receive a request in person for one of our books by a patron living in the Metrolina area, but not a resident of Mecklenburg County. Such a request may be filled after obtaining the personal and bibliographic information usually taken from our own patrons, noting the *book number* of the title in question, and *confirming the transaction by telephone to the patron's home library*. This is a rare exception to standard interlibrary loan procedure and is made only to a Metrolina resident when the need appears to be great, and the work in question is to be used for serious study. Otherwise, the patron is advised to request the book he wants through his own library in the usual way.

CHICAGO PUBLIC LIBRARY
(Chicago, Illinois)

INTERLIBRARY LOAN POLICIES

Interlibrary is a transaction in which The Chicago Public Library borrows library materials or obtains photocopies of materials held by another library. A borrower's card from The Chicago Public Library is needed to request materials through Interlibrary Loan.

In most cases the Interlibrary Loan service is free to users of The Chicago Public Library. However, if the lending library charges The Chicago Public Library, the user will be responsible for such charges upon receipt of the material. The user will be advised of this fact prior to the use of the material. In most cases, it will be a very small fee.

The Chicago Public Library is a member of the Illinois Library and Information Network (ILLINET). Therefore, any material borrowed from other member libraries is sent free of charge and all photocopied material under ten pages is also free. If the photocopied material is more than ten pages, the charges vary. No photocopying will be done if the price exceeds the amount the user is willing to pay.

Outside of ILLINET most libraries charge for photocopying and for mailing materials. These charges vary. Some libraries, such as Harvard, Yale, and Cornell have begun charging a fee ranging from $5–$10 for each request filled. No requests will be sent to these libraries wihtout prior user approval.

The Chicago Public Library will not ordinarily accept Interlibrary Loan requests for:

> More than three titles for one person at a time
>
> Books which The Chicago Public Library owns but which are in circulation or on reserve
>
> Books available only in an inexpensive paperback edition (The Chicago Public Library will consider for purchase.)

In addition, libraries will usually not loan the following kinds of materials:

> Best sellers and new books that have been published within the previous three months
>
> Reference books and rare books
>
> Genealogy books
>
> Magazines and newspapers (Photocopies of specific articles can usually be requested.)
>
> Art prints and other materials which are difficult to package for mailing
>
> Books that are in print (These cannot be borrowed from libraries outside Illinois according to the American Library Association Interlibrary Loan Code.)

The length of the loan period depends upon the policies of the library lending the material to The Chicago Public Library. Most libraries will lend materials on interlibrary loan for two weeks from the date that it is received at the borrowing library. The user will be informed on the length of the loan, when the material is received.

Any requests for specific information, titles, or photocopies that cannot be filled out the local unit of service whether branch, regional, department, or appropriate subject division will be forwarded to the Bibliographic and Interlibrary Loan Center through proper channels. Before forwarding information requests, the resources of the unit must be exhausted. All requests must be reviewed by the person in charge and delivered to the Bibliographic and Interlibrary Loan

Center within 24 hours. Records for all requests will be kept in the originating unit. Materials will be distributed to users through that unit.

All Chicago Public Library Units will accept Interlibrary Loan author/title requests by telephone when a specific citation can be given. At the Central Library, the requests will be handled by the department responsible for materials in the subject area of the request. Information requests must be made in person since an exhaustive search must be done.

These procedures make it possible for each agency to be aware of requests for materials which may not be in their collection and to give consideration to materials for possible purchase.

SERVICE TO SYSTEMS THROUGH ILLINET
(CPL AS A RESEARCH & REFERENCE CENTER)

The Illinois Library and Information Network (ILLINET) is the statewide multitype library network consisting of local public, academic, special and school libraries, eighteen library systems, four Research and Reference Centers, and three Special Resource centers.

As an R & R Center, The Chicago Public Library through the Bibliographic and Interlibrary Loan Center offers the following services to library systems and their members:

Interlibrary loan of books and government documents

Reference and information service

Photocopies of non-circulating materials with first 10 pages copied free of charge

Verification and search of special indexes by professional librarians

Priority handling of
    requests over those from non-network libraries

Referrals to other Research and Reference Centers:
    Illinois State Library, Southern Illinois University (Carbondale), University of Illinois (Champaign-Urbana)

Referrals through the network to Special Resource Centers including: John Crerar Library (including access to the Midwest Health Science Library Network), Joseph Regenstein Library (University of Chicago), and Northwestern University Library.

Search of the Ohio College Library Center (OCLC) data base for titles not found in ILLINET (Locations of titles are given to requesting libraries)

TYPES OF REQUESTS NOT HANDLED

1. Literature searches
   Literature searches which result in tailored bibliographies are
   not considered to be a responsibility of the Research and Reference Centers. However, published bibliographies will be supplied as well as all available information on the requested subject for users who are doing their own literature searches.
2. Term Papers
   Preliminary research for term papers will not be the responsibility of the Research and Reference Centers. It is expected that
   this will be done at the local Library. However, the user who has
   a specific and clearly formulated request for supplemental and/
   or additional material will be assisted.

DUNEDIN PUBLIC LIBRARY
(Dunedin, Florida)

Interlibrary loan service is given at the Information Desk by the
reference staff only. The procedure is outlined in the Interlibrary
Loan Manual.

Reserve cards are used for author, title, and verification information. They are then placed in a 3×5 box labeled "ILL" to be typed by a
specified library assistant who handles all typing, receiving, notification of patrons and returning of ILL's. Any staff questions are referred to the Head of Information Services. It is wise to check with her
on the wording of subject requests and on all photocopy requests.
Requests are seldom made for paperbacks since they are seldom
filled. Bibliographies for genealogical, foreign language, and large
print materials in the State Library of Florida are at the Information
Desk. The patron should be informed that he will have a two-week to
three-month wait for his book. He will be notified as soon as it is
received. He will usually be allowed to keep it two weeks. If he needs
it longer, a renewal must be received at the State Library a week
before the book is due. Each patron may have no more than three
books on interlibrary loan at one time.

MEMPHIS PUBLIC LIBRARY
(Memphis, Tennessee)

REFERRING PATRONS TO THE AREA RESOURCE CENTER
(ARC)

Any time this system does not own or has not ordered a given title requested by a patron, offer to obtain the material on interlibrary loan.

Do not wait for the patron to request this service; it should be extended.

Exceptions to this policy are elementary, high school, undergraduate, and locally enrolled graduate students, since the American Library Association Interlibrary Loan Code does not permit borrowing for these groups.

Because of restrictions in the Interlibrary Loan Code, genealogical requests are not honored by the lending libraries. Therefore, the ARC department does not send requests for such materials.

   a. If the patron is in the library and wants to use the ARC service, call ARC and an assistant will come to the department where the patron is waiting. The assistant can then conduct a direct interview with the patron.

   If the ARC assistant cannot leave the ARC department, accompany the patron to the ARC department, where the ARC assistant can conduct an interview with the patron.

   b. If the patron is on the telephone and requests the services of ARC, take the patron's name and telephone number, saying that ARC will contact the patron. Then transmit the message to ARC, so that the ARC assistant can conduct a direct interview with the patron.

   c. Be sure to inform the patron that although there is no charge for the services of ARC, there may possibly be some financial charge requested by the supplying interlibrary loan agency when photocopying is involved.

   d. A patron in a branch library should contact ARC directly rather than having the branch assistant go through the Branch Office. Explain to the patron that this is done through the Social Science department.

ORLANDO PUBLIC LIBRARY
(Orlando, Florida)

MATERIALS NOT OWNED BY ORLANDO PUBLIC LIBRARY SYSTEM

1. Title is considered for purchase if in print and of value to collection.
2. Interlibrary loan for those materials not in print, or for which there is no need in the Orlando Public Library collection, if material is over one year old.
3. Normally audio-visual materials are not interlibrary loaned. Some exceptions can be made for films and microfilm.
4. Refer patron to other libraries or sources when material is not available for interlibrary loan.

THE FREE LIBRARY OF PHILADELPHIA
(Philadelphia, Pennsylvania)

INTERLIBRARY LOAN REQUESTS

Reference requests from other library systems received through the interlibrary loan system are answered, if possible, by the Interlibrary Loan Department. The more specialized requests may be referred to other departments for assistance or research.

Photocopy

BIRMINGHAM PUBLIC LIBRARY
(Birmingham, Alabama)

PHOTOCOPYING OF REFERENCE MATERIALS

There are some limitations on photocopying of reference materials, particularly rare books and archival materials. Decisions about copying primary source materials are made by the Department Head, based on the condition of the original material.

PUBLIC LIBRARY OF CHARLOTTE & MECKLENBURG COUNTY, INC.
(Charlotte, North Carolina)

SUPPLYING PHOTOCOPIES

When a copy of material held by the Library is desired by the patron, the patron may be directed to the self-service, coin-operated photocopy machine. During office hours, Monday-Friday, the Reference

Librarian can offer the service in the Administrative Offices if the coin machine is defective or if extensive copying is needed, sending a Page to make the copy. If the patron is unhappy with the copy from the coin-operated machine, he may be reminded that we are not a professional copying service and he should be given the names of several local, commercial services.

The Library will not photocopy any material for mailing (except interlibrary loans to another library), if the material carries a legend prohibiting reproduction.

If a non-library request comes in for "copyright material" the patrons should be advised that it is copyright and we cannot photocopy for them; they will have to come in and do their own photocopying.

We do not charge libraries in the Metrolina area. Our photocopying is reciprocal, except in the case of extensive runs, which should be cleared with the Administration.

So that we may have a business record of the transaction, when photoduplicated copies are mailed, and when necessry, billed, they are handled and recorded by the Interlibrary Loan Librarian and the Public Services Secretary. When a Reference Librarian does photocopy a non-interlibrary loan request, he turns it over to the Public Service Secretary to invoice (requesting that a copy of the invoice be returned with remittance) and mail. The Secretary will then turn a copy of the invoice over to the Business Assistant so that she will know what the check is for when it comes in.

When requesting photocopies of material for the use of the Public Library of Charlotte and Mecklenburg (for our files or to replace missing pages, etc.), the request should also go through Interlibrary Loan channels.

When answering telephone questions such as the wording of a poem can be handled more expeditiously by mailing a photocopy of a few pages, this may be done without charge since the cost of collection may be greater than the fee.

Photocopies of materials from other libraries will be requested for patrons and invoiced in the amount charged by the lending library.

CHICAGO PUBLIC LIBRARY
(Chicago, Illinois)

PHOTOCOPY SERVICES

Although the Chicago Public Library does not have a photocopying center, photocopy machines are located in many library agencies for users to make their own photocopies at a charge. When necessary, The Chicago Public Library will fill user photocopy requests by letter in accordance with copyright law provisions. There is an additional charge when copying is done by the staff. There will be no charge if an unsolicited photocopy is sent at a librarian's discretion in response to a subject request.

DUNEDIN PUBLIC LIBRARY
(Dunedin, Florida)

All interlibrary loans for photocopy are handled by the Head of Information Services in compliance with the copyright law.

The procedure for ordering federal documents on microfilm is in the front of *Federal Population Census* 1790–1890 (Ref. 929.3 Uni).

The procedure for ordering photocopies of genealogical materials in the Library of Congress is taped inside the cover of *Genealogies in the Library of Congress* (Ref. 929.1 Uni.).

LOUISVILLE FREE PUBLIC LIBRARY
(Louisville, Kentucky)

PHOTOCOPYING GUIDELINES

Coin-operated copy machines are available in the main library and some branches where users make copies of personal or library-owned material for a fee. Assistance in operating the machines is provided when necessary.

Users should be advised to come to the library to make their own copies if possible; however, staff may make copies for patrons if requested by phone, mail, in person, or through branches, but pre-payment plus postage is required.

Branch librarians may request from the Main Library photocopies of material that can be used to fill frequently asked questions. This will be copied for branches without cost.

ORLANDO PUBLIC LIBRARY
(Orlando, Florida)

When necessary, make available through photocopy those materials which cannot be sent to other libraries in the system or to patron. When sending photocopies to a patron unable to come to the library, staff may copy one or two articles not to exceed ten pages. Copies will be mailed directly to patron with a bill for charges based on administrative policy. Staff does not photocopy materials for patrons who are in the library.

Refunds are given to patrons for unusable copies due to malfunction of the copier. Refunds due to patron error are left to the discretion of the reference staff.

BIBLIOGRAPHIC SERVICES

ANN ARBOR PUBLIC LIBRARY
(Ann Arbor, Michigan)

BIBLIOGRAPHIC ACTIVITIES

1. Bibliographies are compiled by members of the Department to serve the following needs:
   - To guide patrons to library materials in areas of popular interest where the card catalog headings are unusually numerous and complex or non-existent. These titles will tend to be predominantly non-fiction circulating books and the lists will be updated frequently (annually or bi-annually).
   - To facilitate the provision of full answers to commonly asked Reference questions. These titles are usually Reference materials and the lists will be updated frequently (annually or bi-annually).
   - To call attention to a number of similar titles of potential interest for recreational reading. These titles tend to be predominantly fiction titles and the lists are *not* updated frequently, although they may stay in print a long time.
2. The Department will consider suggestions for bibliographies from patrons and local organizations. Bibliographies are not compiled on request unless the suggested list is judged to be useful and desirable for general usage as well.
3. Availability of staff time, as weighed against other departmental projects and other bibliographies, will always be a factor in

determining whether or not a particular list is compiled and updated.

4. For all lists compiled and updated, the Department will try to:
   - Check on availability and condition of copies in collection.
   - Order added copies of significant titles which are missing or constantly in use.
   - Keep track of new titles for addition to future lists.
   - Build the collection by searching out desirable related titles and ordering them.

DUNEDIN PUBLIC LIBRARY
(Dunedin, Florida)

BIBLIOGRAPHIC SERVICES

The Head of Information Services and the reference staff are alert to the needs for bibliographies. The lower right drawer of the Information Desk contains some bibliographies. Others are in their proper folders in the Vertical File.

When an out-of-house bibliography is added, it is brought to the attention of the reference staff. These are checked by a staff member and our holdings are noted by classification number.

In-house bibliographies are prepared on p-slips: further citations are added from current publications and finally a list is typed. Notations are added as they appear.

The bibliographies are photocopied. Five copies are placed in the Vertical File in the appropriately titled folder.

Demand bibliographies originate primarily from students and teachers and may result in reserve materials for a unit project.

The reference staff is on the alert for popular interest topics (child abuse, solar energy, TV violence, for example) to anticipate the public demand.

KINGSPORT PUBLIC LIBRARY
(Kingsport, Tennessee)

BIBLIOGRAPHIC SERVICES

It is the responsibility of the Reference Department (whenever both time and staff are available) to prepare printed, in-house bibliographies and/or bibliographic guides for subject areas of time-proven, or considerable current, interest which would significantly assist a large number of patrons with their informational needs. Bibliographies should not be prepared on behalf of an individual patron, due to the great amount of staff time and resources involved in such endeavors. The final decision for the preparation of such guides and their subject areas lies solely with the Head of the Reference Department.

Reference Department staff should also provide limited assistance, dependent upon time and personnel available and the level of demand, in checking published bibliographies against the Library's holdings. Such bibliographies may be marked with complete library call number or with simply a check-mark denoting ownership and not location.

PUBLIC LIBRARY OF CHARLOTTE & MECKLENBURG COUNTY, INC.
(Charlotte, North Carolina)

BIBLIOGRAPHIES AND READING LISTS

The Reference Section will prepare, upon reasonable request within the judgment of the Reference Librarian on duty (or Head of Reference or Head of Public Services, if there is doubt), bibliographies for individuals, as well as groups and organizations.

The Reference Librarian taking the request for a bibliography will ascertain as many "specifications" of the requester as possible: subject, scope, use to be made of list, whether or not non-book materials are desired to be listed, when and number of copies needed, etc.

The Reference Librarian may at any time consult with the Head of

Public Services concerning the preparation of a bibliography but is asked to especially when the potential bibliography purports to be an extensive and/or expensive one, so that a decision can be made and relayed to the person making the request and also so that if the subject of the bibliography falls more nearly in the area selected by another Reference Librarian than the one taking the request, a reassignment may be considered.

Requests for large quantities of a bibliography or a bibliography to be issued regularly in the form of a periodical must be taken up with the Head of Public Services, Assistant Director and/or the Director.

Any Reference Librarian who prepares a bibliography of any kind, from less than a single page to numerous pages, preserves a copy in a notebook of bibliographies maintained at the Reference Desk.

THE FREE LIBRARY OF PHILADELPHIA
(Philadelphia, Pennsylvania)

Extensive searches of material. Lengthy manual searches of periodical material, bibliographic sources, or searches through extensive reference materials are beyond the Library's resources to perform in most instances. The agency head should consult with the division chief before making an exception to this general rule.

CORRESPONDENCE

ANN ARBOR LIBRARY
(Ann Arbor, Michigan)

INFORMATION CORRESPONDENCE

Questions asked by letter will be answered whenever possible; however, a time limit of approximately thirty minutes will be the maximum spent on an individual letter. Paid individual research may be undertaken by staff on a personal basis with the approval of the Reference Department.

BIRMINGHAM PUBLIC LIBRARY
(Birmingham, Alabama)

GUIDELINES FOR HANDLING INQUIRIES BY MAIL

The policy of the Library is to respond to specific written inquiries for information. Photocopy requests up to fifty copies will be provided and charged at the usual rates. Materials in mircroform will not be researched, although photocopies will be made for requested citations on microform, excluding genealogical materials.

PUBLIC LIBRARY OF CHARLOTTE & MECKLENBURG COUNTY, INC.
(Charlotte, North Carolina)

ANSWERING LETTERS CONTAINING REFERENCE QUESTIONS

The Head of the Division or designated Reference Librarian answers letters involving simple research.

Persons making requests for free material needed for curriculum assignments may be referred to local chambers of commerce, state departments, or other sources.

When a letter requests material to be sent directly to the requester (out of the County), the requester is urged to make his request from his local librarian, who may seek an interlibrary loan.

When a letter requires an answer which would involve time-consuming major research, the Reference Librarian or Head of the Division may confer with the Assistant Director or Director concerning the extent to which the Library may reasonably go in its answer for an *individual* patron outside of Mecklenburg County. However, ordinarily, the Reference Librarian will go as far as resources permit in answering questions from another *library*.

CHICAGO PUBLIC LIBRARY
(Chicago, Illinois)

LETTER POLICIES

Letters should be acknowledged within 7 to 10 days.

1. *Specific Title Requests*
   Books can be loaned to individuals only through regular channels, such as Interlibrary Loan. No books can be sent in response to an individual's letter.
2. *Subject Requests*
   a. *City of Chicago Users*
      The same time frame of 15-30 minutes applies for letters as for telephone service. If the questions relate to Chicago, twice the amount of time may be spent. More time is spent on

Chicago-related material because a public library has a responsibility to document and provide information about its community.

Reference letters from local users may be answered by telephone in order to save time. A notation should be made on the user's letter stating how the question was handled in case there is a need to follow up.

b. *Illinois Users Outside City of Chicago*

Letters from Illinois residents asking about Chicagoana or specialized materials will be answered by the appropriate unit. A copy of the request and response will be forwarded to the R & R Center Reference Librarian in the Bibliographic and Interlibrary Loan Center. The letter will then be counted as a Network request and a carbon copy will be sent to the appropriate unit. When services are provided, the following note should be included: "This service is provided by The Chicago Library System, a member of the Illinois Library and Information Network (ILLINET). In the future please contact your local library which can provide this same service."

If the letter is not Chicago-related or specialized, it will be sent via the Bibliographic and Interlibrary Loan Center to be answered by the appropriate system headquarters. A carbon copy showing what action had been taken will be sent to the correspondent.

c. *Out-of-State Users*

Letters from outside Illinois relating to Chicagoana or highly specialized materials will be answered. Other letters will be returned with a suggestion where the user can contact a local library, state library, or other information source.

d. *Users Outside the United States*

As a courtesy, unless it is a very time-consuming research question, letters from users outside the United States will be answered.

THE DAYTON AND MONTGOMERY COUNTY PUBLIC LIBRARY
(Dayton, Ohio)

MAIL REQUESTS

For non-county residents this service should apply to questions received by letter dealing with local historical material or other information obtainable only in our library system. In such cases where the questions relate to material which is widely available the patron is requested to correspond with local libraries or other institutions in his county or state.

For Montgomery County residents this reference service is handled in the same manner as patron requests received in person or by telephone. All reference questions will receive due consideration and will be referred or answered in a reasonable length of time.

KINGSPORT PUBLIC LIBRARY
(Kingsport, Tennessee)

REFERENCE CORRESPONDENCE

Inquiries received through the mail from persons outside the greater Kingsport-Sullivan County community should be answered only if the question can be answered quickly and briefly, and only if it is obvious that the information requested cannot be obtained from sources closer to, or more appropriate for, the individual requestor (in which case the requestor should be politely referred to such a closer or more appropriate source for the information). Each question should be considered in light of the rest of the Reference Service Policy.

Reference Department staff should make every effort to reply all such inquiries with a typewritten letter mailed no later than one week after the receipt of the inquirer's initial letter. A letter replying to a reference qusestion should be signed by the staff member answering the inquiry. Letters having to do with policies and procedures of the Reference Department should be signed by the Head of the Reference Department. Duplicate copies of all such replies should be made and kept with the inquirer's initial letter in the Reference Department's Correspndence File.

KNOXVILLE-KNOX COUNTY PUBLIC LIBRARY
(Knoxville, Tennessee)

INFORMATION CORRESPONDENCE

The Head of Information Service is responsible for answering written inquiries from individuals. She replies with dispatch, having judged the amount and extent of research necessary balanced with the availability of materials and time.

The Reference Library Assistant handles correspondence involving order information, subscriptions, continuations.

This correspondence is checked by the Head of Information Services before it goes to the Director for approval. All correspondence from the library must be approved by the Director.

THE NEW YORK PUBLIC LIBRARY,
THE RESEARCH LIBRARIES
(New York, New York)

REFERENCE LETTERS AND TRANSMITTED COMMUNICATIONS

Requests for service pour into The Research Libraries by letter and other means. Although The Research Libraries cannot serve as a popular house of answers on an international level, on occasion the correspondent will find only in a collection as large as this the information he desires. Answering such a letter provides a well-tested learning device for the librarian to gain experience in using the catalogs and the collection.

Because of the demands on staff time and the expense involved in replying to many requests, The Research Libraries must limit the number of letters to be answered. To reduce the clerical work in replying to communications for which information cannot be provided, The Research Libraries Administrative Office has prepared form letters. Librarians should consult copies of these replies for their guidance (See Research Libraries Technical Memorandum No. 29, "Library Correspondence: Reference Letters").

There are two kinds of requests to which attention will always be given: first, a reasonable request about Library holdings; second, a request for information on a subject within an area of the Library's responsibility that is not likely to be found in a library otherwise accessible to the correspondent. If the length of the answer to a request exceeds reasonable limits for inclusion in a letter, the writer is advised of the availability of the facilities of the Photographic Service. The amount and method of copying which will be utilized in a reply at the Library's expense are determined by consideration of Library staff convenience and time-cost factors. When the copying is clearly in the Library's interest, the cost should be borne by the Library.

A librarian substantiates his reply by citing his source or sources of information, thereby avoiding the role of authority for himself or The Research Libraries.

A bibliographical item that is not found in the Library's catalogs should be further searched in the hope of identifying the item in case it has not been correctly cited.

If the desired information cannot be found, the librarian suggests other possible sources to the correspondent.

To paraphrase the point of view of the 17th century French scholar and librarian, Gabriel Naude, the ultimate justification for the expense and trouble in building a collection of books is in its use. The Research Libraries share this philosophy but also recognize that this view is best served when facilities and regulations are in balance. These standards are offered to The Research Libraries' staff to help them in seeing that the goal to serve is not lost sight of because of the need to exercise control.

ORLANDO PUBLIC LIBRARY
(Orlando, Florida)

CORRESPONDENCE

Apply the same standards to requests for information received by mail as to those in the other categories.

THE FREE LIBRARY OF PHILADELPHIA
(Philadelphia, Pennsylvania)

LETTERS AND TELETYPE MESSAGES

Letter requests for reference services are an important area of the Library's reference service, and therefore the quality, appearance, and promptness of reply need careful attention.

ROUTING AND ANSWERING LETTERS

1. All reference questions by letter which are not specifically addressed to a particular person or department should be sent (by the Central Public Services Division Office) to the General Information Department. General Information will then determine, if necessary in consultation with the heads of Central departments, whether the questions will be answered. If the question cannot be answered, a statement to that effect will be sent by the General Information Department.
2. If a letter directed to a specific department cannot be answered there, this department will direct it to the appropriate department. If more than one department's material is involved in the request, the letter will be forwarded to General Information which will coordinate a reply.
3. If the letter can be answered by General Information, that department will answer it. If General Information does not have the material, it in turn will route the letter to the appropriate department or departments.
4. The carbon copy of the answer together with the original letter should be forwarded to the Chief of the Central Public Services Division for review, after which they will be returned to the answering agency. Every effort should be made to expedite letter reference questions.

Administrative heads of agencies are responsible for seeing that all written requests are answered within a reasonable length of time. A log of reference questions with date received and answered may be kept in each agency.

SAVING TIME ON REQUESTS

1. When Philadelphia residents' requests for information by letter can be readily answered by a phone call, this is advisable.
2. If more copy is required to answer the request than can be supplied by letter, duplicating services will be mentioned.

ST. LOUIS PUBLIC LIBRARY
(St. Louis, Missouri)

INQUIRIES BY MAIL

1. Inquiries by mail will take third priority. Under the direction of the supervisor of the unit, when the letter requires more than a cursory search, the patron will be notified as to the receipt of the inquiry and given an approximate time if/when he can expect an answer.
2. Conditions under which we will respond by mail:
   - residence outside metropolitan area
   - physical disability which prevents patron's coming to the library
   - special projects
3. Limitations of mail reference questions: In general, our policy of limitations will determine the service offered to mail inquiries.
4. All correspondence should:
   - give source of information
   - be copied and retained for a minimum of one year
   - include name and department of person answering the inquiry

ORIENTATION AND INSTRUCTIONAL SERVICES

ANN ARBOR PUBLIC LIBRARY
(Ann Arbor, Michigan)

LIBRARY TOURS AND ORIENTATION TALKS

Library tours and orientation talks are offered by the Department to all student groups of junior high school age and above, from the area served by the Huron Valley Library System. Tours should be scheduled at least one week in advance and cannot be given after 7 in the evening. Tours and talks will vary from 15 to 30 minutes in length depending on the needs of the group scheduled.

PUBLIC LIBRARY OF CHARLOTTE
& MECKLENBURG COUNTY, INC.
(Charlotte, North Carolina)

Instruction in use of the card catalog, special indexes, photocopying, microfilms, microforms, and special equipment is recorded statistically under Reader's Advisory. Also included in this category is time spent in conduction of informal tours or informational lectures.

TOURS AND LECTURES

The Main Children's Librarian plans for tours of children through the elementary grades. The Young Adult Librarian arranges tours for older students and adults with the assistance of other members of the Main Public Library Services staff or other personnel from the Library system as a whole. Plans for special meetings and lectures should be cleared through section heads, administration, and scheduling authorization.

DUNEDIN PUBLIC LIBRARY
(Dunedin, Florida)

ORIENTATION AND INSTRUCTIONAL SERVICES

Orientation and Instructional Services are an integral part of the answer to most reference questions. When the source of the answer is documented, instruction has taken place. As the staff member uses the card catalog with the patron, as time allows, she indicates call numbers and their locations, subject headings, cross reference and the like. In the stacks further instruction can be given such as: information on the same subject in the reference collection, oversize books, vertical file; referral to the Children's Librarian, for more basic materials or to the Adult Services Librarian for fiction on the topic in question. The reader is encouraged to learn how to use the catalog independently at the same time he is encouraged to ask for reference assistance should he need it.

Formal orientation and instruction for groups of students is handled by the Head of Information Services with the assistance of her staff and occasionally the Children's Librarian. Primary emphasis is placed on instruction in the use of the card catalog and the *Readers' Guide to Periodical Literature*. Other reference volumes are examined as time permits.

NEW ORLEANS PUBLIC LIBRARY
(New Orleans, Louisiana)

Patrons are to be helped at the card catalog as well as in locating information, but staff limitations normally preclude devoting more than 5 to 10 minutes to helping an individual patron.

Research is to be done by patrons. Staff should spend a reasonable time to guide, assist, instruct, etc., a patron on how to get to a subject field or locate material but extensive searching is to be done by patrons. However, it is far better to err giving too much rather than too little assistance! Wherever a patron has difficulty in locating a book, the staff member is to go the shelf and help him.

ORLANDO PUBLIC LIBRARY
(Orlando, Florida)

INSTRUCTION IN USE OF LIBRARY MATERIALS AND EQUIPMENT

Staff will assist patrons in learning how to use library tools (card catalog, subject guide, indexes, vertical file, etc.). They shall also instruct patrons in the use of equipment such as copy machines, microfilm readers and printers, etc.

MISCELLANEOUS

PUBLIC LIBRARY OF CHARLOTTE
& MECKLENBURG COUNTY, INC.
(Charlotte, North Carolina)

HOLDING MATERIAL FOR WHICH THE PATRON WILL CALL

When a patron requests that a certain book or books, other material which can be lent, or a selection made by the Reference Librarian be held 1-3 days for him, and the material is in the Library at the time, the Reference Librarian locates and places the material at the Periodicals Desk, noting the patron's name, date, and initials of the Reference Librarian.

When the material requested by the patron to be held involves Reference books, bound periodicals, or other material which may not be checked out and/or includes written reference to other sources which the patron might find useful, the Reference Librarian places such material behind the Periodicals Desk.

RESERVATIONS

Reservations, or reserves, are made (up to three at a time), at no charge, for books desired by a patron, but not available at the time he calls or comes to the Library. The patron can be a staff member, and receives the same consideration. Reference Librarians fill out and initial cards for reserve requests taken by them, checking the card catalog to verify information. The Reference Librarians are responsible for taking no reservations for books not held by the Library, unless it can be determined that the book is definitely on order.

The Reserve Librarian fills these requests as soon as possible, mailing cards to the patrons, notifying them that the books are being held at the Lending Desk for a period of 5 days from the date of mailing, and arranging books held in alphabetical order (by the patron's last name) on the Lending Office shelves.

DUNEDIN PUBLIC LIBRARY
(Dunedin, Florida)

Donations of materials are handled in the following manner. When a caller wishes to donate periodicals to the library, the Reference Library Assistant III receives the call, determines the titles and dates, and responds according to the library's needs if it is a title already owned. If it is a new title, or if she is not in, the caller is referred to the Head of Information Services. Care is taken to be tactful when an offer is refused, for example: "So many of our friends bring in their copies of 'Reader's Digest' that we have all the additonal copies we can use."

If the caller wishes to donate books, he is referred to the Head of Information Services who attempts to discover the types and condition of the volumes.

THE FREE LIBRARY OF PHILADELPHIA
(Philadelphia, Pennsylvania)

PROMOTION

The public should be made aware of the nature and extent of reference services provided by the library. This should be done through all media of communication, written and oral, and should utilize such vehicles as new stories, films, brochures, and library service talks.

News releases, radio spots, and television interviews should underscore the human needs that bring people into the library to look for information. However, the expertise of the reference worker should be joined to the imagination and ingenuity of the publicist so that the human interest that lies in reference and informational work will be conveyed in accurate and measured statements.

Special multi-media campaigns should be developed for target audiences but care should be taken not to oversell existing library services or to promise services which do not exist or which cannot be handled by current budgets, library staff, and available materials.

Online Policy Statements (Academic, Public and Special)

NATURE OF SERVICE

General Explanation for Public

BRIGHAM YOUNG UNIVERSITY
(Provo, Utah)

WHAT ARE DIALOG, ORBIT IV, MEDLINE AND BRS?

They are on-line, interactive, computer bibliographic search services. The simplest way to describe these on-line retrieval systems is by drawing an analogy to a situation we have all experienced—using the library. When entering a library, a person either knows the subject area, the author, or he may know the number of the document he is seeking. Assuming the person is trying to find subject matter, he goes to the card catalog and looks through an array of cards relating to this subject. Rather than finding one document, he may run across many other references which had not occurred to him originally. With an author's name, the person proceeds in the same manner. DIALOG, ORBIT IV, MEDLINE, and BRS can give a researcher this same information *and more* in a matter of minutes.

WHAT IS THE NEED FOR THESE DATA BASES?

With the continually accelerating growth of information produced by research and various other means, there is a great need in the university community to efficiently handle large numbers of references and successfully retrieve *desired* information from them. In an attempt to more effectively meet the needs of researchers, the Harold B. Lee Library has contracted with Lockheed Missiles and Space Company for the use of its DIALOG Search Service; with Systems Development Corporation for the use of its ORBIT IV System; with the National Library of Medicine for the use of its MEDLINE System; and with the Bibliographic Retrieval Service for the use of its data bases.

HOW DOES IT WORK?

By means of a computer compatible terminal—with a built-in thermal printer—and a standard telephone, we can interact with any of the four search services. Based on subject terms which describe the topic of interest, we send a request to the computer. The computer at the search service then searches the specified data base(s) to find how many references match the request. The computer then sends back a message indicating the number of references which match the request.

We can then print a few of the references to determine whether they are relevant. If the references are relevant, we can then have them printed and mailed to us. If the references are not relevant to the request, we can modify the request until we find references that are relevant; and have them printed and mailed to us.

CITE
(Austin, Texas)

SUMMARY OF CITE (COORDINATING INFORMATION FOR TEXAS EDUCATORS) SERVICES 1980–81

1. Computer searches of ERIC (approximately 50 citations with abstracts)

2. As a follow up to the ERIC search, each client receives, at no charge, 10 ERIC documents on microfiche and 5 journal articles.
3. In addition to the 10 ERIC documents, a client may purchase additional titles for $.20/sheet of microfiche. (Each title averages 2 sheets.)
4. In addition to the 5 articles with each computer search, a client may purchase additional articles for $.15/page. (This is our charge from the journal clearinghouse from which we order.)
5. "Resource Lists" on selected topics. These are bibliographies prepared inhouse of resources available on the subject. They will include an ERIC bibliography, journal articles, chapters from books, TEA publications, and microfiche of curriculum guides or ERIC documents. We can provide multiple copies of the Resource Lists.
6. From the CITE Resource List, a client may order 5 of the items on the bibliography. This will be ordered on the attached Item Order Form.
7. If one of the items on the Item Order Form is the ERIC bibliography or abstracts of curriculum guides, the client may follow up again with an order of 10 microfiche and/or 5 journal articles.
8. A client may order abstracts of curriculum guides on a particular subject.
9. As a follow up to the curriculum guide abstracts, the client may select 10 guides to receive on microfiche.
10. Paper copy of any microfiche document may be ordered for $.15/page.

COLUMBUS TECHNICAL INSTITUTE
(Columbus, Ohio)

CIS (COMPUTERIZED INFORMATION SERVICE)

What: Access to more than 100 computerized databases offering current and historical information on almost all subjects. CIS is used to supplement ERIC material by providing:
1. access to material that has been published more recently than is indexed in printed sources.

2. access to material that is not contained in the ERIC collection.
3. access to material for which manual searching would be extremely difficult and time-consuming.

Where: Educational Resources Center, Reference Section. Interested persons should inquire at the Reference or Circulation Desk.

When: Monday–Friday, 7:30 a.m.–4:30 p.m. Users on Saturday or after 4:30 p.m. are requested to return or call during above hours.

How: Users consult with the Reference Librarian and/or Assistant Librarian for Public Services to determine appropriateness of questions for searching. Users complete a search authorization form and work with the librarian to develop a search profile. Searches are conducted by the librarian, usually within one to two days. Users return to pick up completed search printouts.

Cost: Persons with appropriate questions will receive ten minutes free computer search time. If further searching is desired, users will pay $1.50 per minute connect computer time.

Who: Available to CTI students, faculty and staff.

UNIVERSITY OF CONNECTICUT
(Storrs, Connecticut)

What is a computer search? A way to save time—money—effort. A way to find out what documents or journal articles contain the information you need. A way to begin a research project, grant proposal, thesis, or dissertation.

What does the computer do? The computer, assisted by a trained analyst, searches through all the documents in a particular data base (for example, ERIC or Biological Abstracts) to see which ones meet the requirements you specify. You may request any combination of subjects—example: science education for gifted children in junior high schools in Connecticut. You may ask to have documents selected only from those published during a certain span of years, or in particular journals, or by a certain author. Note: most data bases include articles from approximately 1970 to date—earlier research is generally only available by manual search.

What happens when I request a computer search? First you fill out a rather detailed form, explaining to the search analyst exactly what you want, and telling where and when you can be reached. The analyst will look over your request, determine any additional information needed, and phone you to set up an appointment for the actual search. This appointment can be made for any mutually convenient time between the hours of 8:30 a.m. and 4:30 p.m., Monday through Friday. Then you, the analyst, and the computer meet. The prepared search is typed into the computer, and the computer "discusses" the results with you. At that time, you have the opportunity to briefly review the output of the search, and, if necessary, modify it. The final listing of articles (usually including abstracts) is printed that night by the computer and mailed to the library. It will normally arrive in somewhat less than a week.

Where is the computer? In Scotia, New York. But we talk to it via telephone lines, using a small terminal that looks like a standard typewriter. The Search Office which houses the terminal is located on the first floor near the Reference Desk.

Whom do I contact for a computer search? [Names listed here.]

ENVIRONMENTAL PROTECTION AGENCY (U.S.)
(Cincinnati, Ohio)

INTRODUCTION

The Library of the Environmental Research Center-Cincinnati is the scientific and technical information focal point for the U.S. Environmental Protection Agency. As such, it provides technical information backing to all EPA libraries and all EPA scientists, engineers, and researchers.

Traditional library services have been integrated with new automated services in order to meet the agency's information needs rapidly and efficiently. One of these automated services is using computer databases for literature searching.

Online computer literature searching has been offered at the Cincinnati Library since 1972, when this type of searching first became available nationally. It permits rapid access to millions of bibliographic citations and has proved to be cost effective in terms of both man-hours and dollars. Most of the literature written on a topic within the past 5 to 10 years can be identified in a matter of minutes.

The purpose of this publication is to explain the online searching services available at the Cincinnati Library, to outline the procedure for requesting a literature search, and to provide brief discriptions of the available databases.

This publication is the second edition of *Computer Literature Searching and Databases* and completely revises and updates the 1976 edition. The change in title to *Online Literature Searching and Databases* reflects the fact that almost all of the searching is now done online. Database information is current as of September 1978. Between 1976 and 1978 the number of databases available to the Cincinnati Library has grown from 74 to 124, representing a current total of more than 30 million bibliographic citations or records.

SEARCHING SERVICES

Literature searches are performed in response to specific requests from EPA personnel. They may be either retrospective or SDI (Selective Dissemination of Information).

In a retrospective search all of the years available in the database are searched. The information in most databases covers the last 5 to 10 years, a matter which is determined by the database producer and/or vendor. The searchable years for each database are specified in descriptions of the individual files.

In SDI or current awareness searching a search strategy or profile is run only in the most recent update of a database. Monthly SDI service is provided on request for those who wish to receive the most current information on a topic automatically.

Searches are performed online at a computer terminal, which permits instant viewing of results. Search analysts are reference librarians with expertise in scientific and technical literature, as well as in the operation of computer systems.

Using Boolean logic, the searcher combines terms appropriate to the subject being searched.

COMPUTER PRINTS

Computer prints are custom-made bibliographies or lists of citations on a search topic. A limited number of citations can be provided immediately at the terminal. Offline prints are ordered when a search produces a large number of citations. These are printed at the computer location on the evening of the same day, and are usually delivered within three working days. Prints are sent directly to the requester, whenever possible.

All database citations include author, title, and source of the material. In addition, some include abstracts or summaries, index terms, author's address, language, and other types of data. Since database producers determine the items to be included, the appearance of printed citations from different databases varies widely.

Documents corresponding to the items on computer prints can be supplied at the requester's local library, either from the collection on-site or through interlibrary loan.

HOW TO REQUEST A LITERATURE SEARCH

The search topic should be described in a few sentences on a "Literature Search Request" form (EPA Form 2170-1, rev. 9-76), which is available in all EPA libraries. It is helpful to include a list of the most important keywords and phrases in addition to the titles and authors of several relevant papers.

Databases may be suggested, but this is not necessary. The search analyst will use as many as apply to the subject.

Locations other than Cincinnati. Those desiring literature searches may contact the local EPA librarian, who can provide request forms as well as assistance in stating the request. The librarian will send the request to the Cincinnati Library and will receive the prints when the search is completed.

A search analyst will contact the requester to discuss search strategy and terms. The requester may also be called while the search is in progress. This allows the requester to participate in the interactive process and suggest changes. It there are any questions concerning searches, call 513/684-7701.

Cincinnati. Requester may call the library, ext. 7701, for an appointment. Search strategy will be discussed and at least one database will be searched while the requester is present. This allows live interaction with the computer and the opportunity to review citations. Computer literature searching services through the Cincinnati Library are available to EPA personnel only.

COSTS

Search costs vary, depending on the complexity of the request and the fees for the database used. An average cost of $17.00 has been determined for each database searched. This includes computer connect time and offline print charges. Most searches require the use of 3 or 4 databases. The ERC-Cincinnati Library absorbs the search costs.

DATABASES

Databases used by the ERC-Cincinnati Library are primarily scientific and technical files whose material can support the multiple facets of EPA's mission—environmental research and development relevant to setting standards for pollution control and enforcing these standards within the framework of anti-pollution legislation.

Many of these databases correspond to specific abstracting and/or indexing publications. Some databases include abstracts and others do not. Information as to a database corresponding with a printed product and whether abstracts are included in the computer version is part of individual database descriptions.

Types of material indexed in most databases are: scientific and technical journal articles, government reports, conference and symposia proceedings, dissertations, patents, books, and research projects.

These databases are available to the ERC-Cincinnati Library through contractual agreements with commercial database vendors and interagency agreements with government organizations, making more than 120 databases searchable.

Tables on the following pages provide brief descriptions of the individual databases. In the first column of the database tables abbreviations are used for vendor names as follows: [Here follows a list of five vendors and the database descriptive matter. See p. 440.]

HENNEPIN COUNTY MEDICAL CENTER
(Minneapolis, Minnesota)

REFERENCE AND BIBLIOGRAPHIC SERVICES

The Health Science Library offers a range of reference and bibliographic services including literature searching—both computerized and manual—creating mediographies, and answering reference questions.

Literature Searching

Upon request, Library staff will compile a bibliography on any bio-medical topic. Patrons need merely to call or stop in to request a literature search. Lists of citations are then compiled using several indexes covering medical, nursing, and hospital administration literature available in the Library.

Computerized Literature Searching

As an aid to literature searching, the Health Sciences Library has access to Medline, the National Library of Medicine's computerized on-line bibliographic searching service and several other computerized data bases.

A line to the Medline data base was granted by the National Library of Medicine to the On-line Group of the Twin Cities Biomedical Consortium, of which the Health Sciences Library is a member. Access to other data bases is acquired from Bibliographic Retrieval Services via contract between BRS and the TCBC On-Line Group. The other data bases include Psychiatric Abstracts, ERIC, Inform, NTIS, and many others. When appropriate—e.g., for early time periods, difficult searches or topics which are not covered in the computer data bases—library staff perform manual searches on the several indexes available.

The Library currently owns a Texas Instruments Silent 700 data terminal with which to access data bases. Computer time is paid for on the basis of use. Prime time hours are generally more expensive than non-prime hours. Each month the Senior Librarian receives billing statements from the NTIS and BRS detailing time used. Computerized searches are provided free of charge to patrons. All costs are absorbed by the Library's budget.

At the present time, compiling searches is the responsibility of the Senior Librarian, the Librarian, and the Library Assistant, all of whom are trained to do searches.

Mediographies

Also upon request, Library staff will create mediographies—lists of audiovisuals available on any biomedical topic. A collection of producers' catalogs is maintained in the Library for this purpose.

Reference Questions

Library staff are available to answer general reference questions. Since many of these questions come over the phone or at the Circulation desk, a collection of items pertinent to answering these questions is kept next to the circulation desk. Examples are the Directory of Medical Specialists and the AMA Medical Directory.

With the exception of the Library Page, all Library staff are trained to answer general reference questions and do so as part of their daily responsibilities. Complex reference questions and questions taking longer than a minute or two to answer are referred to the Librarian, Senior Librarian, or Library Assistant.

All bibliographic and reference services are free to Library patrons.

Internal statistics on reference services are kept by the Library staff.

MASSACHUSETTS INSTITUTE OF TECHNOLOGY
(Cambridge, Massachusetts)

COMPUTERIZED LITERATURE SEARCH SERVICE

The MIT Computerized Literature Search Service (CLSS) provides customized literature searching through remote access terminals on a fee-for-service basis. The Service's primary purpose is to serve the research needs of the MIT community. When time permits, however, CLSS is available to non-MIT researchers (including industry) for a surcharge. Industrial Liaison and Associates Program members receive discounts for CLSS services.

Mary Pensyl, Head, CLSS
Susan Woodford, Information Specialist

Hours

Monday–Friday 9 am–5 pm

Location

The CLSS Office is in Room 14SM-48 on the mezzanine above the Science Library (Room 14S-100). The Office may be reached by elevator (press button 1M) or by the stairways within the Science Library Reading Room.

What a Search Provides

The computer has eliminated the need for tedious manual searching; it searches simultaneously all issues (weekly, monthly, annual) of the equivalent printed index for the years covered by the data base and responds in seconds with citations. Computerized searching retrieves information more rapidly than manual searching and often more precisely.

A search can help a user to
- stay abreast of research
- unearth long-lost citations
- research the state of the art on a subject
- compile or extend a subject or author bibliography
- prepare grant, research, or thesis proposals
- learn who is funding which research and how much money is provided
- identify and locate experts in a subject area
- monitor congressional legislation and publications
- obtain forecasts (economic, political, social) and current market and economic information on specific industries
- keep track of ephemeral newspaper articles

Data Bases

Computerized indexes are available in almost every area of science, technology, business, the social sciences, and the humanities. Some information banks cover only a particular type of literature, such as dissertations, technical reports, or research proposals. Interdisciplinary subjects may require searching more than one base. A literature base list can be provided by the CLSS Office.

Citations

Each computerized search produces a bibliography customized the user's interests. Citations may be displayed in various formats at the terminal during the search or printed off-line on 8½ by 11 inch paper at considerable savings. Off-line print-outs are ready within three to five days of the search. Each citation contains a full reference to the printed document (author, title, publication source, work location of the writer). Many information bases supply an abstract as well.

Retrieval

The computer looks for keywords, authors, and special categories of information particular to specific data bases, in combinations specified by the searcher. Boolean operators are used to restrict or broaden the search. Searches may be limited by qualifiers, such as language or year. The search is done from teletype terminals to computers in various parts of the country. The search operates in a question-and-answer mode with immediate, on-line response enabling the user to converse directly with the computer.

Current Literature Alerting Service

Most information banks cover the latest five to eight years; a few go back further. Most of the bases are updated monthly or bi-weekly. Because the printed indexes are made from the data base tapes, citations are available by computer as much as a month before the published equivalent. A special kind of computer search—a regular alerting service—takes advantage of this frequency. A user interest profile is matched to the latest computer update and the user is automatically sent the newest citations in the appropriate field.

How to Arrange for a Search

Users who wish to initiate a search are asked to telephone or visit the CLSS Office to arrange an appointment with a trained information specialist. The wait for an appointment is usually one to two days. Before the time of the appointment the user fills out a questionnaire, which will help formulate the search strategy and minimize the time spent on-line. During the search the user helps to evaluate and modify the search as it progresses, thereby insuring retrieval of the most pertinent references.

Cost

Cost is computed by minutes connected to the computer (average:

about 20 minutes), data base used, and number of citations printed. Because each search is unique, it is difficult to determine exact costs in advance. The CLSS staff will be happy to discuss particular questions about fees. Payment may be made by check, cash, departmental account, or purchase order. Undergraduates working on UROP projects may often obtain funds by applying to their faculty advisers.

Demonstrations

Free demonstrations can be arranged for small groups at MIT. The CLSS staff is happy to do demonstrations at any location at the Institute. (Demonstrations are not available off-campus or for anyone outside the Institute.)

UNIVERSITY OF MISSOURI
(Columbia, Missouri)

The UMC Libraries offer online literature searching of computerized databases. The databases are computer-readable versions of indexes and abstracting services. Online searches are efficient, time saving, and particularly useful when you are searching subjects in combination or a new topic that is difficult to locate in printed sources. The result of an online search is a bibliography tailored to your topic.

The Libraries have access to over one hundred databases covering the fields of science, business, social science, agriculture, and the humanities. The databases include material from journals, books, conference papers, reports, government documents, and other sources. You will likely see familiar titles in the list of databases in this pamphlet. Most databases are updated sooner and more frequently than the corresponding print sources. Other databases do not have a print counterpart.

Searching a topic online goes beyond the limits of traditional manual methods of searching. Not only can one search by author or subject headings but other categories as well, such as author's institution, journal title, company name, date, language, SIC code, conference name, Chemical Abstracts Registry Number, etc.

An online search consists of translating a subject request into groups of keywords. The concepts represented by the keywords are related to each other by logical operators such as and, or, and not. Relationships between concepts may be illustrated by Venn diagrams.

The search service is available to all UMC students, faculty, and staff. The service is available to persons outside of the University on a limited basis. Researchers wanting a bibliography on a topic may request a search at the library branch or division serving their subject area or at one of the locations listed in this pamphlet.

When you request a search, a librarian, or search analyst, will ask you to describe your topic by filling out a questionnaire. All searches are done on an appointment basis; a date and time will be arranged. We request that the patron of the search service be present at the search session.

Before the search, the search analyst will explain costs to you. The libraries must provide searches on a partial cost recovery basis. This means the patron will pay for the direct costs of the search and the library will assume most overhead costs. The cost of a search depends on which databases are searched, and the complexity and comprehensiveness of the topic. An estimate can be provided. Payment for a search may be by personal check, cash or interdepartment order (IDO).

If you are interested in an online search, or would like more information, please contact the librarian in your area or at one of the four terminal locations listed.

SELECTED DATA BASES

[A list, under four subject headings, follows.]

UNIVERSITY OF NORTH CAROLINA
(Chapel Hill, North Carolina)

ONLINE COMPUTER SERVICE

UNC-CH libraries offer online search services utilizing computerized versions of abstracting and indexing publications and other data bases for which there are no printed counterparts. Data bases are available in many subjects—a selective list follows—and are offered through the libraries listed.

ADVANTAGES OF ONLINE SEARCHING

Online searching offers several advantages over manual searching, particularly when the coordination of several subjects is desired. In addition to saving time, this method usually provides more recent information than printed indexes and abstracts. Online data bases are often searchable by more specific vocabulary (words in titles or abstracts) than in their printed counterparts. The computer printout is a bibliography containing not only complete citations, but also abstracts for many data bases. Each search is custom-designed to meet the unique requirements of the topic.

REQUESTING A SEARCH

Reference librarians trained in computer searching are available at each of the locations. They can advise on the suitability of questions for searching, and recommend appropriate data bases. The librarian, in consultation with the requester, prepares the strategy and executes the search. Online retrieval is performed at terminals installed in the various libraries.

PRICES AND METHODS OF PAYMENT

Since these data bases are accessed through vendors, the libraries provide this service to their users on a partial cost-recovery basis. Charges vary according to the data base used and are based on computer connect time, telecommunications, citations printed off-line, and service costs. Average searches last approximately 10 to 20 minutes. Charges range from $.50 to $2.00 per minute.

Payment is required upon completion of the search and may be made by personal check or through University accounts.

For further information contact the appropriate library. [Then follows annotated list of databases by subject.]

THE FREE LIBRARY OF PHILADELPHIA
(Philadelphia, Pennsylvania)

COMPUTER BASED INFORMATION CENTER

The New York Times Information Bank is a computerized index to *The New York Times* newspaper and approximately seventy other sources, covering business, international affairs, newsweeklies and monthlies, and newspapers from metropolitan areas. However, no local newspapers are included.

Virtually all news and editorial material from the Final Late City Edition of *The New York Times* is included in the data base and extends back to January 1, 1969. Current issues are processed within four or five working days. Non-Times material is current within seven to ten days.

Selection Criteria—Normally included are:

- —Significant news items, and interpretive articles of opinion or commentary.
- —Biographical material.
- —Editorials.
- —Business and financial news.
- —Surveys, background, or chronological reviews.
- —Items by or about people of substantial general interest, regardless of content.
- —Commercial and political advertising when of research value.

Selection Criteria—Normally excluded are:

- —Obituaries, except those of well-known individuals.
- —Television listings, sports scores, advice or gossip columns.
- —Letters to the editor, unless written by prominent individuals or dealing with a controversial subject.
- —Paid personal notices.
- —Paid advertising, except when dealing with political or controversial topics.
- —Works of fiction.

The Information Bank is designed to retrieve information quickly and efficiently. It provides detailed, informative abstracts of newspaper and magazine articles. The user can specify the topics to be covered: personal or corporate names, simple subjects or a combination of terms. Because of the amount of detail contained in the abstracts, many questions can be answered directly from the computer print-out, without referring to the full text of the article. Information Bank users who want a large number of abstracts printed or who want an easily readable format can request "deferred print." Such reports are printed on better quality paper without the heavy use of abbreviations characteristic of the on-line print.

THE UNIVERSITY OF SOUTH CAROLINA
(Columbia, South Carolina)

PURPOSE

ACCESS is a computerized reference service. Librarians mechanically search current bibliographic data bases and quickly provide references to recent materials on a wide variety of subjects. This service is just one of many research tools which the Reference Department makes available. Bibliographic citations may also be obtained from the many print bibliographies and indexes in the department.

COVERAGE

The data bases covered by ACCESS are primarily in the natural and social sciences. They include information in biology, chemistry, physics, engineering, business, education, sociology, psychology, history, languages, and literature. New data bases are added regularly. An annotated list of all bases is available in the Reference Department.

WHO MAY USE

ACCESS is intended primarily for students, faculty, and staff of the University of South Carolina campuses. Persons not affiliated with the university may use the serivce, but they will be charged higher fees.

HOW TO USE

1. A request form must be filled out for each search desired. These forms are available at the Reference Desk.
2. Each requester must make an appointment with a search librarian for an interview which is designed to determine exactly what information the requester needs, to formulate a search strategy, and to explain what results are likely. The requester should bring his request form with him to the appointment.

FEES

Partial costs are charged to the user and may be substantial for some topics. The minimum fee is $5.00. For users not affiliated with the University, there is an additional charge.

Users are responsible for the payment of all charges regardless of results.

NOTIFICATION

The requester will be notified by phone (when possible) or by mail when the search results are available. All fees must be paid at the time results are picked up.

INQUIRIES

For further information on ACCESS, contact the Reference Department, Thomas Cooper Library.

SUFFOLK UNIVERSITY
(Boston, Massachusetts)

COMPUTER-ASSISTED BIBLIOGRAPHIC SEARCHING

The service provides access to large subject-oriented indexes stored in computers which can be retrieved at a typewriter terminal in the library. Most of these indexes correspond to printed indexes, many of which the library has. The computerized form, however, permits more efficient and flexible access to the information sought. The result of a computer-assisted bibliographic search is a customized bibliography printed "on-line" (immediately available for use) or "off-line" (available in one week, but significantly lower in cost than on-line printing). Access is accomplished by naming and combining relevant index terms to provide a complete, but specific, bibliography.

The library has selected the Lockheed Company's "Dialog" Information Retrieval Service as its vendor. Dialog currently provides access to 99 information data bases covering almost every area of academic interest in CLAS and SOM. However, since on-line searching is expensive and as yet requires considerable skill and experience to manipulate, the library will in the beginning offer only the seven indexes, or data bases, described on the attached list. These have been selected on the basis of the response solicited from the faculty last Fall. Over time as the staff becomes trained in searching techniques other indexes will be made available.

Until August 1980 no fee will be charged to individuals. Until then, however, the service will be limited to short searches of single indexes among the seven selected. A fee schedule has not yet been devised, but it is expected that individuals will be charged some part of the actual search cost after August.

Computer-assisted searching is not a substitute for, but rather an extension of, the usual search for information in printed sources available in the library's reference collection. Before a computer search is made, an appointment should be made with one of the three full-time Reference librarians for the purpose of developing a useful search strategy. Prior to the interview a Computer Search Request Application should be filled out (available at the Reference Desk) giving an adequate outline of the subject and definition of the problem. Careful planning of a search strategy reduces the cost (since costs are based on the time spent on-line) in addition to producing a more useful bibliography. Expect the staff trained in the use of available indexes to advise you if manual searching is more effective.

Since our staff is not large enough to dedicate one person to computer searching, most searches will be conducted at non-peak hours during the evening and on Saturdays. Therefore, the Reference librarian will inform the requester at the conclusion of the interview when the information should become available.

———————————————

THE UNIVERSITY OF TEXAS AT AUSTIN
(Austin, Texas)

COMPUTER-BASED INFORMATION SERVICES

Computer-based Information Services (CIS) have been offered by the General Libraries to members of the University community since 1972. The services, available only to current UT Austin faculty, students, and staff, are described below.

Lockheed Information Systems, SDC Search Service, and Bibliographic Retrieval Services (BRS). In 1976 the General Libraries expanded its Computer-based Information Services to include online searching of data bases available from Lockheed Information Systems. In 1978 CIS was further expanded to include additional data bases from SDC Search Service and Bibliographic Retrieval Services (BRS). The data bases which cover a wide range of subjects are growing rapidly and currently contain more than twenty-eight million citations.

Many data bases are computerized versions of important abstracting and indexing publications already available in printed form in the General Libraries. Online searching is done by reference librarians trained in computer searching techniques and familiar with the data bases in their printed form. Although some data bases are utilized to retrieve specific information, most are used for computerized literature searching. The typical product of a search is a bibliography with citations and usually abstracts matching the search statement. Computer searching has several advantages over manual searching in addition to providing rapid access to current materials. The linking or coordination of subject terms enables the searcher to narrow the scope of the search and increase the relevance of the results. In addition computerized searching may be more thorough and current since many abstracting and indexing services are updated online several weeks before the printed versions are available.

Searches are done on a partial-cost recovery basis. Rates vary depending upon the data base searched. The scope and complexity of each search also vary so that the cost of each search is calculated at the end of the search. Search costs include only those costs charged the Library by vendors—computer connect time including communication charges and offline printing costs. The General Libraries absorbs the cost of staff time, equipment, supplies, and administrative overhead.

An individual may pay for a search by personal check or funds may be IDT'd from a grant or other University account. Persons paying by personal check must pay at the time they pick up their printout in the Special Services Department, PCL 1.102 (8:00 A.M. to 5:00 P.M., Monday–Friday). Results of searches paid by IDT may be mailed at the user's request and risk. Cash payments cannot be accepted. Searches are printed offline in California or New York and mailed to Austin within twenty-four hours of completion of an online search.

Individuals interested in a computer search should contact an appropriate librarian indicated on the list of *Data Bases Available for Computer Searching* available at public service desks. This librarian can provide additional information, discuss the suitability of your request for computer-searching, and help formulate a search statement.

Current Awareness Services. Current awareness services utilizing the ERIC (education), INFORM (business), Psychological Abstracts, and SPIN (physics) data bases automatically provide users with a list of the most recent literature published on their interests. Each citation includes full bibliographic information and an abstract. Current awareness lists are printed each month by computer and mailed to the campus address of the requestor. There is no charge to the user, but the service is limited to graduate students, faculty, and research staff. If you are interested in this service, a librarian will assist in formulating a subject profile. For information about ERIC, INFORM, or Psychological Abstracts, contact the Special Services Department (PAX 4077 or 471-7539). For information about SPIN, contact the Librarian, Physics-Math-Astronomy Library (PAX 2263 or 471-7539).

ERIC and Psychological Abstracts Retrospective Searching. Retrospective online searching of ERIC and Psychological Abstracts is made available on the Computation Center's CDC 6400 Computer through the time sharing system known as TAURUS. The two most recent years of these data bases are available at specified hours each week. The CIS terminals in the Special Services Department may be used to search these data bases at no charge. However, terminals must be scheduled in advance at the Special Services Department. Demonstrations explaining how to search are given each Monday at 3:00 P.M. in the Special Services Department (PCL 1.102). No appointment is required for a demonstration. These data bases may be searched from terminals outside the Library at additional times by users with account numbers. A schedule of these search times is available in the Special Services Department.

The Information Bank. The Information Bank contains news and editorial material from the daily and Sunday *New York Times* from 1969 to the present. In addition, similar material is included from other major newspapers (*Christian Science Monitor, Houston Chronicle, Los Angeles Times, Wall Street Journal, Washington Post,* etc.) and from selected magazines. Reference librarians in the Perry-Castaneda Library utilize The Information Bank in answering reference questions. For additional information, contact a librarian in the Perry-Castaneda Library Reference Services Department (PCL 2.200) or Special Services Department (PCL 1.102).

OCLC, Inc. OCLC, Inc. (formerly the Ohio College Library Center) provides access to over three million recently cataloged items in approximately 1,800 participating libraries across the nation. The General Libraries obtains the cataloging information of other libraries and inputs much of its recent original cataloging into this data base. A terminal for staff and public use is located in the Perry-Castaneda Library Reference Services Department (PCL 2.200) to aid in bibliographic verification and to provide locations of materials not available at UT Austin. In addition it has proved useful in obtaining call numbers of current books for which catalog cards have not been printed and/or filed in the Public Catalog. Current material is thus made available more rapidly to users.

LEXIS. LEXIS is a computer-based legal research system containing the complete text of recent court opinions from federal courts and appellate courts in twenty states including Texas. Information concerning the use of LEXIS by students and faculty members may be obtained from the Reference Department, Tarlton Law Library (471-7726).

TULSA CITY COUNTY LIBRARY
(Tulsa, Oklahoma)

INFO II is a fee-based research service connected with the Tulsa City-County Library's Business and Technology Department.

INFO II provides a quick and cost-effective alternative to traditional research methods.

INFO II accomplishes this by offering its clients the skills of a trained researcher and the time-saving device of computerized on-line information retrieval.

INFO II has contracts with System Development Corporation and Lockheed Retrieval Service so that it can offer its clients online access to over 100 databases that cover the recent world journal and report literature in fields such as business, social, life and physical sciences, humanities, technology, and marketing.

A computer search of any of these databases provides the client with a list of references on his chosen topic.

INFO II provides other services as well, such as retrieval and photocopying of specific articles and reports, manual searching of printed material, compilation of statistics and current awareness searching.

INFO II is unique in that it can draw upon the resources of the Tulsa City-County Library and other libraries throughout the nation.

In fact, INFO II will try its best to provide the answers to a client's question using all the information sources available.

INFO II provides an alternative to businesses that do not have their own information centers or do not have the time to spend on library research themselves and yet still need to be informed and up-to-date on what is happening in their own area of concern.

INFO II's fees are reasonable: $25/hour for staff research time plus any other fees incurred during the search such as computer searches (average cost is $20–$25), photocopying, or long distance telephone calls.

As an alternative to the $25/hour fee, INFO II has a deposit account system which enables a client to put a minimum of $250 on deposit with INFO II and in return receive a reduced rate of $20/hour as well as priority service.

INFO II offers its clients a confidential service.

INFO II's clients range from large company personnel to students and individuals pursuing specific interests.

STATE UNIVERSITY OF NEW YORK AT ALBANY
(Albany, New York)

INFORMATION RETRIEVAL SERVICES

The University Library has the capability of searching for information on many topics with the assistance of a computer. References to journal articles, books, research reports, and other types of materials have been combined to form databases, many of which correspond to printed indexes and abstracts covering a broad range of disciplines.

Why Use a Computer?

- If your project or research requires a very comprehensive literature search; for example, as background for a master's or doctoral thesis, or extensive term paper; or
- If your topic is so specific that there are no applicable subject headings in the printed forms of indexes; or
- If your research involves the relationship of several subjects or a narrower aspect of a broad subject; or
- If the topic is so new that material is difficult to locate.

What Do You Receive?

The result of a computer search is a bibliography or listing of citations to journal articles, serials, monographs, government publications, etc. related to your topic. Each citation includes full bibliographic information to help you locate items identified by the search. In some cases abstracts or short summaries of the citations can also be printed if you request them. The materials listed are not necessarily available in our library.

How Do You Request and Receive A Search?

1. The librarian at the Main Library or Hawley Library Reference Desks will help you determine if a computer search is needed and what database(s) would be most suitable for your research needs.
2. You will be given a search request form and will be scheduled for an appointment with a librarian who is trained to search the database(s) you need. If you are telephoning for an appointment, please call the Reference Desk (457-8564) first and discuss your research needs with the reference librarian to determine what database(s) are appropriate.
3. Complete the search request form(s) before coming to your appointment. Define your problem carefully in a concise *narrative* statement. Bring the form(s) and a valid SUNYA ID, if you have one, to your appointment. Since the Information Retrieval

terminals are heavily scheduled for consecutive thirty minute appointments, please be prompt. If you are unable to be present for the appointment call the Information Retrieval Section (457-5272) to cancel.

4. During your appointment, you will be interviewed by the librarian, who with your assistance, will formulate a search strategy. The librarian will tell you the number of citations that have been retrieved and together you will review some sample titles. If you are satisfied with the results, the citations will be printed either online at the terminal and made available to you that day or printed offline and mailed to the library. You can pick up your offline print-out at the Main Library or Hawley Library Circulation Desks in four to eight days. Online printing will be made available at the discretion of the librarian.

How Much Does It Cost?

Presently SUNYA users pay *only* the cost of printing citations retrieved from the search. The library absorbs all other search costs such as hourly computer and database charges.

The cost to a SUNYA user will depend on the number of citations retrieved and whether abstracts are also printed. For example, from the ERIC database, a typical printout of 22 citations with abstracts costs $2.34. The same list of citations without abstracts costs $.76.

NON-SUNYA users pay the entire direct cost of the search.

The Information Retrieval pricing policy is constantly being reviewed: due to inflationary cost factors and expanding services, a new pricing structure is being developed.

Current Awareness Service

If you have a continuing interest in your topic, you may wish to request a monthly update of new material retrieval using the same search strategy from your original search. Monthly charges for this service include a $3.00 fee per database, plus the printing cost for each list of citations generated. You may arrange for this service at the time of your appointment.

Locating Materials

A guide describing the elements of each citation will accompany the results of your search. Check the author/title section of the library's card catalogue and/or the periodicals printout to locate book or periodical materials owned by our library. Consult the librarians at the Government Publications Reference Desk for assistance in locating ERIC, NTIS, or government reports.

The Interlibrary Loan Office (Room 110) can usually obtain for you materials not owned by this library.

Databases Available

The attached sheet lists the databases available in our library. The dates of coverage refer to the earliest date covered by the database. In some cases, the print source can be searched manually to much earlier dates than the computerized database.

VETERANS ADMINISTRATION
WEST SIDE HOSPITAL
(Chicago, Illinois)

COMPUTERIZED SEARCH SERVICE POLICY

Staff, house staff, employees, consultants, and students may request a computerized search of the literature. Searches are also done for VA's where a searcher is not available, a computer terminal is not in use, or where a particular data base is not accessible. Searches are done for local hospital libraries and local requesting physicians. If and when these non-VA-affiliated requests become excessive, a charging system will be instituted.

Searches are available of the National Library of Medicine's data bases including MEDLINE, CANCELINE and AVLINE, and of the BRS data bases including MEDLARS, BIOSIS, PSYCH ABSTRACTS, ERIC. The professional librarian searcher reserves the right to say which data base(s) is (are) the proper one(s) for a particular question and to refuse to do a search if it is a "one term" search which can easily be looked up in the printed index corresponding to a data base.

Searches are run at West Side, usually within 24 hours of the request, unless the searcher is away on leave. In that case requests are referred to VA North Chicago or are held for her/his return.

The requester may be asked to help with the search by monitoring results as they come out of the terminal or may wish to do so for the sake of expedience, however, most searches are saved until the end of the day and run as a "batch" by the searcher without the requester present.

Searches are useful for the production of a demand bibliography on a topic related to direct patient care, education, or research. They may also be useful for verification of a particular citation for interlibrary loan or location of an article or for production of a list of articles by a particular person.

Automatic monthly SDI's (selective dissemination of information) from MEDLINE are available on the request of staff, attending physicians, consultants, and employees. These produce a monthly bibliography on a particular topic on which the person needs to be kept current. The search formulations are stored in the computer and output is automatic each month when the data base is updated. Formulations can be changed as the requester's needs change.

General Guidelines for Staff and/or Public

BIRMINGHAM PUBLIC LIBRARY
(Birmingham, Alabama)

PURPOSE OF POLICY

The Online Reference Service Policy is designed to supplement the Reference Service Policy and to serve as a basis for setting procedures and establishing guidelines in those areas of online reference service which are unique from standard reference service due to the nature and cost of data base information retrieval. The Online Reference Service Policy will be revised after a maximum period of six months. (Bracketed material in this policy will apply to an interim period to extend from March 1, 1980 through August 31, 1980, subject to the availability of adequate funding. As set forth below, this interim period of experimentation and adjustment will require some restrictions in the scope and nature of the services offered during the period it is in effect.)

DEFINITION OF ONLINE REFERENCE SERVICE

The greatest difference between online reference service and traditional reference service is that the patron is required to assume part of the expense involved in his/her inquiry because of the high cost of data base information retrieval. Under this policy, the Birmingham Public Library will assume the costs of staff time expended in a computer search and the telecommunication charges, and the patron will assume the costs of connect time and any on- or offline printing required. [During the interim period, the Birmingham Public Library will assume all expenses within the following limitations: each individual or corporate patron will be given a maximum of four searches per month at a maximum of ten citations per search. After the fourth search for a patron in a given month or the tenth citation of a given search, the patron will assume all costs of further connect time. The patron will assume all costs of any offline prints.]

The scope of online reference service may be summarized as follows: 1) advisement of all options in terms of time expenditures and costs between traditional reference service using printed indexes for research of a given question and the various data bases included in the online system(s) under contract by the Birmingham Public Library; 2) advisement of the availability of the material likely to be cited in the data bases and the possibility of obtaining material not owned by the Birmingham Public Library through interlibrary loan and/or through document clearing houses, and any potential time lags involved; 3) advisement of the cost differences between printing citations online and offline; 4) an intensive interview with the patron, arranged by appointment, by a subject area librarian or staff member familiar with the printed indexes in the subject field and a search analyst in order to minimize the time spent online, and thus the cost to the patron, and to furnish the maximum number of relevant citations. (In such cases where the patron is a subject area specialist, the interview may be conducted by the search analyst alone; in such cases where the circumstances of the patron demand an immediate search without the opportunity for consultation, the search may be conducted by the search analyst after he/she advises the patron of the potential difference in quality of such a search performed after full consultation); 5) the actual online search performed by a search analyst, whenever possible done with the patron at the terminal with the analyst in order that the patron may input decisions based on the response of the data base(s) to the search items and strategy provided by the interview; 6) full reference service in aiding the patron to obtain the material cited by the data base(s) employed.

Online Reference Service may also include short searches in "ready reference" situations in those cases where the appropriate printed indexes are not adequate to provide the needed information (e.g., when, because of publication lag, the indexes are not current enough to cover a particular event, person, or fact). This type of search may be made at the discretion of the librarian, based on his/her judgment of its appropriateness. The patron is not charged for this type of service.

It is important that the patron have a full understanding of the nature of data base information retrieval—what the system can and cannot do. The search analyst should be certain that the patron understands that a computer search does not necessarily provide all available citations, and that a retrieval rate of 65% of available citations which meet the specifications with a 65% relevancy rate to the subject terms input by the search strategy represents a computer search operating at peak efficiency, but that a computer search will retrieve a greater number of relevant citations in a far shorter time than conducting the same search by manual menas, and that the computer will also retrieve citations for which no access is provided in the printed indexes.

OBJECTIVE OF ONLINE REFERENCE SERVICE

The objective of online reference service is to provide Birmingham Public Library patrons with the option of obtaining the benefits of a computer search when the printed index resources of the library are insufficient to meet the patron's information needs in terms of 1) time expenditures necessary to search the printed indexes; 2) the incompleteness or other inadequacy of the subject terms used by the printed index covering a particular field (e.g., when the patron's search requires the combination of two or more subject terms;) 3) currency and/or 4) Birmingham Public Library does not possess the necessary printed index.

The decision of whether the Library's printed resources are sufficient for a particular search is made, in all cases, at the librarian's/ search analyst's professional discretion. Free demonstration searches may be conducted for individuals or groups in a manner consistent with the Library's other educational efforts. [Such searches should not exceed the maximum limits outlined above.]

REFERENCE SERVICE INSTRUCTIONS

In general, the reference service instructions for online reference service are the same as they are for traditional reference. However, because of some of the unique characteristics of online reference service (principally, the cost to the patron), the following instructions should be observed in online reference service in addition to the reference service instructions in the Reference Service Policy:

A. In the interest of full and cost efficient online reference service, the librarian/search analyst will undertake to explain all of the following to the patron:

- The benefits and limitations of the computer search.
- The appropriateness of a computer search for the patron's information needs.
- The importance of placing limitations on a search and establishing a maximum cost to the patron.
- The necessity of a full discussion of the subject of the search in order to formulate the most efficient search strategy.
- The development of the search strategy and the selection of the data bases(s) to be used.
- While the Birmingham Public Library reserves the right to maintain copies of all executed searches, all information solicited for the purpose of conducting the search will be treated confidentially, and all copies of searches will be held confidentially in terms of identification of the party who requested the search.
- The nature of the printout, making certain that the patron is able to interpret all references.
- How the cited material can be obtained, including the option of obtaining material the Birmingham Public Library does not possess through interlibrary loan or document clearing houses.

B. Patrons desiring online reference service will be given neither a greater nor a lesser priority than those patrons desiring traditional reference service, with the exception that city and county employees will be given priority when they need reference service in support of their official duties. (During the interim period, "target groups" will be phased in for the purpose of allowing the Birmingham Public Library staff to acclimate themselves to the new service during a period when service is at something less than full capacity, dividing the general public into groups small enough to be fully educated on the service's utility and cost efficiency, and allowing concentrated promotional efforts. The initial target group will consist of city and county employees and the business community. The second target group will include groups and individuals excluded from the first group. Focus on a target group will not deny service to an individual or group that is not a member of the target group, such focus merely being a means to concentrate promotional and educational efforts.)

C. Under no circumstances will a search analyst go to the terminal without a fully developed search strategy in written form.

D. Receipts will be made for all searches, whether for public or in-house purposes.

E. All terminal hook-ups to telecommunications services or data bases will be recorded in the log.

F. Each patron employing online reference service should be furnished a copy of the proper evaluation form and encouraged to complete it.

G. Birmingham Public Library reserves the right to copy all searches in order that search strategies may be evaluated for efficiency and to avoid duplicate searches. Search copies should be maintained and indexed in the vertical file of the appropriate department.

H. "Ready reference" online searches are permitted if printed sources will not yield the necessary information because of publication lag or other insufficiency. In such cases, the short search form may be used instead of the regular form. All appropriate information should be logged and filed.

In recognition that requiring patrons to assume even partial costs for a library service is a radical departure from traditional library practice, and thus limits that service to the public as a whole, the Birmingham Public Library pledges to its patrons a continuing effort to obtain additional funding from public and private sources to make online service as widely available as possible and at as low a cost as possible.

COLORADO STATE UNIVERSITY
(Fort Collins, Colorado)

POLICIES

The CSU Libraries regularly offer on-demand computer-assisted bibliographic searching as a logical extension of the traditional reference functions. The service, known as Computerized Literature

Access-Search Service (CLASS), falls within the purview of the Public Services Division, the administrative unit which has the responsibility for providing interpretive services. The service is supervised, therefore, by the Associate Director of Libraries for Public Services with the assistance of the CLASS coordinator and the Data Base Advisory Committee (DBAC).

The Libraries are capable of offering this service in terms of trained staff and appropriate equipment. There are no restrictions to users who may avail themselves of this service upon payment of a surcharge. All search requests and results, furthermore, are confidential information and are not shared with other patrons.

DOW CHEMICAL, U.S.A.
(Freeport, Texas)

Anyone who has a need to know has access to online searching. We have no other policy statement. Nor do we have any forms.

UNIVERSITY OF SOUTHERN MISSISSIPPI
(Hattiesburg, Mississippi)

PROCEDURES

The following procedures are to be followed by the SCARS (Southern Computer Assisted Retrieval Services) personnel when conducting computer searches.

Step I. Initial Interview
  A. Have requester complete search form.
  B. Discuss computer systems (BRS and Dialog), database content, limitations, costs, etc.
  C. Schedule time for reference interview and terminal session.
Step II. Pre-Interview Procedure
  A. Consult thesauri to ascertain key words for search.
  B. When necessary consult printed indices in subject area for more insight into contents, terminology, etc.

    C. Ascertain from each database guide the unique features to be used, i.e. data limitations, language, procedures for entering numbers, etc.

    D. Formulate possible search strategy.

Step III. Reference Interview

    A. Discuss search statement in depth.

    B. Point out factors to be considered as a result of your literature search (i.e. index terms, subheadings, related terms, etc.).

    C. Discuss formulated strategy with requester.

Step IV. Terminal Search

    A. Record all connect time in each database in log record for each search number. (Be sure you are using the correct log record for the system.)

    B. If offline prints are requested indicate the query number and database in the section of the record for offline services by the search number.

Step V. Completed Searches

    A. Completed Search—On Line

       1. Compute connect charges for on line time use.

       2. If citations are printed online indicate (on the back of the search form and on the citation record) the number of items retrieved and the number in Cook Library. In order to do this you must match the terminal items against our computer printout of periodical titles.

    B. Completed Search—Offline

      • Match the search results against our computer printout to ascertain which items are in our collection and record these numbers.

      • Contact requester to pick up search results.

      • Discuss elements of the printout with requester.

      • Discuss availability of resources.

      • Explain and collect any additional charges.

Step VI. Charges

    A. Consult rate sheet and enter applicable charges for each database connect time.

    B. Add appropriate surcharge

      $1.00—USM Personnel

      $2.00—Other Educational Personnel

      $3.00—Businesses and Industries

    C. Consult Offline chart to ascertain approximate number of pages printed offline and multiply by applicable page or citation rate. Be sure to include citation royalties.

D. Add an additional $1.00 for offline searches.

E. Add $.50 postage & handling for each search.

Step VII. Collecting of Fees

A. Fees should be collected upon completion of each search.

B. Fill out proper forms for interdepartmental charges to accounts.

C. The receipt book should be used for all cash transactions.

D. Make sure the search number appears on all forms whether cash or charge.

E. Record amount received and search number in notebook.

NORTHWESTERN UNIVERSITY
(Evanston, Illinois)

The computerized information retrieval service at Northwestern operates under the acronym of NULCAIS (Northwestern University Library Computer Assisted Information Service). Its primary clients are the faculty, students, and staff of Northwestern University. However, NULCAIS also serves those not affiliated with Northwestern who have been referred through a Datapass. The service is coordinated through the main Library's Reference Department. Searches of multidisciplinary databases (e.g., Environment Abstracts or Comprehensive Dissertation Index) as well as business, social science, and humanities data bases are conducted by librarians in this Department. Due to current staff limitations, searches of applied and pure science data bases (e.g., Chemical Abstracts, Engineering Index, and Biosis) are not presently available through the CACIC Datapass system.

STATE UNIVERSITY OF NEW YORK
COLLEGE AT POTSDAM
(Potsdam, New York)

COMPUTERIZED LITERATURE SEARCHES AVAILABLE

Computerized literature searches are available through New York

State Library to public, academic, and special library patrons from the following bibliographic data bases: MEDLARS, ERIC, BIOSIS, *Psychological Abstracts*, and *The New York Times* Information Bank. In addition, several other data bases have been made available to us. These include *American Statistics Index, Congressional Information Service, National Technical Information Service, Chemical Abstracts Condensates, Physics Abstracts, Toxline*, and several others. The Crumb Memorial Library has been given the opportunity to participate in this project, and the service is available without charge to students, faculty and staff as well as to professional and other members of the community until December 31, 1979. After that date, there will be charges for the service, unless the program is re-funded. There will be a limit of 20 searches per month allotted to the entire North Country 3 R's Council, of which we are a part. Requests from our library will be accepted each month only until the quota is filled.

Implementation of this project will be through regular Interlibrary Loan channels, with the requests transmitted to Albany via the NCRRR Council in Canton. There are some restrictions, mainly the suitability of the topic for a computerized search. Two or more concepts must be present in the same citation in order to retrieve relevant documents. A search topic is not suitable when it is represented by a single subject term or when the single term is not listed in the printed index or in the controlled vocabulary thesauri.

The number of years to be searched will vary with each data base; in some instances, as far back as 1964, in others, only the past two or three years. There will also be a limit on the number of citations provided, varying from 50–80 maximum, depending on which data base is utilized.

Users

GEORGIA INSTITUTE OF TECHNOLOGY
(Atlanta, Georgia)

Search requests are handled on a "first come, first served" basis, except when rush service is specified. Rush requests receive high priority in recognition of their standard 50% surcharge. The normal search process requires an average of 2–3 weeks from initiation until the user receives the results. No average time-frame can be quoted for rush searches. Billing is normally on a monthly basis.

UNIVERSITY OF MASSACHUSETTS
(Amherst, Massachusetts)

COMPUTER SEARCH SERVICE GROUP

Statement of Client Eligibility

The Computer Search Service is available to anyone who is willing to assume the cost of the service and is able to schedule time for both the search strategy interview and the search itself. Requests for computer searches will not be accepted over the phone or by mail, and the actual search will be conducted without the requestor present only in very unusual circumstances.

In the event that demand for the service exceeds the staff or computer time available, priority will be given first to UMass/Amherst faculty, staff, and students; then to the Five College academic community; and then to the public at large (including industrial requestors).

Questions concerning eligibility should be referred to the Associate Director for Public Services.

UNIVERSITY OF NORTH CAROLINA
(Chapel Hill, North Carolina)

CLIENTELE

The Academic Affairs service points (Humanities, BA/SS, Math-Physics, Chemistry) provide service primarily to the faculty, staff, and students of UNC-CH. Service will be provided to others as staff time permits. The Health Sciences Library provides service to anyone. The Institute for Research in Social Sciences and the Carolina Population Center Library serve any Institute member or affiliate.

UNIVERSITY OF NORTH CAROLINA
(Greensboro, North Carolina)

PATRONS SERVED

Members of the Reference and Documents Departments staffs do computerized literature searches for UNC-G students, faculty, and staff on a priority basis. As time allows, they will also do searches for the following, in priority order:

—members of the Friends of the Library, including corporate members;

—other industrial concerns in Greensboro, Winston-Salem, High Point, and Burlington;

—persons who are affiliated with libraries with which Jackson Library has cooperative agreements, but who do not have any access to search services;

—persons affiliated with libraries with which Jackson Library has cooperative agreements, and who *do* have some other access to searching services.

TEXAS A&M UNIVERSITY
(College Station, Texas)

1. The Automated Information Retrieval Service* (AIRS) of the Texas A&M University Library is available to all faculty, staff, and students of Texas A&M University at whatever is the lowest prevailing rate for connect time and offline printing. Payment may be made by cash or by charges to University accounts. Data Processing Center account numbers, however, cannot be used to pay for AIRS services.

2. Users not affiliated with Texas A&M University may use the Automated Information Retrieval Service* under the following conditions:

   a. Non-profit organizations or individuals not representing profit-making firms may use the service on the same basis as Texas A&M University users.

   b. Profit-making organizations may use the service, but a processing fee amounting to an increase of $20 per hour in the connect time rate will be charged.

   c. First priority for service will be given to users affiliated with Texas A&M University.

---

*Excludes searches on the data bases of the National Library of Medicine, for which all users will be charged for connect time and printing costs plus a $1.00 processing fee.

Databases

ENVIRONMENTAL PROTECTION AGENCY (U.S.)
(Cincinnati, Ohio)

EPA, ERC, CINCINNATI, LIBRARY DATABASES

Database Name Years Covered Vendor	Meaning of Name No. of Citations or Records	Producer and Description
ABI/INFORM see INFORM	—	—
ACCOUNTANTS INDEX 1974–Present SDC	— 52,000	AMERICAN INSTITUTE OF CERTIFIED PUBLIC ACCOUNTANTS, New York, NY International coverage of literature related to account- ing, auditing, taxation, data processing, investments, financial management, financial reporting, and

management. Sources are journals, speeches, pamphlets, government documents and books. Corresponds to *Accountants Index*.

AGRICOLA (Formerly CAIN)	*AGRIC*ultural On-Line Access	TECHNICAL INFORMATION SYSTEMS, SCIENCE AND EDUCATION ADM.,
1970–Present	1,150,000	USDA (Formerly National Agricultural Library),
BRS		Beltsville, MD
LIS		Covers worldwide literature
SDC		in agriculture and allied sciences, including general agriculture and rural sociology, agricultural economics, animal science, forestry, plant science, pesticides, entomology, natural resources, and pollution. This file represents the holdings of the National Agricultural Library and cites journal articles, monographs, government reports and special reports, and conference proceedings. Includes the Agricultural Economics file and the *Bibliography of Agriculture* and the *National Agricultural Library Catalog*.
AHL	America: History and Life	ABC-CLIO, INC., Santa Barbara, CA Covers the periodical literature on American and Canadian history, area studies
1964–Present	43,000	nadian history, area studies and current affairs. Beginning in 1974 books and doctoral dissertations are
LIS		included. Corresponds to *America: History and Life*.

AIM/ARM	Abstracts Instructional and Research Materials in Vocational and Technical Education	CENTER FOR VOCATIONAL EDUCATION, OHIO STATE UNIVERSITY, Columbus, OH Abstracts of special material in vocational and technical education, manpower economics and development,
1967–1976	7,500	employment, job training and vocational guidance.
LIS		Beginning in 1977 records which would have been added to this database are included in ERIC file.

[Note: This is the first page of 31 pages of similar descriptive material which concludes the 35 page booklet]

MASSACHUSETTS INSTITUTE OF TECHNOLOGY
(Cambridge, Massachusetts)

All searches are conducted by appointment; see related brochure for specifics or contact the Search Service Office. Rates for service use are available upon request. Monthly updating (current awareness) service is available on all bases. Free demonstrations of any of the bases are available to small MIT groups—details from the Search Service Office.

DATABASES AVAILABLE 1980–1981*

Aerospace

COMPENDEX
DEFENSE MARKET MEASURES SYSTEM

---

*Most subject headings and database listings are taken from *Directory of Online Information Resources*, 6th edition, September, 1980, Rockville, MD: CSG Press. For more information on these databases ask at the reference desk or call the Search Service Office.

NTIS
SAE ABSTRACTS
SAFETY SCIENCE ABSTRACTS
[Followed by 7 pages more of subject division]

UNIVERSITY OF NORTH CAROLINA
(Chapel Hill, North Carolina)

PRIORITIES OF ACQUIRING DIFFERENT TYPES OF FILES

Of first priority for acquisition are those files which are computerized versions of heavily used indexes and abstracts. Such data bases should be offered by the library (in the section which houses the printed versions) since their usefulness has already been demonstrated. Other data bases which are highly specialized (e.g., Geology) should be obtained if the library determines there are sufficient potential users to justify providing the service. A third category of online files, those which encompass multidisciplinary topics (New York Times Information Bank), should also be obtained if the library decides their utility and uniqueness are worth the expense. If the decision is made to acquire a highly specialized or multi-disciplinary data base, then a service point must be established for it.

FACTORS TO WEIGH IN ADDING DATA BASES

When considering whether to add a data base, the following factors should be among the ones evaluated: (1) Potential use determined by current demand for online service, current demand for the corresponding printed versions, amount of current online resources in that subject, or other pertinent factors; (2) Projected demand for the service; (3) Possible duplication by other online files already offered (duplication here is not limited to identical data bases but can include new data bases with essentially the same content as existing files); (4) Proven reliability of the vendor and the system; (5) Financial consequences of the library's commitment including special hook-up or subscription fees, appropriateness of currently held hardware, or any other factor involving extra expense in support services.

UNIVERSITY OF NORTH CAROLINA
(Greensboro, North Carolina)

Jackson Library offers its users a service which can provide bibliographies produced from a large number of computerized data files. Most of these data files correspond to similar published indexes and abstracting services, such as *Psychological Abstracts, Dissertation Abstracts International,* and the ERIC indexes, *Resources in Education* and *Current Index to Journals in Education.* Access to various data files is provided through the Lockheed Information System, Inc., and the National Library of Medicine. Among the approximately one hundred data files available for searching are the following: [Short list of titles follows].

THE UNIVERSITY OF TEXAS/HEALTH SCIENCES CENTER
(Dallas, Texas)

DATABASES

To compile a bibliography, the CARS (Computer Assisted Reference Services) analysts can search any of more than 100 databases available in a wide variety of subject areas. The majority of requests from our patrons are for searches of MEDLINE, ERIC, Psychological Abstracts, or the biomedical databases supplied by the National Library of Medicine. (See the selected list of databases beginning on the next page for specific information.) The search analyst will advise the requester in the selection of appropriate databases for computerized literature searching and alternate sources for manual searching. [Each of the primary data bases, along with charges, is explained in some detail in the remaining pages.]

Service Points

UNIVERSITY OF SOUTHERN MISSISSIPPI
(Hattiesburg, Mississippi)

REQUESTS

A. Any person desiring a computer search must complete a SCARS request form and arrange an appointment with a member of the SCARS staff.
B. Telephone requests will not be accepted, unless the patron agrees to a personal interview prior to the terminal session.

UNIVERSITY OF NORTH CAROLINA
(Chapel Hill, North Carolina)

LOCATION OF SERVICE POINTS

The public and the library can best be served by providing service at several different locations. Reference areas already serving a broad clientele usually provide the best location. The current level of demand seems adequately served by the present five service points— Health Sciences, Humanities, BA/SS, Math/Physics, and Chemistry. (Other service points on campus include the Carolina Population Center Library and the Social Science Data Library of the Institute for Research in the Social Sciences.) If the level of demand increases beyond the capacity of these service points, any recommendation to expand the number should be carefully weighed by the Committee in terms of cost benefit factors, including increased charges, and loss or change in efficiency.

Within this framework data bases should be offered by the currently established service point with the best supporting information collection.

A data base should be offered at more than one service point only if warranted by extremely heavy demand. While realizing that online services are expensive to provide, the Committee feels that, as with certain heavily used reference books, some duplication may be necessary to provide adequate access to different bodies of users. Every effort should be made, however, to meet existing demand for *unique* data bases before duplication is considered.

NORTHWESTERN UNIVERSITY
(Evanston, Illinois)

TELEPHONE REQUESTS FOR SEARCHES

Requests from individual clients for searches will not be accepted over the telephone. Clients must come to the library, accompanied by a Datapass, for the search. In most cases, telephone requests for searches will be accepted from libraries.

STAFF

BRIGHAM YOUNG UNIVERSITY
(Provo, Utah)

The organization is: Library Director/Assistant Director for Information Services/Computer Assisted Research Services Supervisor/ Computer Assisted Research Services Committee. The CARS supervisor does as many online searches as possible and also supervises and coordinates the online searching services. The committee members (currently four subject librarians who have been trained to do searches) serve as backup searchers for the supervisor to do the searches she does not have time to do. [Richard Jensen, Life Sciences Librarian, letter to editor, November 20, 1980.]

COLORADO STATE UNIVERSITY
(Fort Collins, Colorado)

THE COMMITTEE

The Committee exists to recommend overall policy for the functioning of the service. The committee, known as DBAC, consists of:
1. The Associate Director for Public Services, who serves as chairperson
2. The CLASS Coordinator

3. The Fiscal Services Librarian
4. One science subject librarian or assistant
5. One liberal arts subject librarian or assistant
6. One member of the General Reference staff
7. One representative from the Technical Services Division who serves as a communications link between Public Services and Technical Services

THE DUTIES

The duties of the advisory committee are:
1. To recommend policy
2. To recommend publicity and public relations programs
3. To do long-range planning
4. To serve as a center of input for staff opinion and ideas

TYPES OF APPOINTMENTS

All DBAC members are involved in searching or show an active interest in the service.
1. Appointments are made on an annual basis for the academic year.
2. The Associate Director for Public Services and the Fiscal Services Librarian are ex-officio members of the committee.
3. The three Public Services members are appointed by the Associate Director for Public Services.
4. The Technical Services member is appointed by the Assistant Director for Technical Services.
5. The Coordinator is elected annually from among the committee members. The proportion of the time devoted to CLASS by the Coordinator is determined by the Associate Director and the CLASS Coordinator.
6. The Coordinator for the previous year remains a member of the committee for an additional year.

THE COORDINATOR'S RESPONSIBILITIES

1. To maintain the rate tables.
2. To receive all mailings from the vendors.

3. To inform the staff of new developments.
4. To maintain a central file of manuals and other items of interest.
5. To consult on search strategies.
6. To notify the Fiscal Services Librarian when the maintenance of the terminal is required.
7. To develop a publicity program in cooperation with the Libraries' Coordinator of Publicity.
8. To coordinate training.
9. To identify issues for deliberation by DBAC.
10. To compile statistics.
11. To receive all patron payments.

THE SEARCHERS' RESPONSIBILITIES

1. Interview patrons, develop search strategies, and conduct searches.
2. Obtain authorization to conduct a search by means of the patron's signature on the "Request for a Computerized Literature Search" form.
3. Upgrade search skills through training and demonstrations.

UNIVERSITY OF MASSACHUSETTS
(Amherst, Massachusetts)

COMPUTER SEARCH SERVICE GROUP RESPONSIBILITIES OF THE COMPUTER SEARCHER

The computer searcher is a librarian who has been trained in the general techniques of computerized literature searching and in the peculiarities of a set of data bases in particular subject areas.

Scheduling of Appointments and the Interview

Clients seeking detailed information concerning the Computer Search Service are directed to an appropriate searcher depending on the subject field in which the client is interested. Together with the client, the searcher chooses a data base(s), formulates a search strategy, and arranges a mutually convenient time for the search, checking that the terminal is available and adding the intended search to the Search Calendar. The searcher must be sure that the client understands the billing procedure and is aware of the expenses to be incurred. If necessary, a second interview may be held with the patron to review the search strategy.

Charging Searches to University Accounts
(per McDonald memo 6/3/77)

At the time of the search strategy appointment the computer searcher must determine whether the client wishes to charge the cost of the search and the resulting print out (if any) to a University account number. If so, the searcher should provide the client with a copy of the Computer Search Record indicating the areas which must be filled in with the six-digit account number and with the proper authorizing signature. The client should bring the completed form to the search appointment.

Before beginning the search, the searcher must verify the account information provided by the client. This is done by using the large-screen CRT located near the Reference desk and keying in AC3/(six-digit account number). The information displayed includes the name of the principal investigator for the grant or fund in the upper right hand corner of the screen. This name should be the same as the authorizing signature provided on the Computer Search Record.

Searchers in the branch libraries may wish to verify account information *before* scheduling the search appointment by phoning any CSSG member in the Main Library and asking him/her to check the CRT for the pertinent information.

Any problems with this procedure should be directed to the Library's Business Manager.

During the Search

The computer searcher conducts the search, preferably with the client present. After the search has been performed, the searcher arranges with the client when and how any resulting printout will be delivered to him/her. The searcher then escorts the patron to the Public Services Office with the white copy of the Computer Search Record; the yellow copy is filed in the computer search desk file titled "Computer Search Records (fiscal year)." A report of the search is entered in the Search Log. The terminal is then dismantled and stored by the searcher.

Requesting Credit for Dropped Searches

If in the course of a search the system malfunctions, it is the responsibility of the searcher to write to the vendor, explaining the situation and requesting credit. Essential information to be included in the request is: date and time of the search, communications network used, user number, and nature of the problem. Photocopies illustrating problem areas of the search may be made and attached if necessary. Copies of all CSSG-related correspondence are filed in the search desk file drawer folder titled "Correspondence."

Printed Bibliographies

Offline printouts are received by the CSSG coordinator, are distributed to the individual who performed the search, and are delivered to the client by the searcher.

Training

It is the responsibility of the individual searcher to initiate requests to attend workshops and to make *all* the necessary arrangements. Searchers may also utilize a portion of the time allotted for library use of the terminal in order to practice searching techniques and to become familiar with new data bases.

Maintenance of Search Aids

Materials sent to individual searchers from a commercial vendor should be read and filed, and the searcher should be aware of their contents and of any information necessary for the more efficient performance of searchers.

COMPUTER SEARCH SERVICE GROUP
RESPONSIBILITIES OF THE COORDINATOR

Selection and Term of Office

The CSSG Coordinator is chosen each year in June, for a term of one fiscal year, by all members of the Computer Search Service Group. This Group is comprised of all University librarians currently providing on-line computer search services. The librarian designated

Coordinator must be chosen from among the membership of this Group. Consecutive terms are allowed.

Responsibilities of the Coordinator

A. *Compiles Statistics*

1. Statistics on the number of searches conducted and the total number of computer hours spent in each data base and on the number of clients served and their academic status are compiled each month from the information recorded by individual searchers in the Search Log and from the searchers' copies of the Computer Search Record. These statistics are reported to the Head of Reference each month as part of the Coordinator's monthly report using the Computer Search Service Monthly Usage Report form.

2. In addition, the Coordinator maintains a separate statistical record of the number of data bases searched, the hours of use in each one, and the number of clients served. These statistics are recorded monthly on the Annual Computer Searches Usage Report form and are cumulated in June (reflecting fiscal year statistics). This record is maintained in a binder available at the Search Desk.

B. *Reports to the Head of Reference*

1. The monthly report to the Head of Reference consists of:
   - Statistics on the number of searches conducted reported on the Computer Search Service Monthly Usage Report form.
   - A summary of responses received on the Computer Search Evaluation forms reported on a copy of the form itself.
   - A narrative synopsis of activities may be appended to include reports on training sessions, CSSG meetings, demonstrations, new staff appointments, and any other news of recent developments.

2. Copies of these monthly reports are maintained in a binder available at the Search Desk.

C. *Coordinates Publicity*

The Coordinator is responsible for planning all publicity for the Computer Search Service in consultation with other searchers and with the approval of the Associate Director for Public Services. The material produced may be distributed either by the Computer Search Service Group through the Reference Department and the Branch Libraries or by the Public Services Office.

D. *Organizes Demonstrations*

The Coordinator organizes demonstrations of the Service at the suggestion of the CSSG or at the request of other Library, University, or Five College groups and in consultation with the Associate Director for Public Services.

E. *Allocates CSSG Funds*

The Coordinator submits requests for and administers the allocation of funds for brief informational and educational uses of on-line time. These funds cover such activities as practice time in new data bases, informational queries concerning the availability of new data bases, new hours of DIALOG service, and brief use of the DIALOG system for ILL verification or the solution of Reference questions.

F. *Acts as Liaison and Contact Person*

The Coordinator acts as general liaison between and as CSSG contact person for NASIC, for all commercial vendors, and for the Library's Public Services Office. This includes:
1. Responsibility for the circulation of all information from these sources not received by all members of the CSSG (e.g., changes in password, search/save serial numbers, etc.).
2. Channeling general inquiries on policy from the CSSG or from individual searchers to the Public Services Office.

G. *Updates Data Base Information*

The Coordinator is responsible for maintaining a current list of available data bases and searching costs for the use of CSSG members and for the consultation of interested clients when necessary. This may take the form of a supplement to Lockheed's own list of data bases. This record is maintained in a binder available at the Search Desk.

H. *Maintains Supplies of CSSG Forms*

The Coordinator maintains supplies of the following CSSG forms and monitors the need for new copies of them at the Search Desk and in the Reference Staff Vertical File:

1. Search Log (stenographic pad)
2. Calendar of Computer Searches (CSSG-1)
3. Monthly Service Usage Report (CSSG-2)
4. Annual Computer Searches Usage Report (CSSG-3)
5. University Library Computer Search Service Information Sheet (CSSG-4)
6. DIALOG Information Retrieval Service List of Data Bases (available from Lockheed) (Since Nov. 1977 published as a pamphlet: *Database Catalog.*)
7. CSSG Lists of Data Bases: Social Sciences and Humanities, Business/Economics, Science and Technology (CSSG-8/ CSSG-9/CSSG-10)
8. Search Request (CSSG-5)
9. Computer Search Record (CSSG-6)
10. Computer Search Evaluation (CSSG-7)
11. SDI Record (CSSG-11)

I. *Maintains the CSSG Files and Records*

The Coordinator maintains the following CSSG files at the Search Desk:

1. Monthly and Annual Service Usage Reports (black notebook)
2. Monthly Reports to the Head of Reference (black notebook)
3. Computer Search Records (file drawer)
4. Lists of available data bases and searching costs (black notebook and file drawer)
5. Minutes of CSSG meetings (black notebook)
6. CSSG Policies (black notebook)
7. DIALOG Chronolog BRS *Systems Progress Reports*, BRS *Bulletins*, and other newsletters (black notebook and file drawer)
8. Correspondence (file drawer)
9. Other materials as necessary (file drawer)

J. *Terminal Maintenance*

The Coordinator is responsible for arranging for any necessary terminal maintenance by contacting Texas Instruments directly and supplying them with the terminal's model and serial numbers. Records pertaining to service are maintained in the office of the Business and Personnel Manager.

K. *Schedules Meetings of the CSSG*

COMPUTER SEARCH SERVICE GROUP
RESPONSIBILITIES OF THE PUBLIC SERVICES OFFICE

Computing Costs of Searches

The Public Services Office is responsible for computing the cost of each literature search on the basis of the actual computer connect time used and the number of print-outs ordered. The searcher provides the Office with a record of the initial and final clock times and the elapsed time (in decimal percentage of an hour); the number, format, and cost per item of print-outs ordered; and, when necessary, with the hourly charge for each data base and for the communications network used.

Since Summer 1976, DIALOG has computed the cost of each search, including print-outs and connect time, and has printed it at the end of the search after the LOGOFF command has been entered. While this practice continues, the estimated total provided by DIALOG will be entered on the Computer Search Record and charged to the client.

Payment may be made by cash or by check made out to the Library Trust Fund. The cost may also be charged against a funded account providing that an authorizing signature and the proper account number appear on the Computer Search Record prior to the search. If a client is unable to pay at the time of the search, the Public Services Office is responsible for billing him/her or for arranging how the payment is to be made.

Ordering Supplies

The Public Services Office orders and maintains a supply of thermally treated rolls of paper for the terminal (Texas Instruments Silent 700—Model 735).

Client Eligibility for Service

The Associate Director for Public Services shall set requirements for the eligibility of a client for a computer search, and any question concerning eligibility should be referred to the Associate Director.

Approval of Publicity

The Associate Director for Public Services gives final approval to publicity of the Service.

Formulation of New Policy

Questions or problems which are not covered by existing policies should be referred to the Associate Director for Public Services.

MICHIGAN STATE UNIVERSITY
(East Lansing, Michigan)

DATABASE SEARCHES

Entire staff should be able to do computer assisted reference and be knowledgeable about when to use databases. Comprehensive bibliographic searches should be available with specialist assigned for each appropriate new database as it becomes available.

Reference questions efficiently answered and quality bibliographies prepared while number of database search requests increase.

UNIVERSITY OF NORTH CAROLINA
(Chapel Hill, North Carolina)

SERVICE POINT COORDINATOR

At service points where several people search, it is recommended that one person be given primary responsibility for coordination of online searching services. The coordinator's duties would include keeping abreast of new data bases, assigning primary searching responsibilities, scheduling searchers if necessary, providing continuing education for other searchers, handling billing problems (if they arise), providing for public relations, maintaining the quality of finished searches, and representing the service point on the Information Retrieval Committee. Such a coordinator will promote the smooth operation of online services within an existing department, and will serve as a contact for providing input to the Information Retrieval Committee.

TRAINING

The library should provide funds for educational opportunities for librarians involved in online searching. Training may be in the form of instruction provided by the vendor, producer, or by trained searchers, as well as workshops and seminars.

Where there are many searchers at a given access point, each should be capable of searching the data bases essential to their clientele (for example, MEDLINE in the Health Sciences Library or ERIC in BA/SS). However, the Committee strongly suggests that beyond these core files searchers specialize in specific data bases since demand for and complexity of files varies. There should be, of course, more than one searcher trained in any given data base to provide back-up service as necessary. No data base should be advertised unless someone is trained to search it.

INFORMATION RETRIEVAL COMMITTEE

It is expected that questions concerning the above and other related areas will be brought to the campus-wide Information Retrieval Committee for discussion and recommendations. In particular these areas should include: decisions about acquiring data bases; allocating data bases to service points; relocating or expanding the number of service points; and training.

A major function of the Committee is to serve as a clearinghouse for all aspects of information retrieval and to educate the University community in its use.

In addition, the Committee will serve as a place for sharing experiences, problems, information and successes. Discussion in such a forum will help reduce confusion, duplication and misunderstandings.

Membership on the Committee will be composed of at least one representative from each service point on campus. For those service points which have a coordinator, it is expected that the coordinator will be the representative.

THE FREE LIBRARY OF PHILADELPHIA
(Philadelphia, Pennsylvania)

In 1977, the Library received LSCA funds to implement a two-year project of online searching through Lockheed, SDC, and BRS. This project was administered and operated through a section of the Library separate from CBIC (Computer Based Information Center, which houses only the New York Times Information Bank). Over the next couple of months (i.e., from November 1980+), these two operations will be consolidated and moved to larger quarters. [Vilma M. Lieberman, Head, Computer Based Information Center, letter to editor, October 30, 1980.]

THE UNIVERSITY OF TEXAS/
HEALTH SCIENCE CENTER
(Dallas, Texas)

BIOMEDICAL SEARCH ANALYST

The University of Texas Health Science Center at Dallas-Library serves primarily three units: Southwestern Medical School, The Graduate School of Biomedical Sciences, and the School of Allied Health Sciences. Student, faculty, and staff needs in the area of teaching, research, and patient care are principle responsibilities. The Library also serves as administrative headquarters for the South Central Regional Medical Library Program (TALON). The Library consists of three major administrative areas: Technical Services, Public Services, and TALON.

Public Services is comprised of six departments: Reference Services, Computer Assisted Reference Services, Circulation, Medical History,

Interlibrary Loan/Photocopy, and the Learning Resources Center. This division is responsible for providing UTHSCD library users with optimum access to information through the use of diverse media, ranging from the traditional books and journals to audiovisual software and computer searching of specialized data-banks.

The Computer-Assisted Reference Services (CARS) Office produces bibliographies on topics requested by patrons by using the computer to locate and retrieve relevant citations from the millions of literature records stored in databases. The CARS Office also collects from requesters fees which reimburse the Library for the direct costs (connect time and printing) incurred by the Library in researching their topics.

The Biomedical Search Analyst is primarily responsible for providing bibliographic information to patrons by formulating and performing database searches and for informing patrons about the availability, appropriateness and cost of various on-line search services. In addition, this position involves training and partial supervision of clerical personnel as well as creating and revising publicity materials and office forms. The position also requires keeping current with the rapid development of the on-line searching field in order to maintain the quality of the searches.

POSITION INFORMATION FORM

DEPARTMENT:___Library_____ DATE:_____

TYPE OF ACTION (check one): _____ New Position

_____ Review

_____ Proposed Reclassification

INCUMBENT'S NAME (if any): _____

PRESENT TITLE:___Biomedical Search Analyst_____

Principal Duties

In the space below, please list in descending order of importance the principal duties and responsibilities of this position (i.e., those which require at least 10% of the total time on a weekly or monthly basis), *indicating to the left of each duty or responsibility the approximate percentage of time.* Minor or infrequent duties should be listed also, but percentages of time need *not* be indicated. For this reason, time percentage distributions do not have to total 100%. These suggestions may be helpful in completing this form:

A. Number each duty.

B. *Be specific.* Avoid general statements such as "handle correspondence," "compile reports," etc.

C. Omit unimportant details such as "pick up telephone," "open files," etc.

D. Begin each duty with a verb which clearly indicates the action performed such as:

"*Confers* with supervisor to evaluate basis for budget requests."

"*Reviews* damage reports and takes corrective action."

"*Files* documents by subject matter."

DUTY NO. 1

70% 1. Preparation of computerized literature searches which involves:

A. Explaining the cost and process of computer-assisted bibliographic searching to inquirers.

B. Conducting detailed reference interview of persons requesting searches.

C. Selecting or advising the requester on selection of appropriate databases and on-line search systems.

D. Formulating the search by selecting appropriate terms and by constructing search strategy.

E. Performing search on database(s) selected from over 120 possibilities using one or more of four different online search systems.

F. Recording results on search form for permanent statistical record.

G. Calculating cost and charge to requester.

H. Informing patron of search results and charge.

I. Explaining printout format, limits of search, terms used, etc., if necessary.

J. Reviewing results of backfiles and offline prints to insure relevance.

K. Preparing and revising ongoing current awareness searches (SDI's). Store on automatic system or execute monthly.

L. Assisting patrons in the use of indexes, etc., when a computerized literature search is not suitable.

20% 2. Office management duties which include:

A. Training and partially supervising clerical in the performance of duties (responsibility shared with the Head of CARS Office).

    B. Performing public relations activities which involves:
- Planning long-range P-R efforts.
- Creating and revising advertising materials.
- Presenting demonstrations of on-line bibliographic retrieval systems to interested groups or individuals in CARS Office or at other locations.

    C. Creating and revising forms used by CARS Office.

    D. Maintaining files on databases, updating manuals, etc.

    E. Preparing portions of CARS annual report.

    F. Ordering manuals, thesauri, supplies, etc., when necessary.

5% 3. Other library responsibilities which include:

    A. Reference Desk duty on assigned weekends or nights.

    B. Participating in library committees (presently a member of Library Policy Committee and Library Staff Development Comittee).

    C. Attending staff meetings.

    D. Special tasks as assigned by Library Administration, i.e., inventory.

5% 4. Continuing education responsibilities (keeping up with developments and changes in on-line bibliographic searching), specifically by:

    A. Reading newsletters and manuals published by database suppliers and vendors.

    B. Attending workshops, conferences, training sessions, etc.

    C. Reading articles on the subject in the professional literature.

INTERVIEW/ CONSULTATION PROCEDURES

General

UNIVERSITY OF SOUTHERN MISSISSIPPI
(Hattiesburg, Mississippi)

SCHEDULING

A. All appointments should be scheduled no later than the following day of the initial request.
B. As a general rule, the analyst receiving the search request will be the one who conducts the search.
C. Requests for searches at a time when the initial analyst cannot conduct it should be assigned to another searcher and verified as soon as possible. If there is a time discrepancy the patron should be immediately notified.

UNIVERSITY OF NORTH CAROLINA
(Greensboro, North Carolina)

CONSULTATION

Anyone interested in having a search run should arrange for a consultation with one of the Reference or Documents Librarians so that the librarians can:
- —clarify the actual need for a computer search;
- —see that the person is familiar with the related printed indexes and thesauri;
- —make sure he understands the costs and method of payment
- —determine the strategy for the search;
- —obtain a grant or departmental account number if the cost is to be billed.

The librarian on duty at the Reference Desk (who is the only staff member in the department at night and on weekends) cannot provide consultation on searches. Telephone requests are not accepted. Search results short enough to be printed on our own equipment will usually take two or three days to be processed. For those few searches printed off-line and received by mail, the time may be a week.

TEMPLE UNIVERSITY
(Philadelphia, Pennsylvania)

SCHEDULING SEARCHES

Patrons who wish to request a computerized literature search shall fill out the search request form which is available at the Reference desk. The Reference librarian on duty shall answer any preliminary questions and distribute the completed form to the appropriate search unit (i.e., Business, Documents, Social Sciences, or Science). Within twenty-four hours, the designated searcher shall schedule the search with the patron. Although searches are scheduled primarily at the convenience of the patron, other factors, such as library hours, searcher's work schedule, and the availability of the computer, shall be considered. Once the time for doing the search is determined, the searcher shall reserve the computer.

POLICY ON PATRON INTERVIEWS

All computerized literature searchers shall conduct detailed pre- and post-interviews with the patron to ensure high quality results.

Pre-Interview

- A. Carefully question the patron to clarify his/her search request and prepare a preliminary search strategy using the appropriate tools.
- B. Evaluate the search request and recommend to the patron whether or not the search should be done.
- C. Fully explain the on-line and off-line costs of the search and describe the various alternatives which are available.
- D. Inform the patron of the printed counterpart to the data base and that it can be searched manually at no cost.
- E. Go over the preliminary search strategy with the patron to adapt and refine it, being careful to explain:
  - the terms which were chosen;
  - the search process (i.e. boolean logic, etc.); and
  - the capabilities and limitations of computerized searching.
- F. If necessary, further explain and/or adapt the search while on-line.

Post-Interview

1. Go over the search strategy with the patron, indicating which combinations produced which results.
2. Explain the citations and inform the patron how to locate this material in Paley Library.
3. Give a copy of the search to the patron.
4. Distribute an evaluation form to the patron and ask him/her to complete and return it to the library.

THE UNIVERSITY OF TEXAS
HEALTH SCIENCE CENTER
(Dallas, Texas)

REFERRAL PROCEDURE

If patrons request computerized literature searches, do not take the search request. Please refer them the CARS Office staff. Also, if the requester will leave his/her name and number, we will contact him/her. *Under no circumstances, however, write down the topic.* Clear communication between requester and search analyst is the most important part of the search. Bruised expectations cause the library bad PR and extra expense.

Request Procedure

To avoid misunderstanding or delay, the request should be made directly by the person actually needing the bibliography. Requests may be made by phone or preferably in person. By being present while the search is run, the requester may take full advantage of the interactive capabilities of online searching and obtain better results at less expense.

Requesters should also be prepared to assist the search analyst by supplying synonyms or definitions or by selecting subject terms from a thesaurus.

Forms*

BIRMINGHAM PUBLIC LIBRARY
(Birmingham, Alabama)

Patron's Library Card # _____

BIRMINGHAM PUBLIC LIBRARY

COMPUTER-ASSISTED REFERENCE SERVICE

SEARCH REQUEST FORM

Please read this form before completing. Care taken now will facilitate
and enhance the results of this search and will probably lower the cost
to you.   Date _____
NAME _____ Dept. _____
ADDRESS _____ PHONE _____
TYPE OF USER: BUSINESSPERSON ___ CONSUMER ___ PROFESSIONAL ___ CITY/CO GOV ___
    STAFF ___ EDUCATOR ___ STUDENT ___ OTHER(specify) ___
NAME OF BUSINESS, SCHOOL, OR INSTITUTION _____
DATE SEARCH IS NEEDED _____ INTERVIEW APPOINTMENT DATE AND TIME _____

1. PLEASE GIVE A TITLE TO YOUR RESEARCH PROBLEM _____
_____

*Linda Daniels, "A Matter of Form," *Online*, October, 1978, pp. 31–38. The author, after a brief introduction, includes search request forms from MIDLNET (Midwest Regional Library Network) libraries—Ed.

2. PLEASE RECORD A FULL DESCRIPTION OF THE SUBJECT ON WHICH YOU ARE
SEEKING INFORMATION. WHERE APPROPRIATE, INCLUDE ALTERNATE NAMES FOR
CHEMICAL AND BIOLOGICAL SUBSTANCES OR COMPOUNDS, COMMON AND SCIENTIFIC
NAMES OF BIOLOGICAL SPECIES, AND NAMES OR DESCRIPTIVE TERMS FOR
SPECIFIC METHODS OR TECHNIQUES USED IN YOUR RESEARCH. _____

_____

_____

_____

3. LIST IMPORTANT TERMS (WORDS OR PHRASES) AND ANY SYNONYMS OR RELATED
TERMS THAT YOU WISH TO INCLUDE OR EXCLUDE. INCLUDE BOTH SCIENTIFIC/
TECHNICAL TERMS AND COMMON TERMS. PLEASE FEEL FREE TO EXPLAIN TERMS
AND BE AS DETAILED AS NECESSARY. ANY ALTERNATE SPELLINGS THAT HAVE
RELEVANCE SHOULD BE NOTED.

TERMS	SYNONYMS OR RELATED TERMS	EXCLUDED TERMS
_____	_____	_____
_____	_____	_____
_____	_____	_____
_____	_____	_____

4. PLEASE LIST THE COMPLETE CITATIONS, INCLUDING AUTHOR'S FULL NAME, TO
TWO OR THREE OF THE MOST USEFUL ARTICLES ON YOUR SEARCH TOPIC. THIS
WILL GREATLY FACILITATE SEARCHING AND ENHANCE RELEVANCE OF SEARCH RE-
SULTS TO YOUR NEEDS.

_____

_____

5. PLEASE LIST TWO OR THREE OF THE MOST IMPORTANT JOURNALS COVERING
YOUR RESEARCH PROBLEM. _____ _____

6. SHOULD THERE BE LANGUAGE RESTRICTIONS ON THE CITATIONS RETRIEVED?
Does not matter ___ English only ___ English and: _____

7. DO YOU WISH TO LIMIT THE SEARCH TO A PARTICULAR TIME-SPAN?
Does not matter ___ Retrieve only (inclusive dates): _____

8. SHOULD ANY OF THE FOLLOWING DOCUMENT TYPES BE EXCLUDED?
Journal articles ___ Dissertations ___ Conference reports ___
Books ___ Patents ___ Reports ___

9. THE SEARCH SHOULD BE LIMITED TO ___ (number of) CITATIONS OR TO A
TOTAL COST OF _____, WHICHEVER IS THE ___ GREATER ___ LESSER.

10. The Birmingham Public Library reserves the right to maintain copies
of all searches. All solicited information for the purpose of conducting the search will be treated confidentially, and all copies
maintained will be held confidentially in terms of identification of
the party who requested the search.

11. Patron authorization for execution of search (signature): _____

****

FOR LIBRARY USE ONLY
SEARCH STRATEGY

********* **

COMPUTER SEARCH RECEIPT BIRMINGHAM PUBLIC LIBRARY	COMPUTER SEARCH RECEIPT BIRMINGHAM PUBLIC LIBRARY
NAME _____ PHONE ____	NAME _____ PHONE ____
ADDRESS _____	ADDRESS _____
FILE(S) _____ DATE ____	FILE(S) _____ DATE ____
CITATION CHARGE _____	CITATION CHARGE _____
CONNECT CHARGE _____	CONNECT CHARGE _____
TELECOM CHARGE _____	TELECOM CHARGE _____
TOTAL COST _____	TOTAL COST _____
TOTAL CHARGE _____	TOTAL CHARGE _____

CITE
(Austin, Texas)

CITE

coordinating information for Texas educators

REQUEST FORM

Request No._____
In__ _____
Run_____
Out

Name_____Title_____

Affiliation_____ Phone (   )_____

Return Address_____City_____State_____Zip_____

REQUEST STATEMENT:
Please give us a concise statement of your request. You may 1) ask a question or 2) request
specific documents, or both. Include accurate and complete information, explain all abbreviations and acronyms. Specify authors and/or works when appropriate. Supply complete bibliographic citations when ordering.
Information returned to you can only be as accurate as that which you supply us.

_____

_____

_____

_____

_____

PLEASE CHECK THE ONE APPROPRIATE BLANK WHICH BEST SUMMARIZES THE INTENDED PURPOSE OF THIS REQUEST.
__Classroom Use   __Classroom Materials   __Program Planning
__Speech   __Inservice/Staff Dev.   __Professional Awareness/
__District Report   __Personnel Evaluation   Informative Reading
__Project/Proposal Research __Program Evaluation   __Dissertation/Thesis
__Curriculum Development   __Administrative Planning   __College Coursework
        __Other

PURPOSE STATEMENT:
Please write a narrative description of the reason or purpose for which the information and
assistance will be used.

_____

_____

The End User of this material is: Self   Someone else   Group

Year restriction (if applicable) from 19___ to 19___.

CHECK AUDIENCE GRADE LEVEL:
__Pre K   __Middle/Jr High   __Univ/College
__Kindergarten   __High School   __Adults
__Elementary   __Jr/Comm College   __Other (specify)_____

WHAT SOURCES HAVE YOU CONSULTED / WILL YOU CONSULT?
__Public Library   __ESC Subject Specialist   __TEA Publications
__College/Univ Library   __ESC Collections   __Other_____
__District Professional Library   _____

ESC USE: Region_____ Authorization_____
                                          Signature   Date
     Date Requested_____ Request Negotiated By_____

                                          Date Needed_____

HENNEPIN COUNTY MEDICAL CENTER
(Minneapolis, Minnesota)

SEARCH REQUEST

Name_____

Please circle   HCMC   MMC   HCMS   Date

Phone _____

Describe subject matter in your own words for which search is to be
conducted. Define any words which have a special meaning.

____Etiology ____Diagnosis ____Treatment ____Complications ____Other:

Please list any known relevant articles published within the last 3 years,
if available. (Please include author's name)

____Few relevant articles   ____Human

____Comprehensive search   ____Animal experiments

____English only   ____Years to be covered

____Other languages, please specify: (results of searches covering
                                         more than the last three
                                         years may take a week to be
                                         received.)

____ I will check back for the search.

____ Please notify me when the search is ready. Phone _____

____ Please mail the search to me. Address:

Searcher's use:

KANSAS STATE DEPARTMENT OF EDUCATION
(Topeka, Kansas)

KEDDS COMPUTERIZED LITERATURE SEARCH

Name _____ Date _____

Title _____ Institution _____

Address _____USD _____

            city   zip   phone

LINKer: _____ RC _____

□ Mail to Client   □ Mail to LINKer

Describe the topic about which you are seeking information:

Reason for Request:

Educational Level of Topic: ☐ Elementary ☐ Secondary ☐ _____

Sources Investigated Previous to this Search:

Authorities in Field (if known):

FILES & DATA BASES TO BE SEARCHED:				
☐ ERIC Abs.	☐ Kansas File Abs.	☐ Dialog	☐ Accession Numbers Only	# Abstracts _____ COST _____
☐ L & L Bhvr. Abs.	OTHER:	☐ SDC		TIME: _____
☐ Soc. Sci. Abs.	☐ _____	☐ BRS		DATE MAILED
☐ Psych. Abs.	☐ _____	☐	☐ Abstracts Maximum #	
☐ Excep. Child Abs.	☐ _____			
☐ Comp. Diss. Abs.	☐ _____			_____

FORM 0-03-06-108

White copy - KEDDS Resources
Pink copy - LINK Facilitator
Yellow copy - Regional Center

Revised 12/12/79

MASSACHUSETTS INSTITUTE OF TECHNOLOGY
(Cambridge, Massachusetts)

COMPUTERIZED LITERATURE SEARCH SERVICE
Room 14SM-48, MIT Libraries
Cambridge, MA 02139 (617) 253-7746

USER PROBLEM STATEMENT

Name _____   Phone _____

Address _____

Completing this form prior to your appointment will increase the efficiency of the service during your appointment and will probably lower the cost of service to you.

1.   Please give a brief title to your search problem.

_____

2. Please give in your own words a <u>narrative</u> description of the problem to be searched. Be specific; define phrases with <u>special</u> meaning. Append a list to your narrative of any synonyms, closely related phrases, and alternative spellings. Please indicate if any words or phrases have a special use that you wish to exclude. Use scientific and technical as well as common vocabulary. Please underline those phrases which are most relevant to the problem.

_____

_____

_____

_____

_____

_____

_____

_____

_____

_____

_____

_____

3. Please state any topics related to (or applications of, or views of, or approaches to) your specific problem that are <u>not</u> of interest if you wish to exclude retrieving citations to any documents on such topics.

_____

4. Please list two or three of the most important authors (and/or organizations) publishing on your topic; <u>complete</u> names, if known, are helpful. Please indicate if you wish to exclude documents by any of these (or other), authors or oganizations because of prior familiarity with their publications.

_____

5. Please list two or three of the most important journals covering your problem. Please indicate if you wish to retrieve references to documents from <u>only</u> these journals. Please indicate if you wish <u>not</u> to retrieve references to documents from <u>any</u> particular journal, perhaps because you personally receive the journal.

_____

6. Please list the complete citations to two to three of the most useful articles on your search topic. (It may be helpful to bring these articles to your appointment.)

_____

_____

_____

7. Do you wish either to retrieve or not retrieve references to documents written in a particular language? _____ Does not matter _____ Retrieve English only.

    Retrieve only in _____ Do not retrieve in _____

8. Do you wish to limit the search to a particular time span?
    _____ Does not matter _____ only

9. Do you wish to exclude references to particular types of literature?
    Exclude _____ Journal articles _____ Books _____ Patents _____ Reports
    _____ Conference Papers _____ Dissertations

10. Would you prefer: _____ a comprehensive search that retrieves most of the references relevant to your problem, but which may also retrieve many references not relevant to your problem? _____ a narrow search that may retrieve fewer references relevant to your problem, but which also retrieves fewer non-relevant references?

11. Can you estimate the number of relevant documents (a) you think may be present in the literature _____, (b) you would like to retrieve and get references for _____.

12. If you have done a literature search (manually or by computer) on this problem or a closely related problem, please indicate if possible what was searched, what difficulties were encountered, and the overall result of the search.

_____

_____

_____

WORK ORDER   INF. SPEC. _____   Date _____   CLSS Acct. #

      User Name _____   Tel._____ ☐ MIT Acct. #_____

BILL TO   Name _____   ☐ MIT Personal Charge
      Address _____   ID #_____

      _____   ☐ Other Charge/P.O._____

      _____

☐ Non-MIT Rates apply	Service Rate	Units Used	Cost	Acct Object No. Code
CONNECT TIME (system & database)				
ONLINE TYPE				
OFFLINE PRINT				
	SUBTOTAL			
HANDLING & POSTAGE				
TOTAL CHARGE				
Charges Prepaid				
Balance Due				

Thank you for using the Computerized Literature Search Service, the MIT Libraries. Call 253-7746 should you have further questions.

SUBTOTAL

HANDLING & POSTAGE

TOTAL CHARGE

Charges Prepaid

Balance Due

COMPUTERIZED LITERATURE SEARCH SERVICE
         INQUIRY DATA

Date:_____ Receiver:_____

In-Person:____ Phone:____ Mail:____

USER'S NAME:

ORGANIZATION/DEPARTMENT:

ADDRESS:

_____ Administrative Staff

PHONE/HOURS:

_____ Sponsored Research Staff

_____ Research Associate/
      Postdoctoral Fellow
_____ Research Assistant

PREVIOUS USER? Yes _____ No _____

_____ Faculty

UPS Given or Sent _____ Date:_____

_____ Graduate Student

_____ Undergraduate

_____ Other

BRIEF PROBLEM TITLE _____

_____

NOTES:

How did user first learn about the Computerized Literature Search Service?

Colleague referral _____ Librarian _____ Brochure/Poster _____ Other _____

_____

THE FREE LIBRARY OF PHILADELPHIA
(Philadelphia, Pennsylvania)

THE FREE LIBRARY OF PHILADELPHIA   Date_____
Computerized Literature Search Request #____   FLP Department____

Name_____ Home/Business Phone_____

Home/Business Address_____

_____ State_____ Zip_____

Date by which search results are needed_____

____Mail search results ($1.00 fee) OR ____I will pick-up search results

AGREEMENT: I am requesting a computerized literature search. I understand that charges for this search will be based on ½ the cost for database connect fees, ½ the cost for telecommunication fees, and the full cost for citation printing. I agree to pay these charges (NOT TO EXCEED $_____).
Checks should be made payable to THE FREE LIBRARY OF PHILADELPHIA. Payment will be due upon receipt of search results.

            _____ _____
             signature   date

PLEASE TYPE OR PRINT RESPONSES TO NUMBERS 1 THROUGH 10:

1. SEARCH TOPIC. Describe the problem or subject area to be searched.

2. KEYWORDS. List significant words or word stems, terms or phrases, synonyms or related terms describing your search topic. Feel free to list scientific, technical, or common vocabulary. Define terms with special meaning. Indicate terms or meanings NOT to be used in this search.

3. Name important individuals or organizations known to be publishing work related to your topic.

4. Name important journals in which works related to your topic might appear.

5. If known or easily available, provide several references on this topic.

6. LANGUAGE RESTRICTIONS. ____none; ____English only; English and_____

7. TIME PERIOD. ____does not matter; retrive only _____; retrieve from _____ to _____
             year   year year

8. SCOPE OF SEARCH. ____NARROW. An effort will be made to retrieve a minimum number of citations closely matching searc specifications; some relevant citations may be missed.
      ____BROAD. An effort will be made to retrieve a maximum number of citations with the possibility that a relatively high number of non-useful citations will be retrieved.

9. Maximum number of citations to be retrieved _____. If no limit is set, 50 will be the maximum retrieved.

10. May we contact you for a brief, follow-up evaluation of search results? This will be a mailed questionnaire.
____yes; ____no.

THE FOLLOWING SECTION IS TO BE COMPLETED BY FREE LIBRARY STAFF:

Search conducted by_____. Date_____. Vendor: ___BRS; ___LIS; ___SDC
               Telecommunications network: ___Telenet; ___Tymnet
Estimate your OFFLINE TIME for pre-search interview_____
      search strategy formulation_____
      review of search results with requestor_____

Total ONLINE TIME_____. LOGON/LOGOFF TIME(S)_____

DATABASE(S) searched:

____citations printed online; online citation fee (if applicable) $____

____citations printed offline; offline citation print fee $____; date offline prints received_____

USER FEE: $_____. Invoice forwarded_____. Payment received $_____ on_____
         date   date

SUFFOLK UNIVERSITY
(Boston, Massachusetts)

SUFFOLK UNIVERSITY COLLEGE LIBRARY:
Application for Computer Searching

NAME: _____   DATE: _____

ADDRESS OR DEPT. _____
_____

PHONE NUMBER(S): _____

___ Undergraduate   ___ Graduate Student   ___ Faculty   ___ Other (please specify)

Search Title:

Describe the problem or question to be searched. Be as specific as possible.

Define major words or concepts. List synonyms and related terms.

Briefly describe your project or assignment.

Can you cite an article which exactly serves your needs?

APPOINTMENT: _____ for _____   OK_____
              date   time   initials

3/30/80

COMPUTER SEARCHING:
Search Strategy

Search Title:

Comprehensive _____   Format:
Narrow _____   Other limits: (dates, languages)

Data Base to be Searched: File #:

Thesaurus terms   _____   _____   _____
                  _____   _____   _____
                  _____   _____   _____
                  _____   _____   _____

Free text terms   _____   _____   _____
                  _____   _____   _____
                  _____   _____   _____

NOT terms   _____   _____   _____
                  _____   _____   _____

*-terms to E   _____   _____   _____
                  Set #   Set #   Set #

Strategy:

Sample Citation:

SEARCH

Search Results/
Document Delivery

CITE
(Austin, Texas)

coordinating information for Texas educators

Request No._____

In _____

Out _____

**Item Order Form
for
Resource Bibliography**

Send completed form to:
   CITE Resource Center
   Southwest Tower
   211 East 7th Street
   Austin, TX 78701

Name_____Title _____

Affiliation_____Phone (   ) _____

Return Address _____City_____

State_____ Zip_____

ESC Region _____

CITE Resource Bibliography #_____

Only five items are allowed for each Item Order Form. List below the number and title of the items you wish. In the case of microfiche orders, list the item number and the unique identifying number for each document in microform (ex. ED 000 000, or CDL 0*-000.)

ITEM#	MICROFICHE # (when applicable)	TITLE

CITE

coordinating information for Texas educators

Followup

Request No.＿＿＿＿＿

In ＿＿＿＿＿

Out ＿＿＿＿＿

Send completed form to:
CITE Resource Center
Southwest Tower
211 East 7th Street
Austin, TX 78701

Name＿＿＿＿＿　Title ＿＿＿＿＿

Affiliation ＿＿＿＿＿　Phone (　) ＿＿＿＿＿

Return Address ＿＿＿＿＿　City＿＿＿＿＿

State＿＿＿＿＿ Zip＿＿＿＿＿

ESC Region ＿＿＿＿＿

MICROFICHE ORDERS

Ten (10) documents in microfiche are included with each request at no cost. They may be selected from any of our microfiche collections. Documents ordered beyond ten will be billed at 20 cents per sheet of film.

DOCUMENT NUMBER	TITLE

JOURNAL ARTICLE ORDERS

In addition to microfiche documents, you may order up to five (5) journal articles. Article can be provided only when *all* information has been included. Additional articles will be billed at 15 cents a page.

EJ-	Article Title			
	Journal	Vol./No.	Mo./Yr.	Pp.
E J -	Article Title			
	Journal	Vol./No.	Mo./Yr.	Pp.
E J -	Article Title			
	Journal	Vol./No.	Mo./Yr.	Pp.
E J -	Article Title			
	Journal	Vol./No.	Mo./Yr.	Pp.
E J -	Article Title			
	Journal	Vol./No.	Mo./Yr.	Pp.

GEORGIA INSTITUTE OF TECHNOLOGY
(Atlanta, Georgia)

Citations are normally printed offline. More than 15 citations will be printed online only for rush searches. If a user requests that a search be duplicated, re-compiled or re-entered in a data base, charges will be at the discretion of the librarian performing the search. IEC librarians will assist the user in interpreting citations as required. They should advise prospective users of their photocopy service concerning proper format and procedures.

KANSAS STATE DEPARTMENT OF EDUCATION
(Topeka, Kansas)

Form 8-03-06-102
KEDDS/RESOURCES

DOCUMENT REQUEST FORM

☐ **HARD COPY**

☐ **MICROFICHE**

NAME _____ DATE _____

SCHOOL _____ USD _____

ADDRESS _____
STREET   CITY   ZIP   PHONE

Should you desire an ERIC document, list the ED number found in the upper left hand corner of the abstract and the title in the space below:

	ED NUMBER	DOCUMENT TITLE
____	ED _ _ _ _ _ _	
____	ED _ _ _ _ _ _	
____	ED _ _ _ _ _ _	
____	ED _ _ _ _ _ _	
____	ED _ _ _ _ _ _	
____	ED _ _ _ _ _ _	
____	ED _ _ _ _ _ _	
____	ED _ _ _ _ _ _	
____	ED _ _ _ _ _ _	

KEDDS/RESOURCES

JOURNAL REQUEST FORM

NAME _____ DATE _____

SCHOOL _____ USD _____

ADDRESS _____
STREET   CITY   ZIP   PHONE

Should you desire a journal article, list the EJ number found in the upper left hand corner of the abstract and the journal citation and the publication date below:

EJ NUMBER	NAME OF JOURNAL, VOLUME, NUMBER, PAGE NUMBERS, AUTHOR, PUBLICATION DATE
____ EJ _ _ _ _ _ _	
____ EJ _ _ _ _ _ _	
____ EJ _ _ _ _ _ _	
____ EJ _ _ _ _ _ _	
____ EJ _ _ _ _ _ _	
____ EJ _ _ _ _ _ _	
____ EJ _ _ _ _ _ _	
____ EJ _ _ _ _ _ _	

Please keep YELLOW copy, return WHITE and PINK copies to KEDDS/RESOURCES.

NORTHWESTERN UNIVERSITY
(Evanston, Illinois)

DOCUMENT DELIVERY

Northwestern University Library cannot guarantee delivery of, or access to, material cited in the results of an online search for individuals not affiliated with the University. Those not affiliated are welcome to use the Library's collections under its limited access policy outlined in *Libraries and Information Centers in the Chicago Metropolitan Area* (1976 ed.). Clients in need of interlibrary loan services should make requests at their Referring Library.

THE UNIVERSITY OF TEXAS/
HEALTH SCIENCE CENTER
(Dallas, Texas)

SERVICES

Upon request, the CARS (Computer Assisted Reference Services) Office will provide a bibliography, i.e., a list of references, of the literature on a topic or by an author (or confirmation that no references exist in the file being searched). Standard references include author, title, and publication information. Many references have abstracts which can be printed at extra cost.

DELIVERY TIME

Usually the search can be done within a day of the request. Short bibliographies may be printed online at the terminal in the CARS Office and given to the requester at that time. Alternately, the references may be printed offline at the vendor's central computer (on the east or west coast) and mailed to UTHSCD the following day. Online printing provides results sooner. Offline printing takes longer but is cheaper, particularly in expensive databases or when abstracts and/or a large number of references will be printed. Please allow 3 to 10 days mailing time.

PICKUP OF SEARCH RESULTS AFTER THE OFFICE IS CLOSED

A staff member must escort the requester to the office. At no time should patrons be left alone in the office.

Key—The key to the office is kept at the Circulation Desk.

Locating Search Results—Searches will not be left for pickup at the Information or Circulation Desk. They are kept on the third shelf of the corner bookcase in the CARS Office terminal room. The shelf is labeled "Searches Ready for Pickup." Arrangement is alphabetical by last name of requester. Please check the printouts carefully to make sure that another search is not attached by mistake.

Patron Evaluation

CITE
(Austin, Texas)

ACKNOWLEDGMENT OF RECEIPT OF MATERIALS AND PRELIMINARY EVALUATION

Name_____ CITE Search Number_____

Subject of Search_____

Your completing and returning this card to us will assist us in improving our services to you. Please respond to the questions below and return this postage-free card.

1. The material arrived:_____on/before date specified;_____after date specified; ___no date specified.
2. Does the request statement on the yellow CITE search form clearly reflect your original request for information?_____yes _____ no
3. Does a quick scan of the material indicate that it is relevant/useful?___yes_____no
4. If no, please detail below:_____

_____

_____

_____

Verso of the postage paid card: "Approximately six weeks ago you requested a search through the Project CITE Resource Center. The topic of that search request was _____. In order

482

that we may continue to improve our services to the school people of Texas, would you please respond to the questions on the detachable card and mail it to us." [Jan Anderson, manager: "We no longer use this form because of staff reductions, but it had been sent out to every third requester, six weeks later." November 19, 1980]

Please read the instructions on the inside of the card.

1. Did you use the information? ( ) much ( ) some ( ) little ( ) none ( ) not yet

2. To what extent was the information relevant to the subject of your search request? ( ) very relevant ( ) generally relevant ( ) little relevance ( ) off the subject completely.

3. How did you use the information? ( ) in the classroom ( ) in program planning ( ) in inservice planning ( ) in administrative planning ( ) in a college course ( ) for personal improvement ( ) other (describe)

4. What kind of information did you find most useful? ( ) journal articles ( ) reports ( ) program descriptions ( ) curriculum material ( ) brochures ( ) ERIC search ( ) other bibliographies ( ) other (describe) _____

5. Did you seek more information based on references in the search? ( ) yes ( ) no

6. Did you order microfiche/paper copy based on references in the search? ( ) yes ( ) no how many titles? how many pages?

7. Have you initiated another search request since the one listed on this card? ( )yes ( ) no

8. If you have additional requests, would you use the service again? ( ) yes ( ) no Would you recommend the service to a colleague? ( ) yes ( ) no

9. Did you share your information package with others? ( ) yes ( ) no If yes, how many people?

10. If the service were not available through the service centers, would you be willing to pay for the service from another source? ( ) school district funds ( ) personal funds ( ) not interested ( ) other (describe)

11. Comments: _____

KANSAS STATE DEPARTMENT OF EDUCATION
(Topeka, Kansas)

REACTIONNAIRE   Search No. _____

Once you have had an opportunity to look through the material provided in response to your request, please complete the *Reactionnaire* and return it to the KEDDS Resource Component.

Your personal evaluation of each KEDDS search will help us improve computerized search service for all our clients.

1. This search arrived:

   ☐ in time   ☐ too late to be of use

2. The quantity of material received was:

   ☐ sufficient   ☐ too extensive   ☐ too brief

3. The information provided by this search was:

☐ on target ☐ not relevant to topic

4. Do you intend to review documents and/or journal articles from the references listed in this search?

☐ yes ☐ no

Name _____ Topic _____

Address _____

Phone _____

UNIVERSITY OF MISSOURI
(Columbia, Missouri)

University of Missouri-Columbia Libraries
Online Search Service
202 E Ellis Library

Evaluation

In order to continuously improve the UMC Libraries' Online Search Service, please complete this questionnaire and return it in the Campus Mail envelope provided. If you have any questions regarding your search, please contact your search analyst or Jeanmarie Fraser in the Online Search Service office. Thank you.

DEPARTMENT_____

SUBJECT AREA_____

UMC FACULTY____ UMC STAFF____ UMC GRAD.STUDENT____ UMC UNDERGRAD.____ OTHER____

1. How did you learn about the Online Search Service?
   Librarian____ Colleague____ Library announcement____ Other____

2. How many times have you used the service?
   once____ twice____ 3 times____ 4 times____ 5 or more____

3. What databases were searched?
   _____ _____ _____

4. What percentage (approximately) of the results were relevant to your search?
   0-20%____ 21-40%____ 41-60%____ 61-80%____ 81-100%____

5. Do you think online searching is a worthwhile addition to traditional library service?
   Yes____ No____ Not Sure____

6. Would you be interested in a periodic update on your search topic?
   Yes____ No____ Not Sure____

7. Did you receive enough introductory information about the costs, preparation, probable results, etc. of the search?
   Yes____ No____ Not Sure____

8. Did the results adequately meet your expectations?
   Yes____ No____ Not Sure____

9. Do you feel the search analyst was sufficiently prepared to perform the search?
   Yes_____   No_____   Not Sure_____

   If no, please explain.

10. Considering the time it would have taken you to manually search for your
    information, do you feel the cost was reasonable?
    Yes_____   No_____   Not Sure_____

11. Would you use the service again/ recommend it to others?
       Yes_____   No_____   Not sure_____

12. How could the service be improved?

13. Other comments:

Thank you.

Ready Reference Searches

MASSACHUSETTS INSTITUTE OF TECHNOLOGY
(Cambridge, Massachusetts)

DRAFT: GUIDELINES FOR QUICK-REFERENCE USE OF CLSS

Purpose: CLSS will be happy to perform free short searches for reference/bibliographic purposes. This service is not intended as a substitute for regular, user-funded, comprehensive bibliographic searches, but as an aid to reference librarians who have made a preliminary search and are unable to identify, verify, or locate material requested by a user. The purpose of this search is to supplement manual searches or to be used in place of the manual search when that is deemed appropriate. (Some guidelines to determine that use are given below.)

CLSS is keeping a log of "quick-ref" requests in order to evaluate costs and use. Requests will also be analyzed to determine what types of questions are most often answered by the service. Although scheduled appointments must take priority, CLSS will generally be able to respond within 24 hours, and, in most cases, within a much shorter time.

Goals and Objectives:

1. To provide online access to databases as part of a comprehensive

reference service and to further the traditional reference function of assisting the user in identifying and locating relevant information in as efficient and expeditious a manner as possible.

2. To conserve the time of the library staff and users and to promote general productivity.

3. To provide access to a wider range of reference and bibliographic sources than may be available in one's own library.

4. To acquaint reference librarians with and provide access to sources that may only be available in online format.

5. To use this service as a public relations and instructional tool to inexpensively acquaint users with the availability and potential of online bibliographic searching.

6. To attempt to assess the time costs and tradeoffs of answering reference questions via online as compared to manual means.

Guidelines for Use

1. To verify a citation, when a reference is difficult, garbled, elusive, or incomplete, especially when it requires searching several sources for a number of years.

2. When many years of a reference tool must be searched for a piece of specific information, particularly when the cumulations are cumbersome to search, such as "Government Reports" or Dissertation Abstracts. (All years are merged in online files so a term can be culled from a decade of literature automatically.)

3. When the concept is quite new (often a "hot topic" of recent months), or poorly defined (often a buzz-word), and the keywords of abstracts and indexes have not yet caught up (e.g., "gentrification," "burn-out," "genetic engineering").

4. When a very recent citation is needed (the most current issue of an abstract or index is generally in the computer a month or more before it appears in print).

5. When a necessary source is unavailable (a particular volume is missing from the shelves or is at the bindery).

6. To locate the address of an individual or organization, when other directories have yielded nothing (Biography Index, Science Citation Index, the Foundation Directory, Encyclopedia of Associations).

7. When a current piece of factual information may be more likely to be found in a newspaper or popular journal not in one's library (e.g., Infobank, Newsearch, Magazine Index, NDEX, Christian Science Monitor Index [Monitor], etc.).

TEMPLE UNIVERSITY
(Philadelphia, Pennsylvania)

READY REFERENCE

The Reference Department shall utilize the computer to search ready reference questions which are not easily answered through routine methods. Appropriate ready reference questions shall include requests for specific information, new concepts or terminology, acronyms, obscure citations, or any questions for which no answer was found or on which the librarian has spent more than ten minutes attempting to answer. Ready reference questions shall not include requests for directional assistance, call numbers, periodicals, quotations, addresses, bibliographies, or articles for a research question. The library shall absorb all costs for ready reference use of the computer.

SDI

GEORGIA INSTITUTE OF TECHNOLOGY
(Atlanta, Georgia)

Selective Dissemination of Information (SDI, or, current awareness) searches should, when feasible, be done as computer searches. If appropriate data bases are not available, the department head should be consulted before a manual SDI search is offered.

HENNEPIN COUNTY MEDICAL CENTER
(Minneapolis, Minnesota)

CURRENT AWARENESS SERVICE

The Current Awareness Service provides all interested hospital personnel and Hennepin County Medical Society members with a monthly bibliography, based on a profile of the users' specified areas of interest, of the newest citations from the MEDLINE and/or other files.

To participate in this service, users call or stop in the Library and describe their areas of interest and limits which should be placed on the subject(s)—language, human and/or animal experiments, age groups, etc. From this, the Librarian formulates a search strategy which will retrieve relevant citations.

The searches, once formulated and tested on-line, are stored at the National Library of Medicine Computer Center or at BRS. Each month, after new citations for the coming month are added to the files and the SDI (Selective Dissemination of Information) LINE files are regenerated with the newest citations, the stored searches are automatically processed on SDILINE and mailed to the Library.

Maintaining and monitoring this service are the responsibilities of the Librarian with appropriate clerical staff.

During the third week of each month, Library staff review the searches and prepare them for distribution. The searches are mailed to requesters during the fourth week of each month (e.g., the citations for June are mailed the last week of May). Upon receipt of the search, requesters indicate on it those articles of which they would like copies, and return the search to the Library. Library staff, either by xeroxing materials from the Library's collection or by ordering materials through interlibrary loan channels, provide what has been requested.

Statistics are kept on the total number of searches prepared each month. In addition, the number of searches for each institution, the number of searches that were stored, those that were copied (in cases where different individuals have requested similar information) and the number of requests made by each individual are recorded.

The service is evaluated each year by means of a questionnaire which is attached to the November search. Users are asked to rate the service, its value to them, the relevancy of the citations, if they share it with others, and if they wish to continue to receive the searches. At the same time, they are also asked to note any modifications of their profile which they may wish to make.

This service is highly popular. It allows users to remain current with medical information without having to leave their patient care area.

LIBRARY OFFERS CURRENT AWARENESS SERVICE [for the public]

What it is

CAS is an on-going bibliographic service designed to keep you up to date with the literature in your field or in any area of special interest to you.

What it can do for you

CAS can keep you fully informed of new developments in your area of interest by alerting you to any new articles from published media relevant to your research.

How does it work?

1. You provide the Library with a description of your interests, defining them as broadly or as narrowly as you wish.
2. The Library uses your individual Profile to search through Index Medicus and SDILINE (a computerized, online, bibliographic search service), for articles of interest to you.
3. The Library sends you a list of current references each month.

THE UNIVERSITY OF TEXAS/
HEALTH SCIENCE CENTER
(Dallas, Texas)

CURRENT AWARENESS SERVICES

Fight the information explosion with an automatic computerized literature search. Stay currently aware with a monthly or semimonthly update from any one of 26 databases. You can receive references to material on almost any topic or follow the work of an author, an institution, a company, or an organization.

SDILINE

SDILINE is the database most often selected for current awareness service in bio-medicine. It is also the least expensive of the current awareness services. Most subscriptions cost $1.00 or $1.25 a month. SDILINE is an acronym for Selective Dissemination of Information On-line. It is equivalent to the latest month's entries in the MEDLINE file. Therefore, both SDILINE and MEDLINE include references to articles in 3,000 biomedical journals, plus a few selected symposia and published proceedings. Three printed indexes are derived from MED-LINE: *Index Medicus, International Nursing Index,* and *Dental Literature Index.* Abstracts are available for about 50% of the references and may be printed in the SDI at extra cost.

Other Databases with Current Awareness Services: [list follows].

ORDER PROCEDURE

To request current awareness service, come to the CARS Office or call. For best results, please do not delegate the request. Office hours are 8:30–5:00 weekdays. Phone (214) 688-2003 or 2004. Address: Computer-Assisted Reference Services (CARS) Office, Library, University of Texas Health Science Center at Dallas, 5323 Harry Hines Blvd., Dallas, Texas 75235.

FEES

BRIGHAM YOUNG UNIVERSITY
(Provo, Utah)

HOW MUCH DOES IT COST TO DO A COMPUTER SEARCH?

The charge depends upon which data base is used:

DIALOG, ORBIT IV, BRS
1. All Data Bases $5.00 for the first 10 minutes, plus $1.00 for each minute over 10 ($5.00 minimum charge)
2. SDI Service— Monthly Update $3.00 plus 10¢ per citation
3. Off-line Printout of References   10¢ per citation

MEDLINE

	1 to 30 Minutes	31 Minutes Plus
1. Current File— Current 2 to 3 Years	$ 7.50 ($7.50 minimum)	25¢ per minute
2. Backfiles 1966–1968 1969–1971 1972–1974 1975–1977	7.50	25¢ per minute

3. Current and Backfiles	$10.00	25¢ per minute
4. SDILINE Current Month	$1.00 plus 12¢ per page of references	—
5. All other MEDLINE Data Bases	7.50	25¢ per minute
6. Off-line Printout of References	12¢ per page	—

UNIVERSITY OF BRITISH COLUMBIA
(Vancouver, British Columbia)

COMPUTER-ASSISTED BIBLIOGRAPHIC SEARCHES

Charges to on-campus users, i.e., UBC faculty, staff, and students, for searches related to UBC research the cost of the transaction will be shared by the user and the Library as follows:

UBC staff time and equipment costs	paid by the Library, no charge to user.
Cost of computer connect time, communication costs, royalties, and cost of off-line printouts (dependent on data base and carrier charges).	User pays 60%, Library 40% of cost as charged by the data base supplier (minimum billing amount: $2.00).

Charges to off-campus users, and for those searches that are not related to UBC research; in both cases the total cost of the transaction will be paid by the user and calculated as follows:

UBC staff time up to one hour (including initial interview)	$20.00
Additional UBC staff time (charged in half hour increments)	$20.00 per hour
Cost of computer connect time, communication costs, royalties, and cost of off-line printouts (dependent on data base and carrier charges)	As charged to UBC by supplier
UBC equipment costs	$2.00 per hour (in half hourly increments, minimum $1.00).

COLORADO STATE UNIVERSITY
(Fort Collins, Colorado)

THE FISCAL PROCEDURES AND CONTROLS

1. Searchers are responsible for calculating the charges and for completing the Search Request Form, except for the NLM data bases, which are handled by the BMS Librarian.
2. Off-line prints are disbursed from the Coordinator's Office where payments are also made.
3. All payments, accompanied by a copy of the charge sheet (Search Request Form) are forwarded to the Libraries' Accounting Services daily (i.e., cash, checks, accounts receivable, and IMO's).
4. The Coordinator approves all vendor invoices for payment with the exception of NTIS invoices which are approved by the Biomedical Sciences Librarian.
5. The Associate Director for Public Services, the Coordinator, and the Fiscal Services Librarian review the Libraries' surcharge every six months and make recommendations to the Data Base Advisory Committee. If revisions in fees are recommended, the approval of the Director of Libraries is required.

UNIVERSITY OF CONNECTICUT
(Storrs, Connecticut)

FEE STRUCTURE

For each computer search, up to three separate charges may be required. (A "computer search" is defined as a single intellectual query posed in a single data base.)
1. A basic charge for computer time.
2. A per page charge for printing the results of the search.
3. An additional per page or per citation fee, usually referred to as a royalty fee, required by the producer of certain data bases.

DATABASE

	Computer Time Charges	Printing Charges Per Page	Royalty Charges
Agricola	$15	$.16	—
Biological Abstracts	$15	$.16	—
Books Information	$15	$.16	$.05 per page
Chemical Abstracts	$20	$.16	$.08 per cit.
Dissertation Abstracts	$10	$.16	—
Drug Info/Alcohol Use/Abuse	$15	$.16	$.05 per cit.
Environmental Impact Statements	$15	$.16	—
ERIC	$15	$.16	—
Exceptional Children Educ. Res.	$15	$.16	$.05 per page
Inform	$20	$.16	$.10 per cit.
INSPEC	$15	$.16	$.05 per cit.
Management Contents	$20	$.16	$.05 per cit.
MEDOC	$15	$.16	—
Nat. Inst. Mental Health (NIMH)	$15	$.16	—
NIMIS	$15	$.16	—
NTIS	$15	$.16	—
PAIS (Public Affairs Info. Serv.)	$15	$.16	$.05 per cit.
Pollution Abstracts	$20	$.16	$.04 per cit.
Psychological Abstracts	$20	$.16	—
Social Sciences Citation Index	$20	$.16	$.033 per cit.
Smithsonian Science Inform. Exch.	$20	$.16	$.10 per cit.

Users not affiliated with the University of Connecticut will be charged an additional $5.00 per data base. We regret that we are not able to offer searches to private individuals or firms. Requests will be accepted only from individuals affiliated with the University of Connecticut (including its branches and professional schools), Connecticut state agencies, and the four year, technical, and community colleges supported by the state of Connecticut.

DOW CHEMICAL U.S.A.
(Freeport, Texas)

No charge is made for computer time; telephone connect time; nor is a charge made for the searcher's time.

All charges are absored by the library.

A charge is made on the requesting department's account for extensive (10 or more) batch mode off-line citations and extensive (10 or more) online prints of citations.

GEORGIA INSTITUTE OF TECHNOLOGY
(Atlanta, Georgia)

FEE STRUCTURE (1980)

Computerized searches are provided on a flat fee basis with the Library absorbing any additional cost. The fee is payable in advance or, with proper authorization, may be charged to a campus account or project number. In some cases the fee is negotiated if the search is expected to overrun the limits of a "standard" search. The current fee schedule is available in the Reference Department. Citations are printed offline and mailed to the Reference Department. The user is notified promptly when the output is received and is given the option of picking it up or having it delivered via LENDS. This process, from receipt of request to receipt of output, usually requires 7–10 days. If results are needed more quickly, it is possible to print citations online provided the user is willing to pay full cost.

All search requests accepted must have clearly defined cost limits and reporting schedules, mutually agreed upon by the user and the librarian. Rush requests and those for unusually large or complex searches must be cleared with the head of the Information Exchange Center. For the latter, the terms of the search and the time, resources and cost limits must be stated in writing. The IEC is not obligated to accept rush requests or those which, in its judgment, cannot be reasonably supplied.

RECORDS AND BILLING

Departments within each division will maintain separate records. It is highly desirable that each department receive separate invoices from data base vendors. If this is not possible, department heads should cooperate to expedite handling of joint invoices. Invoices must be approved promptly and forwarded to the Administrative Services Department without delay.

Each unit is responsible for the proper recording of its own charges. Off-campus literature search charges (except SDI) will be billed at the end of the month in which results were transmitted to the user. SDI searches require an initiation fee billed at the end of the first month and subsequent monthly, quarterly or yearly billing depending on the number of data bases searched and the amount of the charges incurred. On-campus literature search billing information must be supplied to the Administrative Services Department in time for the regular monthly billing schedule.

Billing for reference and bibliographic service other than literature searching (or verification relating directly to interlibrary loan) is handled by means of the J-charge form. Department heads are responsible for forwarding J-charges to the Information Exchange Center at the end of each month so that they may be recorded statistically. IEC will include J-charges in its regular monthly billing to the Administrative Services Department.

UNIVERSITY OF ILLINOIS
AT URBANA-CHAMPAIGN
(Urbana, Illinois)

ON-LINE SEARCH SERVICES

Computerized bibliographic retrieval to on-line databases, available through BRS and the New York Times Information Bank, are available to library users in the Reference Department. Charges for BRS searches are $3/half hour for non-royalty databases and $10/half hour for royalty databases. Charges for searches on the New York Times Information Bank are on a per-minute basis with an average cost of $1.50/minute. Schedules for interviews prior to on-line search activity can be made with reference librarians by a request at the reference desk or by a telephone call. On-line searches conducted in the Reference Department are in the subject disciplines of social sciences (primarily those not covered by the Education and Social Science Library), humanities and sciences.

MASSACHUSETTS INSTITUTE OF TECHNOLOGY
(Cambridge, Massachusetts)

APPOINTMENT FEES

$75/first 1.5 hr. and $25/hr. or portion of hour thereafter, charged to individual P-card holders, or for-profit organizations, or individuals not belonging to the MIT Membership Plan for Industry, MIT Industrial Liaison Program, or MIT Associates Program.

$25/first 1.5 hr. and $10/hr. or portion of hour thereafter, charged to individuals from academic institutions (including those from the Boston Library Consortium and other Library card holders not cross-registered at MIT), alumni, individuals from non-profit organizations and Membership Plan for Industry.

No appointment fee for MIT users or for users from Wellesley, Woods Hole Oceanographic Institute, the MIT Industrial Liaison Program, the MIT Associates Program, students from other schools cross-registered at MIT, or Draper Laboratory, or government agencies.

Rates for connect time and printout charges and cost estimates on specific questions are available from the staff at CLSS.

UNIVERSITY OF SOUTHERN MISSISSIPPI
(Hattiesburg, Mississippi)

FINANCE

A. All searches are payable upon completion of the terminal session. The fees should include estimates of offline data.
B. Requests for interdepartmental charges by faculty members will be accepted upon presentation of the account number and their signature.
C. Requests for interdepartmental charges by students will be accepted upon presentation of the signature of the expenditure authority for the account number.
D. $10.00 will be kept in the cash box at all times.

E. Money should be reported daily.

F. Interdepartmental charge forms should be reported at the end of each month.

UNIVERSITY OF NORTH CAROLINA
(Chapel Hill, North Carolina)

FEE FOR SERVICE

Online searching is a fee-for-service activity. The costs recovered may vary with the library. Since fees vary for different data bases and different user groups, the fee-for-service rate may also vary. Charges for the same data base may vary among the service points.

DATA BASE PRICE SCHEDULE

Data Base	Online Cost	Communication Cost
ABI INFORM (info)	$.80/minute + $.09/minute + $.10/citation	
DISSERTATION ABSTRACTS (Diss)	$.33/minute + $.09/minute	
ERIC	$.22/minute + $.09/minute	
Exceptional Child Education	$.30/minute + $.09/minute + $.025/citation	
GPO	$.22/minute + $.09/minute	
MANAGEMENT CONTENTS (mgmt)	$.80/minute + $.09/minute + $.05/citation	
NCMH	$.22/minute + $.09/minute	
NY TIMES Information Bank	$1.34/minute + $.09/minute + $.30/citation	
NTIS	$.32/minute + $.09/minute	
PAIS	$.55/minute + $.09/minute + $.05/citation	
PSYCH. ABSTRACTS (psyc)	$.72/minute + $.09/minute	
SSCI (only 77–79 online)	$.80/minute + $.09/minute	

NOTE: For each data base, offline prints are $.16 per page. Administrative fee is $1.00 for each search.

UNIVERSITY OF NORTH CAROLINA
(Greensboro, North Carolina)

COSTS

Users pay for the direct costs of a search, which include computer charges, long distance telephone cost, and the cost of any off-line printing. The cost of an individual search will vary according to the rate for the data file being searched, the time necessary to complete the search, and the length of the print-out of bibliographic material. Most searches fall within the $5–$25 range. Searches must be paid for when picked up. Please make checks payable to Walter Clinton Jackson Library. Visit or call the Reference Department or the Documents Division of Jackson Library for further information.

NORTHWESTERN UNIVERSITY
(Evanston, Illinois)

COMPONENTS OF FEE

1. Service fee (for those who are not current students or staff of Northwestern University) of $30.00 per hour (or any fraction thereof).
2. Per minute cost to search specific data base (includes royalty to data base publisher and telecommunications costs).
3. Citations printed offline.

DEPOSIT

A deposit of $15.00 is required before a search can be undertaken for individuals. This deposit is applied to the service fee noted above.

FORM OF PAYMENT ACCEPTED

Checks, money orders, or cash. Note: *Change is not available; therefore a check is the preferred form of payment.*

TIME OF PAYMENT FOR SERVICES

All fees must be received before a printout is released to individual clients. If the total amount due can be calculated immediately following the search session, then payment is required at that time. Otherwise, the total amount due will be calculated upon receipt of the offline print and must be paid before that printout is released to the client. Charges *cannot* be billed to individuals. Other arrangements may be made for libraries.

DELIVERY OF PRINTOUT

If the client pays for the search at the time it is undertaken, the printout can be mailed to him/her. Otherwise, the client must pick the printout up at the Library and pay for the search at that time.

BILLING FOR INSTITUTIONAL SEARCHES

If a library wishes to be billed for a search conducted for its own institution or one of its patrons, the search and billing process will proceed as follows:

1. Northwestern will use an IRLC identification number to access the data base.
2. The printouts will be sent by the vendor (SDC or Lockheed) to the IRLC office.
3. The IRLC office will notify the requesting institution when the printout is received and will inform them of the total cost of the search.
4. Requesting institution will then indicate whether it will pick up the printouts or wish to have them mailed.
5. The IRLC office will be responsible for collecting the payment and will send a check to Northwestern for the service fee.

THE FREE LIBRARY OF PHILADELPHIA
(Philadelphia, Pennsylvania)

FEES AND CHARGES FOR USE OF THE INFORMATION BANK

It is necessary that the Free Library accept requests for searches of the Information Bank in relation to the rights of all clients, within limitations of library resources. Some extensive searches may be beyond the capacity of the equipment and the size of the staff. It is therefore understood that the staff of the Computer Based Information Center must use professional judgement in order to determine if information searches are reasonably related to the capabilities of the computer information service. Some searches and printings may be declined for good reason or referred to resources elsewhere in the Library.

No searches will be done for students below the 10th grade unless the request is referred to the Information Bank by a Librarian within the Free Library system.

Fees are payable to "The Free Library of Philadelphia" at time of the delivery of the print-out.

1. Five (5) minutes of free search/print-out time per topic will be available to all users. Additional search/print-out time is charged at a rate of $2.00 per minute.
2. The cost of sending printed materials through the U.S. mail is $2.00. These materials can also be sent for pick-up at any branch of the Free Library, or can be picked up at the Central Library, free of charge.
3. Duplicating costs:
   - Paper print copies of enlargements of microfiche texts of *The N.Y. Times* articles abstracted in the information bank: 10¢ per page.
   - Microfiche to microfiche copies of the texts of *The N.Y. Times* articles abstracted in the information bank: 25¢ per fiche.
   - Paper print copies of enlargements of microfilm of newspapers in the Newspaper Department: 25¢ per half page; 45¢ per full page.
   - Paper print copies of enlargements of microfilm texts of magazines: 10¢ per sheet.
   - Vending machine photocopies of printed material: 10¢ each.
4. Group demonstrations are charged at the rate of $60.00 for up to 30 minutes of on-line time. Demonstrations should be scheduled at least one week in advance.

TEMPLE UNIVERSITY
(Philadelphia, Pennsylvania)

PAYMENT FOR SEARCHES [1979]

Patrons requesting a computerized literature search shall be informed that total payment for a search, including any charge for off-line prints, shall be due at the time the search is completed. Patrons may pay with cash or a check made out to Temple University. In addition, qualified faculty, staff, or students may establish a deposit or grant account with the library and have search costs charged to those account numbers. When payment is received, the searcher shall itemize the various costs in triplicate on the COMLIT receipt form. The original shall be given to the patron, one copy shall be sent to the Business Office, and one copy shall be kept for record keeping purposes.

Direct costs shall be passed on to all patrons. These costs include telephone connect rates, various System (BRS, Lockheed, SDC) fees, and source royalties. Users not connected with Temple University shall pay an additional fee to cover in part such expenditures as staff time, equipment charges, and supplies. The following chart outlines the fee structure:

USER	FEE
1. Temple students, faculty and staff	1. Direct charges
2. Antioch students	2. Direct charges
3. Alumni	3. Direct charges
4. Individuals outside the Temple community	4. Direct charges + $10.00
5. Corporations	5. Direct charges + $25.00

TEXAS A&M UNIVERSITY
(College Station, Texas)

The fee structure is basically actual computer connect costs plus $14 per hour for data communications through the Houston telecommunications ports. We will be developing a service policy statement for regular reference service in the near future.

THE UNIVERSITY OF TEXAS/ HEALTH SCIENCE CENTER
(Dallas, Texas)

COSTS

The requester must pay a fee covering direct costs incurred in searching (connect time and offline printing costs). Rates are the same for all requesters. Minimum charge per topic per database is $2.00. The average cost of searching the current MEDLINE file (1979–80) is $4.50. Other databases cost more; however, they usually cover more years. Prices are different for each database and are based on the vendor's charge plus 15%. Cost estimates given by the analyst are not guaranteed.

COST FACTORS

Three major factors influence the cost of a search:
1. The amount of connect time used (charged per minute). Connect time includes search input and any online printing.
2. The number and format of references printed offline and mailed from the computer (charged per reference or per page). Offline printing is much cheaper than online printing.
3. The price charged by the vendor for the database. Some databases are very expensive.

Reference Policy
Statements Reprinted
in Full

Academic Library Reference Policy

RICE UNIVERSITY LIBRARY
(Houston, Texas)
Reference Procedures, October 1980

INTRODUCTION BY RICHARD H. PERRINE

Brief policy statements were written by the Reference Department to suit various purposes in earlier years, but in 1978 a 31-page "Reference Service Policy" was produced. This was inspired by the need for a comprehensive description of reference operations to serve as an orientation tool for new staff members, since there were vacancies to be filled. A copy of the policy was supplied to each one of the five reference librarians added in 1979-80.

During that period there were several changes which affected the validity of the "Reference Service Policy" as written. A library reorganization had created a Reference/Collection Development Department consisting of subject specialists who split their time between the two functions; an on-line search service of data bases had been introduced; and a Committee on Policies and Procedures had established definitions which made the statement appear to be procedure

509

rather than policy. Consequently it was revised and issued in October 1980 as the 33-page "Reference Procedures."

Since then, the Reference/Collection Development department has written a preliminary three-page "Policy Statement" which is to be incorporated in a compilation of policies of all the library departments. This overlaps "Reference Precedures" to some extent and will undoubtedly be revised, both to further distinguish it and to make its format similar to policy statements of other departments.

[The policy reprinted here is based, in part, upon that of the University of Texas and, earlier, from the University of Massachusetts, but the final version is peculiar to the needs of Rice—Editor.]

TABLE OF CONTENTS

B. Service to Individual Readers
   1. First Priority
   2. "On Call"
   3. Telephone Calls
   4. Priorities among Waiting Readers
   5. Pending Reference Inquiries
C. Instructional Services
D. Subject Specialists

IV. Desk Service
  A. General Statement and Instructions
    1. Nature and Extent of Responsibilities of Staff on Desk
      Duty
      a. Priorities
      b. Clipboard Messages
      c. Information Folder
      d. Approachability
      e. Activity during Slack Periods
      f. Staffing Levels
      g. Leaving the Desk Unstaffed
      h. Food and Drink
      i. Holding Materials for Patrons
      j. Assisting Handicapped Students
    2. Handling General Inquiries
      a. General Statement
      b. Directions
      c. Lost and Found
      d. Library Policies
      e. Library Holdings
      f. Information Service
      g. Research and/or Instruction
        1) Amount of Service
        2) Instruction
      h. Suggestions for Library Acquisitions
    3. Handling Problem Inquiries
      a. Questions Received at Closing Time
      b. Genealogical Questions
      c. Questions Relating to Take-Home Exams, Contests,
        Puzzles, etc.
      d. Recommending Reference Books for Purchase
    4. Recording Statistics and Questions
      a. Statistics Report
      b. Unanswered Reference Questions

5. Reporting Problems
   a. Emergencies
   b. Missing Reference Books
   c. Missing Pages
   d. Disorder in Book Arrangement
   e. Public Catalog and Serials List Corrections
   f. Reference Book Problems
   g. Complaints
B. Telephone Inquiries
   1. Incoming Calls
      a. Priorities
      b. Service Standards
      c. Paging Readers
      d. Taking Messages to Carrels
      e. Checking Records
      f. Circulation Information
      g. Questions about Library Policies
      h. Personal Calls
      i. Emergency and Nuisance Calls
   2. Outgoing Calls
      a. General Guidelines
      b. Reader Use of Telephone
C. Circulation of Restricted Materials
   1. Circulation for Use Outside the Library
   2. Renewals, Recalls, Fines
   3. In-Building Use
   4. "Desk" and High-Risk Books
D. Service at Night, Weekends, Skeleton Staff Days
   1. Emergencies
   2. Records in Technical Services Area
E. Inquiries for Material not on Open Shelves
   1. General Statement
   2. Rare Books, Manuscripts, University Archives
   3. Materials in Process or Storage
   4. Search Procedures
      a. Materials in Process
      b. Materials in Storage
F. Referrals
   1. General Statement
   2. Referring Questions to Colleagues
   3. Referring to Other Libraries or Services
   4. Unanswered Questions
G. Assisting Users at the Card Catalog

SECTION I: INTRODUCTION

A. Purpose of Reference Procedures

1. *General Statement*—The purpose of Reference Procedures is to present guidance for providing reference service which will insure a uniform standard of service of the highest possible quality consistent with available resources. This statement will express the understanding between the library administration and the Reference/Collection Development Department concerning the manner in which the Department's responsibilities are carried out. It will conform with the R/CD Policy Statement.

2. *Uses*—The procedures will be used for orienting new staff members, as well as a source of information for reference staff or library administrators with questions concerning departmental operation or responsibilities.

3. *Availability to Readers*—The procedures may be made available to any library user if he or she has a question concerning the service policy of the Department. It will serve as a basis for a briefer statement which will be published and distributed to library users.

4. *Annual Review of Contents*—The contents of the procedures will be reviewed annually by the reference staff and the library administration to insure that policy and practice are in conformity and that changes are made as needed.

B. Goals of Reference Service

1. *General Statement*—Reference service objectives are fully described in the R/CD Policy Statement. Two major goals of the reference service are: (a) to facilitate access to library collections and to the informational content of those collections through direct personal service to the library's users, and (b) to support the University's instructional program through providing formal and informal library and bibliographic instruction.

2. *Basic Philosophy*—As a general rule, because of the size of the library's clientele and the large number of highly specialized (and changing) interests among them, assistance to readers, apart from "ready reference" inquiries, must ordinarily take the form of providing guidance in the pursuit of information rather than providing the information itself. The individual staff member must exercise his or her judgment in determining the

application of this policy in specific situations. The objective situation —i.e., the needs of the user, the amount of time available, and the knowledge upon which the staff member can call— must be the determining factor and not favoritism to any one reader or group of readers.

C. Ethics of Reference Service

The needs of library users must always be taken seriously and treated with the utmost respect. Under no circumstances should there be any discussion of an individual or a group of users, or of any transactions between user and reference staff member, outside of a professional context.

SECTION II: LIBRARY USERS

A. General Statement

No discrimination is made between university and non-university users when giving routine reference service. In the case of a time-consuming inquiry or in the case of special services, the question of the user's affiliation may arise, and some distinctions may have to be made. Guidelines for making these are given below. In applying the guidelines the reference staff member must use his or her own judgment although senior staff members may be consulted.

B. Guidelines for Providing Special Service

1. *Time-consuming Inquiries*—As a general rule, if a library user not affiliated with the University has access to a library intended to serve his needs which is adequate for his purpose, he should be referred to that library for assistance. In cases where the University Library has special resources in staff or materials and the needs of the user seem to warrant it, assistance beyond the routine may be given.
2. *Legal and Medical Questions*—Reference personnel may help a patron find legal or medical reference sources, but may not interpret the material or give advice, due to legal implications. No medical or legal information should be read over the telephone.
3. *Computer Literature Searches*—Online searching of commercial data bases in many subject fields is available through the

R/CD Department for Rice faculty, students, and staff (see Section V.D.). Other library patrons seeking such service should be referred to R.I.C.E. (528-3553).

4. *Letters of Introduction*—A reference librarian will supply a letter of introduction for a Rice student who wishes to make use of some other academic library. The letter of introduction would make clear the status of the person being introduced.

5. *Limited Circulation of Restricted Material*— A reader who has a valid Rice student or faculty ID card may briefly borrow non-circulating materials only in exceptional circumstances. (See Section IV. C. 1.)

6. *Orientation Tours*—Request for library orientation/instructional tours will be honored for university-affiliated groups if staff and time are available. A notice of two working days is required for such requests. If a staff member agrees to schedule a tour with less than two working days' notice, then that staff member will be responsible for giving the tour.

SECTION III: PRIORITIES

A. General Statement

The Reference Department gives priority to all activities involving direct service to library users. Supporting activities, although essential to maintain the quality of these services, must take second place.

B. Service to Individual Readers

1. *First Priority*—As a general rule, service to library users who come to the reference areas takes priority over any other activity. In case of conflict, reference staff unable to meet their reference desk obligations *must* find a replacement. Personal illness is the only exception to this rule. In those cases the person who is ill will notify the reference librarian on duty. Reference staff should try to schedule appointments, meetings, and supporting activities at times when it is expected that library use will be relatively light. All reference staff should leave a schedule of their day's activities at a central location so that they may be found when needed.

2. *"On Call"*—All reference librarians, even though they are not scheduled at the desk, are on call to help during peak periods

and when specific reference questions requiring their subject expertise arise.

3. *Telephone Calls*—In accordance with the rule in paragraph No. 1 above, the user who comes to the reference desk takes priority above the person who calls on the telephone or who has left an inquiry at the desk. For instructions on answering the telephone see Desk Service: Telephone Inquiries: Incoming Calls (Cf. Section IV. B. 1.).

4. *Priorities Among Waiting Readers*—In cases where there are two or more library users waiting, help should be offered first to the person who has been waiting the longest. If it appears that the answer to the inquiry will take a little time, the staff member may deal first with the questions which can be answered immediately, if this is agreeable to the persons waiting.

5. *Pending Reference Inquiries*—If the immediate needs of readers who are in the library or who are telephoning are being adequately taken care of, next priority should be accorded to following up inquiries not answered when they were taken while on desk duty. All such questions must be dealt with immediately by the person who accepted them unless other arrangements have been made or service to users who are waiting interferes.

C. Instructional Services

Library and bibliographic instruction for groups has the second major priority among tasks performed by reference staff. Reference staff are expected to be available when they are not scheduled on a desk or assisting individual readers; this assistance may take the form of actual instruction or the preparation of materials for instructional purposes.

D. Subject Specialists

Members of the Reference/Collection Development Department also have special responsibilities in selection and collection development. As a general rule, service to readers must take precedence if there is a conflict of priorities.

SECTION IV: DESK SERVICE

A. General Statement and Instructions

1. *Nature and Extent of Responsibilities of Staff on Desk Duty*
   a. Priorities—The primary responsibility of reference staff on

desk duty is provision of direct personal service to readers who come to the reference desk reference center for assistance, or who call by telephone. See Section III concerning priorities.

b. Clipboard Messages—Reference staff are responsible for reading the messages attached to the desk clipboard as soon as they come on duty. The purpose of this is to record information and special short-term instructions needed by staff on desk duty that day. Messages should be added to the clipboard by staff on desk duty as appropriate. Examples of such messages are: 1) notes concerning class assignments involving use of reference materials; 2) notes concerning procedures for answering a difficult question being asked repeatedly at the desk; 3) request form for "In Process" material.

c. Information Folder—This folder contains a collection of materials brought together to serve the special informational needs of reference staff on desk duty. Detailed information on specific procedures on the reference desks should be included as well as general information on policies and procedures of other departments in the library and the university.

d. Approachability—Reference staff on desk duty must be constantly aware of how approachable they appear to library users who are in need of assistance. Being approachable is a first step in encouraging users to seek assistance at the desks. Users need to be educated to the fact that individual assistance is the primary responsibility of staff on desk duty, that reference staff members are interested in the problems that face library users and are willing to help. Since the attitude and behavior of staff on duty goes a long way towards creating an image of the entire library, reference staff should strive to make to make that image a positive one.

e. Activity During Slack Periods—During slack periods at the desk, staff may work on collection development details, examine new reference materials, read professional literature, etc., as long as it does not interfere with the provision of desk service. They may walk the floor occasionally to see if they can be of assistance to readers working at the card catalog. Staff must be careful not to become so engrossed in other work that they discourage the approach of users or fail to see readers in need of assistance at the card catalog.

f. Staffing Levels—Staffing patterns and hours of service directly reflect, within budgetary limitations, the needs of the users. Desk hours should be posted in a visible location.

g. Leaving the Desk Unstaffed—Should it ever be necessary to leave the desk unstaffed for more than a few minutes, a sign which states that the person on desk duty will return shortly should be placed in a visible location on the desk. A staff member's absence from the desk should never be so prolonged as to interfere with the rights of others who are waiting for service.

h. Food and Drink—No eating or drinking or smoking is permitted at the reference desk.

i. Holding Materials for Patrons—Reference books, materials that have been collected to answer a reference question, or "in process" materials may be held for patrons in designated areas behind the reference desk. Each item being held should contain a slip stating for whom the item is being held and how long it should be held. The Circulation Department will hold circulating materials behind the circulation desk for patrons. Personal belongings will not be held behind the reference desk.

j. Assisting Handicapped Students—Reference staff should aid handicapped students with the card catalog and book retrieval when requested.

2. *Handling General Inquiries*

a. General Statement—It is expected that judgment will be used in determining which questions can be handled to completion by the staff and which ones are best answered by providing guidance in selecting sources to consult. In the first category are directions, general questions concerning library holdings and ready reference questions involving specific facts easily determined from standard sources.

b. Directions—In giving directions, explanation should be given when possible with reference to appropriate printed aids available at the desks so that the explanation will be as clear as possible and the user can, if he wishes, find his own way the next time he has a similar question. When necessary, staff members accompany users to the needed areas or information sources.

c. Lost and Found—Lost items should be delivered to the circulation desk as soon as they are discovered. Inquiries about lost items should also be referred to that desk.

d. Library Policies—Follow the instructions in Section IV. B. 1. g. in giving information on library policies and service. When the user comes to the desk in person it may be preferable to

make the inquiry for him if it is necessary to refer to another
service point for full information.

e. Library Holdings—In giving information on library holdings, the reference librarian should not give a negative answer without fully verifying the item requested and checking
in all appropriate sources. This applies especially to periodicals which are often inaccurately cited. The card catalog
should be checked for periodical titles not appearing in the
Current Periodicals List or the Texas List. If the requester
does not want to wait until this can be done or is satisfied
with a less than complete search, be sure to indicate that a
more thorough search might locate the material wanted.
When it has been established that material needed by a
reader is not available in the library, suggestions may be
made concerning other possible locations which may be appropriate, such as another library, a bookstore, etc.

f. Information Service—Answers to questions should be based
on data in standard reference sources whenever possible. The
printed information should be shown to the reader or, in the
case of a telephone inquiry, the source of the information
should be cited. The reference librarian should not vouch for
the accuracy of a particular answer or source, although in
some instances an indication of its reliability may be given.
The reference staff will not normally cross-verify answers
except in the case of obvious discrepancies.

g. Research and/or Instruction—In a second category are questions which require much longer, more detailed answers; e.g.,
questions concerning search strategy for information in a
specific field, perhaps involving several forms of material
(periodical articles, books, government documents, etc.) or
questions which will require a search through a number of
specialized sources which are located some distance away
from the desk area.

When these more complicated, time-consuming questions
arise at the desk, there are several possible procedures to
follow: for example, (1) arrange for another staff member to
take your position at the desk, (2) ask a subject specialist to
take over the problem, (3) inform the reader courteously that
the question will probably take considerable time to answer
fully and ask if he or she is willing to come back later for an
answer, or for individual help in locating the answer. The
reference staff member is expected to use his or her own

judgment in determining the most appropriate response and also to be considerate of the reader and any colleague who is asked for assistance.

1) Amount of Service—The amount of service that can be given at any particular time will vary, depending on such factors as how busy it is at the desk, how many other reference staff members are available to help, etc. What is practical at one time may not be at another; it is important, however, that an effort be made to provide adequate service. Some guidelines that may be followed are given below:

   a. Always try to suggest some sources and specific headings (in the public catalog, an appropriate index or bibliography, etc.) and encourage the reader to come back for further suggestions if the results are not satisfactory.

   b. If the student is beginning his own search and is unfamiliar with the relevant sources, the librarian may want to suggest that he make an appointment with one of the reference staff for a conference on how to make full use of library resources in that field. Such a conference will enable a reference librarian to give much more assistance to an individual student than is possible on the spur-of-the-moment at the busy reference desk.

   c. If you are unfamiliar with what sources might be available and wish to investigate when you have more time, write a description of the subject and arrange to report to the reader on the question later.

   d. When likely sources of information are known but a search of them will be very time-consuming, or require specialized knowledge which no one on the staff has, you should suggest that the reader do the search for himself or employ an outside research assistant, or request the services of the Regional Information and Communication Exchange (528-3553).

   e. When the search appears to require a quick check of a large number of potential sources which would be difficult to explain to a reader, the reference staff member may, if the purpose of the question seems to justify it, invest a reasonable amount of time on the research.

2) Instruction—Informal instruction in the use of library

records, bibliographic tools, and other sources in the reference collection should be a routine part of reference service. Encourage the reader to follow your steps as you seek out the information or sources, but never force instruction on a reader who asks a simple question which can be answered by reference to one or two sources. Reference staff should be alert to the kinds of questions that indicate a need for instruction; in general they will fall into two main categories: (1) occasions when a reader is looking for material for a paper, speech, or other project; (2) when a reader seems unfamiliar with the use of a particular reference tool and indicates an interest in learning how to use it effectively. Reference staff should also be alert to questions indicative of class assignments where formal library instruction for the entire class might be more fruitful than answering individual questions at the reference desk. If possible, attempt to determine the nature of the assignment, the due-date, and the name of the instructor. This information should be referred to the appropriate librarian, who will then judge whether the instructor should be contacted.

h. Suggestions for Library Acquisitions—Reference librarians will remove completed order slips from the box on the reference desk labeled "Suggest Books for Library Purchase." Completed forms will be given to the appropriate Collection Development Librarian for processing.

3. *Handling Problem Inquiries*

a. Questions Received at Closing Time—Whenever possible, handle questions received at closing time to completion, even if it means working overtime. However, if the question seems very involved, or you have other commitments which prevent you from working overtime, ask the reader to return for assistance at a time when the desk will be staffed. (Reference desk hours should be posted in a visible location.) Fill out a reference question form, summarizing the main points of the inquiry, so that you or the staff member coming on duty in the morning will be able to handle the question to completion at the time agreed upon with the reader.

b. Genealogical Questions are those which involve the tracing of lines or details of family history, and not just the identification of a person, or the finding of brief biographical "who's who" type information. Such tracing questions are referred

to the Clayton Branch of the Houston Public Library.
  c. Questions Relating to Take-Home Exams, Contests, Puzzles,
     etc.—The reference staff will not aid persons in finding an-
     swers for take-home exams, or for radio, newspaper, or TV
     quizzes and puzzles. In some cases, the basic reference tools
     that might be used to find needed answers could be indicated.
  d. Recommending Reference Books for Purchase—If a reader
     asks that the reference staff member recommend an encyclo-
     pedia, dictionary, or other reference work for purchase, an
     opinion may be given on the reputation of a specific work, but
     the opinion should always be supported by a review or com-
     ment in a standard reference source, such as the "Reference
     and Subscription Book Reviews" in *Booklist,* or *Choice,* etc.
     The reader should always be advised to examine the library's
     copy of the work to see if it meets his individual needs and
     expectations.
4. *Recording Statistics and Questions*
  a. Statistics Report—It is the policy of the Reference Depart-
     ment to keep statistics on inquiries received at the desk in
     order to provide a factual base for review of reference service.
     One of the duties of all reference staff scheduled for desk
     work is to keep an accurate record of inquiries received.
  b. Unanswered Reference Questions—It is the responsibility of
     persons assigned desk work to record questions they are
     unable to answer while on desk duty.
5. *Reporting Problems*
  a. Emergencies—Reference staff are responsible for reporting
     emergencies by following the instructions on file at each
     service point. In general, the following guidelines should be
     observed. Security and medical emergencies requiring *im-
     mediate* action should be reported directly to Campus Police
     (3333/3334). Building emergencies and security problems
     should be reported to the Administrative Office during the
     day and to the Campus Police on nights and weekends. Such
     building emergencies would include fires, electrical hazards,
     and water leakage.
  b. Missing Reference Books—Temporarily missing reference
     books should be reported by filling out a missing book form
     for the missing volume and giving it to the circulation staff
     member who is assigned this duty for searching. The circula-
     tion records should always be checked *before* the book is
     reported "missing."

c. Missing Pages—Pages missing from books or periodicals may be noticed by or brought to the attention of a reference librarian. Since library policy does not generally permit the replacement of mutilated pages because of the cost of borrowing, copying, rebinding, etc., the reference librarian will, if the reader wants the missing information, suggest another library or interlibrary loan as the source. The reference librarian will write at the top of an adjacent page, "Mutilation Noted," giving the date and initialling the note. The publication will then be given to catalog maintenance for statistical recording and reshelving.

    If the missing pages appear to be due to a publication error, and if the book or periodical has been recently received, then the reference librarian will take the item to the order section (if it is a monograph) or the serials department where a replacement will be requested for the imperfect copy.

d. Disorder in Book Arrangement—Since disorders in book arrangement can cause serious inconvenience to users, the reference staff should pay continuous attention to maintaining the collection in good working order. Occasionally, there will be breaks in the system set up to accomplish this. Shelving problems should be reported to the staff member responsible for collection maintenance. When there is a temporary pileup of heavily-used reference books, staff members should attempt to keep the collection in good working order, reshelving books as necessary.

e. Public catalog and Serials List Corrections—Reference staff, like other library staff, are responsible for reporting to technical services any errors discovered in the Public Catalog and in the Current Periodicals List.

f. Reference Book Problems—Reference staff are responsible for notifying the appropriate subject librarian of any reference book problem requiring some kind of follow-up activity off the desk. For example, while working at the desk you may have occasion to use a reference work you suspect is outdated, and perhaps should be removed from reference, or be replaced by a newer edition. Such discoveries should be reported on a memo form and given to the appropriate subject librarian.

g. Complaints concerning policies or functions of library should be referred to the appropriate Department Head (or, in the case of an absence, to the Acting Head of the Department).

B. Telephone Inquiries

1. *Incoming Calls*
   a. Priorities—As stated in Section III. B.3., the user who comes to the desk takes priority over the person who calls on the telephone. However, the phone should be answered even if all the desk staff are working with readers, since constant ringing will disturb the whole room. If the phone call interrupts service you are giving to a reader at the desk, ask the person on the phone if he can wait or if you can phone back later with the answer to his question. If the desk staff are helping readers in other areas of the floor, the phone may be left to ring. However, the phone should serve as a reminder of the need to return to the desk as soon as possible.
   b. Service Standards—The telephone is one of the most important means of providing and arranging for service to library users. Members of the reference department are responsible for maintaining the best possible standards of telephone service. Since the manner in which telephone inquiries are handled has a direct bearing on both the operation of the department and the public impression of the University Library, it is important that the telephone techniques outlined below be practiced:

      DEVELOP A PLEASING TELEPHONE MANNER
      —Make the caller's first impression a good one.
      IDENTIFY THE DEPARTMENT
      —So that the caller knows immediately he has reached the right department.
      GIVE PERSONAL SERVICE
      —Treat callers as individuals. Take the time to be polite.
      —Do not leave a person holding the line for more than a few minutes while you search for an answer. If a search is going to take more than 2–3 minutes, arrange to call the reader back if it is a local or Texas call, or have the reader call back at a specific time. Explain that the information will be left with the staff member then on duty.
      HANDLE CALLS TO COMPLETION (see also Checking Records below)
      —Many callers do not know the person who can help them. You may have to transfer them to the right person. Calls

may be transferred but give the University switchboard and the extension numbers to the caller in case you are cut off in trying to transfer the call.

—If you know that the information a caller wants is to be found in specialized sources and can be better provided by another department, make sure the caller knows whom he should consult and the type of service he can expect. In some cases it is best to refer the caller to a specific person by name and title.

RECOGNIZE SERVICE PRIORITIES

—Answer all general information calls which can be answered in a few minutes' time without questioning the status of the caller. Whenever possible, answer the inquiry rather than switch the call to another extension.

—Complicated questions are often better answered if the caller is encouraged to come in person to the library.

c. Paging readers—The reference department will not page readers.

d. In the case of an emergency, the Circulation Department can be asked to leave a message on a carrel.

e. Checking Records—The reference department receives a number of phone requests each day for catalog information. Requesters should be informed that no more than three titles are to be verified in the card catalog for each caller.

If additional verification is needed, do not refer callers to technical services departments. Whenever possible, call the area on another extension or consult the records yourself.

f. Circulation Information—If a caller inquires about whether a specific book for which he has obtained the call number is actually in the library, inform him courteously that it is not possible to look on the shelves, but that the circulation records can be checked to see if the book is checked out.

g. Questions about Library Policies—Answer questions concerning general library policies if the inquirer simply wants to know what the policy is. However, if the question concerns interpretation of policy, or an individual problem affected by a policy, refer the inquirer to the department responsible for carrying out that policy.

h. Personal Calls—Staff members who make or receive personal calls at the reference desk should use an extension other than 4800 and keep the calls brief. If a person on duty on a reference desk receives a personal call, he should ask the caller to call again when he is off duty.

Transfer or refer calls for other members of the library staff to the correct department and give the number to caller for future use. If the person called is not listed in the Faculty/ Staff Director, refer the call to the Administrative Office.

   i. Emergency and Nuisance Calls—In an emergency situation, such as a bomb threat, try to obtain as much information as possible from the caller and write it down. Notify the Campus Police at once (Extension 3333), then the Administrative Office. (See also Section IV. D. 1.) Nuisance calls should be dealt with as quickly and unemotionally as possible. If they persist, notify the University operator.

2. *Outgoing Calls*

   a. General Guidelines—When placing official calls, always identify yourself as a member of the Reference/Collection Development Department of the University Library.

   b. Reader Use of Telephone—Telephones at the reference desk are available for official library business only. Readers should be encouraged to use the telephones on the second landing of the front stairway.

C. Circulation of Restricted Materials

1. *Circulation for Use Outside the Library*—In general, restricted materials are not circulated outside the library, so that they will be accessible to as many users as possible for the whole period the library is open. Many such materials, e.g., periodical indexes, the latest editions of standard encyclopedias and almanacs, are in such constant demand and they cannot be taken from the building without causing severe inconvenience to other library users. The reference needs of the majority must take priority over the needs of a single individual.

However, since some restricted materials are in much less demand than others, reasonable requests to borrow less heavily used titles for brief periods of time may be granted, e.g., to take the item to another building for copying purposes. Eligible borrowers, after receiving approval from a reference librarian, must leave a valid patron ID number at the circulation desk until the item is brought back.

2. *Renewals, Recalls, Fines*—Reference material checked out of the building may be renewed if an extended loan period is not

likely to inconvenience other users. Renewal of reference material must be approved by the appropriate subject librarian. Reference books are subject to immediate recall by phone if urgently needed by someone else regardless of the hour due. There are no fines for overdue reference materials unless the material has been recalled, in which case the same fines are levied as for reserve materials.

3. *In-Building Use*—In general, reference books should be used in the area in which they are shelved so that they can always be located quickly when needed by others. Reference books should be reshelved periodically throughout the day to help insure eficient use of the collection.

4. *"Desk" and High-Risk Books*—Unlike reference books shelved in other locations, the dispositon of books shelved behind the reference desk in the "ready reference collection" must be known to the reference staff. Any reader making use of such books can be asked to sign for them or leave identification. The purpose of this is simply to maintain control of these books since they are often in heavier demand than other reference books, and it is vital for the staff member to know which of these books is in use at any given time.

D. Service at Night, Weekends, Skeleton Staff Days—Problems

1. *Emergencies*—The reference librarian on duty nights and weekends is responsible for emergencies involving building security and the security of patrons. Such emergencies should be reported by the reference staff to the Campus Police Department. The librarian on duty nights and weekends is responsible for interpreting library policy, except circulation policy, and dealing with any patron conflict with these library policies.

2. *Records in Technical Services Area*—Records kept in the Technical Services area (such as the shelflist and the central serials record) will generally not be accessible at such times. If a reader needs information from these sources, make a record of the request and follow it up the next working day.

E. Inquiries for Material not on Open Shelves

1. *General Statement*—Reference libraries will advise or assist readers who are seeking material not available to them on open

shelves, including rare books, manuscripts, university archives, and materials in process or in storage.

2. *Rare Books, Manuscripts, University Archives*—Readers who inquire about these materials, including books with call numbers preceeded by an asterisk, "Axson," "Bartlett," or "Masterson," will be referred to the Woodson Research Center.

3. *Materials in Process or Storage*—Readers requesting such items will be asked to fill out the appropriate form at the reference desk. If technical services (or the storage area) is closed, or if the work load at the reference desk does not permit the reference librarian to leave, the inquirer will be informed of a time when the item will be availabe at the reference desk and the filled-out form will be placed on the clipboard.

4. *Search Procedures*

   a. Materials in Process—When a reference librarian is able to pursue this search, it will be by the book number on the location shelves in technical services. If the book is not found there or at any other logical place, the form should be given to the Order Receiving Supervisor for further searching.

   When a book is found, slips should be removed and given to the Order Receiving Supervisor. The book should be taken to the marking table where Rice ownership stamps and the barcode will be added. It can then be taken to the reference desk to be given to or held for the requester.

   Rice faculty and students are permitted to charge out such books at the circulation desk. Other readers may only examine an uncataloged book, leaving an identification card at the reference desk if it is taken away. The book, when returned by the reader, will be taken to the location book truck in technical services, or to the Order Supervisor's desk if slips were removed. Forms for volumes which are further searched by the Order Receiving Supervisor will be returned to the reference desk with the status indicated. Forms will be held on the clipboard until the information has been given to the requester. All forms will then be filed with other such forms.

   b. Materials in Storage— A reference librarian, when able to leave the reference desk will search for the requested volume in the basement storage area. When removing anything from this area, its call number and volume number, the day's date and the librarian's initials will be marked on the sign-out sheet in the area. The reader requesting the volume will be instructed to return it to the reference desk. A reference librarian will then reshelve it in the storage area, marking through the notation on the sign-out sheet.

F. Referrals

1. *General Statement*—A reasonable effort must be made to answer every reference question. When the staff member receiving the question has been unable to answer a question satisfactorily after having consulted the known source or has reason to believe that the question cannot be answered by sources at that reference point, if possible he or she should refer the reader to another source of information.

2. *Referring Questions to Colleagues*—The staff member on duty should ask colleagues for advice and/or assistance as necessary, but should not refer readers to the latter without first notifying them of the problem, and telling them what sources have already been checked. Verbal communication is best, but if this is impossible, leave them a short note so that they will be aware of the problem when the reader returns.

3. *Referrals to Other Services*—In general, do not refer a reader to a colleague in another department, another library, or to a service without calling ahead to make sure they can be of assistance. This is a courtesy to both the library user and the person or institution to which he is being referred.

4. *Unanswered Questions*—Incompletely answered questions, or those for which information does not appear to be available, should be recorded and discussed with other staff members. The person who received the question originally is responsible for seeing that the question is handled promptly to completion. All reference staff members should be informed on these questions whenever possible, since they are a useful stimulus to education in the use of less frequently consulted reference materials.

G. Assisting Users at the Card Catalog

1. *Responsibility*—One of the chief responsibilities of the reference staff is instruction in the use of the public card catalog. Since an understanding of the catalog is a key to self-sufficiency in library use, the staff member on desk duty should, when

possible, accompany the reader when he or she has a question concerning the catalog.

2. *Kinds of Problems*—When a person cannot find a specific entry in the catalog, it may be that:
   (1) his information is incomplete
   (2) he doesn't understand the library's filing system
   (3) the card for which he is searching has been misfiled [a search under title as well as under author is wise]
   (4) the library does not own the book
   (5) the item wanted is owned by the library but not represented in the catalog [e.g., some microforms, documents, maps].

If the information is incomplete or possibly incorrect, try to verify the item before informing the reader that the library does not own it.

The reader may need help in establishing the correct subject heading. This is the time to introduce him to the *Library of Congress Guide to Subject Headings,* and to other ways of identifying the appropriate subject entry.

3. *Offering Assistance*—If someone appears to be having difficulty at the catalog, ask him if he needs help. Each staff member should use his own judgement in identifying such a situation.

H. Donations of Books or Periodicals

1. *General Statement*—Occasionally donors, unaware of the existence of Gifts & Exchanges, will contact the reference desk, with their donation in hand, or with questions.

2. *Material Brought to Desk*—Books or periodicals brought to the reference desk by donor can be accepted by a reference librarian. A slip bearing the name and address of the donor, the day's date and the number of items will be placed with the gift which will be delivered to Gifts and Exchanges. A book delivered to the reference desk wrapped in white paper with "Dr. Carrington" written on it will be taken to Gifts & Exchanges.

3. *Telephone Inquiries*—Callers will generally be referred to Gifts & Exchanges (extension 2583). Those wanting to leave materials at the loading dock will be instructed to include a slip with the name and address. Gifts & Exchanges and Shipping & Receiving should then be altered.

SECTION V: BIBLIOGRAPHIC SERVICES

A. Reference Initiated

When time and resources are available, the preparation of bibliographies by staff members is authorized.

B. User Requests

1. *Preparation of Bibliographies*—Bibliographies are occasionally prepared for faculty members as an aid to class instruction. Such bibliographies are not to be done for a faculty member's research, due to the heavy demand of desk and other duties on the reference staff. (For computerized literature searches, see V. D.) Requests for bibliographies are handled on an individual basis by the subject librarians.
2. *Checking Bibliographies*—Reference personnel will provide limited assistance, dependent upon time and staff available, in the checking of bibliographies against the library's holdings as an aid to class instruction or collection development. If the lists are long ones, library users will be aided in performing this task for themselves. Subject librarians will handle requests for checking bibliographies and reserve book lists.

C. Current Awareness

At present, there are insufficient time and resources available for the manual compilation and dissemination of a "current awareness" bibliographic service to the University community; however, library users will be given assistance and suggestions regarding commercial services which are available. (See V. D.)

D. Computer-based Information Service [i.e., AIRS (Automated Information Retrieval Services)]

Searches of on-line data bases are available on a cost-recovery basis. Any interested party should be referred to the appropriate librarian. AIRS personnel prefer a first meeting with a patron requesting a search wherein the search is discussed and then a date and time for the search are established.

SECTION VI: REFERENCE CORRESPONDENCE

A. Who Drafts Replies

Incoming inquiries to reference are referred to an appropriately qualified librarian for reply.

B. Signature

A letter replying to a reference question is signed by the individual librarian answering the inquiry. Official letters, i.e., correspondence having to do with the policies and procedures of the department, are signed by the head of the department.

C. Copies

Letters are typed in duplicate so that one copy may be retained in the departmental correspondence file.

D. Policy for Handling Request

Not all inquiries asking for general information ought to be answered by reference. In general, the policy is not to provide information for the general public that can be obtained from local libraries unless the questions can be answered quickly and briefly. Nor will the reference staff complete homework assignments for students. However, replies to inquiries that are not answered should suggest a more appropriate local source of information.

The reference staff will attempt to answer letters as fully as possible when they come from inquirers who are considered authorized library users; i.e., members of the University community, particularly the staff, alumni and trustees; also state government officials, librarians and faculty from Texas colleges and universities, and people from the local area.

E. Promptness in Answering

Replies should be mailed back to inquirers no later than one week after receipt. When suitable, the inquirer may be invited to use the library in person, in the event that we have neither staff nor time to answer the inquirer fully.

F. Requests from Holdings Information

Specific, easily answered requests to check library records and report holdings (e.g., what title does the library own relating to a particular, narrowly defined subject) will be referred to a subject specialist for reply.

G. Supplying Photocopies

The library will not normally supply more than five free pages of photocopied material as part of a reply to a reference inquiry by letter, within the limits of the copyright law. If more copying is necessary, bibliographic information concerning the source should be supplied to the inquirer, with the suggestion that he request the material through interlibrary loan, or come to the library to use the material here.

SECTION VII: ORIENTATION AND INSTRUCTION

A. General Statement

The coordinator of user education and instruction is responsible for planning and developing programs of orientation and instruction in the use of library resources, and for coordinating library instruction offered within the University Library.

B. Responsibilities of Reference Staff

A coordinator of user education may call upon reference staff (and, in appropriate circumstances and with the permission of the relevant supervisor, upon other members of the library staff) for assistance in orientation and instruction activities.

1. *Orientation*—Orientation activities include:
   (a) Guided tours of the building
   (b) Preparation of publications describing the layout of the library building and the service points within it
   (c) Preparation of nonprint media which may complement or offer an alternative to tours and publications [such as library graphics, slide-tape programs].

2. *Instruction*—Instructional activities include:
   (a) Course-related sessions for undergraduate or graduate classes
   (b) Subject- or discipline-oriented workshops or mini-courses
   (c) Preparation of publications and nonprint media related to the above activities.

C. Policy and Procedures

1. *Orientation*—Reference staff should be sufficiently familiar with the route of the standard tour of the building to be able to conduct a group through it expeditiously.
   Individuals requesting tours of the library should be referred to the calendar of scheduled tours or the coordinator of user education. Requests for group visits should be referred to the coordinator of user education or the appropriate subject librarian. (See Section II. B. 6.)
2. *Instruction*—Faculty-initiated requests for library instruction for their classes should ordinarily be routed to the appropriate subject librarian.

SECTION VIII: REFERENCE COLLECTION

A. General Statement

It is the responsibility of the Reference/Collection Development staff to assure that the reference collection is developed to meet the needs of the academic community at Rice University. Activities to accomplish this must take second place to service to library users.

B. Selection Procedures

These procedures are described in "Reference Collection Development Policy."

C. Classification Decisions

Some volumes being processed through technical services are brought to the attention of the reference staff for classification decisions, i.e., whether a particular volume is to be marked "Reference," "Restricted," or to be permitted to circulate. The decisions will be made by the pertinent subject specialist with the approval of the department head. Each item will be marked accordingly, and returned to the process line.

D. Criteria for Decisions

The following criteria will govern the decison:

1. Inclusion in Sheehy's *Guide to Reference Books* (for any book published prior to 1974). Not all Sheehy items will be classified "Reference." Some may be considered not sufficiently relevant to the teaching and research programs at Rice. Some may be too narrow in scope, or too specialized, or too esoteric to belong in Fondren's reference collection. Such items will generally be classified as "Building Use Only."

2. Reference nature of the book, i.e., used for finding of single definite facts and not used for consecutive reading. This characteristic is not always clearly distinguishable and in some cases is an arbitrary interpretation. There are some books which, while intended primarily to be read through for either information or pleasure, are so comprehensive and accurate in their treatment and so well provided with indexes that they serve also as reference books, e.g., *Cambridge History of English Literature*. There are others with a reference-like title which because of their content, treatments or relationship to other library holdings are permitted to circulate, e.g., *Dictionary of Hymnology, Encyclopedia of Draw Poker*. The most probable use of such works will have to be carefully weighed by the subject specialist who may seek the opinion of a faculty member.

E. Collection Organization

Reference materials are organized in the manner most appropriate their type and form and with a view toward efficient retrieval and effective use.

F. Collection Maintenance

Reference materials will be examined, both as they are used and during inventories or reading of the shelves, for condition, usefulness, and currentness. They will then be either repaired, retained, discarded, reclassified, or replaced. At the same time, gaps in the collection will be noted and needed items will be ordered.

Public Library Reference Policy

LOS ANGELES PUBLIC LIBRARY
(Los Angeles, California)

Reference and Advisory Service Guidelines, January 1980

TABLE OF CONTENTS

Multiquestion letters
Responsibility for reply

Information Files, Updating Information
Anticipating Questions

REFERENCE AND ADVISORY SERVICE GUIDELINES

Service Philosophy. Reference and information service is a part of the Library's commitment to serving the needs of the residents of Los Angeles. Within limits defined in this document, equal effort should be made for all questions regardless of originating source. The confidentiality of the origin of questions should be respected and discussion with others should be restricted to seeking assistance in finding the desired information. The information given should be documented, even when the staff member is sure of sure of the correct answer.

REFERENCE DESK SERVICE POLICIES

General guidelines for in-person reference service

1. Librarian should respond to requests for service in the order received, whether in person or by telephone.
2. Any work performed at the reference desk should not become a barrier to the public.
   a. Librarian should not appear too busy to be interrupted.
   b. Librarian should walk through agency when possible and volunteer service.
3. Give active assistance in answering or locating materials.
   a. If questions cannot be answered in a reasonable amount of time, provide possible sources and return periodically until patron can work independently.
   b. Provide instruction in use of tools and resources as needed.

TELEPHONE REFERENCE

General guidelines. Telephone reference service is usually limited to supplying the kind of information that is readily available, does not require extensive searching, and which may be accurately imparted over the telephone. If the question cannot be answered quickly by telephone, the patron should be asked to come to the Library for assistance; or, if appropriate, the question may be taken as a call-back and/or referred to another agency.

Ready reference. Ready reference requests are defined as those inquiries which can be accurately answered in three to five minutes while the patron waits.

Call-backs. A call-back is defined as a question which can be answered appropriately by telephone but requires more than three to five minutes to complete. If the situation seems to warrant it and there is insufficient time to answer a question while the patron waits:

1. The patron may leave his/her name and telephone number and will be called when the information is available. If more convenient for the patron, or if the call is long distance or an extended area call which cannot be placed over tie lines, the patron may be asked to call. The patron should be instructed exactly how to place the return call.
2. In general, the librarian taking the question is responsible for completing it and calling the patron unless other arrangements are made.
3. Whenever possible, call-backs should be completed the same day or within 24 hours unless specific arrangements are made otherwise.

TELEPHONE REFERENCE SERVICE LIMITS.

Ready reference questions per call. *Three* ready reference questions per call is a recommended guideline; however, exceptions may be made depending on how busy the agency is.

Checking lists of books. Not more then *three* book titles are usually checked against the catalog (and shelves, if necessary) per telephone call. The patron may, of course, call again and have three more titles checked.

Quotations for stocks or other securities, currency exchange rates, etc. *Three* quotations are answered per telephone call or five if they should all be on the same date.

Sources checked. The number of sources checked will depend on the time limit guideline and how busy the agency is.

Time limit
1. Ready reference
Three to five minutes per call is a recommended guideline.
2. Reference call-backs
Generally, no more than one hour should be spent working on a reference call-back. If appropriate, the question may be referred for further searching (see *Referrals*).

Items held at reference desk. Materials which may circulate are held for patrons until closing time the following day. On request, time may be extended. Reference items which do not circulate should not be held at the desk, except for reference items borrowed on interlibrary loan, etc., which are held for in-house use.

Interlibrary loan requests by telephone. Telephone requests for items to be sent by interlibrary loan to other Los Angeles Public Library agencies will be filled only if the requested item is on the shelf at the time of the call. If not on the shelf, patron is advised to call other agencies, including Central Library. (See *Branch Manual,* Chapter 27: "Reserves and Interlibray Loans"; or, Central Library Interlibrary Loan Committee. *Interlibrary Loan Manual for Central Library.* 1977.)

Reserves. Reserves are accepted by Central Library subject departments for items not on shelf at time of the call. A postal reserve card is completed by the librarian on duty at the telephone. It is explained to the patron that upon receipt of the reserve postal, he/she is to come to Central Library for the material and at that time will be responsible for paying the fee for the postal reserves. At present, branches do not accept postal reserves by telephone.

Photocopy requests. For details see "Photocopying Services—Branch and Central Sections" in *General Manual.*

Telephone directories, city directories, social registers, criss-cross directories, etc. Personal names and addresses are not supplied by telephone from telephone directories, city directories, social registers, and criss-cross directories. Such information is read, however, if it appears in bibliographical tools. Patrons are advised to visit the

Library if the appropriate directory is in the collection; or, appropriate referrals are made.

REFERENCE QUESTIONS WHICH REQUIRE
SPECIAL APPROACHES

School assignments. These are handled in the same manner as any other reference question; i.e., same number of sources checked, same amount of time spent on question, except:

1. With complex school assignment questions, librarian should make tactful suggestion to telephone patron, or to parents of students, that the student come into the Library for personal assistance and to do his/her in-depth research.
2. In dealing with college and university students, librarian should assist them in the use of library materials and should also be certain that they are aware of the resources and services of their college or university library.

Contest questions. These questions are answered the same as other questions except that, if it is known to be a contest question, callbacks—and the search involved—are not made. (In the interest of public relations, the information that the Library does not allow call-backs for this kind of question is not volunteered. It is, of course, supplied as a statement of policy if the patron asks to have the Library look up an answer and call him back later.)

RATINGS AND EVALUATIONS

Consumer information. Care should be exercised in giving answers over the telephone to consumer questions. Patrons asking for product ratings in such sources as *Consumer Reports* may be given the brand names and model numbers of products rated acceptable. If a patron asks for information on a specific product, the evaluation may be read. Patrons should be encouraged to come to the Library to read the entire article. Such limitations as the date and context of the rating should be pointed out.

Evaluations of dictionaries, encyclopedias, etc. The Library does not recommend one dictionary or encyclopedia over another. Brief descriptions will be read over the telephone of those which seem to meet the patron's needs. The patron should be urged to come to the Library to use the file of dictionary reviews, *Encyclopedia Buying Guide*, and other reviewing sources and to examine the various dictionaries and encyclopedias in the Library's collection.

Other ratings, recommendations, and evaluations. Before supplying ratings, recommendations, or evaluations by telephone, explanations given in sources should be read in detail. Patron should be encouraged to come to the Library if interpretation is required. Personal opinions should never be given.

Values of art works, antiques, rare books, coins, stamps, currency, etc. Appraisals of the value of art works, antiques, rare books, coins, stamps, currency, and other collectibles are never given. Sources are made available which give prices; i.e., auction records, catalogs, etc. Lists of appraisers or other appropriate referrals are made available if necessary.

Critical analyses, etc. Personal critical analyses, interpretations, or judgments of the merit of literary or other works are not done for patrons by Library staff. However, published analyses are made available and, if brief, will be read by telephone. Reader's advisory service is offered (See *Reader's Advisory Service*).

Medical, legal, statistical, and technical information. The librarian should not *interpret* material of any type related to these fields, including tables, charts, equations, conversion formulas, laws, taxation and regulatory information, or legal and medical definitions. When providing information related to the above material by telepone, the librarian will read the information and indicate the source, but the patron must interpret the information. The librarian should feel free to indicate to the patron that he/she does not have the specialized knowledge to give positive or absolute answers. Patrons should be advised to read the materials themselves. Referral suggestions may be made if assistance is needed in interpretation. See *Information Files, Updating Information, Anticipating Questions*.

Patent and copyright searches, etc. Patent and copyright searches are not performed by Library staff, nor does staff attempt to ascertain whether a published work is in the public domain. Basic instruction is offered to the patron on how to do such searches, however; and/or referral lists of patent attorneys, etc., are made available.

Genealogies. Genealogies are not prepared for patrons by Library staff. Published genealogies are read by telephone only if readily available and reading can be done within three to five minutes.

Translations. Translations too lengthy to be done within time guidelines (see *Time Limit*), or too technical for the level of staff expertise, are not performed. A list of outside translators is made available from which the patron may choose.

Compilations and literature searches. Extensive compilations (bibliographies, lists, statistics, etc.) are not prepared for patrons by Library staff, nor are exhaustive literature searches undertaken. Assistance is offered to the patron while doing the work in the Library; and/or lists are provided of persons or firms available on a fee basis.

Mathematical calculations. Library staff should not do mathematical calculations for patrons. Information from tables and formulas can be read, but patron should do own calculations.

OTHER ASPECTS OF REFERENCE DESK SERVICE

Circulation Functions at Reference Desk

Reference books, periodicals and other restricted materials. While items designated as reference are not generally loaned to the public, exceptions may be made when the owning agency determines that such a loan is warranted. The final decision rests with the agency head.

Special loans. Special loans are made according to the policy stated in *General Manual*.

Vertical File, uncataloged and unprocessed materials. The agency head determines if this type of material is to be loaned and whether it is to be loaned through the regular circulation procedure or by special loan.

Card catalog service. Before a patron is referred to the card catalog, it should be determined if he/she will need assistance in using it. The librarian should be aware of any patron who may need help using the card catalog and offer as much assistance as needed and possible.

Special information resources. The librarian should be aware of and know how to use special information sources such as indexes, documents, and microforms within the Library and in his/her agency as well as resources of other libraries and other agencies in the community. It is the duty of the librarian to inform the patron of all information sources in the Library and elsewhere that may help satisfy his/her needs.

Referrals. Within the Los Angeles Public Library system, the normal referral process for questions that cannot be answered in the local agency is to the regional library, then to Central Library or to the regional resource center; i.e., Southern California Answering Network (SCAN).

Bibliographic Services

Verification and location. If an item of library material is not available within the Los Angeles Public Library system, and if the patron desires to locate it, an effort is made to verify and to locate it. If the patron wishes, an attempt is made to borrow the material. (See *Branch Manual*, Chapter 27: "Reserves and Interlibrary Loans"; or, Central Library Interlibrary Loan Committee. *Interlibrary Loan Manual for Central Library.* 1977.)

Bibliographies
1. Agency initiated
   The head of an agency may authorize the preparation of bibliographies by staff members when the results would contribute significantly to the work of the agency.
2. Patron requests
   a. Preparation of bibliographies
      Because of the heavy demand of desk and ancillary duties, staff members are unable to undertake the preparation of bibliographies on behalf of individual patrons.
   b. Checking bibliographies
      Dependent upon time and staff available, limited assistance will be provided in the checking of bibliographies against the Library's holdings.

Southern California Interlibrary Loan Network (SCILL). Assistance to all patrons in the verification and location of materials is available through the bibliographic services of SCILL. (See also *Verification and location.*)

Reader's Advisory Service. As part of their duties, librarians help patrons select materials. This function is unavoidably judgmental; however, it should not be a matter of casual judgment but should reflect a thorough and up-to-date knowledge of the collection.

MAIL REFERENCE

General guidelines for mail reference service
1. It is the Library's policy to respond to all reference inquiries received by mail. The agency head has the responsibility of deciding what is a reasonable amount of time (usually a maximum of one hour) to be spent on each letter.
2. The following limitations must be placed on all mail reference service:
   a. No extensive searches through unindexed materials such as newspapers and periodicals.
   b. No preparation of long bibliographies.
   c. See also *Reference questions which require special approaches.*
3. Requests from persons living outside Los Angeles:
   With the following exceptions, requests from persons living outside the City of Los Angeles are returned to the sender, who is advised to use his/her local library. If special materials, collections, or information unique to the Los Angeles Public Library are involved, or, if it is presumed or known that the patron has no local library or that the library has no material on the particular subject, an effort will be made to answer the question or to make available appropriate referrals which may do so.

Multiquestion letters. Letters containing several questions which require answers from more than one agency are routed by the agency originally receiving to the other agencies concerned. The latter attach(es) answers and return(s) them to the original agency for reply to be made to the patron. If most of the material involved is in an agency other than the first recipient, the reply may be made by the agency holding the bulk of the material.

Responsibility for reply. Unless given special permission, agencies do not send out letters without the signature of the agency head, who is responsible for matters of policy involved and for letter content (See *General Manual*); however, in the case of replies to mail reference requests, the name of the person preparing the reply is also included. For letter form, see *General Manual*.

Information Files, Updating Information, Anticipating Questions. Each agency establishes and maintains files reflecting current local interests. These and standard reference tools must be continually updated. These files include other information sources that may be of assistance in meeting the patron's needs if the local agency is unable to do so. The librarian should verify regularly any dated or incomplete referral information and, if in doubt, call before referring.

[Index follows—Editor.]

Online Library Reference Policy

UNIVERSITY OF HOUSTON
(Houston, Texas)

Policy Manual for a Computerized Search Service in an Academic Library

POLICY MANUAL FOR A COMPUTERIZED SEARCH SERVICE IN AN ACADEMIC LIBRARY—DRAFT PROPOSAL—by William J. Jackson

Libraries are finding it increasingly necessary to establish the capability to do on-line searching for their patrons, yet this service has not existed so long that a firm idea exists as to what should and should not be done. It is quite easy to begin the service without any formal statement of policy or procedures. Doing so can easily lead to chaos.

As of March, 1979, there were only two documents indexed in *Resources in Education* which address this problem directly. The first, ED 127 912, David M. Wax, *A Handbook for the Introduction of On-line Bibliographic Search Services into Academic Libraries*, could be of great help to those who have not actually begun the service. It provides a number of useful suggestions for those who are already in operation. The second document, ED 144 557, is a copy of the policy manual used by the University of Massachusetts at Amherst. Their manual was found to be helpful in preparing this proposed manual; some of their sentences were used verbatim, and the general structure was copied. However, the University of Massachusetts at Amherst is organized and administered differently from the University of Houston Central Campus, and these differences show in a comparison of the two manuals. Even the location, urban vs. rural, has an effect on the operations of the two services.

It is hoped that, with the publication of this proposed policy manual, others will be able to see elements which are common to more than one search service operation as well as be able to get contrasting ideas on how to solve problems which have been treated differently in the two manuals.

STATEMENT OF PURPOSE

The Computerized Information Retrieval Service exists to support the research efforts of the University of Houston System.

GENERAL QUESTIONS

General questions about the operation of CIRES will be answered by the Coordinator. The Coordinator will normally refer patrons who have questions about a specific data base to an appropriate searcher.

PATRONS SERVED

A. All faculty, enrolled students, and staff of any University of Houston System campus are eligible for service.
1. Should the question of eligibility arise, the burden of proof shall be upon the patron wishing to be served. Proper identification must be supplied upon request.
2. Special consideration will be given to the University of Houston student working on a dissertation, thesis, or other research project who is *temporarily* not enrolled (e.g. during the summer). Doubtful cases will be decided by the Coordinator.

B. Service will not be given to anyone who is not in the above categories. This includes the following people, who will not be served:
   1. Persons affiliated with other universities
   2. Alumni
   3. Courtesy card holders (including Friends of the Library)
   4. The general public and business community
C. CIRES equipment and terminals will not be used by anyone not employed by the central campus library. Members of the staffs of other libraries may be excepted from this prohibition by the Coordinator. No other exceptions will be made.
   1. Persons who are granted exceptions must be fully trained to use data base systems and must have their own password.
   2. Persons who are not employed by libraries or are not fully trained may not use CIRES equipment and terminals. No exceptions.

COST

A. All persons normally eligible for service (faculty, enrolled students, and staff) will pay on the same basis, without regard to status.
B. Rates will be based upon the rates charged by the various data base vendors.
   1. Rates charged by vendors are data-base specific; therefore, rates charged will vary according to the data base used.
   2. Rates charged by the vendors may be subsidized or surcharged by the library, depending upon the revenue needed to adequately fund the service. However, any subsidy or surcharge will be applied to all users in a uniform manner, except for those mentioned below.
C. Should exceptions be made to provide service to someone not normally eligible, or should such a person unknowingly be provided service and later discovered to be ineligible, that person will be charged cost plus 25% or cost plus twice the amount of any surcharge currently being charged normally eligible users, whichever is greater.
D. Financial obligation
   1. Patrons are financially responsible for all services requested.
   2. If a patron charges a search to a departmental account and the department refuses to pay, then the patron is responsible for all charges.

RESPONSIBILITIES OF SEARCHERS

A. Maintenance of searching skills
1. Searchers are members of the library staff who have been trained in the techniques of using one or more on-line data base system(s). It is the searcher's responsibility to keep informed of the latest developments and new techniques for effective searching by reading the bulletins issued by various data base vendors as well as through the reading of professional literature. Periodic review of the search manuals and guides is recommended, particularly for searchers who search less than weekly.
2. It is the responsibility of the individual searcher to initiate requests to attend workshops and to make all necessary arrangements. Requests for action to attend workshops should be addressed to the person or committee responsible; e.g., the travel committee for travel funds, the department head for time off, the Coordinator for selection in cases of limited enrollment or other problems specifically related to workshop enrollment or attendance. The Coordinator will not handle problems (such as travel) which would be encountered in attending a non-data-base-related function. The Coordinator will strive to keep searchers informed of workshop and convention possibilities.
3. Searchers should not hesitate to consult with other searchers or with the Coordinator should problems arise or be anticipated with a search strategy or with on-line techniques.
B. Scheduling of appointments and the interview
1. Patrons seeking detailed information about the search service will be referred to an appropriate searcher, depending upon the subject of interest. The searcher will arrange a convenient time to interview the patron. During the interview, the searcher and the patron will discuss the problem to be researched and choose the data base(s) to be used. If convenient, a search strategy will be devised at that time and the search will be performed. The searcher may also elect to defer preparation of the search strategy until after the patron leaves when other patrons or business must be attended to, or when the strategy will be difficult and/or time-consuming to prepare, or when the patron is not able or does not desire to wait. In such cases, if the searcher would like the patron to be present during the search, a second appointment should be made.

2. Searches are normally done on an appointment basis. However, searchers may elect to do a search for someone without an appointment. This will be completely at the searcher's discretion in each case.
3. In cases where a search involves material with which the searcher is totally unfamiliar, delaying the actual search is recommended if the searcher feels that time to consult printed reference sources to provide background might improve the search effectiveness.
4. Searchers should anticipate problems which may arise on-line and discuss these fully with the patron before doing the search. Such problems should include the possible need to narrow, broaden, or otherwise modify the strategy as well as the question of the number and format of the citations to be printed. Failure to do this results in an unnecessary discussion of such matters while on-line and is an irresponsible waste of patron money.
5. Searchers will discuss the procedure for payment before the on-line search is begun. The patron should be made completely aware of the financial obligation involved.
6. The searcher should discourage searches which can easily be done manually. This is an excellent opportunity to introduce a patron to the printed resources available.
7. It is strongly suggested that the search interview be done in person rather than by telephone. However, many persons in the UH system would be greatly inconvenienced by the necessity of a trip to the central campus. Therefore, searchers may conduct interviews by telephone. The decision to accept telephoned searches is left to the discretion of the individual searcher.

C. The search
1. The presence of the patron during the search is optional. Searchers are encouraged to have the patron present when searching areas in which their personal knowledge is limited.
2. In deciding when to do the search, the searcher should consider factors which may affect cost, such as computer response time. Searchers should take whatever actions are possible to control costs.
3. If annoyingly slow response time is encountered on-line, the searcher should discontinue searching and try at a later time. Temporary search saves should be used to avoid duplicating efforts. Searchers should always check before

beginning a search on techniques needed to cost-effectively abort searches.

D. Post-search
  1. Cost computation and search log
     a. It is the searcher's responsibility to compute the cost of each search except in those cases in which an offline printout it to be received from a vendor which charges by the page, or when a search of an offline file is to be performed at an unknown cost.
     b. The searcher should enter information concerning each search into the search log(s) as soon after the completion of the search as possible.
  2. Patron payment should be made when all work is completed.
     a. Procedures for making payments are listed in Appendix A.
     b. Payment at time of search—search completed with patron present.
        i. If the search is completed to the point that the patron need not return (i.e., no offline prints), then the searcher should make sure that the patron knows how to pay for the search.
           a. For cash or checks, the searcher should accept payment in full, or, if necessary, ask the office secretary to accept payment. Payment by check is always preferred and should be suggested. The search number(s) must appear on the record of payment (either the check or the cash receipt).
           b. If payment is to be made by IDT (Independent Transaction), the searcher should explain in full the necessary procedure. The patron should be provided with the search number(s) and the total amount due. The patron should be instructed to call the Coordinator or the office secretary with the number of the IDT being sent, along with the search number(s) being covered by the IDT number given.
        ii. The searcher is totally responsible for assuring that payment has been made or that the IDT process has been explained if all work is completed and the patron is not expected to return again.
     c. Delayed payment
        i. Searches falling into this category are those for which an offline printout has been ordered, a search of an offline file has been requested, an SDI search, or a

search which has been done with the patron absent. The common characteristic of all these cases is that the person will return at a future time to retrieve the results and make payment. Any search which includes offline printing or searching will be included in this category, even if some on-line results are given to the patron.

    ii. Collection of fees for such searches is the responsibility of the office secretary.

d. Deposit accounts

    i. Patrons who have established a deposit account with the Coordinator may charge searches against the account.

    ii. The Coordinator will have information about deposit accounts readily available so that it may be quickly verified. The patron should sign a receipt when charging a search to a deposit account. The receipt should be sent to the Coordinator.

e. Mailed out searches

    i. Searches may be mailed to patrons who find it difficult to visit during operating hours. This applies primarily to persons affiliated with UH campuses other than the central campus.

    ii. It is preferred that payment be received before the search is mailed. However, if the patron's need seems urgent, the search results may be mailed before payment is received. Searches should be referred to the Coordinator for mail-out.

        a. Collection problems connected with mailed searches are the responsibility of the Coordinator.

        b. When choosing a data base vendor for a search which will involve offline printing, Dialog or Orbit should be used rather than BRS since the cost of the offline print is known immediately. The patron can then mail payment before the printout is received and thus reduce delays.

3. User instruction

a. After a search is done, the searcher is responsible for making sure that the patron will be able to read and use the results. If the results of the search are printed on-line, the searcher should explain the printout before the patron leaves. If the patron is to return later to pick up the search results, the searcher should encourage the patron to telephone or come to the office should there be any problems in using the information.

b. The patron should be encouraged to ask for additional searches or bibliographic help if it is needed. The searcher should inquire as to whether the patron is aware of other useful resources available in the field being researched. Additional instruction should be given when warranted.

RESPONSIBILITIES OF THE COORDINATOR

A. The Coordinator is selected by the Assistant Director for Public Services and Collection Development in consultation with the head(s) of the reference department(s). The Coordinator reports to the head of General Reference.

B. Statistics—service
   1. The Coordinator will compile service statistical reports on a monthly basis. Statistics reported will include but not be limited to:
      a. Number of searches performed in each data base.
      b. Number of searches performed by each searcher.
      c. Number of searches performed in each system (vendor use).
      d. Number of searches performed by status (faculty, graduate student, etc.).
   2. These statistical reports will be sent to the head(s) of the reference departments(s).

C. Statistics—financial
   1. The Coordinator will compile financial statistical reports on a quarterly basis. Statistics reported will include but not be limited to:
      a. Sources of asset debits
         i. Revenue from fees based on connect time charges.
         ii. Revenue from surcharge fees.
         iii. Revenue from discounts received from vendors.
      b. Sources of asset credits
         i. Expenses for connect time charges
         ii. Expenses for operations, including terminal repairs, search aids, training, etc.
         iii. Expenses for printing and other publicity.
         iv. Expenses for costs written off
            a. Bad debts expense.

      b. Bad searches for which the patron is not charged.

      c. Research by library employees for operations/publication.

      d. Searches to answer reference inquiries.

    c. Balances in any accounts (if such accounts are established and budgeted) for equipment repair, training, etc.

  2. These financial reports will be sent to the head(s) of the reference departments(s).

D. Liaison and contact

  1. The Coordinator is the person who conducts all business, arranges all agreements and contracts, and resolves all problems with data base vendors.

  2. The Coordinator circulates new information about the data base systems to all searchers and keeps them informed of all changes in procedures or other matters.

  3. The Coordinator keeps all information necessary for smooth operation up-to-date; e.g., the Coordinator maintains a list of all data bases available with the current prices.

E. The Coordinator is responsible for arranging for any repairs or maintenance to the terminal and other equipment. The library business office will assist the Coordinator with the necessary vouchers.

F. The Coordinator will determine a fee schedule necessary to provide adequate revenue to operate the service. The Coordinator will request funds to be used for subsidies, equipment, training, demonstrations, or any other activity for which it might be deemed desirable not to charge patrons. The Coordinator will administer all funds of the service and will have total responsibility for the collection and disbursement of money as well as for the overall sound fiscal condition of the service.

G. The Coordinator will perform or supervise all accounting operations for the service, including analysis and checking of the monthly Budget Activity Report (BAR), and will act to correct any errors or problems in the accounting operations of the service.

H. Publicity: the Coordinator will be responsible to adequately publicize the service in order to make those who might benefit from it fully aware of its existence. Such publicity might include flyers, posters, newspaper articles or advertisements, or demonstrations for selected users.

I. Supervision of paper flow and daily operations

  1. The Coordinator will design all forms necessary to make the

operations of the service as smooth as possible.
2. The Coordinator will direct the activities of the office secretary in those duties which pertain to the service (see section VII).
   a. The Coordinator will organize a logical method of record keeping for the secretary which will produce the needed statistical and financial information with a minimum of difficulty.
   b. The Coordinator will resolve any problems arising for the secretary as a result of this statistical gathering.
3. The Coordinator will receive all offline prints, verify the accuracy of the prints for delivery, and give the prints to the secretary to have patrons called.
4. Patron complaints and inquiries (e.g.: about an overdue offline print) will be directed to the Coordinator for resolution (see section IX).
5. The Coordinator will pursue overdue accounts by whatever means are available and will act to prevent anyone who does not pay for a search from receiving additional service.
6. The Coordinator will maintain all files and records pertaining to the operation of the service.
7. The Coordinator will assure that all needed supplies are ordered.
8. The Coordinator will mediate disputes between individual searchers and refer serious problems to the appropriate department head.
9. The Coordinator has final responsibility for all daily operations, including the accuracy of search cost computations.
J. Maintenance of searching quality
1. The Coordinator will suggest to searchers, when appropriate, methods of improving the quality of searching or of reducing the amount of connect time for a search.
   a. The Coordinator will not participate in other searchers' on-line sessions unless asked; however, deficient techniques which are noticed will be mentioned.
   b. The Coordinator may choose searches at random to review the strategy in an effort to suggest ways to improve searching techniques.
2. The Coordinator will work with searchers who have deficient search skills and will suggest methods and techniques for improving those skills.
3. If the Coordinator determines that an individual searcher

consistently performs badly, the Coordinator may recommend to the appropriate department head or assistant director that the searcher be permanently prohibited from further searching. Destructive negative publicity resulting from poor searching must be prevented.

4. The Coordinator will recommend any changes in equipment and implement any changes in procedures necessary to maintain searching quality.

5. The Coordinator will arrange and plan all workshops and training sessions which are to be held in-house.

K. The Coordinator will recommend and/or implement any changes necessary in personnel, policy, equipment, or procedures to assure the overall success of the service.

RESPONSIBILITIES OF THE OFFICE SECRETARY

A. Service to patrons

1. The secretary will answer telephone inquiries by patrons who wish to find out if their search results are ready to be picked up.

2. In the absence of the Coordinator, the secretary may refer patrons wishing a search to an appropriate searcher if the subject of the inquiry can be determined.

3. The secretary will call patrons to notify them that search results are ready.

4. The secretary will deliver search results to patrons who come to the office and collect the specified fee for the search. The secretary will encourage payment by check. Procedures for payment are listed in Appendix A.

   a. The secretary will be responsible for fees collected until the money is transferred to the Coordinator.

   b. The secretary will arrange for someone to deliver searches to patrons during absences from the office.

B. Record keeping

1. The secretary will collect all the data needed by the Coordinator to complete the required statistical reports. Forms for this purpose will be supplied by the Coordinator.

2. The secretary will keep an accurate account of the funds received in payment of a search.

C. The secretary will serve as the typist for the search service.

D. Other regular or special duties may be assigned with the approval of the secretary's supervisor.

RESPONSIBILITIES OF THE LIBRARY ADMINISTRATION

A. The library administration will provide adequate staff to support the needs of the service.
1. Reference staffing will be maintained at a level which allows searchers to devote adequate time to each search request.
2. Services which may be affected by computerized retrieval (e.g., Interlibrary Loans) will be monitored to assure that the final result of searches does not become unnecessary frustration to patrons unable to retrieve materials cited.
B. The library administration will provide funds or assist in obtaining funds necessary to maintain equipment or other hardware at a level of quality which will assist in service excellence.

COMPLAINTS

A. Complaints about service should be directed initially to the searcher who performed the search.
B. Patrons who remain dissatisfied after speaking with a searcher about a complaint should be directed to the Coordinator.
C. If the Coordinator is unable to resolve a patron complaint, the patron will be referred to the Assistant Director for Public Services and Collection Development.

POLICY APPROVAL AND CHANGE

A. This policy will go into effect when approved by the Coordinator and the library administration.
B. Questions arising about policy which are not covered by this written service policy will be decided by the Coordinator and subsequently added to the policy.
C. All changes must be approved by the Coordinator.

APPENDIX A (to be revised in final draft)

UNIVERSITY OF HOUSTON LIBRARIES/CIRES

Payment of Computer Searches

PAYMENT IS DUE WHEN THE SEARCH IS COMPLETED AND THE RESULTS PICKED UP

All payment is handled in the General Reference Department Office, room 111 of the Main Library (749-1217).

Methods of Payment

> *Check:* This is the preferred method of payment. The checks should be made out to the "University of Houston Libraries."

> *Cash:* Payment in cash must be for the exact amount. We cannot make change. You may call beforehand to determine the exact amount due. A receipt will be made out upon payment.

IDT (Interdepartmental Transaction): This method of payment is only available to those authorized to draw on University funds.
  Please note the following points:
  1. An IDT is to be issued for the exact amount of the search or for an estimated amount given by the searcher.
  2. All three authorizing signatures are required on the IDT ("Requested by," "Authorized by," and "Received by").
  3. Direct the IDT to "Library/CIRES." This is typed in the "TO" box near the top of the form.
  4. Send the IDT to accounting for encumbrance. It will be forwarded to use by that department.
  Search results may be picked up before we have the IDT in hand. In this case, however, give us the IDT number when you receive your results.

ALL QUESTIONS ABOUT PAYMENT SHOULD BE DIRECTED TO EITHER ALAN PFEIFFER-TRAUM OR HELEN TATMAN AT 749-1217.

Index

Columbia University, xxix
Columbus (OH) Technical Institute,
    online reference service, 403–04
"A Commitment to Information
    Services: Developmental
    Guidelines, 1979." *See* Ameri-
    can Library Association,
    Reference and Adult Services
    Division.
Committee,
    advisory, online reference service,
        447–48, 457–58
    reference services policy develop-
        ment, xxvii, 22–4
Community information, 345
Community services, academic
    libraries, 52, 53, 62, 63, 64–71,
    75
Complaints, 298, 299, 524
    objectionable materials, 263–64
    online service, 31, 558, 560
    procedure memorandum on, 266
*A Comprehensive Program of User
    Education for the General
    Libraries, The University of
    Texas at Austin*, 201–02
Confidentiality,
    online service, 31, 431, 433
    reference service, 13, 204, 205,
        236, 261, 319, 515
Connecticut, University of,
    online reference services,
        explanation, 404–05
    fees, 493–96
Consumer Index, 294
Consumer information, inquiries,
    281, 283, 288, 294–96, 317,
    322, 541
Consumers' Reports, 288, 322
Contests, inquiries, 84, 106, 108, 109,
    275–78, 317, 328, 543
Continuing education, staff, xxxi, 12,
    80–1
Controversies, resolving, xxiv
Cooperation,
    among library departments, 166,

181, 524
    interagency, 10, 11, 173, 175, 213
    with local schools, 271, 272–73, 274
Coordinating Information for Texas
    Educators. *See* CITE.
Copyright law, interlibrary loan,
    158, 180, 377
Copyright searches, 544–45
Correspondence, 186–91, 292,
    384–91, 533–34, 547–48
    form letters, 388
    letters of introduction, 188, 516
    outgoing requests for information,
        188–89
    standards, xxiv
    statistics, 117
County of Orange (CA) Public
    Library. *See* Orange County
    (CA) Public Library.
Current awareness. *See* Selective
    dissemination of information.

DIALOG Search Service, 401, 402,
    419, 555
Daniels, Linda, "A Matter of Form,"
    466
Databases, 401–02, 403, 404, 408,
    409, 411, 413, 417, 420, 426,
    435, 436
    lists, 440–44
    priorities for acquiring, 443
Davis, University of California at,
    xii
Dayton and Montgomery County
    (OH) Public Library, xxii
    correspondence, 386–87
    inquiries, 262
        contests, 276
        school assignments, 271–72
    nondiscrimination statement, 235
    reference materials, circulation,
        356
    telephone inquiries, 321–22
    catalog checking, 338
Deaf, 241
Demonstrations, online reference